The New Country Music Encyclopedia

TAD RICHARDS & MELVIN B. SHESTACK

A Fireside Book
Published by Simon & Schuster

New York   London   Toronto   Sydney   Tokyo   Singapore

FIRESIDE
Simon & Schuster Building
Rockefeller Center
1230 Avenue of the Americas
New York, New York 10020

Copyright © 1993 by Melvin B. Shestack and
Tad Richards

DESIGNED BY BARBARA MARKS
Manufactured in the United States of America

10 9 8 7 6 5 4 3 2 1

Library of Congress Cataloging-in-Publication
Data

Richards, Tad.
    The new country music encyclopedia /
Tad Richards, Melvin Shestack.
        p.   cm.
    Includes index.
    1. Country music—Bio-bibliography
—Dictionaries. I. Shestack, Melvin.
II. Title.
ML102.C7R5   1993
781.642′092—dc20
    [B]   93–17689
                                    CIP
                                    MN

ISBN 0-671-78258-4

Acknowledgments

Thanks . . .

To Pat Richards, Shari Doherty, Cindy Bell and Ann Winfield for help up in the mountains; to Jessie Gifford and Donna McLaughlin Wyant for help down in what we country folks call Noo Yawk City. To Darlene Ondesko in Reba Country. To Nathan Humbard of WGRV in Greeneville, TN.

To a whole lot of people in Nashville, almost too many to name, so I'll let a few names stand for a bunch more. To Art Sparer, for friendship, knowledge, and "the writer's couch." To Sandy Neece and Sarah Brosmer, standing for a lot of wonderful and helpful people at the record labels. To the folks at the Evelyn Shriver Agency, standing in for a lot of very helpful publicists, and a special thanks to Sharon Allen. To the wonderful Hazel Smith. To Mike Campbell, for an act of graciousness when we were just starting out. To Robert K. Oermann, for steering me in the right direction on more than one occasion. To the Country Music Foundation and Ronnie Pugh, for *being* the right direction for so much information. To Lee Marsh at RETNA for great photos, wonderful cooperation.

To Steve Price, for helping to get this book off the ground, and to Dave Dunton, for knowing about music and prose, and for being worth talking to on both subjects. To Bill Quirk for everything.

To everyone we talked to in putting this book together. You were *all* highlights in our minds, so you'll forgive us for mentioning just a few highlights: Ricky Van Shelton, Holly Dunn, Rodney Crowell, Duane Allen and Joe Bonsall, Mary-Chapin Carpenter, Billy Joe Royal, Donna Fargo, Jo-El Sonnier.

Introduction

In 1974, Mel Shestack published a book called *The Country Music Encyclopedia*. Back then, the big news in country was a new sound coming out of Texas by a couple of rebels who had left Nashville, dejected over their inability to make their kind of gritty music in a town in love with the string-sweetened Nashville Sound.

Their names were Willie Nelson and Waylon Jennings. Waylon had just put out an album called *Honky Tonk Heroes,* destined to become a classic. Willie had just organized his first Fourth of July picnic in Dripping Springs, Texas, and was "back in Texas now, living quietly." Mel thought they were important enough stars of the future to write up major entries on them, but nowhere in those entries will you find the word *outlaw*. That wasn't to come for another couple of years.

Nineteen seventy-four was the heyday of the first great wave of woman singers. Loretta Lynn, Tammy Wynette, and Dolly Parton changed forever the way audiences and the industry would think about women, and this was a lot more important than whether or not Tammy's "Stand by Your Man" message was out of step with the feminist vanguard. A black singer, Charley Pride, had been named Enter-tainer of the Year in 1971. It was a pivotal time in country music.

I met Mel in the early eighties and spent the next several years trying to convince him to update his original encyclopedia. It'll be an easy job, I argued. Just bring the entries up to date and add a few new ones. Mickey Gilley, all those hot new Urban Cowboys. Country music doesn't change that much.

Meanwhile, the story was slipping away. The Urban Cowboy fad disappeared, and no one outside a hundred-mile radius of Nashville cared about country music. By the mid-eighties, the *New York Times* wrote country music's obituary. It was finished forever as a genre, as a vital part of American popular culture.

But the pundits of the media were a little premature. In 1990, Simon & Schuster signed up this project, and we were in business.

But what business? Just update the old book, tell everyone what Dave Dudley and Wanda Jackson and Freddie Hart[1] were up to now? Not a chance. It was a whole new

---

[1]Freddie Hart, an educated and sensitive man whose big hit was "Easy Loving" back in 1971, now runs a school for handicapped children in California.

ball game. Most of the people who were around in 1974 were gone from the scene. The players were all new. Not just one, but two or three different revolutions had swept across the face of country music since then.

Certainly it wasn't the country that Mel first fell in love with as a high school student in the forties, when he conducted his now-legendary interview with Hank Williams, Sr., for his high school newspaper (which refused to run it—a hillbilly in *our* school paper?). No one was writing about country music back then; in fact, that was the only interview Hank, Sr., ever gave.

But those were the years that shaped the future of country music. In the Southwest, Bob Wills and others were creating Western Swing, a blend of country and big-band jazz that was as musically progressive as it was danceable—the first fusion, the first crossover. In Kentucky, Bill Monroe hired Lester Flatt and Earl Scruggs into his Bluegrass Boys and brought a level of instrumental virtuosity into country that rivaled that in any other form of music. (Bluegrass has always led a separate, parallel existence to mainstream country, but many of today's new musicians, from Ricky Skaggs and Keith Whitley to Emmylou Harris to Marty Raybon of Shenandoah, have a bluegrass background and have brought its sensibility into the mainstream.)

And in Nashville, Hank Williams, Sr., along with his publisher and the shaper of his genius, Fred Rose, was creating a timeless style and a body of songs that will stand up against any songwriter in any genre.

It was Hank's work that brought country its first wider audience, as pop singers from New York and Hollywood began to cover his songs—or, as some would say, rip off the culture of the white South the way they ripped off black culture when guys like Pat Boone had hits with watered-down versions of Fats Domino and Little Richard.

Margaret Whiting, the great cabaret singer, and the first pop star to record in Nashville ("Slippin' Around," a duet with movie cowboy Jimmy Wakely), agrees in retrospect that there may be some truth to that, but she points out that the artists meant no disrespect, nor were they trying to rip anyone off. "We wanted to sing the songs because they were, and are, such great songs."

But the Margaret Whitings and the Tony Bennetts and the Jo Staffords were about to be pushed off center stage by a revolution: the 45 rpm record, the emergence of a vast teenage record-buying market, and a new music to fill that market.

A lot of purists thought that rock and roll was the death of country, but it wasn't. Elvis and Carl Perkins and Jerry Lee Lewis and the Everly Brothers brought a new excitement to music; and at heart, they were solid country.

This was where I came in. As it was for so many lonely teenagers of the fifties, the radio was my best friend, and the songs I heard over it were the most important tool I had for figuring out what life was all about. Radio was my Voice of Experience, my guide to the secrets of a larger world out there.

I knew I couldn't count on teenage pretty boys like Fabian to tell me the secrets of life. But Fats Domino could, and so could groups like the Turbans and the Cleftones, who sang from the urban streets. And so could Jerry Lee Lewis, who knew some wild, dark inner secret.

And so could the mainstream country singers who found their way onto the pop charts in the wake of the rockabillies—guys who knew about the sadness of the human soul, such as Ferlin Husky and Jim Reeves.

Rock and roll collapsed around 1960, and Bobby Rydell, Connie Francis, and Bobby Vinton certainly weren't going to tell me anything about life. Anyway, I was in college then, and I was cool: I was listening to Miles Davis and Charlie Parker. But country hadn't collapsed. Johnny Cash and Sonny James, Kitty Wells and Patsy Cline, Marty Robbins and George Jones . . . country was still squarely on the side of real life.

Real life changed in the sixties. The kids weren't Lesley Gore and Frankie Avalon anymore; they were Bob Dylan and John Lennon, and suddenly you could learn from the Voice of Innocence as well as the Voice of Experience. (Maybe we didn't learn enough—is being able to snicker at the naïveté of kids who put flowers in the barrels of guns really such progress?)

Johnny Cash carried the banner of country music through much of those days. Bob Dylan listened to him. Johnny Cash carried on his own form of social awareness, singing about the American Indian and playing benefits in places like San Quentin prison, where a young convict named Merle Haggard heard him.

Merle Haggard was the antithesis of sixties culture. The self-proclaimed Voice of Experience in the sixties was Jimi Hendrix; the message was from a traveler returned from inner space. Haggard was just the opposite: a voice from the heartland of America, but a flat-out honest voice. The fugitive, the branded man. In a time when kids were blaming the older generation for their problems and the world's problems, Haggard blamed himself.

In Woodstock, The Band knew what Haggard was talking about. Robbie Robertson wrote songs like "Tears of Rage," about the plight of parents trying to reach their children. On the West Coast, Crosby, Stills and Nash had some inkling of what Haggard was talking about when they wrote "Teach Your Children." In the Midwest, John Prine knew, when he wrote songs of the deepest respect for his elders, such as "Grandpa Was a Carpenter" and "Hello in There." And the hippy-dippy Grateful Dead knew, when they recorded Haggard's songs. And when Haggard recorded the hippie-bashing "Okie From Muskogee," the counterculture embraced him as much as it vilified him. In the best of the "Okie" answer songs, "I'll Change Your Flat Tire, Merle," a hippie comes to Haggard's rescue because, "Merle, you've got soul."

Janie Frickie was a student at the revolution-tossed University of Indiana in the sixties, but was so involved with her music, she says, that she barely noticed the outside world. But the role models for a young woman country singer—Loretta Lynn, Tammy Wynette, and Dolly Parton—were presences that the outside world couldn't fail to notice. And at the same time, a Rhodes Scholar/West Point instructor turned dropout headed not for San Francisco but for Nashville: Kris Kristofferson got a job as a janitor in a Nashville recording studio and started writing songs that would become classics in both country and rock.

A strange phenomenon afflicts the country music community from time to time:

11

crossover mania. Country has always looked for a way to expand its audience. Identifying itself as the music of America's heartland, proclaiming its pride in its roots, country has always had a bit of an inferiority complex about those roots. That's why when it thinks about crossing over, it always thinks of crossing in the same direction: uptown. Café society, the carriage trade. Vegas.

In the fifties, that country establishment liked what Eddy Arnold was doing, dressing up in a tuxedo and singing at supper clubs. It was terrified of what Elvis and Roy Orbison and those guys were doing, bringing funky, low-rent, black music into the country tent. It turned to the"Nashville Sound," devised by Chet Atkins and others, in which brilliant musicians got together and created a Muzak overlay to country arrangements.

By the late sixties, country had gotten used to the rockabillies and had welcomed singers as diverse as Jerry Lee Lewis and Conway Twitty back into the fold—though not, for some reason, Roy Orbison, who is almost completely absent from the country charts.

The rockabillies weren't scary anymore, but a new generation of teenagers had become even more menacing. As Hank Thompson put it in "Ace in the Hole," an updated parody of an old Tin Pan Alley song: "Those hippies and demonstrators / Draft dodgers and agitators / Want old-age benefits at twenty-one."

As the Vietnam War and the Generation Gap divided America, the music of America's heartland and working people bifurcated in what would seem to be a strange way, if you were only listening to the music. Hank Williams and Woody Guthrie are close kin in musical heritage, style, and attitude, but in the sixties, some-

thing called "folk music" represented youth, liberalism (this will be a difficult concept for the eighties generation—youth and liberalism?), and the antiwar movement, while something called "country music" represented middle age, social and political conservatism, and support for the war.

At the same time, country performers were getting to be a big deal on TV. Johnny Cash and Glen Campbell had their own network shows—and for a teenaged California Beatles fan named Rosanne Cash, this was something of an embarrassment. Actually, Cash, like Willie Nelson and a number of other country singers, was a political liberal, but the image of country music was closer to Hank Thompson's message. Or Johnny Wright's message, in "Hello, Vietnam," or Staff Sgt. Barry Sadler's in "The Ballad of the Green Berets,"[2] or most dramatically, Merle Haggard's in "Okie From Muskogee" and "Fightin' Side of Me." It's questionable whether these songs accurately represented Haggard's philosophy—he's a subtle and thoughtful man—but they became anthems of the political right.

If the country establishment hated the hippies, not all the hippies felt the same animosity. Bob Dylan journeyed down to Nashville to make an album and started a pop music fad for Nashville as a recording center and for the Nashville Sound (John Sebastian and the Lovin' Spoonful reflected this in their song "Nashville Cats"). Johnny Cash and Dylan formed a mutual admiration society. The Byrds, the Nitty Gritty Dirt Band, Asleep at the Wheel, the Grateful Dead, and Com-

---

[2]Also a number one pop hit; Sadler was later involved with some sleazy mercenary gunrunning in Latin America and ultimately killed himself.

mander Cody were just some of the pop acts who loved country music, but you won't find any of them on the country charts for that era.

Which is not to say, as the sixties rolled over into the early seventies, the Nixon years, that the country charts did not embrace pop acts. They just didn't embrace those long-haired, dope-smokin' hippie pop acts. Again, country crossover dreams were uptown dreams, attached to such shining hopes as John Denver and Olivia Newton-John. When the two of them swept the Country Music Association Awards in 1974 and 1975 (Denver was Entertainer of the Year in '75), a lot of real country artists got disgruntled enough to talk about forming a new organization.

The Outlaw Years happened at the same time. Willie Nelson and Waylon Jennings grew their hair long and hung out with hippies and rockers such as Doug Sahm, Asleep at the Wheel, or Delbert McClinton at the Armadillo World Headquarters in Austin, Texas, the center for the new coalition. And the Nitty Gritty Dirt Band went to Nashville in 1971 to record with the conservative stronghold of old-fashioned country music, with Roy Acuff and Vassar Clements and Mother Maybelle Carter and Earl Scruggs and Doc Watson. All this stuff made the country establishment nervous, too, but Waylon and Willie made their way under the tent.

Others didn't. During this same era, even as potential second-generation country stars such as Rosanne Cash, Carlene Carter, and Pam Tillis were turning away from country, trying to find music that was more relevant to their generation, young working-class Southern whites were developing a new kind of music. Like the rockabilly of Elvis and Johnny Cash, it was blues and country based; but these young guys had listened to Jimi Hendrix and acid rock as well. The Allman Brothers and the Marshall Tucker Band and Wet Willie and Lynyrd Skynyrd played something called Southern Rock, and it had every bit as much right to be called country as "Have You Never Been Mellow." Although only the Charlie Daniels Band, of all the Southern Rockers, ever made the country charts, their sound left its mark in the work of Hank Williams, Jr.

But the kid at the gas station in North Carolina was listening to the Southern rockers, not to John Denver, not to Barbara Mandrell. By cutting them out (as well as white Midwestern working-class rockers such as Bob Seger), country music lost a huge chunk of its new generation of potential listeners.

The establishment guys were still looking for that magic uptown crossover secret, and they seemed to have finally found it in 1980, with the Urban Cowboy craze, in the wake of the movie of the same name. Bars all across the country started installing mechanical bulls, yuppies started wearing yoked shirts and fringed boots, records by Mickey Gilley, Eddie Rabbitt, Johnny Lee, T. G. Sheppard, and Alabama shot up the pop charts. The country music network TV series for this era featured the Vegas-glitzy Mandrell Sisters. The multitalented Barbara Mandrell became country music's face for the TV audience (a face that played the tenor saxophone, among other things); a lot of people in Nashville were sure that the millennium had finally come, and country music had attained its rightful place in the universe.

It didn't happen. The country establishment had put too much faith in an audience that didn't really exist, a vision of America that was an illusion. Ronald Reagan's secretary of the interior, James Watt, misread the American spirit in the same way when he declared that the Beach Boys represented immoral, un-American values, and that their Fourth of July appearance on the Washington Mall should be scrubbed in favor of a concert by a real American, Las Vegas celebrity Wayne Newton. And like James Watt, country music found its credibility in a shambles.

Interestingly, the seeds of country's rebirth were being sown on the back forty even as the gentlemen farmers of the Urban Cowboy movement were sipping their mint juleps on the front porch. An unfashionable cowboy singer from Texas was pleasing country audiences, even if he wasn't crossing over to the pop charts. A brilliant bluegrass picker from Kentucky made records featuring traditional instruments and bluegrass-influenced locals; he didn't make the pop charts, either. Nor did a second-generation country performer, making a comeback after a near-fatal accident, who used his family pedigree to play wide-open Southern Rock to a country audience. A rodeo queen from Oklahoma was having spotty success with the "contemporary country" that producers and record company execs wanted her to sing; she kept trying to move in a more traditional direction.

George Strait, Ricky Skaggs, Hank Williams, Jr., and Reba McEntire represented the future of country music, even if no one recognized it right away. And in the same period—1980, to be precise—a veteran of a quarter century in the business, an unreconstructed and unreconstructable stone traditional country singer, George Jones, released the closest thing we have to a consensus choice for the greatest country song of all time: "He Stopped Loving Her Today."

In 1984, as the industry leaders continued to hold on to their Urban Cowboy dream, a mother-daughter team from Kentucky by way of California rediscovered traditional harmony singing in a way that was so unique they could almost be said to have invented the form, and the following year, a former juvenile delinquent from North Carolina with a voice like a down-home angel turned his life around, focused his talents on music, and began to make his mark. The Judds' first number one came on their second single release, in 1984. Randy Travis only made it to No. 67 with "On the Other Hand" in 1985; rereleased the next year, after he'd caught the public's attention with "1982," it went straight to number one.

The New Traditionalism was turning country around, artistically and commercially; but there are two other important factors worth mentioning if you're going to trace the history of country's renaissance in the eighties: country cable television networks and Farm Aid.

TNN, the Nashville Network, started broadcasting in 1983, with eighteen hours a day of country variety shows, country talk shows, country amateur hours, country videos, and live country music. All the new sounds, new performers, changes, and counterchanges that were to take place in the next decade would take place in America's living rooms, before an ever-expanding audience—by January 1992, TNN reached more than 54 million households.

In 1985, Willie Nelson's crusade to save American family farms took concrete shape in the form of Farm Aid, a huge benefit concert featuring top rock and country stars. Farm Aid publicized the plight of the American farmer to the cities and suburbs; it also brought country music to the attention of those audiences. TNN broadcast the entire twelve hours of Farm Aid live.

So country was on the way back. The music was getting stronger, the performers were getting better, there was a new spirit of excitement in Nashville. But who was the new audience?

There was still the traditional core from the rural South and Midwest, but that audience was getting older, and their kids listened to arena rock and heavy metal. There was a new suburban audience, as well—not exactly the audience that Urban Cowboy had gone after, but the audience that had fallen in love with the great pop singer-songwriters of the seventies, the James Taylors and Carole Kings and Dan Fogelbergs.

A Boston music writer, in the early eighties, tried to find out whether the sixties generation was still listening to music and buying records, and if so, what? He reported that if those avid Beatles / Stones / "In-A-Gadda-Da-Vida" buyers of the sixties had bought anything at all during the preceding year, it was most likely to have been "a Willie Nelson record," even if they couldn't always remember exactly which one. And the eighties, the era of the graying of the baby boomers, saw a record-buying public that increasingly included men and women over thirty.[3]

So in the late eighties, not one but two healthy winds swirled through Nashville. The New Traditionalists carried the banner of George Jones and Merle Haggard. The new singer-songwriters loved that Jones-Haggard tradition, but they came from a variety of different, and highly personal, directions.

The names of the singer-songwriters go through this book like a litany: Nanci Griffith, Lyle Lovett, the O'Kanes, and particularly the savage god of the new generation, Steve Earle. They shook things up; they inspired other writers and performers; they got the national media talking and writing about the new country music.

And for one reason or another, they didn't quite last—at least, not in the country mainstream, which more and more came to be represented by country radio.

The New Traditionalists, on the other hand, the godsons of Jones and Haggard, got bigger and bigger—a particularly interesting phenomenon in view of the new audience they were appealing to, yet another new country audience, and a surprising one.

The audience began to get younger. The Nashville Network was showing music videos on a regular basis, and a new cable network, Country Music Television (acquired by TNN in 1981), showed vid-

---

[3]There was another significant audience of one for country music: the president of the United States, George Herbert Walker Bush. He explained why, in an article for *Country America* magazine: "So many country songs have that upbeat, optimistic sound to them . . . it's like a good game of horseshoes—I can't help but have fun and loosen up!" This is, if I remember right, the musical form that brought us "He Stopped Loving Her Today," "I Guess I'll Just Stay Here and Drink," and "She Even Woke Me Up to Say Good-bye."

Well, we don't really expect our leaders to be even remotely in touch with the real world, do we? Ronald Reagan thought Bruce Springsteen's "Born in the USA" was a patriotic affirmation of his policies and Harry Truman thought his daughter was a great singer.

eos around the clock. Videos appeal to young viewers, and that young audience liked the younger performers, particularly the good-looking young guys in cowboy hats. The labels started signing more and more of them: Ricky Van Shelton, Alan Jackson, Dwight Yoakam, Clint Black, Mark Chesnutt, Joe Diffie . . . and a young Oklahoman named Garth Brooks.

How big was the country audience? Bigger than a lot of people thought, as the entertainment world discovered in 1991, when *Billboard,* the bible of the music industry, changed the formula by which it tabulated its hit charts. The new system used bar coding at the point of sale and created a much more accurate list. Country was already making a strong showing on the Top 200, but it exploded on the new charts. Garth Brooks's *No Fences,* which had been in the twenties the week before, was No. 2 on the first new chart. And that fall, Brooks's new release, *Ropin' the Wind,* astounded everyone by making its debut at number one on the pop charts—something no country album had ever done.

You didn't see a Garth Brooks single on the pop charts, though—nor a single by any other country artist. The singles charts, reflecting radio play, remained totally format-driven—and for the first time, country radio was a more popular format that Top Forty. "Why should we promote Garth Brooks to pop radio?" asked Jimmy Bowen, president of Brooks's label, Capitol Records. "We're a stronger format than they are, anyway."

"Why should we play Garth Brooks?" Top Forty programmers were saying. "It'll just be a plug for the country stations, and they're taking too many listeners away from us anyway."

Country radio was doing just fine with Garth Brooks and a few others—fewer and fewer, as playlists began shrinking. Perhaps the first salvo against the wide-open playlist was sounded by KRVN in Lexington, Nebraska, which announced that it would boycott the records of k. d. lang because of her "fanatical antimeat stance." Actually, lang, like a lot of the other new artists of the eighties, was already beginning to disappear from radio, but this announcement certainly suggested one reason why: the same old reason. Fear of the wild element. You'll get respect, you'll get crossover respectability, if you play it safe.

That's not it, say the radio programmers. "We have a fairly broad playlist," I was told by Bud Walker, owner of radio station WRWD in Highland, New York, "but it's because we're the only game in town. When you have two country radio stations competing for the same market, the one with the shorter playlist will always do better in the ratings."

Interestingly, TNN, which is the only all-country cable variety network, has retained a marvelously broad "playlist." Their keystone program, "Nashville Now," starring veteran disc jockey Ralph Emery (whose autobiography was a surprise national best-seller in 1992), features everyone from oldtimers to unknowns. TNN shows such as "Texas Connection" and "American Music Shop" have presented cutting-edge performers such as the Flatlanders, the Texas Tornadoes, Delbert McClinton, and John Prine, playing live music before live audiences.

At this writing, country music is more popular than it has ever been, and the movers and shakers in the industry believe it's here to stay—this is no Urban Cowboy phenomenon, you hear over and over.

We're not diluting the product, we're play-ing real country music, and the audiences are coming to us.

They could be right. We hope so. Through all the cynicism and reportorial detachment, we love country music. Along with rhythm and blues and jazz, it represents the very best art that American culture has produced.

TAD RICHARDS
Saugerties, NY
1993

Alabama

RANDY OWEN
b. 12/13/49, Fort Payne, AL

TEDDY GENTRY
b. 1/22/52, Fort Payne, AL

JEFF COOK
b. 8/27/49, Fort Payne, AL

MARK HERNDON
b. 5/11/55, Springfield, MA

Style
Slick, catchy pop-rock. Country harmonies on top of shake-your-booty party licks that have been known to drift toward the conventional.

Memorable songs
"Mountain Music," "If You're Gonna Play in Texas (You've Gotta Have a Fiddle in the Band)"

Awards
ACM—Vocal Duet/Group 1981–85, Album of the Year and Album coproducer 1982 (Feels So Right), 1983 (The Closer You Get), 1984 (Roll On), Entertainer of the Year 1981–85, Artist of the Decade 1980s; CMA—Album of the Year 1983, Vocal Group 1981–83, Instrumental Group 1981–82, Entertainer of the Year 1982–84; Grammy—Country Vocal Performance–Duo or Group ("Mountain Music") 1982, ("The Closer You Get") 1983; MCN—Album of the Year 1982, 1984, Band 1983–84

Nobody likes Alabama but the public, and the public likes Alabama a whole lot. How much? Actually, that's not hard to describe, as long as the phrase *most popular band in the history of country music* is still in the language. Their brand of undemanding, party-time country rock has struck a responsive chord with an amazing number of people. An Alabama concert is not just a gathering of the Fan Fair faithful. Most of the time, you'll find an equally healthy representation of Fort Lauderdale–Spring Weekend–Tastes Great–Less Filling types.

Jeff Cook, Teddy Gentry, and leader Randy Owen were all cousins and homeboys from the cotton-mill town of Fort Payne, in northeastern Alabama. They began their professional existence in the early seventies as Wild Country, along with another local Alabama boy, Bennett Vartanian.

It was Wild Country that gravitated to the resort community of Myrtle Beach, South Carolina, and landed a regular job playing at a club called the Bowery. The gig stretched into an eight-year run, where they played marathon sets (sometimes all day and all night), worked out their style, and began to define their audience.

Vartanian left the group in 1976 and was replaced by "six or seven drummers who came and went in the coming years," their official bio says. Actually, one of them, Rick Scott—who cowrote "Why Lady Why," later a number one for the group—stayed for a good three years, but he was ultimately replaced by New Englander Mark Herndon, a rock and roll drummer who was developing a reputation playing in party bands around Myrtle Beach.

By this time, the group had been renamed the Alabama Band and had charted its first single at number 77, on an independent label. Two more indie releases over the next couple of years won them a major-label contract with RCA in 1980.

The rest is The Land of Wildest Dreams: number one the first time out of the box with "Tennessee River," a string of number one hits that had passed two dozen before the decade ran out (including twenty-one straight, a record no one has even approached). They've been three-time Country Music Association Entertainers of the Year, five-time Academy of Country Music Entertainers of the Year, they've won two Grammys, they've been named three times by *People* magazine's readers as favorite group of any musical style, and in 1989, they were chosen by the ACM as Artists of the Decade. They hit a slump in record sales as the eighties wound down, but made a strong comeback with their 1989 album, *Southern Star,* and its follow-up, *Pass It On Down.*

Alabama have represented themselves on record as a regional band ("Tennessee River," "Mountain Music"), a party band ("If You're Gonna Play in Texas"), a romantic band ("When We Make Love"), and even a socially conscious band ("Song of the South," "Forty-Hour Week (For a Livin')," "Pass It On Down.") Always,

though, they've been first and foremost a band.

Today, that doesn't seem strange. Contemporary, rock-style bands are all over the charts, and Alabama is the godfather of Exile, Sawyer Brown, Shenandoah, Highway 101, and a whole slew of others. But back in the midseventies, a self-contained band was not only unheard of in country music circles, it was downright subversive, and a lot of major labels shied away from Alabama for exactly that reason. As Jeff Cook explains it in Tom Roland's *The Billboard Book of Number One Country Hits,* the powers that be in conservative Nashville seemed to feel that "if you were a band, you would have a hit record and then have internal problems and break up."

Of course, country music has always prided itself on fan loyalty and the longevity of its stars' careers, so these were the models that the guys behind the desks understood. Bread-and-butter stars. It made sense to sign a Randy Owen, provide him with a backup band of competent, nameless, replaceable pickers, and count on him to have five years or so of Top Ten hits, then go on as a huge draw at the county fairs for the next twenty years.

Alabama didn't go for it. They made their decision to stand or fall as a band, and the Artist of the Decade award is proof enough that they confounded the skeptics. Whether they've contributed to a major shift in the profile of the country music star, and the country music world, is still open to question. A lot of observers say that bringing pop/flash to country is a mixed blessing. Country music audiences are growing closer and closer to pop music audiences—they're making one-hit wonders, flash-in-the-pan careers, totally forgotten superstars.

Alabama, of course, is a group that's lasted. But for that matter, megastars though they are, what kind of a mark will Alabama leave when they're gone? Will they inspire a future troubadour to sing, as George Jones did about his generation's idols, "Who's Gonna Fill Their Shoes?"

We'd guess maybe not. If Alabama were a movie, they'd be *The Poseidon Adventure:* an all-star cast, lots of flashy scenes and effects, big box-office, but not much of an artistic impact, and hard to remember clearly ten years later.

It's worth mentioning before we take leave of them that Owen, Cook, Gentry, and Herndon have given back, for almost as long as they've been on top. Their June Jam, which they began in 1982 in their hometown of Fort Payne, has raised over $2 million for state and local charities; they've backed up their environmental sentiments in "Pass It On Down" with statements and personal example; and in 1987, the group was given the Bob Hope Humanitarian Award for public service and contributions involving children.

Danielle Alexander

b. 12/2/54, Fort Worth, TX

Style

Pop country

On her album covers, Danielle Alexander appears dressed for a ritzy cocktail hour, personifying somebody's archetype of sophistication. In person, with her Buddy Holly glasses off, she's a long, tall Texan with an engaging, down-to-earth manner and a face that suggests rough times she doesn't talk about.

Music was Danielle's direction out of a life headed nowhere special, and country was her answer to a life in music that was starting to look much the same. She was playing cocktail piano in LA and Vegas lounges, until she looked at herself "in the mirror one day and saw myself playing at a piano bar, fifty years old, probably somewhere in San Francisco, living above the bar with my mother, both of us drinking Scotch, playing 'New York, New York,' and at midnight, going home and watching the late show," so she headed for Nashville.

She arrived in 1986, got a publishing contract as a songwriter, and was still on the scene two years later when Mercury Records went looking for another K. T. Oslin and found her playing a Writer's Night at Nashville's Bluebird Cafe.

Mercury has presented her as a solo artist, and as half of a duo with Butch Baker. She hasn't found the style that will establish her as a presence on record yet, but Danielle Alexander is a good old girl, and here's hoping she does.

Deborah Allen

b. 9/30/53, Memphis, TN (*Deborah Lynn Thurmond*)

Style

Collaborative (well, sort of)

Deborah Allen made her mark as a duet singer on three successful pairings with Jim Reeves in 1979/80. If Reeves was pleased with the results, he didn't say—he'd been dead for fifteen years. She had a couple of solid hits of her own, with "Baby I Lied" and "I've Been Wrong Before" in 1983/84, before fading into obscurity—at least as a singer. She's a successful songwriter and is married to another: Rafe Van Hoy.

John Anderson

b. 12/13/54, Apopka, FL

Style
Solid

Memorable songs
"I'm Just an Old Chunk of Coal (But I'm Gonna Be a Diamond Someday),"
"Swingin' "

Awards
CMA—Single of the Year 1983
("Swingin' "); Horizon Award 1983

There was a time when John Anderson was a breath of fresh air in country music. He was the new Great Voice, the heir to the tradition of Jim Reeves, George Jones, Merle Haggard: simple, honest, affecting. The guy who had worked as a carpenter on the glitzy new Opryland was the new favorite singer of those who loved the old values—the same values that were to be reborn in the eighties as the New Traditionalism.

Anderson sang about the down-and-dirty truths of life, about The Girl at the End of the Bar, the girl who Just Started Likin' Cheatin' Songs. His breakthrough song, in late 1980, was "1959," and he followed that up with the mournfully optimistic "I'm Just an Old Chunk of Coal," which captured a down-in-the-gutter-looking-at-the-stars feeling as well as any song has.

"Wild and Blue," in 1982, was Anderson's first number one record, but it was the next one, "Swingin'," that was the monster: the biggest-selling country single in Warner Brothers history. "Swingin' " had a rhythm-and-bluesy drive and a stone country energy, combined with a cheerful raunchiness. It won the CMA's Single of the Year award, and it won Anderson the Horizon Award as the hottest new entertainer of the year.

But Anderson would never have another year like 1983. There were bad career choices in the areas of management and material, some negative publicity, and a weight problem that didn't enhance his golden-tressed, boyishly bearded image. He's younger than a lot of today's new stars, and he paved the way for their success, but—almost incomprehensibly for a guy with a voice as great as his—Anderson saw his career melt away and had to struggle to pull it back together. He seemed to succeed in 1992 with a hot comeback album, *Seminole Wind*.

Lynn Anderson

b. 9/26/47, Grand Forks, ND

Style
Smooth MOR belter; solid performer, but perhaps she seemed more distinctive in an era when there were hardly any other women stars in country music.

Memorable songs
"Rose Garden," "Rocky Top"

Awards
ACM—Female Vocalist 1967, 1970;
CMA—Female Vocalist 1971;
Grammy—Country Vocal; Performance-Female 1970 ("Rose Garden")

Lynn Anderson, short version: Second-generation country performer (mom Liz Anderson wrote "All My Friends Are Gonna Be Strangers" for Merle Haggard);

crossover star of "Rose Garden" and Lawrence Welk fame; rodeo queen and horse-farm owner; painful and losing custody battle with second ex-husband (whom she describes as "the real J.R."), in which her mother testified against her.

In the days when Lynn Anderson was a reigning queen of country music, it was easier to get her to talk about her horses. These days, with more to look back on than ahead to (although she's only in her early forties), she's thoughtful and articulate about the country music scene and her place in it.

On the old days: "Girls weren't allowed to have their own bands when I started. Dolly Parton worked for Porter Wagoner, Loretta for the Wilburn Brothers—everybody was somebody's girl singer, and they'd walk out at their appointed time, sing their three or four songs, and disappear."

On these days: "Those of us who are ladies in the country music field cannot expect to be cute little things out there onstage when we're seventy. Unless we gain some kind of a stature like Minnie Pearl and can inject some humor, then our ability to communicate with the audience diminishes to a large extent. But these days you have ladies with gray hair on the cover of *Vogue*. And the advent of a George Jones, who can sing from the point of view of someone who's made some mistakes, and lived through them, may open up things for some of us girls, and we'll see more of a place for, well, character roles."

On the future: "I aspire to working behind the scenes—A and R or something like that. I'm a song person, always have been. I've always had pretty good taste in songs, I believe. In fact, I've established an excellent track record of hits for other people—songs like 'True Heart' [number five for the Oak Ridge Boys] and 'Tender Lie' [number one for Restless Heart], which I recorded but were never released."

Lynn Anderson's list of the greatest songs of all time: "I Can't Stop Loving You," "Yesterday," "Cryin'," "Wind Beneath My Wings," "Unchained Melody."

Eddy Arnold

b. 5/15/18, Henderson, TN

Style
"Countrypolitan"—country's first crooner

Memorable songs
"Cattle Call," "Jim, I Wore a Tie Today"

Awards
ACM—Pioneer Award 1983; CMA—Entertainer of the Year 1967; Hall of Fame 1966

The last person you expected to make a comeback in the nineties was Eddy Arnold. For one thing, although the New Traditionalism was the watchword of the era, the emphasis was on the "new" part, the handsome guys in cowboy hats. It was the old sound, but no one was rushing out to sign up a bunch of old guys such as Hank Thompson or Warner Mack to major-label contracts. For another thing, if they had been signing up the Old Traditionalists, Eddy Arnold wouldn't have been one of them. Arnold was the progenitor of the now-discredited Nashville Sound, smooth strings, lush arrangements, and pop-style crooning. But RCA, Arnold's label since 1946 (with a break of a couple of undistinguished years in the midseventies on the now-defunct MGM), released a new Eddy Arnold album in 1990, and another in 1991.

Arnold was seventy-one when *Hand Holding Songs* came out, and seventy-two for the release of *You Don't Miss a Thing*. The former was all Tin Pan Alley standards like "As Time Goes By," and frankly, it was a pretty terrible album. On *You Don't Miss a Thing* he went for newer material (can you imagine some twenty-two-year-old songwriter being told, "We're holding one of your songs for the new Eddy Arnold album"?), and although the album wasn't about to yield any new Top Ten hits, it was really not bad at all.

The forties, when Arnold began his career, was the decade of a number of legends of country music. Bob Wills, whose Texas Playboys defined the style known as Western Swing (kept alive today by Asleep at the Wheel), was still in his heyday, and Western Swing bandleaders, like big-band jazz and pop bandleaders, were immensely popular. Tex Williams ("Smoke! Smoke! Smoke! That Cigarette" was Capitol Records' first-ever million seller); Spade Cooley, who would later be convicted of murdering his wife, was the ace of California Western Swing (the godfather of the Merle Haggard/Buck Owens Bakersfield sound); Hank Thompson, who would achieve his greatest success in the sixties, was the new Western Swing kid on the block, taking "Humpty Dumpty Heart" to number two in 1948. Merle Travis's songs about real working people and their lives ("Sixteen Tons," "Divorce Me C.O.D.") affected future songwriters, while his guitar playing has influenced succeeding guitarists from country to jazz. Singing cowboys Gene Autry, Roy Rogers, Tex Ritter, Jimmy Wakely, and the Sons of the Pioneers were movie idols as well as recording stars (Autry, over his

own strenuous protests, recorded a throw-away novelty number called "Rudolph, the Red-Nosed Reindeer" in 1949). The great stylists of the era included Ernest Tubb ("I'm Walkin' the Floor Over You"), originally a protégé of Jimmie Rodgers's widow; Roy Acuff; yodeling Elton Britt (who sang "There's a Star Spangled Banner Waving Someplace" for FDR at the White House); and—last but not least—Hank Williams.

If RCA, in 1990, was simply giving the venerable Mr. Arnold a sort of vanity production, they could certainly afford it just by taking it out of the profits Eddy Arnold had made for them over the years.

How big a success was he? Arnold's name doesn't exactly have the mystique of Willie or George, Hank or Lefty, and he isn't the first artist who comes to most people's minds when they make their lists of the greatest of all time. That's why it came as such a surprise in 1989, when Joel Whitburn's book *Top Country Singles 1944–1988* (essential for any country aficionado) came out, that the most successful country music performer of all time was Eddy Arnold.

Whitburn used a formula based on number of charted records, highest chart position reached, total weeks on the charts, and total weeks (if any) at number one. His Top Ten artists were:

1. Eddy Arnold
2. George Jones
3. Johnny Cash
4. Merle Haggard
5. Conway Twitty
6. Ray Price
7. Webb Pierce
8. Willie Nelson
9. Marty Robbins
10. Dolly Parton

With over 85 million records sold, Arnold ranks behind only Elvis and the Beatles in total sales. He is also, by most people's reckoning, the richest man in country music.

Asleep at the Wheel

RAY BENSON
b. 3/16/51, Philadelphia, PA

Tim Alexander, John Ely, Michael Francis, Larry Franklin, Jon Mitchell, David Sanger, Cindy Cashdollar

This is the current group—as Benson says, essentially the post-1985 group. There have been something like seventy-five members altogether, going back to its founders: Benson, Leroy Preston, and Lucky Oceans (Reuben Gosfield). "The group has changed considerably," says Benson, "and yet there are elements that are exactly the same . . . me."

Style

Western Swing

Memorable songs

"House of Blue Lights," "Texas Fiddle Man"

Awards

ACM—Touring band (cowinners w/Sons of the Pioneers) 1977; Grammy—Country Instrumental Performance 1978 ("One O'Clock Jump"), 1987 ("String of Pars"), 1988 ("Sugarfoot Rag")

We remember Ray Benson's Asleep at the Wheel from 1971 at the Château Liberté, a hippie dance hall in northern California's Santa Cruz Mountains. We were younger and wilder then, and Asleep at the Wheel played a red-hot, crowd-pleasing, foot-stomping brand of unadulterated Western Swing.

Somehow in the ensuing twenty years we got older and more subdued, but we did catch Asleep at the Wheel recently at New York's Bottom Line, and if we've gotten twenty years older, Ray Benson doesn't seem to have: he and his new lineup played a red-hot, crowd-pleasing, foot-stomping brand of unadulterated Western Swing.

Western Swing was Texas's response to the big-band era of the thirties, combining the traditional country-and-western sounds of the Southwest with the swinging ensemble arrangements of jazz innovators such as Fletcher Henderson and Benny Goodman. As pioneered by such bandleaders as Milton Brown, Spade Cooley, and above all Bob Wills, it was sparkling, sophisticated, and you could dance your booty off to it. The glory days of Western Swing had faded by the end of the forties, but you could still find the music on records if you looked for it, and if you were a kid named Ray Benson, growing up in Pennsylvania as the fifties turned into the sixties, you might well be looking for it.

Especially if you were already listening to Faron Young, Ferlin Husky, Stonewall Jackson, and Patsy Cline on the radio—and Jerry Lee Lewis when you turned to the rock and roll stations.

Ray Benson and his sister started playing hootenannies when he was eleven—they were even offered a record contract, "but our parents wouldn't let us take it because we would have to travel." In his teens, he played square dances around New England, and then, after a short stint at Antioch University in Ohio, and an apprenticeship as a film ed-

25

itor in New York, he gave himself totally over to the Western Swing that had won his heart.

Asleep at the Wheel was formed in Paw Paw, West Virginia, in 1969. Commander Cody, a New York artist turned country/rock cult figure, brought the group out to the San Francisco area around 1970. Willie Nelson heard them play and suggested they move to Austin, which they did in 1973.

"Austin was a dream world back then," Benson remembers. "Hippies, cowboys, state legislators . . . and everybody seemed to tolerate each other. I went out every night of the week, either to play or see somebody play. The Thunderbirds, Doug Sahm, Stevie Ray Vaughan . . . older guys like Willie, Jerry Jeff Walker, Michael Martin Murphey. And all the Western Swing guys were there. I got to meet guys like Jesse Ashlock, Al Stricklin, Leon McAuliffe [all former Texas Playboys]—hundreds of guys, a lot of whom have since passed away. The music scene had so much tradition, and yet it was so new."

Asleep at the Wheel released its first single, "Take Me Back to Tulsa," in 1973. It went nowhere, but as Benson says, "we started out recording the kind of music we wanted to play, and that's what we've always done. A lot of people have told us to try other stuff, but we never listened. A career in music is two things—one, are you playing music for the pure enjoyment of it, and as a reflection of your lifestyle, or do you play music to feed the entertainment machine? We wanted to do both, and we were naive enough to think that we could, so we did. I've always considered myself a clown, and a music scholar. And I tried to mix the two so the people would be entertained."

Asleep at the Wheel's first real chart success came in 1975 with "The Note That Johnny Walker Read," still their only Top Ten hit. Then came a period of doldrums in late seventies and early eighties when it seemed nobody wanted to listen to Western Swing. Still, "we didn't change anything," Benson remembers, "except that we did get better. Willie Nelson financed us during those days. He really kept us alive."

During those years, Nelson suggested they record an old favorite song of Benson's called "House of Blue Lights."

Benson's piano player at the time was from a different style, "but then we got a hot piano player, and then out of the blue, Huey Lewis's manager called and said, 'You ought to record "House of Blue Lights." ' So I said, 'Hey, here's two guys who know what they're talking about,' so we went in and cut it in a mobile home—in fact, I cut it as a duet with Willie, but the record label said no, let's cut Willie off it, he's already got two records out now. Which made Willie real mad—at them, not us—but it became our comeback hit, so to speak."

Comeback hit is accurate—it came out in 1987 and was their first chart Top Twenty since "Johnny Walker" in 1975. But it's more than that to Benson: "It turned out to be one of those records where you just do it, and then you listen to it back, and you say to yourself, 'That's what Asleep at the Wheel is—that record says it all.' "

Ray Benson's list of the greatest songs of all time (he barely pauses as he pulls one song after another from the jukebox of his mind): "Crazy," "There Will Never Be Another You," "Midnight Train to Georgia," "Sally Gooden," "Take the 'A' Train."

Chet Atkins

b. 6/20/24, Luttrell, TN

Style

Guitar wizard

Memorable Songs

"Poor Boy Blues," "Sails"

Awards

ACM—Pioneer Award 1982, Guitar player 1986, 1987; CMA—Musician 1967–69, 1981–85, 1988; Grammy—Instrumental Performance 1967 (Chet Atkins Picks the Best), Country Instrumental Performance 1970 (Me and Jerry w/Jerry Reed), 1971 ("Snowbird"), 1974 (The Atkins-Travis Traveling Show, w/Merle Travis), 1975 ("The Entertainer"), 1976 (Chester and Lester w/Les Paul), 1981 (Country— After All These Years), 1985 ("Cosmic Square Dance," w/ Mark Knopfler), 1991 ("So Soft, Your Goodbye" w/ Mark Knopfler), 1992 (Sneakin' Around w/ Jerry Reed), Country Vocal Collaboration 1990 ("Poor Boy Blues" w/ Mark Knopfler), Hall of Fame, 1973

After a career of close to half a century as a professional guitar picker, you might think that Chet Atkins would have gotten a little tired of six strings and a wooden box; you might not be surprised to hear that he was just going through the motions on the guitar these days, while pursuing his true passion of raising Arabian horses or collecting Japanese art or restoring Hepplewhite furniture, or any one of those pursuits that gentlemen with as much money as Mr. Atkins tend to indulge.

Uh-uh. "I really have no interests other than music," Atkins says. In fact, even within the field of music, Atkins has focused his attention. Once a producer and A&R man who oversaw Elvis Presley's first sessions for RCA, once a record-company executive, he is now centering all his energies on dancing with the love that brought him to the ball—that guitar. And Atkins has played it in virtually every style and format that anyone has ever dreamed up—country, jazz, classical, blues.

Chet Atkins got his first guitar in a trade for a pistol. He began playing professionally in the early 1940s and made his first appearance on record in 1945, backing a group called Wally Fowler and his Georgia Clodhoppers (they would later come to be called the Oak Ridge Boys). He made his first recording for RCA in 1946.

By the 1960s he was the head of RCA's country music division, and producer of some of Nashville's most significant artists. He was also the originator of one of country music's most historic innovations: the Nashville Sound, a smoother, more urbane reworking of the country concept, in which the classic hillbilly fiddle and Dobro guitar instrumentation was abandoned in favor of pianos and string sections.

The Nashville Sound has been swept away in recent years, first shaken by the Outlaws of the early seventies, then blown out the door by the New Traditionalists. Atkins told us recently: "I'd rather play country than any other kind of music. But I play jazz and light classical and New Age because I can get radio play in those formats." But enough of those Traditionalists have enough respect for the old CGP (certified guitar player) to make Atkins's duet album with rock guitarist Mark Knopfler (Dire Straits) one of the surprise hits of 1990.

Hoyt Axton

b. 3/25/38, Comanche, OK

Style

Old pro folkie, gruff good humor

Memorable songs

"Joy to the World," "Never Been to Spain," "The Pusher" (as writer)

Who wrote a number one hit song whose mother also wrote a number one hit song?

Perhaps you can win your next game of Trivial Pursuit with this: it's our boy, Hoyt Axton, who wrote "Joy to the World," and his mama, Mae, who wrote "Heartbreak Hotel."

And don't think Mama wasn't an influence on young Hoyt. "I got interested in songwriting when I was about fourteen," he told us. "My mom started writing back in '49, and I was fascinated by the whole process. From the time I was in junior high, she was constantly having guys come by who could really play guitar and write well. This was in Florida, where Mom taught English and drama in high school. I saw how much fun she was having writing those songs—and after "Heartbreak Hotel," when I saw those royalties coming in, I thought to myself, 'Gol-ly, you mean you can make a living doing this?' "

Some can, and some can't, and it wasn't long before young Mr. Axton had a chance to find out for himself. When he was eighteen, "My dad said, 'I'm tired of paying for you, boy, you eat too much. Why don't you go on the road?' " Hoyt headed for Los Angeles, where he became a folk singer, performing at the Troubadour, a seminal club of that era.

In 1962, he became a successful writer for the first time, when the Kingston Trio took his "Greenback Dollar" to number one.

Depending, that is, on how you define success. "I got eight hundred dollars from 'Greenback Dollar.' I had a crooked publisher. You live and learn. So the next year I formed my own publishing company and went to work for Screen Gems Publishing in Hollywood, writing one song a month on contract from '63 to '65. No hits, although I had two songs recorded by Glenn Yarborough.

"The next song I wrote that had any success was 'The Pusher Man.' I used to sing it at the Troubadour. John Kay was the dishwasher there, and he told me later that he used to come out of the kitchen with that wet towel over his shoulder and listen to that song. And he told himself that if he ever had a band, he'd like to record it."

Kay got a band a few years later, Steppenwolf, and his version of the song exploded off the sound track of *Easy Rider* in 1969.

During this same period, the LA-based folksinger got his first acting roles, in a "Bonanza" episode and then in a Western called *Smoky,* which starred Fess "Davy Crockett" Parker. "I couldn't act my way out of a wet paper sack. When I saw myself on-screen in *Smoky,* I said, 'I don't want to do this.' I didn't act again for ten years."

Axton's broad features and solid presence come across well on film, as he has shown most notably in Steven Spielberg's *Gremlins.* Nevertheless, he says, "Acting doesn't make my soul sing the way music does."

Axton's connection with the world of big-time pop music has always been a little tenuous, as well. "I canceled my subscription to *Rolling Stone,*" he told us, "the day they said, 'Three Dog Night takes Hoyt Axton's songs out of the realm of unfocused silliness and puts them in proper musical perspective so the masses can enjoy them.' "

So perhaps the Florida folk rocker has always belonged in country, although his only two Top Ten hits on the country charts came in 1974, followed by some scattered chart action through the rest of the seventies and early eighties. He completed a new album in 1990, called *Spinning the Wheels,* "a song I started at the big Harley gathering in Sturgis, South Dakota, in '89. I had some films fall through right about the same time, and my agent couldn't understand why I wasn't more upset. I said, 'It doesn't matter, I'm writing music.' "

Hoyt Axton's list of the greatest songs of all time: Bach's Suite for Solo Cello in G Major, "Life Is Like a Mountain Railway," "Joy to the World" ("I was driving through upstate New York back in '69 and I heard a classical station out of New York City playing 'Joy to the World.' Then the announcer came on and said you've heard such and such by Debussy, and so and so by Bach, and 'Joy to the World' by Axton, and such and such by Mozart, and I thought, 'Yeah, that sounds good'"), "City of New Orleans."

Baillie and the Boys

KATHY BAILLIE
b. 2/20/51, Morristown, NJ

MICHAEL BONAGURA
b. 3/26/53, Newark, NJ

Style

Girl/boy harmonies

Memorable songs

"Treat Me Like a Stranger"

It's not as unusual as it once was to have country stars from New Jersey, but it's still not the norm, either. The success of Kathy Baillie and Michael Bonagura is very much a product of this era.

Country music stars of the Ray Price/Webb Pierce era, of the Loretta/Tammy era, basically drew on country for their influences—Hank Williams, Hank Snow, Mother Maybelle Carter. The new stars grew up in the rock and roll era. Over and over, in asking performers about their influences, we heard "Hank Williams and the Beatles . . . Elvis . . . Ray Charles," and from a still newer generation, the singer/songwriters of the seventies: James Taylor, Carole King, Dan Fogelberg, Jim Croce. "If those people came along today, they'd be in country," we've been told, and maybe it's true. Kathy Baillie and Michael Bonagura aren't country folk influenced by King and Fogelberg, they could have been King and Fogelberg: sub-urban folkie background, suburban folkie foreground. As Kathy Baillie told *Country Music* magazine's Bob Allen: "I don't really have any country roots. My mother liked Patsy Cline, and that was about all my exposure. I grew up on Connie Francis and Judy Collins and Joan Baez and Cat Stevens and Brenda Lee."

Well, Brenda Lee's kinda country, but the rest of the names represent the classic progression of a Jersey girl from the sixties into the seventies, definitely on the folk-pop singer-songwriter track. But Kathy and Michael ended up in Nashville, and perhaps they were always headed that way. During her New Jersey gigs, as she told David Zimmerman of *USA Today,* "I'd sing a rock and roll cover song and somebody would say it was country and ask if I knew any rock and roll."

Baillie, Bonagura, and Alan LeBoeuf headed for Nashville in 1982, with a job waiting for them with Jim Croce's former producer Tommy West: singing backup on an Ed Bruce album that West was producing, and that yielded Bruce's Top Ten hit, "My First Taste of Texas." After that, Bonagura remembers, things slowed down: "The phone didn't ring for a year."

Gradually, things started to turn around. Bonagura sold a song called "There's No Stopping Your Heart" to Marie Osmond, and it became one of her biggest hits. The group got a few more backup jobs and quickly rose to the elite ranks of Nashville's top studio singers, adding a distinctive sound to the tracks they appeared on. They backed up Anne Murray, Dan Seals, and Vince Gill; they sang on Randy Travis's first three albums.

In 1986, they signed with RCA, and the pace of life started to pick up for them. Their first, self-titled album came out in September of 1987; their first hit was "Oh Heart." Touring behind the album turned out to be a little tricky for the group. Kathy Baillie, their star attraction, was pregnant.

She was able to stay with the tour, however, until seven and a half months into the pregnancy, and on April Fools' Day, 1988, she delivered Alyssa Baillie Bonagura. Mom and Dad were back on tour within a month, Grandma Baillie traveling with them to help out.

In 1989, Alan LeBoeuf left the group, worn out by the demands of stardom. He was replaced by Lance Hoppen, who had made his reputation with the highly regarded seventies pop group Orleans, who had megahits with "Still the One" and "Dance With Me" (and who have recently re-formed, giving Hoppen something of a dual career). Since the group is still called Baillie and the Boys, that gives Lance a sort of equal billing as the other boy, but the group is really a husband-wife duo these days.

Moe Bandy

b. 2/12/44, Meridian, MS (*Marion Bandy*)

Style
Drinkin', cheatin', rodeoin' good ol' boy; gravel-voiced storyteller

Memorable songs
"Hank Williams, You Wrote My Life," "Just Good Ol' Boys" (*with Joe Stampley*)

Awards
ACM—New Male Vocalist 1976, Song of the Year 1979 ("It's a Cheatin' Situation"), Vocal Duet/Group 1979, 1980 (w/Joe Stampley); CMA—Vocal Duo 1980 (w/Joe Stampley)

Surprisingly soft-spoken in person, Moe Bandy declines to take credit for actually living that life which Hank Williams wrote. "Some of it's me, I guess—there's got to be a part of you in anything you do—but generally I haven't lived it, at least the drinking and cheating parts. I have rodeoed a lot. And the good old boy—some of that, but not a lot.

"What is, once you get a hit like 'Cheatin' Songs,' you want to follow it with another, so I just got every drinkin' and cheatin' song in the world. I still do story songs, but I've tried to get away from those negative subjects. Lately I've done things like 'Till I'm Too Old to Die Young' and 'Americana.'"

Bandy grew up in San Antonio, Texas, in a rodeo family: his brother went to the national finals seven times as a bull rider. Moe tried his hand at riding bulls, too, but soon gave it up for the easier—some would say rougher—life of playing music in Texas honky-tonks, while keeping his day job as a sheet-metal worker. He and his band played behind Bob Wills—"that was one of the biggest thrills of my life"—Webb Pierce, Charlie Pride, Loretta Lynn, "back when it was just her and Mooney traveling together."

If the Moe Bandy on record is a combination of self-assured and fatalistic, rowdy and hell-bent, the Moe Bandy in person is a different story. Of his first success, he says: "It scared me to death. I didn't know what to do next. I was flat broke—I'd spent all my money on going to Nashville and doing the session. I couldn't even afford a plane ticket to go on the road—back then, the labels left you kind of on your own as far as financing a tour went. That first hit is a very rough point in a guy's career. You think it's when he has it made, but . . . you go out and do a medley of your hit, and then you've got to figure out the rest of the show."

Bandy's career flourished from 1974 to 1983, as a single and in a series of duets with Joe Stampley ("It was great at first—the first album was fun all the way through, but then the record companies kept pushing us to keep it up—and you can't force fun"). After that: "It was scary. All of a sudden the records weren't going past fifty on the charts, and it scared me to death. You're afraid your career's over."

Bandy resurfaced in 1987 with "Till I'm Too Old to Die Young," another solid, gravel-voiced rendition of strong material in the classic Moe Bandy tradition, but perhaps a last hurrah in this age of youth. In 1991, he planned two moves that suggest a shift to Country Music Mount Rushmore. He built a nine-hundred-seat theater in Branson, Missouri, where he'll do two shows a day, six days a week, from April to October. And he's rerecorded all his hits for a TV package.

Bobby Bare

b. 4/7/35, Ironton, OH

Style
Growly, open

Memorable songs
"Detroit City," "Please Don't Tell Me How the Story Ends"

Awards
Grammy—Country Record 1963 ("Detroit City")

One of the best shows ever presented on the Nashville Network was the one in which Bobby Bare, in his jeans and battered hat, sat around and talked with songwriters on songwriting. It was honest, casual, intelligent, and informative. It didn't last, but it's fondly remembered.

But then, Bobby Bare has always been a class act. Unpretentious and untemperamental, he not uncommonly toured without even a guitar, just borrowing one from someone backstage before he went on. His first hit song, "All American Boy" (in 1959) was released under someone else's name, but Bare has never quite gotten around to insisting that the labeling mistake be corrected.

Known as "the songwriter's friend," he has always been open and encouraging to young songwriters. He was one of the first in Nashville to recognize Kris Kristofferson's talent and recorded his "Come Sundown" and "Please Don't Tell Me How the Story Ends."

Songwriter Fred Koller says, "I love hearing a guy like Bobby Bare singing my songs because I know he's going to do it with integrity."

"Detroit City" was Bare's first major hit (under his own name) in 1963. Other notable recordings have been Ian Tyson's "Four Strong Winds," Tompall Glaser and Harlan Howard's "Streets of Baltimore," Tom T. Hall's "Margie's at the Lincoln Park Inn," and two Kristofferson songs, "The Winner" and "Dropkick Me, Jesus."

The Bellamy Brothers

HOWARD BELLAMY
b. 2/2/46, Darby FL

DAVID BELLAMY
b. 9/16/50, Darby, FL

Style
Smooth harmonies, topical in their own way

Memorable songs
"Let Your Love Flow," "Old Hippie"

The Bellamy Brothers still live at home, on the working cattle ranch in central Florida that their family has owned for over a hundred years. And if sticking by your roots is the secret of success and longevity in the music business, the Bellamy Brothers are living examples of it. They've been consistently on the charts, country and pop, since 1975: not a year has gone by when they've failed to have more than one record on the charts. As of 1991, they've had twelve number one country hits and a number one pop hit ("Let Your Love Flow").

Their first music-business success came out of a teenage incident: "We were living in the bunkhouse on our ranch," Howard recalls, "and we came in one night just a little on the twisted side, and I woke up in the morning with a big old rat snake in my bed, and spiderwebs all over the wall. It gave David an idea for a song, 'Spiders and Snakes.' We sent the tape to this guy we knew who had produced the group Lobo—he was the only guy we had ever heard of who produced records. He threw it in the reject pile, but then Jim Stafford stopped by the studio and saw it on the pile, and he kind of liked the title."

Royalties from "Spiders and Snakes"

financed the brothers' move to Hollywood, where "it was total culture shock. We moved from an area where your goal was to grow grass for cattle, to Beverly Hills where you had to keep your grass half an inch tall. We planted a sunflower garden in our front yard, and some oats, and we got a letter from the health department saying we had to cut our yard because it was attracting rodents."

It was also the mid-seventies, the Eagles were the kings of country rock, and the Bellamys had a style that suited the pop market of the day. "Let Your Love Flow" came out in 1976 and went straight to the top. Then, recalls Howard, "disco came in, and the same people who'd been recording us were telling us go home and forget it, cowboy songs are dead forever. So we went back to the ranch in Florida and went on making the same music."

But now for a country audience. "Country accepted us right away," Howard says. "We might have been the first long-haired hippies in country music, but they accepted us with open arms. We had a couple of minor hits, and then number one in 1978 with "If I Said You Had a Beautiful Body (Would You Hold It Against Me?)"

In succeeding years, the number one hits kept coming: "Sugar Daddy," "Dancin' Cowboys," "Do You Love As Good As You Look," and so on . . . more number ones than any other male duo. But let's face it . . . something is number one every week of the year, and some of those are a lot less memorable than others. When was the last time you thought about "In My Eyes" or "I Got Mexico" or "Don't Underestimate My Love for You"? Can you even remember who did them? But they each had a week at number one in the mideighties.

The Bellamy Brothers, at around the same time, had two songs that people do remember and that captured the spirit of the sixties generation growing older better than any pop singer has been able to do.

The first was "Old Hippie," which came out in 1985 and peaked at number two. "We were working with Jimmy Bowen at that time, and I have a feeling any other label head would have pitched that song out the window, but Bowen was an old hippie, too. He'd been just as wild and crazy as we were.

"We recorded the song with a line, 'he's just too friggin' old.' We've always been on the liberal side, and we saw no harm in the line . . . maybe we just wanted to see if we could get away with it. Anyway, we're out on tour in Seattle, Washington, and Bowen calls us and says you boys have to fly back in and change that friggin' line—radio won't play it. So we had to fly back all the way across the country to change one friggin' word—to 'just too damn old'—and now every time I hear the song on the radio, they play the 'friggin' ' version anyway."

The second song, "Kids of the Baby Boom," was "basically lines that were left over from 'Old Hippie,' " according to David, who wrote both songs in the same day. "Kids" apparently struck an even more responsive chord. It spent two weeks at number one and established the Bellamy Brothers as the definitive boomer chroniclers.

"Their songs chronicle the pleasures and problems of the latest decade," observes *Billboard*'s Gerry Wood, "and they are quick to put their talents on the line to raise money to help the homeless, feed the hungry, aid the environment, and teach the children."

Howard Bellamy's list of the greatest songs of all time: "Silver Wings," "Mama Tried" . . . "I could name all Haggard songs, but we'll do some different artists just to mix it up." "The Air That I Breathe" by the Hollies, "You've Got a Friend" (the James Taylor version), "Lovesick Blues."

Matraca Berg

Style
Plaintive, sensual

Memorable songs
"Lyin' to the Moon"

Matraca (pronounced Ma-TRAY-sa, and she describes its origin as "exotic hillbilly") Berg is a real Nashville show business story.

"I was raised on Music Row," Matraca describes it. Her mother, Icee Berg, was a respected but unheralded career professional in the music business, a songwriter and backup singer. "My mother used to say that she paid my dues," Matraca told UPI feature writer Jim Lewis.

"My aunt and uncle were in the music business, too, and they did well. I watched the business for many years from the inside. I watched people come and go. I watched what they went through during each transition. I don't think I have any illusions at all."

Matraca's mother was undoubtedly the most important figure in her development, which led her more or less naturally into the music business at an early age: she was seriously writing songs by the time she was fifteen.

"If I have anyone to thank or credit," she says, "it's my mom. She was definitely there to coach me when I made up my mind that songwriting was what I wanted to do. She used to take me down to all the publishing companies and make me play my songs for people. She really believed in me and the songs I was writing, and people could sense that, so they'd listen to me."

Matraca was only eighteen when her mom introduced her to Bobby Braddock, the veteran songwriter whose credits include George Jones's "He Stopped Loving Her Today." Braddock invited her to try writing with them, and they came up with "Faking Love," which went to number one for T. G. Sheppard and Karen Brooks.

When Matraca was twenty, Icee Berg died of cancer. "She was pretty much all I had," Matraca says now. "I felt like I'd lost an arm or a leg. I turned to songwriting, and it made me look at places where I hadn't looked before for songs. I grew up."

Berg's "Appalachian Rain," a song about an unwed mother going off to have her baby, and the fate of the father who abandoned her, is "what happened to my mom; and in the song I tried to deal with how she must have felt, and what I wished had happened to my father."

"Appalachian Rain" is on her first album, *Lyin' to the Moon,* released in 1991 to widespread critical praise. For such a focused and committed songwriter, Berg more or less drifted into singing, after RCA executive Joe Galante, hearing one of her demos, suggested she cut the song herself.

She wasn't sure. "I was a songwriter," she says. "I had no commitment to being an artist." But the idea of having her songs done exactly the way she envisioned them finally won her over. A year after Galante's offer, she finally signed with RCA.

Clint Black

b. 2/4/62, Long Branch, NJ

Style
Tough, intelligent, traditional

Memorable songs
"A Better Man," "Killin' Time"

Awards
ACM—Male Vocalist/New Male Vocalist 1989, Single of the Year 1989 ("Better Man"), Album of the Year 1989 (Killin' Time); CMA—Horizon Award 1989, Male Vocalist 1990; TNN/MCN—Star of Tomorrow 1990, Album of the Year 1990

In 1991, Clint Black made news for two significant duets. In his professional life, he teamed up with Roy Rogers for "Hold on Partner," the biggest hit off the comeback duet album from the King of the Cowboys. In his private life, on October 20, he teamed up with "Knots Landing" star Lisa Hartman on the marital front. In other words, Clint Black was more than just a country music star. He was a media event.

He probably deserved it, if that was what he wanted. Of the talented new superstars who hit the scene as the eighties wound down (Garth Brooks, Alan Jackson, and Black would be the big three), Black is far and away the most talented. His voice is dead on target, with an easy beat and a hard edge, and his songs (frequently cowritten by Hayden Nicholas, his longtime collaborator and guitar player in his band) are as haunting and memorable as they are catchy and danceable.

Speaking of songs . . . one of the easiest and commonest cheap shots against country music goes something like this: all those songs are about the same clichéd themes, generally involving drinkin' and cheatin', lovin' and hurtin'. Well, they say that every great novel or play ever written is a variation on one or another of seven basic plots, so it's hard to figure out why someone who writes two-and-a-half-minute stories set to music should be criticized for mostly dealing in variations on a half dozen or so themes, especially if he or she does it with style and feeling. Anyway, it occurred to us that if country music is put down for having such limited subject matter, other forms of popular music must be a lot more diverse, right? So we checked out a few albums at random, starting with classic American pop, as represented by Natalie Cole's tribute to her father, *Unforgettable*. We found songs on the themes of lovin' ("The Very Thought of You," "This Can't Be Love," "For Sentimental Reasons," "Our Love Is Here to Stay"), hurtin' ("Paper Moon," "Mona Lisa," "Don't Get Around Much Anymore," "Too Young"), ramblin' ("Route 66"), and an inspirational ditty about makin' the best of life ("Smile").

We checked out classic British rock—the Beatles' *A Hard Day's Night*. We found workin' (the title track), lovin' ("I Should Have Known Better," "I'm Happy Just to Dance With You," "And I Love Her"), cheatin' ("Tell Me Why"), hurtin' ("I'll Cry Instead"), and an inspirational song about livin' life with the right set of values ("Can't Buy Me Love").

Or how about a classic American singer-songwriter, Bruce Springsteen? In *Born in the USA*, Springsteen writes and sings about workin' ("Workin' on the Highway," "Downbound Train"—actually workin' and hurtin'), lookin' for love ("Cover Me," "I'm On Fire," "Dancin' in

the Dark"), tough times ("My Hometown," the title song), ramblin' ("Bobby Jean," "Darlington County"), and an inspirational song about livin' life with the right set of values ("Glory Days").

Surely, we'd find more variety from an acknowledged genius of American song like George Gershwin? We dug up an old album called *Chris Connor Sings Gershwin* from the back of the shelf and found lovin' ("Love Walked In," "A Foggy Day," "Love Is Here to Stay"), cheatin' ("I Love You Porgy"), playin' music ("Slap That Bass"), and an inspirational song about family values ("Summertime").

Clint Black's first album, *Killin' Time*, came out in 1989, and it had some extraordinary songs on it. "A Better Man" was the first single, and it was a hurtin' song, but one with a bittersweet silver lining. Drawn from the breakup of a long-term relationship, it carried a ring of truth inside a two-step rhythm, and it shot up to number one on the charts within two months of its release. Black became the first artist to ride his debut single all the way to number one since 1975, when Billy Swan ("I Can Help") and Freddy Fender ("Before the Next Teardrop Falls") had done it in rapid succession.

"Killin' Time" was a drinkin' and hurtin' song that didn't moralize, but nevertheless took a close, clear-eyed look at getting pie-eyed. It went to the top, too, as did "Nobody's Home," "Walking Away," and "Nothing's News," all of them hurtin' songs, but each of them unique, particularly the moody and powerful "Nothing's News," about a guy who's pining for a lost world of smoky old poolrooms and barroom brawls.

This last, incidentally, was written to prove a point to his father, who told him, "You haven't done enough living—shooting pool, drinking beer, and getting in fights" to write a real country song. Dad G. A. Black advised his son to stick with material by real songwriters, such as Harlan Howard, or else "got get drunk and get into fights."

Instead, as Black told *Los Angeles Times* writer Mike Boehm, he got ornery. "I went home and in twenty minutes I wrote 'Nothing's News' to show my dad that the proverb was true—you don't have to stick your hand in the fire to know how it feels."

Radio and Records magazine credits Clint Black with being the first artist in any format to score five number one singles off a debut album. Milli Vanilli came close at around the same time with four, but even if they'd gotten one more, Black would still have been the first artist to actually sing five number one singles off a debut album.

Born in New Jersey, Black is Houston bred and raised, and he started out playing folk clubs around the Southwest, playing a repertoire that centered around Jimmy Buffet and James Taylor, Dan Fogelberg, and the Eagles, in addition to his own material. "I didn't grow up with Bob Wills and Hank Thompson," he told John Morthland in *Country Music.* "I grew up with the people that grew up with them, like Merle Haggard and Gene Watson and George Strait. It's kind of like your grandfather . . . I never gave those older guys like Bob Wills any thought, but I'm starting to think about them now."

After he met Hayden Nicholas, he began to hone his songwriting skills further, and in 1987, he was introduced to Bill Ham, the managerial genius who had guided ZZ Top's career. Ham, an avid country fan, had always wanted to manage a country act, but had never found the

right one until Black. Ham's managerial skills appear to have been fine up to a point. In late 1992, he and Black parted company acrimoniously, with lawsuits and countersuits. Well, these things happen.

Black's second album, *Put Yourself in My Shoes,* was a solid career step forward. It contained songs about lovin' and drinkin' and workin', all of them sharply realized, emotionally complex, and all of them aspects of what Black describes as his favorite theme, "life and its effects," a broad but effective theme that Black has continued to examine in subsequent albums. And 1992's *The Hard Way* showed Black mostly sifting through the effects of relationships, finding that they're never going to be quite what you expect. His 1993 release, *No Time To Kill,* showed him opening up both musically (including a duet with Wynonna) and thematically. But then, as he put it in "Happiness Alone," one of the album's stronger entries, "Unpredictable me—Like I swore I would be—Nothing's ever written in stone."

Suzy Bogguss

b. 12/30/56, Aledo, IL

Style

Chirpy/folkie, but she can belt one

Memorable songs

"I Want to Be a Cowboy's Sweetheart," "Outbound Plane"

Awards

ACM New Female Vocalist 1988

Suzy Bogguss set out to carve out a career on the road, living in a van and wandering through the West, but she's quick to tell you, "I wasn't really a rebel, I was just adventurous. My mom always knew where I was . . . sort of."

Suzy's upbringing was the "sort of Beaver Cleaveresque community" of Aledo, Illinois, "that gave me a wide-eyed outlook on life." When she was twelve years old, she visited her grandparents in California and met their good friend Roy Rogers, a meeting she says "had a real profound influence on me." In college, where she majored in metalsmithing, she read Tom Robbins's *Even Cowgirls Get the Blues* and Douglas Adams's *Hitchhiker's Guide to the Galaxy,* and it's anyone's guess how they affected the wide-eyed Beaver Cleaverette from Aledo, Illinois.

Legends do seem to take to Suzy. Here's Chet Atkins: "I don't like hot dogs and I don't like anchovies. I don't like people who say there are too many guitar players in the world, and I especially don't like singers who sneak up on their notes. But I like Suzy Bogguss. She is always in the tone center, her voice sparkles like crystal water, and she ain't all that bad looking, boys and girls—she's only one of the best."

Suzy spun her wheels for a few years after her New Vocalist award, but 1992 saw her reach stardom with a hit album, *Aces.*

Larry Boone

b. Cooper City, FL

Style
Neotraditional

Larry Boone is a direct descendant of Daniel Boone's brother, which makes him some kind of relative of Pat Boone's as well. But his country role model is fellow Floridian Mel Tillis, whom Boone credits with "sticking his neck out for me a few times."

He started college on a baseball scholarship, which he lost due to injury, so he turned to singing in a local steak house to work his way through. He majored in journalism, but was "disillusioned by the regimentation of journalistic writing and decided to be a songwriter instead." He switched to education, took his degree, and headed to Nashville to teach school and write songs.

Arriving "just when everyone was doing the Urban Cowboy stuff," he spent his first few years doing more teaching than anything else, but gradually "I guess there's a sort of changing of the guard that happens all the time in Nashville."

"I haven't had the breakout success of a Randy Travis or a Mark Chesnutt," Boone is the first to admit, "but I've sold some records, and I think it's because there's always been a core audience for traditional country music, and there always will be, as long as the industry allows it." His biggest chart success was "Don't Give Candy to a Stranger," in 1988; as a writer, he's responsible for Don Williams's "Old Coyote Town."

Larry Boone's list of the greatest songs of all time: "Over the Rainbow," "Crazy," "Sunday Morning Comin' Down," "Almost Persuaded," "The Way We Were."

Brooks & Dunn

KIX BROOKS (*Leon Eric Brooks*)
b. 5/12/55, Shreveport, LA

RONNIE DUNN
b. 6/1/53, Tulsa, OK

Style

Hard country

Memorable songs

"Brand New Man"

Sounds like a booking agent's dream act for the nineties: "Hey, we got this great act. Guy named Brooks . . . guy from Oklahoma." Of course, we don't have to mention that the guy named Brooks and the guy from Oklahoma are two different people, and neither of them is named Garth.

Of course, it didn't happen that way. But Kix Brooks and Ronnie Dunn are two guys who were looking for a career, after both of them had not quite managed to break through as solo artists.

Brooks's first push down the country road came from a neighbor in his boyhood home of Shreveport, Johnny ("Battle of New Orleans") Horton. Later, following the advice of another Horton classic, he took a year off from college, went North to Alaska, and worked on the pipeline while singing in Fairbanks honky-tonks. Moving to Nashville, he became a successful songwriter, hitting number one with John Conlee and "I'm Only in It for the Love," the Nitty Gritty Dirt Band and "Modern Day Romance," Highway 101 and "Who's Lonely Now." His own album on Capitol, however, went nowhere.

Ronnie Dunn started out studying to be a Baptist minister, "but I got caught playing honky-tonks, and they threw me out."

Dunn came to Nashville after winning the 1988 Marlboro Talent Contest. That may seem like a sort of wimpy, corporate way to break into the rough and tough world of country music, especially for Dunn, who's the tough edge of the duo ("Ronnie is probably a little closer to Lefty Frizzell, and I'm more on the Glenn Frey side of things," Brooks says). But there's a refreshingly bizarre twist to the story. Eric Clapton's drummer, Jimmy Oldecker, saw the Marlboro entry form in a convenience store and, on a whim, entered his pal Ronnie Dunn. "When he told me about it, I just laughed," says Dunn. "But we sent them a tape, and a few weeks later we got a letter saying we qualified for the regional finals in Tulsa. We put together a band, learned three songs real fast, and won the regional. We came to Nashville for the finals and won that, too."

Arista Records' Scott Hendricks had been one of the Marlboro judges, and he stayed in touch with Dunn. Arista head Tim DuBois put him together with Brooks as writing team, and the rest is history: commercial success, and critical raves. Ken Tucker, writing in New York's *Village Voice,* put it this way: "Every time I went back to double-check something on this album, I ended up playing it all the way through."

Garth Brooks

b. 2/7/62, Tulsa, OK

Style

Billy Joel comes to Nashville

Memorable songs

"Friends in Low Places," "The Dance"

Awards

ACM—Male Vocalist 1990, Album of the Year 1990 (No Fences), *Song of the Year 1990 ("The Dance"), Single of the Year 1990 ("Friends in Low Places"), Video 1990 ("The Dance"), Entertainer of the Year 1990; CMA—Horizon Award 1990, Video 1990, 1991 ("The Thunder Rolls"),*

Album of the Year 1991 (No Fences),
Single of the Year 1991 ("Friends in Low
Places"), *Entertainer of the Year 1991;
Grammy—Country Vocal Performance
—Male 1992* (Ropin' the Wind),
TNN/MCN—Video 1991 ("The Dance")

At the 1991 Rock and Roll Hall of Fame
induction show, Lars Ulrich leaned into a
TV camera and asked, "Who the hell is
Garth Brooks?"

So who the hell is Lars Ulrich?

Lars Ulrich is the lead singer of Metallica, one of the perennially hottest heavy
metal groups. Those are those guys who
wear skintight leather jeans and vests with
no shirts, swing mike stands around their
heads, put on flamboyant, earsplitting
concerts, and have dominated the *Billboard*
Hot 100 pop charts ever since people put
away their love beads and fringed bell-
bottoms.

Metallica put out a new album in September 1991—their strongest album in
years, the rock press said. No doubt about
it, this is the album that will put Metallica
back on top of the charts.

But a funny thing happened on the
way to the top. That same week, a chubby,
cherubic-looking guy with thinning hair
under a big cowboy hat released an album,
and when *Billboard*'s September 28 issue
came out, Garth Brooks *Ropin' the Wind*
had made its debut at number one on the
pop charts, something that no country album had ever done.

The next week, the new album by
Guns n' Roses was released. Who the hell
is Guns n' Roses? Guns n' Roses were the
bad boys of rock, the group that had gotten more negative publicity than the
Rolling Stones, the Doors, Jerry Lee
Lewis, and 2 Live Crew put together—
and as we all know, for a heavy metal

rocker, negative publicity is the best you
can get. The Guns n' Roses album was
the media-hype event of the year. Their
label arranged for leading record stores
across the country to stay open all night,
to sell nothing but the new Guns n' Roses
album. And it worked. Guns n' Roses
went to number one on the charts . . .
for one week. The following week Garth
Brooks was back on top, and he stayed
there for seven weeks.

In January 1992, Brooks starred in his
own TV special, a videotaped concert in-
tercut with brief interviews with family
and colleagues, all giving their explanation
of the Garth phenomenon. During the
course of the special, Garth smashed guitars, doused himself with water, swung
out over the audience on a rope, and sang
a bunch of his hits, including an extra verse
of "Friends in Low Places" in which he
invited the stuffed shirt from the black-tie
affair to kiss his ass.

"Welcome to the nineties," Brooks
told the larger-than-core-country audience. The special was one of the top-rated
shows of the week, and with it *The New
York Times* declared, "the singer effec-
tively did away with decades of country
stereotypes and helped usher the music
into a new era."

Brooks became the biggest thing ever
to happen to country music; and like every
supernova, he drew his detractors. The
funniest putdown we ran across was *Rolling Stone*'s: "Garth Brooks is the Vanilla
Ice of country music."

So, is Garth really any good? Has he
really done enough to deserve all the
adulations, the Garthmania? Is he really
that much better than anyone else around
him?

Dumb question. An artist isn't responsible for living up to media hype (although

Brooks, a marketing major in college, is given a lot of credit for shaping and building the image behind the Garth phenomenon), only for creating good art, and what Garth hath wrought is plenty good.

Brooks is a combination of intensity and ordinariness. He's you, he's your husband. But if he's you, he's the you who could go over the edge at any moment; if he's your husband, he's the husband who could turn into the demon lover and take you over the edge at any moment.

"It's funny how a chubby kid can just be having fun, and they call that entertaining," Garth Brooks said as he accepted the CMA Entertainer of the Year award, but a chubby kid grabbing a rope and swinging out over an audience, all by itself, could be a clip from an old Abbott and Costello movie. Always right there, bubbling under the surface, at electric moments breaking through the surface, is the Garth Brooks who described this moment to *Time* magazine: "Sitting in the parking lot of a damn fire station back in Hendersonville, Tennessee, beating my head as hard as I could because I had snapped, and Sandy screaming at me to quit. I was crying, she was crying. I calmed down, and we went back home."

This was six months before Brooks finally broke through, signing a contract with Capitol Records.

He's chosen some songs that strike home. "The Dance," by Tony Arata, has become one of the most requested songs at funerals. Like weddings, funerals are ceremonies that call forth our deepest inner emotions, and Brooks's sensitive delineation of the value of life with all its pain seems to have comforted many people during those moments.

In "If Tomorrow Never Comes," by Brooks and Kent Blazy, he captured a tender but intense rumination on the importance of seizing the day, even in an ongoing love relationship. Then he backed up the sentiments in his own life. Brooks, who has been honest about the strains that a show business career and the demands of exploding stardom can put on a marriage, took off the winter and spring of 1992 to be with his wife, Sandy, during the last few months of her pregnancy and after the birth of their first child.

"The Thunder Rolls," by Brooks and Pat Alger, struck a powerful enough chord that the video was banned on both the Nashville Network and Country Music Television. The song was about a battering husband whose wife finally turns on him and kills him. Brooks played the part of the battering husband in the video, and if its graphic violence was too much for the commercial cable networks, it won praise and thanks from thousands of women's shelters across the nation, where the video was used in counseling sessions.

Brooks's strong on-screen portrayal of the unsympathetic husband was nearly as important to the impact of the video as his singing; his acting talents have been noted by others, too. Steve Zuckerman, who directed him in a guest shot on the TV sitcom *Empty Nest,* said, "He sees the whole scene, not just his words."

That's an acute and important observation. In his music as well, Brooks's strength lies in his ability to convey the whole picture of the song, to find all its depth and complexity. That's true of moody, sensitive songs such as "The Dance," "If Tomorrow Never Comes," and "The Thunder Rolls." It's equally true of a raunchy romp such as his honky-tonk classic, "Friends in Low Places."

"Friends in Low Places" paints a picture of a guy using a fierce pride in who he is as a shield against pain. It plays off the idea of getting high as a defense against feeling low, but there's a wistfulness that undercuts his defenses in the plaintive way Brooks sings "as high as that ivory tower that you're livin' in"— he'll never get as high as that ivory tower; it's an unrealistic goal because the ivory tower is a fantasy world, probably a more destructive fantasy than the one that says you can get drunk and solve your problems. It's like the punch line of the old joke: Tomorrow I'll be sober, but you'll still be ugly. Tomorrow I'll be sober, but you'll still have traded real life for snobbish social position.

But for the guy, there's another choice. He can get low down to fight against feeling low down . . . and that *will* work. The booze will help, the friends will help, the ability to turn his back and walk out on the phony arena of social competition will help a lot—but more than anything, it's the raunchy, irresistible, indomitable will of the guy himself, and it's Brooks's raunchy, irresistible energy that supplies that. Garth Brooks's "Friends in Low Places" could have been the number one song in any format it was released to. It's early in the decade yet, but we're confident in nominating it for Best Song of the Nineties.

Frankly, we'd love to sign off on that note, because our own taste runs to low places, but in the interest of chronicling the full scope of Garth's music, we must mention that his 1993 album, *The Chase*, really does take country music into new areas of social awareness. Brooks—who took most of 1993 off to be with his family—seems genuinely poised to start the new century.

Marty Brown

b. 7/25/65, Owensboro, KY

Style

Mainstream neotraditional

Marty Brown seems to be positioning himself to be the next John Conlee. "I'm common as dirt," he sang on his hit, "Wildest Dreams," and he set out to prove it in his first promotional tour.

It's too early to tell whether Marty Brown is going to have any staying power as an act, but he did come up with an interesting promotional gimmick. Taking a cue from Tiffany, America's teenaged Long Island princess of the eighties, who made a name for herself by touring suburban malls, the blue-jeaned Kentucky boy made his bid to become the common man of the nineties with a tour of Wal-Marts. He drove from one to the next in a 1969 Cadillac, which was ultimately given away to a lucky fan in a drawing.

Brown has a real hillbilly singing style, and a persona to match. "I went to Noo York City just once," he told host Ralph Emery on "Nashville Now," "and I felt like I ought to have a passport. I thought I was in a foreign country."

T. Graham Brown

b. 10/30/54, Arabi, GA

Style

Country Motown

Memorable songs

"Come as You Were," "I Tell It Like It Used to Be"

That T. Graham Brown has a sense of humor is shown by the nickname he has for himself, "His T-ness," not to mention the name of his early group, Rack of Spam. That his roots are not entirely country is demonstrated by the fact that Rack of Spam was a flat-out soul group.

Brown is a graduate of the University of Georgia, which perhaps accounts for his fraternity-boy image and his love of the Motown soul sound. He arrived in Nashville in the early eighties, where he found quick success in the jingle and demo business (his Taco Bell commercial is widely requested at his live shows) and won a record contract with Capitol. Brown was capable of singing straight-ahead country—you more or less had to be, if you wanted to make a go of it in the demo business—but Nashville was open to new sounds in the latter half of the eighties, and Capitol gave him a chance to do his own kind of music, which he describes as a combination of Otis Redding and George Jones.

His T-ness had the ability to make it work, and he came along at the right time, when the baby boomers who had fallen in love with soul in the sixties and seventies were increasingly turning to country for the music they were no longer finding on the pop scene. In 1985, Brown had his first Top Ten hit, "I Tell It Like It Used to Be."

During the 1980s, he scored three number one hits, "Hell and High Water," "Don't Go to Strangers," and "Darlene." He also managed a highly credible remake of Otis Redding's "Dock of the Bay," a song that it's hard to imagine anyone remaking successfully, and he's made three films—*Greased Lightning, The Farm,* and *Heartbreak Hotel.*

Success and the temptations of excess that accompany it took something of a toll on T. Graham, but he's worked at drying out and making a comeback. He gives much of the credit for his new sober lifestyle to two people: his wife, Sheila, and his role model, Sheriff Andy from "The Andy Griffith Show."

Jann Browne

b. 3/14/54

Style
Honky-tonk dance hall

Memorable songs
"Mexican Wind"

Jann Browne's first major success was as a vocalist with Asleep at the Wheel. She toured with the Western Swing group from 1981–83, then went back to the California honky-tonks she'd started in and continued to try for a solo career. A recording contract with Curb Records led to a 1990 album that won critical raves, but didn't break through.

"I haven't had much radio play," she admits. "If I dwelt on the odds against making it, even given that I've gotten as far as I have, I'd have a lot of sleepless nights, so I try not to think about it. On the bright side, I've had a lot of video play."

We asked her a question that we asked a number of people: What's the story with country radio in the nineties? Why don't so many deserving artists get played? Her response: "The truth is I'm like anybody else—I don't understand it. There's a lot of wonderful talent, female and male, just begging to be heard, and sometimes it feels like a law—you can't break through.

Looking at guys like Rodney Crowell and Vince Gill, who are incredible talents, and how long it took them to break through, gives me some hope."

Ed Bruce

b. 12/29/40, Keiser, AR

Style

Rugged

Memorable songs

"Mamas, Don't Let Your Babies Grow Up to Be Cowboys," "Texas (When I Die)" (*both as writer*)

Ed Bruce has had a long career as a singer, with some solid highlights including a number one hit in 1981 ("You're the Best Break This Old Heart Ever Had"). He began his career in the fifties as a rockabilly singer for Sam Phillips's legendary Sun Records in Memphis. His distinctive yet generic voice has given him a solid career as a commercial jingle singer, and he's no slouch as an actor, either, with several TV-western roles, including a regular part in the unsuccessful return of "Maverick" in the early eighties.

But Bruce's most important career has been as a songwriter. He's written not only some of the biggest hits, but some of the most memorable and distinctive songs of our time: "Working Man's Prayer," "The Man That Turned My Momma On," "When I Die, I Want to Go to Texas," and the unforgettable "Mamas, Don't Let Your Babies Grow Up to Be Cowboys."

Glen Campbell

b. 4/22/36, Billstown, AR

Style

Smooth

Memorable songs

"By the Time I Get to Phoenix," "Gentle on My Mind"

Awards

ACM—Male Vocalist 1967, 1968, Single of the Year 1967 ("Gentle on My Mind"), 1975 ("Rhinestone Cowboy"), Album of the Year 1967 (Gentle on My Mind), 1968 (Glen Campbell & Bobbie Gentry), TV Personality 1968, 1971; CMA—Male Vocalist, Entertainer of the Year 1968; Grammy—Vocal Performance Male, Contemporary Male Solo Vocal Performance 1967 ("By the Time I Get to Phoenix"), Country Recording, Country Solo Vocal Performance—Male 1967 ("Gentle on My Mind"), Album of the Year 1968 (By the Time I Get to Phoenix)

In the sixties and early seventies, there was no bigger country star than Glen Campbell. Discovered by the Smothers Brothers as a summer replacement for their hugely successful variety show, Campbell became a huge TV star in his own right and remained on the air after CBS pulled the plug on the Smothers Brothers for controversial topical humor. If Barbara Mandrell (the Glen Campbell of the eighties) was

Country When Country Wasn't Cool, then Campbell was Slick When Country Wasn't Slick, perhaps the original prototype of the Urban Cowboy. Or the Rhinestone Cowboy, as he called himself in his 1975 number one hit.

Campbell left home as a teenager to try to make it as a musician. He played in a band in Wyoming, then put in a four-year stint in New Mexico with a band led by his uncle, Dick Bills, before heading for Los Angeles. For a country boy from Arkansas and high-school dropout, Campbell was a serious and sophisticated musician who had closely studied the techniques of such jazz guitarists as Django Reinhardt and Tal Farlow, and he quickly became a successful studio musician.

Campbell joined The Champs, a group that hung on through the fifties on the strength of one huge instrumental hit, "Tequila," and that became the spawning ground for a number of performers, including Campbell, Seals and Crofts, and Rich Grissom. Later, as a result of playing on a number of Beach Boys' sessions, he toured sporadically as a Beach Boy.

In one year as a studio musician, he told an interviewer for *Seventeen* magazine, he worked on 586 sessions, "and of all those records there were only three hits. I sat down and analyzed what the trouble was with the others. There was a lot of good music there, but out of all those singles I worked on that year, only three of them had lyrics that meant something!"

Campbell learned the lesson well; as he

started to become a hitmaker on his own, he chose songs with strong, memorable lyrics. "Gentle on My Mind" by John Hartford, which became the theme for his TV show, described the special relationship between a drifter and the one woman who could tame his heart. "By the Time I Get to Phoenix," which began his working relationship with LA songwriter Jim Webb, portrayed a man leaving a woman with a cold-bloodedness that masked heartache. The psychological ambiguity was provided by the emotion in Campbell's voice.

Campbell is a superb musician and a flexible singer, and he was the perfect interpreter for Webb's complex, sophisticated melodies, as the two of them were to show again in such songs as "Wichita Lineman" and "Galveston," both of which were big pop hits as well as being number one on the country charts in 1968 and '69.

At the same time, Campbell parlayed his TV success into a plum movie role, as second banana to John Wayne in *True Grit*. He made one other movie, with Joe Namath, but acting never became an important part of his career, perhaps because his clean-cut good looks and nonthreatening style came across more on the small screen, where he could fit comfortably into the Dreams of the Everyday Housewife (a 1968 hit).

Campbell's TV career ended in 1972. His next big career peak happened in 1975, when "Rhinestone Cowboy" soared to number one on both the country and pop charts, followed by a string of hits through 1977's "Southern Nights," written by Allan Toussaint, master of New Orleans soul music, which also hit number one across the board.

Campbell has never exactly faded into obscurity. Although he's always been LA and not Nashville, he's always been around and respected. He's had hits off and on through the eighties, including a 1987 duet with Steve Wariner, "The Hand That Rocks the Cradle."

Paulette Carlson

b. Northfield, MN

Style
Hot voice, cowboy boots, white eyelit trim

See HIGHWAY 101.

Mary-Chapin Carpenter

b. 2/21/58, Princeton, NJ

Style
Intelligent

Memorable songs
"This Shirt," "Opening Act"

Awards
ACM—New Female Vocalist 1989; Grammy—Country Vocal Performance —Female 1992 ("I Feel Lucky")

It's not often that one live performance of one song catapults a performer into stardom—*You're going out there a waitress, but you're coming back a star!*—but it happened to Mary-Chapin Carpenter at the 1990 CMA Awards show.

Mary-Chapin Carpenter was not exactly a waitress in 1990, of course. She'd put out an album called *Hometown Girl* for Columbia in 1987, which we, to our discredit, had dismissed in our column for the *Middletown* (NY) *Times-Herald-Record* as schoolgirl stuff. She'd put out a second album in 1989, about which we wrote:

"She's replaced a breathless schoolgirl striving after originality with a smoky solidness in her writing. Her singing style has matured, too. She can tell a story or deliver an emotional message with authority. On *State of the Heart* she fulfills the promise that we, in all honesty, hadn't realized was there. Good thing somebody did."

She'd put out a third album in 1990, *Shooting Straight in the Dark,* and by now it was hardly a secret that she was something special. Still, no one expected the sensation she would cause when she stepped out in front of the audience and the cameras with her guitar at the CMA Awards show. The producers of the show hadn't expected it— they had called her at the last minute as a fill-in act and asked if she'd sing that funny song about being an opening act. "I said no," she recalls. "Partly out of fear, partly because I didn't know how to edit it down to a minute and thirty seconds, and partly because everybody knows that if you're lucky enough to get a spot on that show, you sing something that people have heard before [she's never recorded "Opening Act"]. But they were very persuasive, and given that I basically feel it's okay to live dangerously, I finally said yes. And then even while I was onstage singing it, I was so scared I had my eyes closed the whole time, so I didn't know how it was going over, and it wasn't till I was finished and I opened my eyes and saw that people were standing up and cheering that I realized I'd gotten over."

Mary-Chapin Carpenter had gone out there a promising singer-songwriter and come back a hyphenated legend.

Who was the star she sang about? Uh-uh. She's not saying. "The morning after the awards show, I ran into Mike Campbell, who was Ricky Van Shelton's manager then, and he said, 'It's all over Nashville how you trashed Ricky on the show.' I almost died until I realized he was kidding."

Given her talent, it's not surprising that Mary-Chapin is a star. What may be a little surprising is that she's a country star.

She doesn't have anyone's idea of a country background. Born in Princeton, New Jersey, raised partly in Japan, where her father was publisher of the Asian edition of *Life* magazine, educated in the Ivy League at Brown University . . . country? Not normally.

Does she consider herself country? Where would she describe herself in relation to country music?

"I'm okay with it," she says. "I mean, I tend to shy away from categorization in general, but I understand the reality of it. A couple of weeks ago *Time* did a review on *Shooting Straight,* just a little blurb, and described it as a country-and-western album, and that didn't seem quite right. But on the other hand, sometimes people describe me as a folkie, and that doesn't sound right either.

"If I try to figure out how I ended up in Nashville, the best I can come up with is that it had something to do with timing. When I was sending my tape around in 1986 and '87, the tape that ended up being my first album, Nashville was in a period where it was welcoming a wide range of acoustic musicians and singer-songwriters. I think that's starting to change now, but back then Nashville was one of the few places where they'd listen to that kind of music."

She made the tape more or less casually. "I was working for a small philanthropic foundation during the day, and at night I was playing music in bars, which was pretty much what my life had been for a long time, and I just wanted to make a tape I could stick in my back pocket and sell at gigs. It was really just for me. I'd write a song and say, 'Hmm, I think I'll put this on the tape.' "

The tape found its way to Columbia Records in Nashville, and to her surprise, they called her and told her they wanted to sign her up.

Mary-Chapin Carpenter still lives in Washington and still records in Washington—although not as casually as she recorded her first album. She works with her friend and coproducer John Jennings, and her own musicians.

She deals with the problem of celebrity by not having any problems of celebrity. "Before I had a record deal I didn't have much of a glamour life, and now, it's pretty much the same. I read, I ride my bike, I try to find time to write."

Mary-Chapin Carpenter's list of the greatest songs of all time: "Well, this is an April morning and I just had my coffee, so right at this moment it would be 'Norwegian Wood,' 'Rollin' and Ramblin',' 'The Death of Hank Williams,' by Robin and Linda Williams, 'Willie Short' by John Jennings, 'Steady On' by Shawn Colvin."

Carlene Carter

b. 9/26/55, Nashville, TN

Style

Rockin' traditionalist

Memorable songs

"I Fell in Love," "Me and the Wildwood Rose"

In Edward Albee's play *The Zoo Story*, a philosophical drifter explains that "sometimes it's necessary to go a long distance out of your way to come back a short distance correctly," and that could be Carlene Carter's motto. She was born into country music's oldest and most revered family, the Carters (Mother Maybelle Carter was her grandmother, June Carter is her mother, her father is Carl Smith, one of the biggest country acts during the fifties; her stepfather is Johnny Cash, and Rosanne Cash is her half sister).

But more than Rosanne, more than Pam Tillis, more than anyone, Carlene moved away from her roots. After a failed youthful attempt at marriage, she took up with British rocker Nick Lowe and moved to London in the late seventies. She released several rock albums produced by her husband, a couple of them to considerable critical acclaim, and she made a solid mark as a songwriter. Emmylou Harris's "Easy From Now On" was written by Carlene, and she had songs cut by such pop superstars as the Doobie Brothers and the Go-Gos. We were actually big Carlene fans during that period and still deeply regret having lost our copy of *Musical Shapes* somewhere along the way; but she never established a major career, perhaps in part because of a serious battle with drug and alcohol abuse.

Gradually, during this time, she was moving back to an appreciation for the country music she had rejected. She spent a year on the London stage in a production of the country-flavored *Pump Boys and Dinettes*. Then, when the Carter Family came to London on a tour, she found the opportunity to move back into the family, and into country music. Her aunt Anita took sick, and she filled in for a night. Then she remained with the family group for the next two years. "I sort of wormed my way in with them," she told David Zimmerman of *USA Today*. "I was away for a long time. I needed to know all those stories and to learn where what comes out of me naturally comes from."

In 1990, Carlene cut her first country album, *I Fell in Love,* for Warner/Reprise Records. The album was solid rootsy country. Of the two songs she didn't write or cowrite, one was by songwriting legend Leon Payne, the other was A. P. Carter's "My Dixie Darlin'." Her own songs include the touching family tribute "Me and the Wildwood Rose." At the same time, she showed that she hadn't lost her pop savvy. In addition to such all-star country session men as James Burton, Jay Dee Maness, and Albert Lee, she called on rockers Dave Edmunds, Levon Helm, Jim Keltner, several of Tom Petty's Heartbreakers (including Howie Epstein, who produced), and Kiki Dee. The combination seemed to work for country fans: the title cut hit number three on the charts and returned prodigal daughter Carlene Carter. At the year's end, the album made a whole lot of people's ten-best lists, including *Time* magazine's, where it was slotted in between Beethoven, Robert Johnson, Enrico Caruso, and Frank Sinatra.

Carlene has not only returned to Nashville, she has truly returned to the bosom of her family. She currently lives in a house that once belonged to her grandmother, Mother Maybelle Carter.

Carlene Carter's list of the greatest songs of all time: "Layla" by Derek and the Dominoes, "He Stopped Loving Her Today," "Like a Rolling Stone" by Bob Dylan, "The Waiting" by Tom Petty and the Heartbreakers, "Crazy."

Lionel Cartwright

b. 2/10/60, OH

Style
Singer/songwriter

Memorable songs
"I Watched It on the Radio"

Lionel Cartwright's ambition in Nashville, he says, "is to plow new ground. Country music has an incredible history to draw on. What I want to do is to take the music to interesting places, but always retain that country edge."

The interesting places are the singer-songwriter places that we went to in the seventies with such guys as Paul Simon, James Taylor, and Billy Joel, whom Cartwright names as his influences, along with Merle Haggard, Buck Owens, and those two great cornerstones of virtually all the new acts of the eighties: the Beatles and Hank Williams.

Cartwright got to those places over a route that had some solid country signposts. He worked for the WWVA Jamboree in Wheeling, West Virginia, starting as a backup piano player and ending up as the show's musical director.

After moving to Nashville in 1982, he became part of the cast of one of the Nashville Network's less inspired efforts—a sitcom with music called "I-40 Paradise." During this time, he became a sort of protégé of Felice and Boudleaux Bryant ("Rocky Top," "Bye Bye Love"), for whom he sang on demo tapes.

His self-titled first album on MCA came out in 1988. There weren't any monster hits from it, but one number, "Give Me His Last Chance," was a solid Top Ten song.

Of his second album, *I Watched It on the Radio*, we wrote in the *Middletown (NY) Times-Herald-Record:*

"Okay, you heard it here first: Lionel Cartwright is not destined for country immortality. Fifty years from now, nobody is going to be making TV movies about his life, and there won't be any country songs about a hillbilly heaven with 'On one side . . . Hank Williams, and on the other side . . . Lionel Cartwright.'

"No, we're afraid this fellow is a lightweight. But his new lightweight album is better than his first lightweight album. His lyrics, especially in the title song, are apt in their choice of details. His music leans overmuch into the syntho-pop school for our purist tastes, but it retains a country feel."

Johnny Cash

b. 2/26/32, Dyess, AR

Style
Johnny Cash

Memorable songs
"I Walk the Line," "Folsom Prison Blues"

Awards
ACM—TV Personality 1969–70, Song/Single of the Year 1985 ("Highwayman," w/Kris Kristofferson, Willie Nelson, Waylon Jennings), Pioneer Award 1990; CMA—Album of the Year 1968 (At Folsom Prison), 1969 (At San Quentin), Male Vocalist 1969, Vocal Group 1969 (w/June Carter), Single of the Year 1969 ("A Boy Named Sue"), Entertainer of the Year 1969; Grammy—Country Performance–Duet, Trio, or Group 1967 ("Jackson," w/June Carter), Country Vocal Performance–Male 1968 ("Folsom Prison Blues"), 1969 ("A Boy Named Sue"), Country Vocal Performance–Duo or Group 1970 ("If I Were a Carpenter" w/June Carter), Album Notes 1968 (At Folsom Prison), 1969 (Nashville Skyline–Bob Dylan), Best Spoken Word or Non-Musical Recording, (Interviews From the Class of '55 Recording Sessions w/Carl Perkins, Jerry Lee Lewis, Roy Orbison, Johnny Cash, Sam Phillips, Rick Nelson, & Chips Moman); MCN—Country TV Show 1969, Living Legend 1989, Hall of Fame 1980

Some highlights from Mercury Records' Johnny Cash fact sheet:

- Johnny Cash has placed more than forty-eight singles on *Billboard*'s Hot 100 pop charts. Some of the acts who have not had as many pop singles include Barbra Streisand, Billy Joel, Kenny Rogers, the Everly Brothers, Chicago, the combined total of Paul Simon, Art Garfunkel, and Simon and Garfunkel, Michael Jackson, including his Jackson Five hits, Rod Stewart, and Hall and Oates. (They didn't mention Zager and Evans or Rick "Disco Duck" Dees, but we guess they didn't have to.)
- He has duetted with Bob Dylan, hosted "Saturday Night Live," produced a movie about the life of Jesus, starred in over a dozen other films, written best-sellers such as *Man in Black* and *Man in White*, about the conversion of the Apostle Paul, entertained U.S. presidents, and fished with Mick Jagger.
- He placed twenty-six albums on the pop charts between 1955 and 1972, the same number as the Beatles during that time span.
- He has placed at least two singles on the country charts for thirty-five consecutive years.

• Both "Folsom Prison Blues" and "I Walk the Line" have been certified by BMI as million-performance songs, and "I Walk the Line" has been recorded by over one hundred artists.

Johnny Cash's career spans a lot of eras. Collectively, they add up to the rock and roll era, which is an era he helped to usher in. He was one of the voices of the new Southern style that Sam Phillips recorded for Sun Records in Memphis, some rhythm and blues mixed with some country. The young guys whom Phillips signed up for his label included Cash, Carl Perkins, Jerry Lee Lewis, and Elvis Presley. When they all sat down in the Sun Studios together to harmonize on some favorite gospel, country, and R&B numbers, they were called the Million Dollar Quartet, an estimate that probably shortchanged their value by several hundred million dollars. Most of those tapes have disappeared (may they show up one day in our attic!), but the records that Sun released on Cash include "I Walk the Line," "Folsom Prison Blues," "Ballad of a Teenage Queen," and "Big River."

In the sixties, when social and political consciences were being raised, Cash made his own political statements, giving concerts at Folsom and San Quentin prisons. They became albums that were not only successful, but important.

From 1969–71, Cash had his own TV show. He and Glen Campbell were the first to bring country music to network TV, to put it right square in the mainstream of mass entertainment.

You could include the drug era, too. Amphetamines and barbiturates took their toll on Cash over the years, and in 1984, as his daughter Rosanne was facing up to and dealing with her cocaine addiction, Cash entered the Betty Ford clinic.

In 1985, Cash made one more ascent to number one on the charts, with the group that came to call itself the Highwaymen, after their number one single: Johnny Cash, Willie Nelson, Waylon Jennings, and Kris Kristofferson.

And Merle Haggard wrote in his autobiography: "I'm not a fan of many people. But I'm a true Cash fan. There's a certain magic that must have been born in him. He can grab an audience and hold them right till the last chorus."

Rosanne Cash

b. 5/24/55, Memphis, TN

Style

Confessional

Memorable songs

"Seven Year Ache," "The Way We Make a Broken Heart"

Awards

Grammy—Country Vocal Performance–Female 1985 ("I Don't Know Why You Don't Want Me"), Album Package 1988 (King's Record Shop)

The inner landscape of Rosanne Cash's pain—especially her twelve-year marriage to Rodney Crowell—is so much a part of her professional life that you can't talk about one without the other.

She was born around the time that her father, Johnny Cash, signed his first contract with Sun Records. By the time she was two years old, he had hit the big time with "I Walk the Line." He was off touring constantly—and in some ways he was even more of a problem on his rare visits home. Rosanne has described those early Christmases as a nightmare, with an amphetamine-addicted father roaring around their house on a tractor, playing Christmas carols at full blast from huge outdoor speakers. Before long, her parents were divorced, and Rosanne's mother had moved her to California to start a new life.

California gave her a different life and a different set of problems from, say, Pam Tillis. Tillis had an absentee father, too, but everyone in her world adored him and assumed she must be the luckiest little girl in the world to have him as a father. To Rosanne's Valley Girl friends, country music was uncool, and Johnny Cash was a figure of ridicule. "I was a California girl," Rosanne explained to Michael Corcoran in *Request.* "Into rock 'n' roll and beaches and convertibles, and country music was real Southern, real hokey. I didn't like country music when I was growing up."

Nevertheless, there was a pull. Back to Nashville at first, where she enrolled at Vanderbilt University as a theater major. Then back to a relationship with her father, as the purple-haired California punker went to work for her father as a laundress and part-time backup singer. "He'd play all those great country songs for me, giving me a crash course in country," she told Corcoran. "That's when I started to appreciate it."

After a move to London to study acting (she never quite enrolled once she got there), she recorded her first album for a German label. The album was produced by Rodney Crowell, whom she had met at a party in Nashville. The album was never released, but meanwhile, she and Crowell fell passionately in love. He left his wife, and they were married in 1979.

That same year he produced a new album for her, this time for Columbia Records, which produced a few minor hits, including the duet "No Memories Hangin' Round" with Bobby Bare.

By her second album (*Seven Year Ache,* 1981), she had apparently been married to Rodney long enough to begin the confessional phase of her career. The album's title cut chronicles a fight that she and Crowell had had in a Los Angeles restaurant; it went to number one.

As time went on, she raised the emotional/confessional stakes. In "Hold On" (1986), off her fourth album, she hurled a challenge directly at Crowell: "If you want to keep a woman like me / You'd better hold on."

Cash's career might be hampered somewhat by her determination not to repeat her father's mistakes. She limits her tours, spending as much time as she can at home with her family. She did repeat the sins of the fathers in another area, however. In 1984, as Johnny Cash was taking a cure at the Betty Ford clinic, Rosanne admitted herself to Ridge View Institute in Atlanta for treatment of cocaine addiction, while Rodney fought the same battle on his own.

But her talent has always proved to be stronger than her rationed commitment to her career. She had a solid string of hits between 1981 and 1986, and in 1987, when she took time out from her inward odyssey to make a straightforward country album, *King's Record Shop,* she had a smash: four number one singles (a feat never before accomplished by a woman), including a wonderfully upbeat remake of her father's "Tennessee Flat Top Box."

She recorded the song without knowing that her father had written it, and the event provided one of the upbeat moments in her rocky family saga. The week it hit number one, the senior Cash took out an ad in *Billboard,* which read: "A lot of people have made such a big deal of the fact that you didn't know that I wrote 'Tennessee Flat Top Box' when you recorded it. I'm glad you didn't.

"I could never put into words how much it means to me that you recorded my song. Your success with 'Tennessee Flat Top Box' is one of my life's greatest fulfillments. I love you, Dad."

After that, it was back to introspection, and a three-year struggle to produce *Interiors,* a deeply personal album that expressed those innermost parts of her soul that she needed to express, most of which seemed to relate to her marriage and her sense of herself within it. For the first time in her career, Rosanne jettisoned Rodney and took over as her own producer.

A lot has been made of how Rosanne and Rodney have hammered each other back and forth in their songs, but it does seem as though the hammering has mostly struck in one direction. Rodney's "If Looks Could Kill" takes a dig at a woman who expresses her anger with a cold silent treatment, a theme echoed by Rosanne in "Mirror Image," on *Interiors:* "A woman frozen and a man still on fire."

While Rodney was still capable of puppy-affectionate ditties such as "I Couldn't Leave You If I Tried," Rosanne's *Interiors* was unrelenting:

"I'm reaching out to you but I'm keeping my hands clean" ("On the Inside").

"Don't give me your life, I have one of my own" ("Dance With the Tiger").

"The things we believe in, we just throw them away / On the surface, everything's okay" ("On the Surface").

"I don't want to hide my light so yours keeps shining / If you don't want to face the truth / You're not gonna like what I do" ("Real Woman"). This one seems particularly harsh in view of the fact that Rodney was just having his first

success in 1990, while she'd been a star for some years.

"We threw the best parts of life away" ("What We Really Want").

"We hang on a noose / Of subtle abuse" ("Land of Nightmares"). Nice line.

"I walk away the fear and anger / I'm talking through the tears each day" ("I Want a Cure").

And finally, in "Paralyzed": "I picked up the phone, you were both on the line / Your words to each other froze me in time / A lifetime between us just burnt on the wires . . . Our faces in pieces, facades on the floor / The pretenses between us for a moment destroyed."

Autobiographical? The source for the hurt and bitterness? Rosanne won't be specific. Pressed for details, she quotes the Irish poet W. B. Yeats: "It is inappropriate for an artist to limit the suggestibility of his own work" by tying it to the realness or unrealness of specific events.

In early 1991, both Cash and Crowell agreed that her *Interiors* catharsis had strengthened their marriage and their commitment. By the end of the year, they had separated—a move which, according to Rosanne, also strengthened their relationship.

CeeCee Chapman

Style
Emotion with a touch of humor

Memorable songs
"What Would Elvis Do," "Everything"

CeeCee Chapman, who came to Nashville from the Washington, D.C.–Maryland–Northern Virginia circuit (much like Mary-Chapin Carpenter), where her father played guitar in her band (somewhat like Barbara Mandrell), has a distinctive style, though her first album fell short of rocketing her to the top of the heap.

We first noticed Chapman through the video of her single, "Everything," in which she's mistaken for Tracy Chapman by a guy with a cigar who wants to make her over. We were completely charmed by her, and we were charmed by her version of Pam Tillis's "What Would Elvis Do." Chapman managed to win a couple of awards in 1989—*CashBox* magazine's New Female Vocalist Award, and as her publicists describe it, "named by the European music community as Best New Artist for 1989." Not exactly the Grammys, but not chopped liver, either.

Ray Charles

b. 9/23/30, Albany, GA

Style

Rhythm and blues

Memorable songs

"I Can't Stop Loving You," "Seven Spanish Angels"

Awards

Grammy—Male Vocal Performance, Single 1960 ("Georgia on My Mind"), R&B Recording, R&B Solo Vocal Performance Male or Female 1966 ("Cryin' Time"), Lifetime Achievement Award 1987. These are Ray Charles's country-related awards.

Ray Charles is one of the greatest singers and most profound influences in the fields of rock and roll, rhythm and blues, soul and jazz, so it shouldn't come as a surprise that when he released *Modern Sounds*

in Country and Western Music, in 1962, he became one of the most profound influences in the field of country music as well.

Charles's early country recordings were at first looked on as curiosities, an unexpected slumming self-indulgence from a man capable of better things. Well, they couldn't have thought he was serious, and not just because he was a black man singing white folks' music long before anybody had ever heard of Charley Pride. Nobody much took country music seriously back in 1962. But Charles was absolutely serious. He'd grown up listening to country music; he had always loved it and had wanted to pay tribute to it for a long time.

Modern Sounds in Country and Western Music never made a dent on the country charts, but it didn't go away, either, and if the average country fan wasn't listening to it, people like George Jones and Willie Nelson were—just as singers like Otis Redding and Stevie Wonder were taking in everything that Charles had to offer in the fields of R&B and soul.

Clint Eastwood, a fan of both jazz and country, tabbed Charles (and another R&B legend, Fats Domino) for the predominantly country sound track of his rowdy redneck comedy, *Any Which Way You Can*. It led to country-chart appearances for both Domino and Charles—in Ray's case, as part of a duet with Eastwood.

Not long after, Charles signed a deal with Columbia Nashville and began a run as a country singer, hitting number twenty on the charts in 1983 with a song called "Born to Love Me."

But it was his duet album, *Friendship,* released later that year, that finally won him mass success with country music audiences. Charles teamed with Hank Williams, Jr., the Oak Ridge Boys, George Jones, Chet Atkins, Janie Frickie, B. J. Thomas, Ricky Skaggs, Mickey Gilley, Merle Haggard, Johnny Cash, and Willie Nelson. The album went to number one and yielded two Top Ten singles. The first, "We Didn't See a Thing," teamed Charles with George Jones. The other, "Seven Spanish Angels," with Willie Nelson, was the real smash, giving Ray his only number one country record.

Charles has once again moved on from his Nashville period. He continues to feature some of his best-known country songs as part of his act, and his legacy remains at the heart of—and certainly, at the soul of—country music.

Mark Chesnutt

b. 9/6/63, Beaumont, TX

Style

Jones

Memorable songs

"Too Cold at Home"

Country music is song-powered, and if anyone doubts the power of a great song, just look at the Mark Chesnutt story. A lot of people in Nashville knew Mark was a good kid and a good singer, and they expected he'd make an impact when they signed him to MCA, but they figured to bring him along slowly. They released "Too Cold at Home" as a single in July of 1990, figuring that they'd let the song kick around for a while, rouse a little curiosity, and then they'd release the album and start touring him the following January.

But it didn't quite work out that way. "Too Cold at Home" was a great song, quite likely destined to go down, with "Friends in Low Places" and "Life as We Knew It," as one of the classics of its era. Everyone who heard it flipped out, from fans to talent buyers, and everybody wanted more Mark Chesnutt *now*—the album, the tours, the whole nine yards.

We caught up with Mark just as the first wave of excitement was cresting. It was a rare moment: he was close to the hottest thing in Nashville, and he was still an innocent kid. He sat in the office of his publicist, Sharon Allen, in a small frame building on Music Row, and told us his story:

"I still live at home, in Beaumont. I wouldn't live in Nashville because the people would drive me crazy. I feel like the industry would swallow me up. I'd get too involved in all this, and then I'd change, and I wouldn't be the same. That's the same reason George Strait doesn't live in Nashville.

"I was born in Beaumont, Texas, September sixth, 1963. The first singer I ever remember hearing was my daddy. He was pretty good, and they were trying to get him with a major label, but then he just quit and went into the used-car business. He decided he would rather stay home and raise his two boys. So he had some experience with the business, and he told me what to expect.

"He told me it ain't easy. It's hard to get into the business, and it's even harder once you get in. He knew what he was talking about because every single thing he told me was going to happen has come true.

"Like staying in Beaumont. He said, 'You don't need to move to Nashville to try to make it because there's already too many there. Your time will come, they'll find you.' I used to get so mad at him, and I'd say, 'I need to be in Nashville. I need to move to Nashville.' But I never did.

"I never even had to come up and do a showcase. I worked in clubs around Beaumont and southeast Texas for twelve years. That's all I ever did. I had a couple day jobs for a few months, but the rest of the time I was singing—five, seven nights a week.

"I've never written a song in my life. I first heard "Too Cold at Home" when I cut a demo on it. It was written by Bobby Harden, and he'd had big, big hits by Reba McEntire and Loretta Lynn. I told him, 'That's the greatest song I ever heard, and if I ever get a record deal, I hope you'll let me record it.' Bobby kind of laughed and said, 'Son, you don't understand. I'm out of it. I haven't had a hit in years—nobody listens to my stuff anymore. You want that damn song, you can have it.'

"So I kept that song. I sang it in beer joints for four years, and then I finally cut in on an independent label in Houston.

"They played it in my hometown a few times, but you know how it is with a small-label release. But I had this guy who played drums with me for a while; he used to be with George Strait, and I hired him because I thought it would be kind of neat to have George Strait's ex-drummer in my band. He quit after a while because he just wasn't into that small-club circuit, but about a year later he showed up and said, 'Man, I heard your record. I know some people if you want to do something about it.' The next thing I know Tony Brown from MCA is down in Beaumont to see me, and five months later I'm in the studio doing the album.

"I had dinner with George Jones last night. We're friends, now. He was singing 'Too Cold at Home,' and the way that man sang my song, I got chill bumps all over me. I tell you what, we've been getting a lot of great songs since this record. All these great songwriters are coming up to me. And I've got another song of Bobby Harden's called 'Old Country,' which is going to be the title cut on my next album.

"I've never been into anything except singing. I don't care to be an actor. I don't care to produce. I don't even really care to write songs. I just want to be the best singer I can be. I started singing professionally when I was sixteen, and that was all I knew. When my friends would be sitting around talking about baseball, football, basketball, all this stuff, I never could join in, and I guess I used to think I was pretty strange, because it seemed like I didn't know anything about anybody. If they talked about some sports figure, I wouldn't even know who he was. But if they asked me about who was singing what, or anything about George Jones, I could tell them all about it.

"But I guess, starting to work full-time in music when I was sixteen, I really was different. People look at you as different, and you lose a lot of friendships along the way. It pretty much ended my first love affair. I got a card from that girl the other day. I just laughed and laughed."

Mark Chesnutt's list of the greatest songs of all time: Hank Williams's "Your Cheatin' Heart," George Jones's "The Race Is On," another George Jones, "When the Grass Grows Over Me," another George Jones, "A Good Year for the Roses," Merle Haggard's "Swinging Doors."

Guy Clark

b. 11/6/41, Rockport, TX

Style
Folk

Memorable songs
"Desperadoes Waiting for a Train,"
"Heartbroke" (*as writer*)

Guy Clark is as much of a Nashville institution as anyone who's lived in a town for twenty years can be, but he doesn't feel like one. "I'd go back to Texas in a second if I didn't have to be here for the business," he says.

But while he concedes that living in Nashville is a compromise, as far as his music is concerned, "I write for myself. If other people do my songs, that's great, it makes me a fair living, but I never try to compromise or write in a certain direction, and when I do, it doesn't work. The only money I've ever made has been in writing for myself. I don't hear anyone else doing my songs when I write 'em. I write 'em for me."

Clark has had big hits by the Highwaymen on "Desperadoes Waiting for a Train" (he prefers the Slim Pickens version), Ricky Skaggs on "Heartbroke" (he prefers the George Strait version), Rodney Crowell on "She's Crazy for Leavin'." He's been recorded by such artists as Jerry Jeff Walker ("L.A. Freeway"), John Conlee ("The Carpenter"), and Johnny Cash ("The Last Gunfighter Ballad" and "Let Him Roll," a powerfully melodramatic ballad that was clearly not written for mainstream radio, containing lines like "Her name was Alice / She used to be a whore in Dallas").

Guy Clark's list of the greatest songs of all time: "Most of Townes Van Zandt's songs. He's my favorite writer."

Roy Clark

b. 4/15/33, Meherrin, VA

Style
"Hee Haw"

Memorable songs
"I Never Picked Cotton"

Awards
ACM—Comedy Act 1969–71, Entertainer of the Year 1972–73, TV Personality of 1972, Jim Reeves Memorial Award 1976, Guitar player 1977; CMA—Entertainer of the Year 1973, Instrumental Group 1975–76 (w/Buck Trent), Musician 1977–78, 1980; Grammy—Country Instrumental Performance 1982 ("Alabama Jubilee"); MCN—Instrumentalist 1969–72, 1974–80

Roy Clark's Top Ten hits (fewer than you'd think, considering the amount of recording he's done) all came in the seventies, although he continued to put out recordings throughout the eighties. The big story on Roy (besides his instrumental skills, which are impressive) is "Hee Haw," and if you're not sure how relevant that is in the nineties, consider Alan Jackson's description of a moment of self-revelation, when he realized: *Here I am, coming out of the cornfields. I guess I've really made it in this business.*

Clark has been the host of the long-running syndicated show since it began in 1969. He's toured all over the world, including the Soviet Union. He was the first country star to guest-host the "Tonight" show, and he was named the first national ambassador for UNICEF. He has two honorary doctorates, has an airport named after him in Oklahoma, and is the visiting Artist in Residence at Longwood College, Farmville, Virginia.

Oh, yes, and in 1991 "Hee Haw" changed its image and got rid of the cornfields.

Patsy Cline

b. 9/8/32, Winchester, VA
d. 3/5/63

Style

Classic

Memorable songs

"Crazy," "I Fall to Pieces"

Patsy Cline died March 5, 1963, and she's still on the charts. Her popularity has never declined, and it doesn't have to do with any sort of death mystique. It has to do entirely with her singing, which combined musicianship with emotion with a sense of phrasing worthy of the great jazz singers—in fact, there are record, tape, and CD collections all over the country that belong to young people, and in many of these you'll find a couple of albums by Billie Holiday and a couple of albums by Patsy Cline.

Patsy had six Top Ten hits before she died in a plane crash, which also claimed the lives of country singers Cowboy Copas and Hawkshaw Hawkins. The hits included "Walkin' After Midnight," "I Fall to Pieces," and "Crazy." She had two more Top Ten hits after she died: "Sweet Dreams" and "Faded Love."

The fifties, when Patsy Cline came to

prominence, began as the decade of Hank Williams and ended as the decade of Elvis Presley.

Williams first hit the charts in 1947 ("Move It On Over"), and he died on New Year's Day, 1953, on his way to a concert in Canton, Ohio, just after the release of "I'll Never Get out of This World Alive." His songs and records are as fresh now as they were then, and he is as great an influence on today's singers as he was back then.

Lefty Frizzell rivaled Hank's popularity in his lifetime, and his influence on the New Traditionalists is second only to Hank's. One week in 1951, Frizzell had four singles in the Top Ten at the same time: "Always Late" (recently covered by Dwight Yoakam), "Mom and Dad's Waltz," "I Love You a Thousand Ways," and "Traveling Blues." Willie Nelson recorded a tribute album (*To Lefty From Willie*) in 1976 and took "If You've Got the Money I've Got the Time" to number one all over again, and "Long Black Veil," the best ever love and death country song, has been recorded over and over, most notably by The Band.

Webb Pierce, who died in 1991, had twelve number one hits and thirty-seven Top Ten hits during the fifties. In 1954, "Slowly" spent seventeen weeks at number one; in 1955, "In the Jailhouse Now" made it for twenty-one weeks. That can't happen anymore. There are too many artists, too much pressure for quick turnovers at the top. Since 1980, the only song to last as many as three weeks at number one has been Randy Travis's "Forever and Ever, Amen"; the last time a song held on for more than five weeks was 1977 (Waylon Jennings's "Luckenbach, Texas"). But seventeen and twenty-one weeks were remarkable even back then.

Hank Snow ("I'm Movin' On"), Tennessee Ernie Ford ("Shotgun Boogie" and later, "Sixteen Tons"), and Hank Thompson ("The Wild Side of Life") were major stars of the early fifties; so was Kitty Wells, whose "answer song" to Hank Thompson, "It Wasn't God Who Made Honky Tonk Angels," made her the first woman star. Ray Price ("My Shoes Keep Walking Back to You") was Hank Williams's protégé, and in 1970 he became the first performer to score a number one hit with a Kris Kristofferson song ("For the Good Times"). Jim Reeves recorded arguably the best song ever written, "He'll Have to Go." Like Patsy, he died in a plane crash (in 1964), and unreleased material kept him in the Top Ten through the early seventies. An electronically mixed duet with Patsy, "Have You Ever Been Lonely," made the Top Ten in 1981, and Deborah Allen had a series of successful electronic duets with Reeves in 1979/80. Faron Young, a hard-bitten Louisianan who called himself the Singing Sheriff, was the first performer to score a number one hit with a Willie Nelson song— "Hello Walls," in 1961. Later that same year, Patsy Cline took Nelson's "Crazy" to the top of the charts. Faron is still touring, these days with a stage act heavily dependent on Catskill Mountains comedy.

And there was a guy named George Jones. He's still around, too.

Patsy Cline's album sales averaged seventy-five thousand a year through the sixties and seventies, and after two movie portrayals of her—Beverly D'Angelo in *Coal Miner's Daughter* and Jessica Lange in *Sweet Dreams*—her popularity soared even higher. It shows no sign of going away.

Mark Collie

b. 1/18/56, Waynesboro, TN

Style

Intelligent, basic, driving

Memorable songs

"Another Old Soldier," "She's Never Comin' Back"

In 1989, MCA records released a debut album called *Hardin County Line*. The album didn't zoom to the top of the charts (it did okay), but it had one of the best collections of songs to come from the pen of a new writer in recent times, right up there with Lyle Lovett and Clint Black.

"The good news is she loved me," went the refrain of the first cut on the album, "the bad news is she's gone . . . she said her mama said when things got rough to come back home." The next song was a bright play on words about a girl all too ready for the altar: "She wants something with a ring to it, like a church bell makes"; and it contained lines like "My baby did but now she don't, and if I don't say 'I do,' it's a safe bet that she won't." There was more of the same on succeeding songs: "What I wouldn't give is more than she could take," "Where there's smoke you'll find my old flame."

But there was more: dark surrealism in the guise of a blood-and-guts car-racing song ("Hardin County Line"). And a complex and emotionally wrenching tribute to his father and other veterans, "Another Old Soldier," about which *Chicago Tribune* columnist Jack Hurst wrote: "virtually everybody, from a Rambo hawk to an activist dove, must empathize with the song's wounded military hero for the cost of his devotion to duty."

"Waynesboro's about halfway between Nashville and Memphis, so I grew up with country and R and B," Collie says. "I loved music all my life, but never really thought, 'Well, I'll grow up and be a singer-songwriter.' I mostly just grew up thinking about getting out of Waynesboro. I thought about going into the military, but I found out I was a diabetic.

"When I started playing music seriously, I moved to Memphis. That was in the late seventies, and I wasn't too crazy about what was going on musically in Nashville. I went to Memphis looking for whatever it was that Carl Perkins and those guys at Sun Records had. There was no music industry in Memphis, but I did get to play with all kinds of players, rhythm and bluesers, rock 'n' rollers—there wasn't anything you couldn't do down there.

"I started writing songs the first time I picked up a guitar, and right from the beginning I was influenced by Hank Williams, Jimmie Rodgers, John Lennon, and Paul McCartney. I think every country artist today is influenced by rock 'n' roll, and anyone who says, 'I never listen to anyone but Roy Acuff and George Jones,' is living in denial. Country and blues and jazz and hillbilly and gospel are what is rock 'n' roll, so if we say we're not influenced by rock 'n' roll, we're kidding ourselves. I never met a guy who ever picked up a guitar who couldn't play the opening riff to 'Johnny B. Goode.'

"Today, country music has become such a great outlet for creating an American art form—country, rock 'n' roll, country rock. Because rock today is so splintered—head-banger rock or heavy metal or glitter rock or rap—and you don't have anybody like John Fogerty or even as pure as the Rolling Stones were.

"My girlfriend, Anne, joined me after I'd spent about a year in Memphis, and we got married. Then, as guys like Ricky Skaggs and Randy Travis started to make it in Nashville, she encouraged me to make the move. Then we had a child, and I was writing bad songs, trying to write what I thought other people would want, and going no place. Around 1986, I told Anne I was going to give up the chase. But she told me if I gave up music, she was gonna leave me. She didn't give me any choice; she was serious.

"So I went back to writing the kind of songs that I liked to hear, that I didn't mind singing. I got my old band from Memphis back together, and we started playing around."

He played at Nashville's Douglas Corner for about a year, and suddenly he was discovered overnight. "One night there were fifteen people in the audience. The next there were a hundred and fifty, and six or eight of them were record company people."

Two of those were MCA Nashville's president Bruce Hinton and vice president Tony Brown, and Hinton took advantage of a break between sets to call MCA in Los Angeles and inform the head guys that he was signing up a new artist.

That's the Mark Collie story, except for one thing: he has a collie named Amos who's appeared on every one of his videos except "Let Her Go," and "people complained so much we put him back, and he's been there ever since."

Mark Collie's list of the greatest songs of all time: "Amazing Grace," "I'm So Lonesome I Could Cry." "Those are probably the two greatest songs. Probably the greatest records ever made were 'Whole Lotta Shakin' Goin' On' by Jerry Lee Lewis, 'What'd I Say' by

Ray Charles, and 'Don't Be Cruel' by Elvis."

John Conlee

b. 8/11/46, Versailles, KY

Style
Common

Memorable songs
"Common Man"

Awards
ACM—New Male Vocalist 1978

Ten years of solid popularity began to wind down for Conlee as the new stars of the late eighties rushed past him, and if it turns out that his career as a major star is ready to be laid to rest, he might be able to do the job on himself. Before he got into the music business, Conlee was a mortician in his home state of Kentucky, and he still has a valid mortician's license.

Conlee also worked as a radio announcer in Kentucky and originally came to Nashville to take a radio job with a local station, WLAC (famous in the fifties and sixties as the clear channel voice of rhythm and blues across the South and Midwest). His first hit record was "Rose Colored Glasses" on ABC (later merged with MCA) in 1978. It was one of only two hits he wrote himself. The other, "Backside of Thirty," hit number one the next year.

Conlee is most famous for "Common Man," number one in 1983, the song in which he described himself as a common man who drove a common van, and which gave him his official nickname. You guessed it: the Voice of the Common Man.

Rapidly gaining as his second-most-

famous number is "Busted," the old Ray Charles song, which Conlee made a Top Ten country hit in 1982. When he sings it, fans have taken to coming up to the stage and giving him dollar bills. Conlee donates them to the Feed the Children charity in Oklahoma.

Earl Thomas Conley

b. 10/17/41, Portsmouth, OH (*"Roy Rogers's hometown"*)

Style
Smooth but sensitive

Memorable songs
"Somewhere Between Right and Wrong," "Too Many Times"

You spend some time talking to Earl Thomas Conley, and before long you realize you're hearing a lot more about his music than his personal history. You ask him about it: Earl, you seem to be a guy who'd rather talk about your art than your life.

"My life is my art," he says in a matter-of-fact tone that's striking for its absence of vanity. "My art is my life. I'm always an artist. Look where the industry is today, right at this point. There's pressure all around you to conform, but God, I can't. I'm an artist, I was an artist from day one, and it kills me if I'm not able to be an artist. I studied at the Dayton Art Institute in Ohio before I went into music as a career. I saw paintings by Monet there for the first time, in the early sixties. The French impressionists—I love those pieces."

By the late sixties, Conley had gone from art to real life, working in an Ohio steel mill, commuting back and forth to Nashville but unable to open any doors. In 1974, he moved to Huntsville, Alabama, "to be closer to Nashville."

He worked hard at the music business, putting out a series of singles on a small independent label. They made some noise on the lower end of the charts, making enough of a name for Conley that Warner Bros. signed him up.

The name he was making for himself in the midseventies was Earl Conley. Unfortunately, John Conlee and Con Hunley were making names for themselves at the same time, and it started to get hard to tell which name was which. So Warner started to experiment: Earl Thomas Conley on his next release, the ETC Band on the one after that. Then they dropped him.

Earl Thomas Conley—the version he has continued to use—went back to Huntsville and hooked up with his old producer, Nelson Larkin, who had just started his own independent label, Sunbird. With Larkin coproducing (he was to remain Conley's coproducer for many years), he recorded the 1981 album that launched him as a star, *Blue Pearl,* which yielded two smash singles, "Silent Treatment," which went to number seven on the charts, and "Fire and Smoke," his first number one.

After "Fire and Smoke," Conley began his long-term (and profitable) association with RCA, and the process of building a country music career. He toured as an opening act for Charley Pride, then RCA's hottest star. "Being on the road was a challenging experience for me, and a wonderful education—and horrifying, too, at first, because I was an extremely introverted person when I first started. And different—his band was fifteen feet behind him, and of course that really works for him. So it was hard for me be-

cause I like the communication and the rapport that goes back and forth with the band. But I tell you what, for the year and a half I worked for him, I actually made more money that I'd ever made working on my own. They kept giving me raises, and I didn't have any expenses. So I had money all the time, and it was fun to work with them because they treated me real good. And his wife, Rozene, is just a precious person. She's a great lady and so is Charley, a great person."

Conley went on to open shows for Hank Williams, Jr., and after that he was headlining his own shows, and putting out hit record after hit record (eighteen number one hits as of 1991).

Conley traces his musical influences back to his father. "My father played by ear. He didn't play good, but he played great for what he played because he didn't give a flip about technicalities. We only cared about the emotional values that songs had to offer, so it was great when you could talk him into picking up a guitar or a banjo, or an organ or a piano if there was one around. He played that real old-fashioned, old-timey mountain music."

After that, Conley recalls a wide range of influences. "I grew up listening to Nat King Cole, Brook Benton, Sam Cooke, all that stuff from the fifties. In country, you had Jim Reeves at that same period of time, and I think that Jim Reeves was influenced by those people, too, because he has such a smooth, silky voice. I listened to rock and roll, too—Jerry Lee Lewis and Conway Twitty and Elvis, but at the same time I was listening to Hank senior in the late forties, before he died. So I go back a long way with country music, too. I didn't just look at one person. I looked at all of them. I kept a good view of what was happening everywhere, to the point where I don't even remember all my influences unless someone mentions a name, and then I say, 'Yeah, I remember that.' So I'm an accumulation of all the things I've seen or touched or felt, and I think everybody else is, too, but people tend to pigeonhole other people in groups. I don't think I want to do that.

"When I first went out on the road with my own band, I had a pretty hard-edged sound, with two rock and roll guitar players. When I toured back near home in Ohio and Indiana in the early eighties, where they had a pretty traditional, conservative crowd, I used to scare those people to death."

Conley came along in the early eighties, at a time when a lot of country music fans, including the authors of this book, found our attention drifting away from that era's Urban Cowboy country stars, and that included Conley's smooth, carefully crafted stylings. We didn't really start listening to him until his 1986 duet with Anita Pointer, "Too Many Times," and it was then that we focused on the subtle musicianship and emotional precision underneath the smoothness.

"She was a great lady, and that was a great song," Earl recalls. "I love that song because of the message. Anita Pointer was in town looking to open some doors, and I said, yeah, I'd help, because I was pretty hot at the time and pretty much unintimidated by the industry, so it was just a real nice challenge for me. And it was something I believed in. I thought it was time people put the flesh-tone colors out of life and go for the soul. I hear it on the radio occasionally now, and I say, 'God, that was a great record.' When you're recording all this stuff, you get so caught up into the creative thing that I don't think you realize how good something is until you get away from it. You know if it's bad right off the bat, but you're not sure it's good until it's already done what it's gonna do as far as commercial success.

"'Too Many Times' was probably one of the biggest highlights of my career. Another was my duet with Emmylou Harris ['We Believe in Happy Endings,' number one in 1988]. I like to work with artists who challenge me creatively. Just to see what kind of extremes that I can put into the marketplace."

Rob Crosby

b. 4/25/54, Sumter, SC

Style

Sensitive New Age Guy

Memorable song

"She's a Natural"

Rob Crosby has sensitive, sincere good looks, and a way of looking straight into your eyes and telling you that he loves you just the way you are: a little graying, maybe, but a proud, self-actualizing woman. It's hard to imagine Crosby singing over a knife-and-broken-bottle fight in a Texas honky-tonk, but the self-actualizing New Age women he sings to probably don't hang out in those places anyway.

Like many singers his age, Crosby's influences are rooted in sixties pop, and his real introduction to country music was through the Beatles.

Today, music videos and the explosion of young talent have lowered the average age of the country listener, but it's still music for adults. Rosanne Cash, who grew up in southern California, has talked about how it was a little embarrassing to admit to her friends that her daddy was this hillbilly singer on TV; but kids in the South weren't that much different. "I was inspired by the Beatles," Rob Crosby says. "I was inspired by Dylan, the Kingston Trio, Paul Simon, James Taylor. Not so much the Rolling Stones. They were competent as writers, but not trendsetters. Led Zeppelin and Jimi Hendrix paved the way for the heavy metal of today, and the Beatles paved the way for everything else, including today's country."

Crosby has always been successful as a singer, doing so well in local South Carolina clubs that it was hard for him to break away and go to Nashville. In 1984, a group of Atlanta businessmen agreed to sponsor him. In return for a percentage of the publishing contracts on his songs, they supported him to the tune of $700 a month until he got on his feet.

"I didn't consciously set out to write songs with a specific attitude toward women," he says of his music. "But the women in my family were strong and brought us all together. So, while I think I can be as stubborn and crude as the next guy, I'm probably on the other end of the spectrum from a rough and rowdy guy like Hank Williams, Jr.

"And there are still a lot more people out there buying rough and rowdy songs by Hank junior or 'love to lay you down' songs by Conway Twitty, so there must be a very powerful appeal to that sort of thing. Actually, while I get letters from girls saying they were touched by a song like 'She's a Natural,' I get an equal number of letters from guys saying it reminds them of their wife or girlfriend."

Maybe American men are changing.

Rodney Crowell

b. 8/7/50, Houston, TX

Style
Literate honky-tonk

Memorable songs
"She's Crazy for Leavin'," "Leavin' Louisiana in the Broad Daylight" (as writer)

Awards
ACM—New Male Vocalist 1988; Grammy—Country Song 1989 ("After All This Time")

Try to beat this for an earliest memory: "When I was two years old, my father took me to see Hank Williams. I was sitting on my dad's shoulders, and I just remember the light—I can close my eyes and imagine music coming out of that light, and I think that was the point at which there was no turning back for me. There was nothing else I would ever be interested in."

Crowell spent a long apprenticeship as a cult figure before he finally hit superstardom in 1988 with his superb album *Diamonds and Dirt*. He was known for his skills as a writer (for songs like "Leavin' Louisiana in the Broad Daylight," recorded by a number of singers before the Oak Ridge Boys finally took it to number one in 1979). He was respected as a sideman (for Emmylou Harris's Hot Band, which also included Ricky Skaggs, Albert Lee, former Eagle Bernie Leadon, and future Desert Rose bandsman Herb Pedersen) and performer (his early group, the Cherry Bombs, featured Vince Gill and Rosanne Cash). He was admired for his work as a producer (particularly with his wife, Rosanne Cash, from whom he's since separated), and he gained some celebrity from his in-laws (particularly his father-in-law, Johnny Cash). And he had recorded four albums under his own name, to ever-increasing critical acclaim, without getting a single past number 30 on the charts.

His 1986 album, *Street Language,* was intricate and layered with sound. It was a producer's album, and perhaps more a critic's album than a listener's. We say "perhaps" because we reviewed *Street Language* at the time and found ourselves wishing that we liked it more than we did. He was such a talented guy, and he'd obviously worked so hard . . .

Perhaps too hard. *Street Language* was a flop. The Irish poet W. B. Yeats had it right when he talked about what happens when you make a song sound as though you'd labored over it: "A line may take us hours . . . yet if it does not seem a moment's thought, our stitching and unstitching has been nought." Crowell learned that lesson. A year and a half later, he came out with *Diamonds and Dirt,* an album that sounded as easy and natural as fresh air, and finally, it was the album everyone had been waiting for. Crowell was a star.

"Raised in a honky-tonk," as he describes it, Crowell is open and articulate, a fountainhead of stories and opinions. In his own words:

"I'm a real romantic about country music. For me country music is at its best coming out of the dashboard of a '49 Ford. That's the way Hank's records sound, and Lefty Frizzell . . . that's how I first heard "I Walk the Line" when I was six years old, going fishing with my dad and my grandfather in the back of a '49 Ford.

"Houston has a man-made ship channel, and my grandfather would take me down there to the merchant marine sailors'

bars and honky-tonks—he'd tell my mother and my grandmother he was taking me for a haircut. I can remember all his old cronies—sailors with eye patches and earrings. I was five years old. It was great, it was poetry. There I'd be with my grandfather, be getting attention from all these characters, and I'd look up and there'd be my grandmother and my mother banging on the window and dragging me out by my ear.

"I played my first gig when I was eleven, with my dad, in a beer joint around Houston. My dad was a local musician, he played honky-tonk dance music in bars. He used to say, 'If there's one thing I can do, I can keep the dance floor filled.' He took a lot of pride in his ability to read a dance floor, play the right mix of fast songs and slow songs. They'd put a cigar box on the floor in front of the bandstand, and whatever went in that cigar box was what they made. People would request stuff like 'Don't Let Me Cross Over,' 'Walkin' the Floor,' Hank Williams songs, the real honky-tonk music that I think Hank Williams personified. My dad died the day my fourth song off *Diamonds and Dirt* was number one.

"I grew up with a lot of R and B, too—I think that Big Joe Turner and Hank Williams come from the same honky-tonk place. In rock and roll at its best, like country music at its best, the language gets right on the melody and rides the melody, the way Hank Williams did in 'Honky Tonk Blues,' or Chuck Berry in 'Maybellene.' I love rock and roll. I'm not talking about rock music—there's a difference. Rock is a more corporate, studied kind of music.

"I went to Nashville originally in August of 1972, and the first people I met were Townes Van Zandt and Guy Clark and Mickey Newbury. Those three guys were brilliant, and when I got there, my songs were not any good, but lucky for me, Guy Clark took a liking to me, took me under his arm and showed me around. And I spent a lot of time by myself, reading everything I could, and listening. I was already listening a lot to Dylan. And with my country honky-tonk roots and the education I was getting from these great working songwriters, I started digging deeper. So when I went to California in 1975 to become a performer with Emmylou, I took this valuable experience I had in the writing area and brought it into the performing area. I started producing just by using my common sense—when Rosanne asked me to produce a record, I said, 'Okay, let's go,' and we just flew by the seat of our pants, and it worked.''

Rodney and Rosanne were introduced by Guy Clark's wife, Susanna, and it was not an easy family for a young honky-tonker to slip into. ''When I first met Johnny Cash, I got so nervous I got real drunk on the plane, and by the time I got there I was drunk and crazy, and I think he could see a kindred spirit. John and I have always gotten along real good because he intimidates me . . . and I think I intimidate him, too. I don't say this in a presumptuous way, because you don't intimidate Johnny Cash. It's more that we're uncomfortable with each other on a certain level that revolves around him. I try to make him laugh, and he tries to make me laugh, and when we're making each other laugh, it's real comfortable. And if I can't get a laugh out of him, I'm intimidated.''

About his success, Rodney says: ''It behooves me to operate from the point of view that there ain't no big time, because if you sell yourself on the idea of the big time, you're going to give away the innocence and the mysticism of what it's all about. And I don't deny what I've done. As a songwriter, I've made my contributions and I'm very proud of them, but by the same token, it's much more important to me that I think in terms of not having done a damn thing, because . . . well, we go around looking under rocks anyway, because that's what writing and creating is all about—and if you start thinking that you are the rock, you're no longer looking under the rock. I admire a great artist like Tennessee Williams because whatever happened to him, it was worth it for the beauty of what he created.''

About the future of country music: ''You know that loyalty thing that everyone is always attributing to country music, that once you've earned the loyalty of the country music fan, you'll always have it—I think that's slowly becoming a thing of the past, and it's becoming more that you're only as big as your last single. And if that's the way it is, I can function within it, but I think that if the aura of the human condition gets moved aside for commercial reasons, if radio programming becomes not a matter of love and devotion as much as protecting ratings for your advertising dollar, then the very foundation of country music suffers. It starts to weed out that human element, that inarticulate speech of the heart, and I think that as an artist, if you're dedicated, if it's something that lives and breathes and beats in your heart, then you've got to go ahead and do it anyway. I don't know what's going to happen in the future, but my hope is that everyone who's a country music artist can hold on to that pure artistic vision of Hank Williams, and then I think that the spirit and the atmosphere and the romance and the poetry of country music is going to survive beyond programmed radio and video.''

Rodney Crowell's list of the greatest songs of all time: "Dear John (I Sent Your Saddle Home)" by Hank Williams, "Like a Rolling Stone," "I Walk the Line," "And Your Bird Can Sing" by the Beatles, "She Even Woke Me Up to Say Good-bye" by Mickey Newbury.

Billy Ray Cyrus

b. 8/25/61, Flatwoods, KY

Style
Sexy, unsubtle

Memorable songs
Could you respect us if we didn't say "Achy Breaky Heart"? Could you respect us if we did?

After the heady whirlwind surrounding Billy Ray Cyrus's first release, "Achy Breaky Heart," began to slow down just a bit, the less than enchanted began to have their say. One of the best lines came from "Saturday Night Live": as pictures of Madonna, Kevin Costner, and Cyrus were flashed on the screen, "Weekend Update" anchorman Kevin Nealon said "Everyone here who's still going to be famous a year from now take one step forward—not so fast there, Billy Ray."

Well, Billy Ray's rise had certainly been meteoric. His first single release, "Achy Breaky Heart," debuted in the spring of 1992 and zipped up the charts with a speed heretofore unknown *by* an unknown. In fact, what Billy Ray matched for speed of ascendancy was "To All the Girls I've Loved Before" by Willie Nelson and Julio Iglesias (a feat noted by *Rolling Stone*'s Rob Tannenbaum as "a genuinely dubious achievement"). By May his al-bum, *Some Gave All,* had leapt past Kriss Kross and Def Leppard to hit Number One on the pop charts in only two weeks, and no release had done that in thirty years.

Did Mercury know what they had with Billy Ray? From the evidence of the album, they may well not have had a handle on it when they brought him into the studio. *Some Gave All* is a jumble of songs in a hodgepodge of singing styles, from Alabama-style country rock to Harry Chapin-style folk, including a song that had been a flop for a group called the Marcy Brothers the year before, called "Don't Tell My Heart."

But somewhere along the line, someone must have figured out that they had a potential hot property here. Maybe it was when they saw him on stage. Maybe it was when someone remembered having seen him on stage a few years earlier (rumors abound that he was once a Chippendale's dancer).

Anyway, a marketing major (like Garth Brooks) would have to admire the way Mercury built up Billy Ray. First, they released a video in which Billy Ray is brought to a disco in a limo. He is mobbed by panting women, screaming and reaching out for him as he does his (Chippendale's?) moves on stage.

At the same time, another segment of the audience in the video appears to be breaking into a spontaneous but complicated line dance—a dance that was created by a choreographer especially for the video.

It all worked. There's always, it seems, a market for a sexy guy if he's hyped properly. And the Achy Breaky line dance became a sensation.

Country audiences are dancers, anyway. They love to dance, and what they do has nothing to do with the gingham-

and-crinoline barn dancers of the old fashioned stereotype. Modern dance club audiences dress up in their George Strait jeans and rhinestone studded shirts, their Emmylou Harris fringed skirts and fringed white boots, and show off their mastery of the intricacies of the Texas Two-Step, or the Cajun waltz, or the Fade, or any one of a variety of line dances. And a TV show like TNN's "Club Dance" (the "American Bandstand" of country music) gives a pretty good demonstration of how smooth and pretty good country dancers can look.

Billy Ray admits (with a smile) that he can't actually do the Achy Breaky himself.

Not everybody loves the boy from Flatwoods, to be sure. Travis Tritt sneered that Cyrus "degrades country music by turning it into an ass-wiggling contest." Radio stations in Cyrus's native Kentucky responded by boycotting Tritt, and he eventually apologized, but Billy Ray may not have been completely mollified: at a 1993 awards ceremony, he gave this message to his critics: "Here's a quarter, call someone who cares."

Others who were less than swayed: Critic Jay Orr in the Nashville *Banner* likened "Achy Breaky Heart" to the 60's trash hit (by the Trashmen) "Surfin' Bird." Bob Oermann, in the Nashville *Tennessean,* was tactful: "He's certainly not the world's greatest singer." And Donna Mann, an Arkansas teenager, put it this way: "His song just kinda got old, like New Kids on the Block, and he went with it."

In case anybody missed the Billy Ray phenomenon, the singer's second video drew attention to itself with a fervor bordering on desperation. Virtually every other shot in it was a closeup of a headline in one newspaper or another trumpeting the success of Billy Ray in concert or Billy Ray on the charts.

Does this mean that someone's trying too hard, that someone is not so sure that Billy Ray is going to stay hot on nothing but his own merits?

Not necessarily. But does anyone want to bet that five years from now Billy Ray won't be playing whatever is the 21st Century equivalent of the county fair circuit, still stripping down to his sleeveless undershirt on cue, still thanking dwindling audiences from the bottom of his achy breaky heart?

Lacy J. Dalton

b. 10/13/48, Bloomsburg, PA (*Jill Byrem*)

Style
Worldly wise, with a fire burning inside

Memorable songs
"Hillbilly Girl With the Blues," "Crazy Blue Eyes"

Awards
ACM—New Female Vocalist 1979

Nobody has ever doubted Lacy J. Dalton's talent, and nobody has ever doubted her heart either. But it's seemed to most people that she's had more rough breaks than most people, and a lot of people have wondered if this petite lady, with the voice that combines rough-and-tumble with sensitivity in a manner unmatched by anyone this side of Waylon Jennings, will ever make it to the heights that she deserves.

Lacy laughs this off. "There's a Charley Pride song where he says, 'Some folks say that life is rough, I wonder compared to what.' Well, since I have nothing to compare it to, I wonder if my life is any rougher than anyone else's, and it probably isn't, so maybe I just talk about it more."

Nah; we can't buy that. We first heard the singer who became Lacy J. Dalton around the Santa Cruz Mountains in the early seventies. Her name was Jill Croston, then. There was a vital, exciting musical scene in northern California then (Asleep at the Wheel were regulars on the circuit), but she stuck out. We still get chills remembering her supercharged reworking of an old English ballad, "Little Mattie Groves," and we can kindle a warm glow recalling her song about a "Mellow Mountain Mama." And there was a song that everyone thought should be a hit . . . a number called "Crazy Blue Eyes."

At the same time, she was keeping her career aspirations on a low key, as she devoted herself to caring for her husband, who had suffered a broken spine in an accident.

Lacy traces her country music roots to her Pennsylvania family, lovers "of country music and Perry Como. My dad's favorite song was 'Give Me Forty Acres and I'll Turn This Rig Around.' "

But she had to find her way back to those roots. In high school and college (first Brigham Young University in Utah, then back home to Bloomsburg State College in Pennsylvania), she listened to the folksingers of the day—Bob Dylan, Joan Baez, and Judy Collins—and to such early blues singers as Robert Johnson and Leadbelly. After that, "I went to California when I turned twenty-one with a guitar player who was my boyfriend, and we became part of the hippie movement. We were going to do psychedelic rock, but I started to write, and what came out were these country songs. And I found that people really enjoyed them, in that mixed format out there—just as now, all these new influences are coming into country, and people enjoy them. I'm talking about artists like Steve Earle and Rodney Crowell. They're so talented and innovative, and they've brought a whole new audience to country music."

In 1979 she signed with Columbia and had her first hit with "Crazy Blue Eyes." By the next year, she was hitting the Top Ten regularly. "Takin' It Easy" was her most successful, reaching number two in 1981. After her remake of Roy Orbison's "Dream Baby" in 1983, the hits stopped coming, as Columbia seemed to lose interest in promoting her.

In 1989, she moved over to Capitol, where she's working at reviving her commercial career; but she's philosophical about such trivial matters as success or failure: "Personally, I just can't believe that one lifetime is enough for us to get it all together. I don't even know if I could believe in God if I didn't believe in reincarnation. There are just too many things, like babies being born blind, deaf, and dumb and supposed to find meaning in the same amount of time that I have with all the gifts I've been given . . . the universe is constructed in such a sensible way, with all those molecules and atoms governed by laws of nature, to believe that someone isn't steering the ship. On the other hand, you read about the newest theories of quantum physics, about how things change on the subatomic level just by your speaking about them changing—I recently asked my son, Adam, who wants to be a physicist, "Don't you think that this might be evidence that we're supposed to be learning to be cocreators with God on some level—that maybe we're baby gods?"

Lacy J.'s all-time favorite songs: "Desperado," "The Last Cowboy Song," "Pancho and Lefty," Charlie Daniels's "Leave This Long Haired Country Boy Alone," *and just about anything by Steve Earle.*

Davis Daniel

b. 3/1/61, Arlington Heights, IL

Style

Light

Davis Daniel comes from the heartland, a small Nebraska farm in that windswept part of America where in the winter, if you're living on the margin, you have to break the ice in the toilet before you can use it in the morning. It's the kind of background you'd work hard to move up from, and Daniel worked hard at his music, learning chords from a Willie Nelson songbook and playing the bars and American Legion halls around Denver, and eventually Nashville.

Sometimes hard work pays off, and sometimes luck pays off, too. As the nineties rolled around, the success of music videos and the success of the rugged, sexy cowboy-hat guys seemed to dictate that the perfect new country star prototype would be Alan Jackson: a strikingly handsome guy who's also a terrific singer. If you can't quite find that combination, you can get a guy who's a great singer and pretend that he's a good-looking guy. That would be Garth Brooks. Or you can take a great-looking guy and pretend he's a good singer.

That would be Davis Daniel. Well, why not? It worked for Fabian. But if you look at him on the one hand, and Garth Brooks on the other, it's pretty clear which way works best.

Charlie Daniels

b. 10/28/36, Wilmington, NC

Style
Fiddles over a seventies Southern Rock base

Memorable songs
"The Devil Went Down to Georgia"

Awards
ACM—Touring Band 1979, 1980; CMA—Single of the Year 1979 ("The Devil Went Down to Georgia"), Musician 1979, CMA Instrumental Group 1979–80; Grammy—Country Vocal Performance–Duo or Group 1979 ("The Devil Went Down to Georgia"); MCN—Band 1980

Charlie Daniels has a reputation as a colorful guy and a great fiddle player, both of them somewhat overrated. His reputation as a fiddle player comes from having defeated the devil in a fiddling contest, but—and this may come as a shock to some—he didn't really do it.

Daniels and his band (Tom Crain, guitar, Joe "Taz" DiGregorio, keyboards, Charlie Hayward, bass, and Jim Marshall, drums) have bounced back and forth between rock and country since they made their debut in 1973 with "Uneasy Rider," a song that did a whole lot better on the pop charts than the country charts. All in all, not such a surprise, given its redneck-baiting theme—a hippie has to think fast when he accidentally wanders into a working-man's bar. Some fifteen years later, when Daniels was courting those same rednecks, he recorded a new "Uneasy Rider," in which the narrator is a good old boy who accidentally wanders into a gay bar.

The white, soul-based Southern Rock sound was hot in the early seventies, and it was changing the demographics of the Southern audience. The kid who worked in the gas station in a small Southern town wasn't sticking Eddy Arnold, the Tennessee Plowboy, or Sonny James, the Southern Gentleman, into his eight-track: he was checking out the Allman Brothers, Lynyrd Skynyrd, or "Jim Dandy" Mangrum of Black Oak Arkansas.

That audience was gone, and country music never really got it back—or tried to compete for it. Country radio didn't play those groups or try to extend its musical scope to encompass them. This had happened before in the fifties, with rockabillies such as Buddy Holly and Roy Orbison; it would happen again in the eighties with blue-collar rockers such as Steve Earle.

But Charlie Daniels did manage to keep his nose under the country tent, even with more or less insulting stuff like "Uneasy Rider," which got as far as number 67 in 1973 on the country charts, while it made the Top Ten in pop.

By 1979 the handwriting was on the wall for Southern Rock as a pop chart phenomenon, and Daniels made a big move toward the country audience. He already had an industry reputation as a fiddle player for a number of sessions, most notably Bob Dylan's *Nashville Skyline* album, and now he decided to feature his fiddling in a big way. He chose a song called "The Devil Went Down to Georgia," which became not only a number one country song, but his biggest pop hit as well, peaking at number three.

By the late eighties, Daniels seemed to have been around forever and had created an image of himself as a beloved, uncompromising outlaw in the Waylon–Willie–Hank, Jr., mold, but he wasn't, really. He had never repeated his "Devil" success; he was a one-hit wonder, floundering between rock and country, certainly not unsuccessful, but not a major act, either. Finally, in 1989, Daniels found a new formula for megasuccess.

It was a disturbing one. Daniels reconstructed himself as a comic-book, one-dimensional version of those rednecks he had once mocked. He released an album called *Simple Man,* in which, among other things, he advocated lynching and called for the assassination of Gorbachev.

Simple man? Simpleton is more like it.

Gail Davies

b. 4/4/48, Broken Bow, OK

Style
Professional

Memorable songs
"Blue Heartache"

Gail Davies remains known as a singer's singer in Nashville, someone whose flexibility and musicianship goes back to her days as a jazz vocalist, someone who still gets called upon for session work and duets, someone who has not been counted out for a revival of her career.

Davies came to Nashville from LA in the midseventies and had a run of a half dozen years or so as a significant player in the country music game, with five Top Ten hits: "Blue Heartache," "I'll Be There (If You Ever Want Me)," "It's a Lovely, Lovely World," "Grandma's Song," and "Round the Clock Lovin'." She's been dropped by labels and picked up by other labels; she's had some success as a songwriter.

She is also believed to have been the first woman producer in Nashville.

Mac Davis

b. 1/21/42, Lubbock, TX

Style
Smooth

Memorable songs
"In the Ghetto" (*as writer*)

Awards
ACM—Entertainer of the Year 1974

We can never quite remember whether it was Mac Davis who stole Glen Campbell's wife or Glen Campbell who stole Mac Davis's wife.

We do remember that although Campbell, Kris Kristofferson, and Davis all had some degree of success in the movies playing characters of laid-back cowboy competence, and that although Campbell, Johnny Cash, and Davis all had country-music-centered TV variety shows, Davis is the one who was never the important figure in country music that the others were.

Not to say that Davis has not made his mark in the American entertainment world. He wrote "In the Ghetto," which was Elvis's comeback song to the Top Ten on the pop charts in 1969, and later had another Elvis hit with "Don't Cry Dad." He cowrote "White Limozeen" with Dolly Parton.

He was natural and appealing in the role of a pro football quarterback, costarring with Nick Nolte, in *North Dallas Forty.* He has all sorts of good credits to recommend him.

But he ain't country.

Paul Davis

b. 4/21/48, Meridian, MI

Style

Collaborative

Producer and seventies pop singer Paul Davis is better known (and highly respected) for his behind-the-scenes contributions as producer and songwriter ("Ride 'em Cowboy," "I Go Crazy"). When he's lent his own duet-singing talents to artists he has produced, he's made some successful contributions to the male-female duets that became such a big thing in the mid-eighties. His collaborations with Marie Osmond ("You're Still New to Me") and Tanya Tucker ("I Won't Take Less Than Your Love") both went to number one—"You're Still New to Me" while Davis lay recovering from a gunshot wound suffered during a holdup attempt.

Billy Dean

b. 4/2/62, Quincy, FL

Style

Pop

Memorable songs

"Billy the Kid"

A recent review of Billy Dean in concert reads: "The basis of Mr. Dean's music is the still-popular traditional country sound with a serious acoustic flavor. His voice is smooth and strong, bringing to mind a young Larry Gatlin, yet the album *Young Man* shows traces of California pop, and even—dare I say it?—funk." What's Dean's response?

"My response is, I love it, because nobody can pin me down to one thing." But Dean thinks his versatility may have been a problem, too: "I didn't get a record deal five years ago because I wasn't country enough, and I'm thinking, how country do I need to be? I've got all the background, like everybody else. I grew up poor, I'm from a farming community, my roots are about as country as you can be, but I've worked hard trying to study different kinds of music. I learned a lot of my guitar-playing style from guys like James Taylor and Dan Fogelberg, and my songwriting style from guys like Don Henley, and the California-pop style of well-written songs.

"But I can probably tell you what songs that guy was thinking about. Traditional country: 'She's Taken'; serious acoustic flavor: 'Somewhere My Broken Heart' or 'Brotherly Love'; young Larry Gatlin: 'Only Here for a Little While'; California pop: 'Young Man'; funk: 'Tear the Wall Down.' "

Billy Dean's first album, *Young Man*, came out in 1991, after the young man had won the Wrangler Star Search and impressed industry insiders at the New Faces Seminar in Nashville. Dean's decision to take this music business approach to the top, rather than the traditional honky-tonk route ("although I've played in my share of honky-tonks too," he says), was deliberate. "I felt I had to prove myself to the industry before I went out to the public. I found my biggest challenge in getting where I wanted to go was to gain the respect of my peers, because I knew that they knew what was really good. I wanted to get it right technically first, to have my peers saying that's a well-written song, that's a great piece of work. And yet you can be too much of an artist to be commercial. You've got to be slick enough and clever enough to get through to the industry, and at the same time you've got to be simple and honest enough to get through to the public."

Billy Dean's list of the greatest songs of all time: "Wind Beneath My Wings," "Desperado," "You Are So Beautiful," "My Way"—"I learned that in the tenth grade and vowed I would sing it at my graduation, and I did"—"Amazing Grace."

Martin Delray

b. 9/26/49, Texarkana, AR

Style
Cash-influenced

Memorable songs
"Get Rhythm"

With all the new singers on the scene who are making hugely successful careers out of sounding like Jones or Haggard, you'd think someone would get the idea of looking for other country legends to sound like. How come nobody sounds like Webb Pierce? Or Conway Twitty? Or Roger Miller? Or Johnny Cash?

Well, actually, there is someone who sounds like Johnny Cash: Martin Delray, who even has the Man in Black making a guest appearance on the video of his remake of "Get Rhythm."

Delray made his first success in 1978 as writer of the Kendalls' hit, "Old Fashioned Love," but it was another dozen years before the University of Arkansas graduate finally got his own career off the ground. Meanwhile, he'd been developing a style based on a mixture of hard country and hard rock: "I suppose if I had to classify myself as a performer," he says, "it would be kind of a cross between Johnny Cash and Eric Clapton. Strictly a guitar-playing singer."

Iris DeMent

b. 1/5/61, Paragould, AR

Style
Mountain voice, poetic sensibility

Memorable songs
"Mama's Opry," "Our Town"

What would it sound like if Nanci Griffith had been raised by wolves?

Our guess is it would sound a lot like Iris DeMent, who was actually raised by good churchgoing folks. Her parents listened to nothing but country gospel, and her older sisters were gospel singers. But there's a wild strain to that old time religion, and you can hear it in Iris's voice, along with a natural, piercing purity.

The DeMent family followed a latter day *Grapes of Wrath* route from Arkansas to California, where Iris played piano and sang in church. But the California of Bakersfield and that town south of it was never much of a musical or cultural influence on her. As a young woman, she moved back to the heartland—to Kansas, where she began writing songs at the age of twenty-five, and singing them at local open mike nights in Kansas City.

A move to Nashville brought her to the attention of John Prine, who said, "I can count on three fingers the number of people who impressed me as much the first time I saw them live." Her first album, *Infamous Angel,* came out in 1992 to critical raves, and she returned home to Kansas City, but not to obscurity.

Desert Rose Band

CHRIS HILLMAN
b. 12/4/44, San Diego, CA

HERB PEDERSEN
b. 4/27/44, Berkeley, CA

JOHN JORGENSON
b. 7/6/56, Madison, WI

BILL BRYSON
b. 11/10/46, Evanston, IL

STEVE DUNCAN
b. 7/28/53, Knoxville, TN

JAY DEE MANESS
b. 1/4/45, Loma Linda, CA

Style

Tight country rock

Memorable songs

"Love Reunited," "He's Back and I'm Blue"

Awards

ACM—Touring Band 1988–90, Drummer 1988–90 (Steve Duncan), Steel Guitar player 1974–76, 1980, 1982–83, 1986–90, (Jay Dee Maness), Guitar Player 1990 (John Jorgenson)

"I believe that Desert Rose Band is the best group in country music today, bar none," says Jeff Hanna of the Nitty Gritty Dirt Band.

A lot of people in country music today would agree with Hanna. One of them is Chris Hillman, and this is in no way meant as a knock on Hillman for runaway ego. No one has worked harder or longer than Hillman at his art, and there aren't many performers who've had so much critical tri-

umph that hasn't necessarily translated into commercial success. So you don't take Chris Hillman lightly when he talks about the Desert Rose Band being a continuation, a refinement, an extension of the music that he pioneered with the Byrds' *Sweetheart of the Rodeo* album and the Flying Burrito Brothers: twenty years' worth of work toward the goal of creating the best group he could create, "and who wins the CMA Award for Group of the Year? A bar band!"

With all due respect to the rowdy, good-time sounds of the Kentucky Headhunters, one can understand Hillman's feelings.

Chris Hillman, one-third of the front line of the Desert Rose Band, began his career as a teenaged California bluegrass player in a band led by Vern Gosdin and his brother, Rex. From there, he went on to become a cofounder of the Byrds, the southern-California folk-rock group that in 1991 was inducted into the Rock and Roll Hall of Fame.

The Byrds represented a lot of styles and influences, but Hillman's country roots didn't find expression until Gram Parsons joined the band, and they recorded *Sweetheart of the Rodeo*. The album was a commercial failure, but it signaled the reinjection of country music into rock's mainstream, and *Rolling Stone* magazine has called it one of the one hundred best albums of all time.

Parsons and Hillman then moved on to form the Flying Burrito Brothers. The Burritos never achieved commercial success either, but they were arguably the most influential group in the history of country rock. They lasted from 1969 to 1971, and after that Hillman went on to associations with two successful but short-lived groups, Manassas with Stephen Stills, and Souther-Hillman-Furay (J. D. Souther, noted for duet singing with Linda

Ronstadt, and Richie Furay of Buffalo Springfield and Poco).

In the midseventies and early eighties, Hillman withdrew from the rock super-group scene to form his own acoustic band and get back to his roots. During this period, he recorded two albums for the prestigious independent Sugar Hill Records and began putting together a new group of musicians who could play at the level of skill and intensity he needed. Two of these were John Jorgenson and Bill Bryson.

Bassist Bill Bryson is an instrumental virtuoso who's played behind artists from Doc Watson to Dr. John, with a lot of credits from that southern-California country rock scene: Ry Cooder, David Lindley, Emmylou Harris. John Jorgenson is a multi-instrumental genius, born in Wisconsin but raised in southern California, who as a teenager played clarinet and bassoon behind such jazz greats as Benny Goodman and Doc Severinsen, and who subsequently won a national collegiate competition to become the featured artist at Disneyland.

In 1985, Hillman was asked to bring his new group and join an old friend in backing up Dan Fogelberg on an album. The old friend was Herb Pedersen, who was a musician on a par with the newly convening group. How good was Pedersen? Well, here's a credit on his bio that caught our eye: 1967—fills on banjo for Earl Scruggs in Flatt and Scruggs. Pedersen stuck with Hillman for a tour with Fogelberg, and the front line for what would become the Desert Rose Band—Hillman, Pedersen, Jorgenson—was complete. They added Steve Duncan and Jay Dee Maness, two more award-winning musicians (Duncan was voted drummer of the year by the West Coast–based Academy of Country Music in 1988–90; Maness has been the ACM's pedal steel player of the year twelve times).

In 1987 the group's first album came out from MCA/Curb.

In 1988, Chris Hillman was honored by BMI for "twenty-one years of hit songwriting," and in 1991 he was inducted into the Rock and Roll Hall of Fame, which you don't qualify for until twenty-five years after your first recording.

That's a long time to be scrapping away in the music business. It's a long time to be refining your craft, too, and it's given Chris Hillman the hard-nosed attitude that an artist gets after a lifetime spent looking inward on his/her work, with half an eye cocked outward at the audience and popular acceptance. "Andy Warhol says everyone will have fifteen minutes in the spotlight," he says. "I don't think my fifteen minutes are up yet."

Diamond Rio

MARTY ROE
b. 12/28/60, Lebanon, OH

DAN TRUMAN
b. 8/29/66, St. George, UT

GENE JOHNSON
b. 8/10/49, Sugar Grove, PA

DANA WILLIAMS
b. 5/22/61, Dayton, OH

BRIAN PROUT
b. 12/4/55, Troy, NY

JIMMY OLANDER
b. 8/26/61, Palos Verdes, CA

Style
Bland

The members of Diamond Rio have some interesting credentials. Lead singer Marty

Roe was named after Marty Robbins and learned to sing Merle Haggard's "The Fugitive" when he was only three. Gene Johnson played mandolin and fiddle with David Bromberg and J. D. Crowe and the New South. Lead guitarist Jimmy Olander has backed up Rodney Crowell, Foster and Lloyd, and the Nitty Gritty Dirt Band. Bassist Dana Williams is a nephew of the Osborne Brothers.

But put them together and there's no style, no sound, no originality—at least not on the basis of their 1991 debut album, or their bland number one hit, "Meet in the Middle."

Diamond Rio was discovered by Arista/Nashville vice president Tim Du-Boi, who also created Restless Heart.

Joe Diffie

b. 12/28/58, Tulsa, OK

Style

Jones

Memorable songs

"If the Devil Danced in Empty Pockets," *"Home"*

Diffie was one of the Class of 1990, that watershed year when the country music establishment decided that there was no such thing as too many good young singers with solid traditional roots and a sound reminiscent of Jones or Haggard.

They didn't have far to look for Joe Diffie. He was right there in Nashville, and everyone knew about him. Throughout a good chunk of the eighties, Diffie was busy building a reputation as the best, most reliable demo singer in Nashville.

That's a tough job. Generally, a songwriter has an idea of his/her song in terms

of a recognized star. Here's a George Jones type song; here's a Keith Whitley; here's an Alabama. Sing it like that, will you, pal? The session lasts until the producer/ writer is satisfied, and the pay can be as little as ten bucks. For a top demo singer, a Kathy Mattea or a Joe Diffie after they've made a reputation, maybe a hundred. But producers and executives listen to demos, and a distinctive voice—a Diffie, a Mattea, a Matraca Berg—will gradually start to catch their attention.

No one can make a song sound better than it is, but a good demo singer should be able to capture everything that's good about a song, to make a producer or artist or record company executive stop, listen, and figure out, without too much of a leap of faith, how the song will sound with their guy doing it. If a songwriter or an independent producer commissions a demo, he/she will want as good a representation of the product as possible; if it's a major label or producer, they already like the song and they want to hear it with a quality production. So Diffie's talents were no secret—it was just a question of when someone would decide to tap him.

Which meant that someone had to decide that his particular talents were marketable at a particular time.

As Diffie tells it, Bob Montgomery, vice president of Epic Records, was the first to contact him. Montgomery is the producer of Vern Gosdin, among other acts, and he offered Joe a contract with Epic if Joe would wait until he could open up a spot on Epic's talent roster for him.

This makes a record label sound a little like a big league ball team. If Garth Brooks suddenly found a loophole in his contract with Capitol, declared free agency, and contacted Epic, you can bet they'd find a spot on the label for him. But Diffie had to wait a year before Epic finally called him up to the big leagues, and in the meantime, he turned away expressions of interest from other labels, waiting for Montgomery.

That has to be a gamble. As good a singer as Diffie is, fashion is fickle, and a rush to sign up traditional, Jones/Haggard-style cowboy-hat guys can result in a glut, and it can't last forever. Diffie may have come close to waiting too long. As he put it when we talked to him, with self-effacing humor, "Sometimes I turn on the car radio and for a second I'm not sure if it's me or Mark Chesnutt or Alan Jackson or whoever."

Diffie was born in Tulsa but raised in the small town of Duncan, Oklahoma, with some detours—his family lived in Texas, Washington (the state), and Wisconsin during his youth. It's said that he could sing harmony by the time he was three years old. Well, Mozart composed "Twinkle, Twinkle, Little Star" when he was three years old, and you'd probably have to give the nod to him as a musical prodigy, but singing harmony at that age is damn impressive.

After a short stint in college, Joe went to work in a foundry back home in Duncan and spent his evenings writing songs and singing in local bars. A country career was no more than a distant fantasy in those days, but he did sell a song to Hank Thompson—"My mother sent it to him," he relates.

After nine years at the foundry, he was laid off. Jobs were hard to come by in Duncan, so, what the heck, he decided to give Nashville a try. If Hank Thompson liked his songs, maybe others would, too.

He fell in with a group of young songwriters, who remain his closest friends and cowriters today ("I'm much more comfortable cowriting with somebody," he says. "I guess you could say I'm codependent.") With two of them, Lonnie Wilson and Wayne Perry, he wrote "There Goes My Heart Again," which Holly Dunn took to number four in 1984.

When his debut album, *A Thousand Winding Roads,* finally came out in 1990, Diffie showed decisively that it wasn't too late for one more traditional singer to make it. His first single, "Home," went straight to number one, and he's stayed hot. He's also continued to show his versatility in a 1992 duet with country folkie Mary-Chapin Carpenter.

Dean Dillon

b. 3/26/55, Lake City, TN

Style
Well, it's not really his style that you think of.

Memorable songs
"Nobody in His Right Mind Would Have Left Her"

It says something about Dean Dillon's career that he was only able to take his biggest hit, "Nobody in His Right Mind Would Have Left Her," to number 25 on the charts. Perhaps it says more about his career that George Strait took the same song to number one, along with "The Chair," "It Ain't Cool to Be Crazy Over You," "Ocean Front Property," and "I've Come to Expect It From You," all Dillon-penned tunes. Dillon, who's been a successful Nashville songwriter since the late seventies, had his first number one as writer with "Lyin' in Love With You," which Jim Ed Brown and Helen Cornelius went all the way with in 1979. He's written "Miami My Amy" for Keith Whitley, "Tennessee Whiskey" for George Jones, "Is It Raining at Your House?" for Vern Gosdin—all of which goes to show that he knows how to connect with a great voice.

But his own career has always been middle-of-the-charts. Nevertheless, he continues to pursue it.

Holly Dunn

b. 8/22/57, San Antonio, TX

Style

Neotraditional from a decidedly contemporary woman

Memorable songs

"Daddy's Hands," "You Really Had Me Going"

Awards

ACM—New Female Vocalist 1986; CMA—Horizon Award 1987

It's hard for Holly Dunn to imagine what life was like for a girl singer in the old days, but she appreciates what those pioneers went through: "By the time I got here, people like Loretta and Dolly and Tammy had really pioneered for women in country music. They'd finally gotten it away from, 'Here, darling, you stand here and you sing this.' All we women could participate in back then was the singing of the song, but Loretta and Dolly wrote their own songs, and they and other songwriters helped blaze the trail for people like me. Now we do everything. I cowrite my video scripts, produce my albums, direct every aspect of my career, and nobody even blinks an eye at it.

"I love to sing, obviously, but I'm very realistic about it. I'm constantly thinking about what happens afterwards. And I figure if I can stay current and keep a finger on the pulse of the music community, I can write forever. Harlan Howard's been writing hit songs for thirty or forty years."

Doesn't sound like the classic image of the hard-livin' artist? Wait, there's more: "I find that artists in my age bracket are much more concerned with the business end—we're not just getting the money and then squandering it on fancy cars. We tend to be a little more conservative about what we do. I think the realities of the business now are a lot more apparent to some of us, and we realize the gravy train could stop at another depot at some point."

This is the new face of country, all right. Holly Dunn is trim, sophisticated, cosmopolitan. She graduated with honors from Abilene Christian University, with a degree in advertising and public relations. Her brother and frequent collaborator, writer/producer Chris Waters, studied at the University of Liverpool in England "on a Broadbury scholarship," has a master's degree in creative writing, and has taught English at the University of Colorado.

Does all this business acumen affect the way she and the artists of her generation make music? Holly considers the question carefully, then sighs, "Boy, I don't know. I don't know."

If so, it's hard to say the effect is a negative one. If it gave her a more sophisticated worldview, that didn't get in the way of the emotional directness of a song like "Daddy's Hands," written as a Father's Day gift for her father, a Church of Christ minister. But it did make her think twice after women's groups protested her

"Maybe I Mean Yes," a song she ultimately pulled from circulation.

Dunn's first musical influences were "the Beatles, things which my brothers would bring home. When I grew up a little bit and my brothers left home, so I gained possession of the radio, I got into James Taylor, Carole King—singer/songwriters. Of course pop music back in the late sixties and early seventies was not a lot different than what we're doing now in country music."

She came to Nashville in 1979, right after she graduated from Abilene Christian. Her brother Chris, who had arrived three years earlier, had begun to establish a career as a songwriter, and he opened a few doors for her. She was able to land a staff writing job with CBS Music, "the only staff female songwriter in the entire company—we're talking West Coast, international, everything." But she languished unrecorded there for over three years, growing frustrated and depressed, until "finally, bless her heart, Louise Mandrell, who had a pretty viable career then, recorded a song I wrote with Chris called 'I'm Not Through Loving You Yet,' which is still her biggest song to date, and I started getting songs recorded after that and got a record deal and publishing contract with MTM, and from that point on, it's been steady as she goes."

Steadier for her than for MTM Records, which folded in 1988. But by then Holly had won a CMA's Horizon Award as most promising newcomer of 1987 and established herself as a solid presence on the charts. Moving to Warner Brothers, she released a new album, *The Blue Rose of Texas,* which yielded her first number one single, "Are You Ever Gonna Love Me."

Today, Texas-born Holly lives in Nashville, which she loves on those occasions when she's there: "What's a social life? Seems to me I remember that word somewhere. I love my career, but every now and then I get a little cranky when I take off on the road. I miss my home, I miss my friends, and I do get jealous sometimes."

She's unmarried. "I know my mother would like a son-in-law. She has three daughters-in-law. And I think if I were married, they wouldn't worry about me so much. But they don't make a big deal out of it. I'm a real independent spirit, and they accept that."

But most of all, this college honors graduate, who looks with such a clear business eye at her career, is "a country singer. Even in my formative years, when I was listening to pop music, the songs I was writing were much, much closer to country in lyric and melodic content than they will ever be to pop—and now pop has gone so far in the other direction that I can't really even relate; it seems like a foreign language to me.

"I just always try to be real. I did not grow up in a tar-paper shack in the hills of Tennessee, but I'm country. And the most gratifying thing to me is when some young kid, maybe thirteen or fourteen years old, who's been dragged to a concert by their parents, will come up and say, 'I always hated country music, but I really like what you do.' That's like the greatest compliment I can get."

Holly Dunn's list of the greatest songs of all time: Dolly Parton's "To Daddy," Emmylou's version of "Making Believe," everything on Willie Nelson's Stardust album.

E

Steve Earle

b. 1/17/55, San Antonio, TX

Style

Springsteen/Mellencamp working-class country rock

Memorable songs

"Guitar Town," "The Devil's Right Hand"

A lot of tough, semi-irreverent, rock-edged traditionalists in Nashville in the nineties—the kind who don't wear cowboy hats, guys like Mark Collie or David Lynn Jones or Kevin Welch—are likely to tell you something like, "I had to convince the record-label executives that I wasn't another Steve Earle."

They don't like Steve Earle in Nashville one little bit. Too rock 'n' roll for them.

It's not really his music, either. Rock 'n' roll is the base for half the new music in Nashville, from Rodney Crowell to Alabama to Ricky Van Shelton, and Earle is as much a deep-down, dyed-in-the-wool lover of the country idiom as any of them. The guy has too much of a rock 'n' roll attitude.

Earle had a long apprenticeship in Nashville: he arrived there in 1974, did some songwriting (Elvis was supposed to record one of Earle's songs, but never showed up for the session), some demo singing, some work for a publishing company. In the early eighties, he released a few singles for Epic Records that failed to catch fire. Then, in 1986, MCA Records put out a single called "Guitar Town," from an album of the same name, and it was a sensation.

"Guitar Town" had one of the hottest guitar riffs of recent memory, a free-wheeling but friendly rebel attitude, and a major league level of energy. The single (with the line "Everybody knows you can't get far / On twenty-seven dollars and a Jap guitar" awkwardly overdubbed to "and a cheap guitar") only made it to number seven on the charts. But the ripples it made were far greater. Everybody was talking about this explosive song-writing/performing talent with the explosive personality. *Rolling Stones* named Earle Country Artist of the Year in 1986, and Epic rereleased the singles and demos he had made for them in the early eighties as *Early Tracks.*

One other single from *Guitar Town,* "Good-bye's All We Got Left," made the country Top Ten, but after that, things stopped happening for Earle in Nashville. His next album, *Exit 0,* didn't get much country airplay. He embarrassed the country establishment by getting arrested in Texas. MCA moved Earle from its Nashville division to its New York division and more or less gave up the fight to promote him as a country artist, just as they did with Nanci Griffith and Lyle Lovett—all of them artists who have tremendous appeal, record sales, and critical acclaim, but who are gone, gone, gone from country radio. In 1990, Earle toured with Bob Dylan.

Earle talked about his career in and out of country music with Harold DeMuir, in *Pulse!* magazine:

"With 'Guitar Town' I was convinced that I could cross over to rock radio from a country base, and it turned out I was wrong. My attitude was, whatever format gets the job done, but MCA didn't see it that way. I still haven't given up on that idea, but I couldn't convince MCA to ship singles to country radio on *Copperhead Road*. I'm asking them to ship to country radio on the new album; whether they do or not remains to be seen. [The new album was *The Hard Way*; they didn't.]

"It's not drum sounds or guitar sounds that are keeping me off country radio. It's what the songs say, and it's the promotion people and the radio station management concerned about what their advertisers will accept. They get nervous when they hear a song about a Vietnam vet holed up in the hills growing marijuana ['Copperhead Road']. I don't think 'Long Black Veil' or 'I'm So Lonesome I Could Cry' could get on country radio these days.

"The thing is that in the old days, when pop music was totally inane, country music was saying something. Country music acknowledged the fact that people live, people die, people hurt, people get divorced and cheat on each other. Nowadays, country music doesn't do that, but I'm convinced they would accept it if it did . . . the bottleneck is at radio and at the labels; it's not the audience.

"With MCA Nashville . . . I tried to keep my perspective, and I was never bitter. I learned a lot from Jimmy Bowen [then head of MCA/Nashville], and I have a lot of respect for him on one level, but I don't think Bowen has any respect for artists . . . he had a little vendetta against me because I didn't do what he asked me to do, which was to cut an album with two or three things that would be tailor-made for country radio, and then I could do whatever I wanted with the rest of the record. I think he just assumed that I was so ambitious that I'd be willing to work that way, but I see an album as an overall work, and I'd rather not make records at all than make records that way. . . .

"I've never claimed to be working class. But one of the main reasons I still live in a small town outside Nashville is that it's easier to hang on to real life and function a little more normally with regular people who work for a living. The people there just accept me as the local hillbilly singer, and they're kind of protective of me. . . . It's important to be around other artists, but if that's all you know, then you risk losing touch with the very thing that fuels your work. . . .

"I thought I was doing something for country, but they didn't see it that way. I think stuff I've done has had something to do with changing things a little, and I'm happy about that. . . . I don't know if the country community considers me a part of country anymore, and I don't really care. No matter what anybody says, I'm basically just a hillbilly singer with delusions of grandeur."

Steve Earle's ten favorite songwriters: Townes Van Zandt, Guy Clark, Gram Parsons, Bruce Springsteen, Don Henley, Tom Waits, Harlan Howard, Roger Miller, Paul Vanderberg.

Joe Ely

b. 2/9/47, Amarillo, TX

Style
Texas rebel

Memorable songs
"Honky Tonk Masquerade," "Musta Notta Gotta Lotta"

In 1971, a group called the Flatlanders made an album in Nashville, and the album was, in due time, released. Nothing much unusual about that—lots of albums get recorded in Nashville and released in due time. But usually the due time is less than twenty years. The Flatlanders' album came out in 1990, by that time titled—appropriately—*More a Legend Than a Band*.

In 1971, the Flatlanders—chiefly Jimmie Dale Gilmore, Butch Hancock, and Joe Ely—were way outside mainstream tastes. When the album was finally released by Rounder Records, they were still outside mainstream tastes, but the fringes were wider and more inclusive by then, and a Flatlanders reunion show made The Nashville Network.

In the interim, Jimmie Dale Gilmore moved to Denver and studied with an Indian guru, Butch Hancock became an architect and continued to write unusual, haunting songs, which have been recorded by Emmylou Harris and others.

Joe Ely stayed in music, moving from Texas to New York and back to Texas. He recorded a couple of albums for MCA in the late seventies, which failed to make a ripple in the commercial country music, but made Ely a cult favorite—particularly the album *Honky Tonk Masquerade,* still prized by collectors.

In the early eighties, his career took a particularly unusual turn for a country artist, even a cult country artist. He was discovered by the Clash, one of the leading British punk rock groups of the early eighties, and a favorite of the critics for their biting lyrics and driving rock and roll. The Clash had recorded a song called "I'm So Bored With the USA," but they weren't bored by Ely, who represented a freewheeling frontier spirit to them, the America of Woody Guthrie and Buddy Holly.

His experience with the Clash gave Ely a harder edge and a more rock-oriented, electric sound—a precursor of country rebels like Steve Earle.

Ely continued to perform throughout the eighties, and by the end of that decade he was an elder statesman of the Texas honky-tonk crowd—an elder statesman who was still as raw and rockin' as ever, as shown by his 1990 MCA release, *Live at Liberty Lunch.*

Skip Ewing

b. 2/6/64, Redlands, CA

Style
Country/folk

There's a generation of singer-songwriters in the age range of, say, Rodney Crowell, who grew up listening to Bob Dylan, and there's a younger generation of singer-songwriters to whom Bob Dylan is a vague memory from the distant past. This generation listened to James Taylor and the Eagles when they were little kids, but their real singer-songwriter role model is Dan Fogelberg.

Skip Ewing is of that generation, and

although he says he "was hooked on country the first time I heard Merle Haggard sing," his style owes more to the sensitivity of seventies folk than the hard-edged real life of a Haggard. Ewing came to Nashville right out of high school, got a job singing at Opryland, and very quickly started building a career as a songwriter, with songs cut by such masters as George Jones, George Strait, and Charley Pride.

His debut album in 1988 was entitled *The Coast of Colorado,* and his first hit was "I Don't Have Far to Fall." By 1991, he had released his fourth album, some sort of an indication that at least some folks in Nashville think he's got staying power.

Exile

SONNY LEMAIRE

STEVE GOETZMAN

LEE CARROLL

PAUL MARTIN

MARK JONES

Exile has had more major personnel changes than most groups in their front-line guys (as opposed to, say, Asleep at the Wheel, which has always been Ray Benson and sidemen). Key exiles from Exile are founder J. P. Pennington, Les Taylor, Mark Gray, and Marlon Hargis.

Style
It's changed over the years, but it's never strayed too far from pop.

Memorable songs
"Kiss You All Over," "Woke Up in Love"

Exile went country because they weren't selling records to the pop audience anymore. They'd spent a month at number one on the pop charts in 1978 with "Kiss You All Over," they'd toured as the opening act for arena-rockers Aerosmith, but their subsequent pop releases sputtered, their venues got smaller and smaller, until they came to the point where . . . well, Sonny LeMaire, with the group since 1978 and now its senior member, puts it this way: "You're searching for ways to keep it all together, and literally the last-gasp effort of the band was, you know, 'Boys, we gotta play because that's what we do.' But there's no place for us to play on the road. Well, I'd played at a bowling alley in Lexington, Kentucky, right before I joined Exile, and I knew the owner real well, so I went to him and said, 'You know, we need a place to hole up and play till we can get our act together.' "

Not bad—Madison Square Garden to a bowling alley in three years. And at the same time, the personnel of the group had changed. Jimmy Stokely, their flamboyant rock and roll lead singer, had left the group, and Mark Gray and Les Taylor had joined it, "so the focus shifts from this singer going wild on stage to everybody playing an instrument, so we weren't quite as mobile as we had been. J. P. started to sing, Les was singing, Mark was singing, I was singing just a little bit, but the songs began to take a different slant. I can see it very clearly now, but I couldn't at the time, and there was more R and B coming out in the music and more country beginning to come out."

If the guys didn't notice that their music was changing, other people apparently did. One of their pop flops, "Take Me Down," was recorded by "an up-and-coming country group named Alabama" and went straight to number one on the country charts. Dave and Sugar, then a hot country act, and Kenny Rogers had success with Exile songs as well, "and we're in the bowling alley just going crazy. It was bizarre. I mean, in some ways it was a slight vindication that we really did do good material, but on the other hand it was painful because it wasn't us having the success."

It wasn't a real leap for them to start thinking about country. They were all Southern boys who'd played a lot of music while they were growing up: "You went to one band, you played country, you went to another and played rock and roll. It was no big deal. In fact, when we were still a rock and roll band, Les, who was a great mimic, used to imitate George Jones, and it would break us all up."

Mark Gray left the group during the bowling-alley years. "Mark never had a band background like the rest of us," LeMaire said. "He was a solo guy, he'd done a lot of gospel, I think we may have been the first band he was really ever in. It's difficult in a band—there's a lot of politics, there's a lot of give-and-take." Gray went on to a solo career that peaked with several Top Ten hits in 1984 and '85, including a duet with Tammy Wynette.

Meanwhile, Exile was petitioning Epic Records in Nashville, and in 1983, they were signed by CBS Records' Rick Blackburn to an Epic contract. By then, "The Closer You Get," another Gray/Pennington composition that had failed as a pop single, had gone to number one for Alabama.

In the mideighties the country music establishment seemed particularly open to the slicker elements of pop-rock. Alabama's version of "The Closer You Get" featured a rock arrangement; Dan Seals's

"Bop" was virtually disco. Exile first hit the charts in 1983 with "The High Cost of Leavin'," and their next release, "Woke Up in Love," went straight to number one.

From 1983 to '87, Exile ruled the roost, sending one single after another to the top of the charts, ten in all. But the personnel changes started to pile up. Marlon Hargis left in 1985, replaced by former Judds bandleader Lee Carroll.

In August of 1988, Les Taylor left. Taylor, a strong vocalist, had shared the lead-vocal role with J. P. Pennington, but he wanted to do more as a singer. Taylor, who describes his style as "rhythm and bluegrass," signed a solo deal with Epic, but has yet to come up with a breakthrough hit.

Epic Records came close to dropping the group after Taylor's departure, but they decided to hold off and see how his replacement, Paul Martin, worked out as a single partner to J. P. Pennington. But by the end of the year, Pennington left the group, too.

Pennington had been the founder of Exile, their mainstay, their lead singer and songwriter. "J. P. had been on the road forever," LeMaire theorizes. "He wanted to take it easy and regroup, and I think he was tired of the band situation." Pennington, after a year off, went to work on a solo career and issued his first solo album on MCA in 1991.

Epic Records had not bargained on Exile with neither Taylor nor Pennington, and they dropped the group. LeMaire and the others—including Martin, who had assumed he was joining a high-flying group and was stunned when he returned from his honeymoon to discover that its head honcho had quit—decided to hold the group together.

It can't have been an easy decision. Imagine Charlie Watts and Ron Wood being told that Mick Jagger and Keith Richards had quit, but deciding to go ahead with a group that they'd still call the Rolling Stones. The new bunch cut a demo with LeMaire and Martin as the front guys and took it back to Epic, who rejected it: "Doesn't sound like Exile."

The new group kept playing—not quite the bowling alley, but some anxious times nonetheless—and shopping their new material around, until after about a year, in late 1989, they signed with Arista.

Their first Arista release yielded a number one single, "Yet," giving the group a measure of justification. A lot of people have dismissed their music a shallow pop posturing, and we're not sure we'd disagree, but perhaps there'll always be an Exile.

Sonny LeMaire's list of the greatest songs of all time: "Heartbreak Hotel" by Elvis, "I Fall to Pieces," "These Arms of Mine," by Otis Redding, "I Can't Help It If I'm Still in Love With You," "Honky Tonk Women."

F

Donna Fargo

b. 11/10/49, Mt. Airy, NC (*Yvonne Vaughan*)

Style

Upbeat

Memorable songs

"The Happiest Girl in the Whole USA," "Funny Face"

Awards

ACM—New Female Vocalist 1969, Female Vocalist 1972, Album of the Year 1973 (The Happiest Girl in the Whole USA), Song/Single of the Year 1972 ("The Happiest Girl in the Whole USA"); CMA—Single of the year 1972; Grammy—Country Vocal Performance—Female 1972: MCN—Most Promising Female Artist 1972

Donna Fargo was a young schoolteacher in California when she went to audition for a music producer named Stan Silver. Fargo hadn't done much singing up until that point, and she didn't exactly know what kind of singer she was.

Silver only needed to hear the recent arrival from North Carolina once. "You're country," he told her.

Silver taught her how to play the guitar, coached her in country stylings, and married her. They are still together, through twenty years of ups and downs.

The ups came quickly. Her first release, "The Happiest Girl in the Whole USA,"
went to number one, and her career had hit the ground running. Five more number ones in the next five years, pop crossover success, CMA and ACM Awards, a Grammy, her own syndicated TV show.

The downs came just as suddenly. In 1987, she was stricken with multiple sclerosis, a crippling degenerative disease of the central nervous system, for which there is no cure. Fargo fought her way back from it, though, and while she has never regained the momentum of her earlier career (although she can once again perform her highly galvanized stage show, she must conserve her energy), she had continued recording and limited touring and had a modest chart success on a duet with Billy Joe Royal, "Members Only," in 1987.

Forester Sisters

KATHY FORESTER
b. 1/4/55, Lookout Mountain, GA

JUNE FORESTER
b. 9/23/56, Chattanooga, TN

KIM FORESTER
b. 11/4/60, Lookout Mountain, GA

CHRISTY FORESTER
b. 12/21/62, Lookout Mountain, GA

Style

Family harmony

Memorable songs

"(That's What You Do) When You're in Love," "Men"

Awards

ACM—Vocal Group 1986

Kathy Forester is quietly proud of her master's degree in music education, and why shouldn't she be? A postgraduate degree is a substantial accomplishment by anyone's standards; and of course, it's not her only accomplishment: she and her sisters brought the girl-group concept, which had long been a staple of other forms of popular music, into country. And they've stayed on top in an industry that has traditionally been a lot more hospitable to men than to women.

We caught up with the Foresters on their tour bus, backstage at a summer music festival. And if your fantasy of life on a tour bus comes from old Willie Nelson movies, with a bunch of good old boys passing guitars, bourbon bottles, and bimbos around, you'd have to reformat that fantasy about two seconds after you stepped onto the Forester Sisters bus, into the homey chaos of babies and toddlers, nannies and mommies. A star attraction's tour bus is no small place, but it's still cramped quarters to manage four families in; nonetheless, we felt that we might have been sitting at Kathy Forester's kitchen table, in a household presided over by your typical 1990s superwoman: a bright, maternal career woman with a master's degree and country common sense, and a household open to nieces, nephews, and cousins, grandchildren and friends, and even the occasional journalist if he minded his manners.

By this unlikely hearth, the Forester women talked about growing up in Lookout Mountain, Georgia, as very much local folks in what was very much a tourist-oriented, artsy-craftsy community. They had a family-oriented, church-oriented upbringing, with a window on a larger world that was unusual for small-town Southern girls.

The Foresters began singing, and learning about harmony, in church. Kathy, June, and Kim went on from church and college to music-business careers as band singers before deciding to join forces as a group. When little sister Christy left college in 1982 to join the group, the family unit was complete.

In 1983, the Judds hit the country music charts, and the charts were never the same again. There had never been a great female country harmony group before, but now there was one. Generally speaking, there's only one thing that will cause a major label to take a chance on a new sound: if it's not quite new, if someone else has already made it work. So female harmony groups had their chance, and Warner Brothers snapped up the Foresters.

They've never had cause to regret it. The Forester Sisters hit the charts first time out with "(That's What You Do) When You're in Love," and their next single, "I Fell in Love Last Night," hit number one. It was the first of an impressive string of hits for the ladies from Lookout Mountain.

The sisters have held close to their church roots, recording a briskly selling, TV-marketed collection of hymns and spirituals. And they've hit with a hugely popular and appealing signature song, "Men," in which they dish up the dirt with no holds barred on that other sex.

We happened to review "Men" on the same week that we also reviewed the Bellamy Brothers' *Rollin' Thunder* album, which contains a song called "She Don't Know That She's Perfect," and we wondered, "Incidentally, has it struck anyone that both these sibling acts are singing a shared secret about the opposite sex—but the guys are singing about how women don't know how perfect they are, and the women are singing about how guys don't know how far from perfect they are?

"A sign of the times? Or has it always been this way?"

Foster and Lloyd

RADNEY FOSTER
b. 7/20/59, Del Rio, TX

BILL LLOYD
b. 12/6/55, Bowling Green, KY

Style

The Beatles come to Nashville

Memorable songs

"Crazy Over You"

Foster and Lloyd disbanded in the winter of 1990, as country music radio tightened its stranglehold on its playlists, so that, as one industry insider put it gloomily, "there just wasn't room anymore for acts with intelligence."

Foster and Lloyd's intelligence took the form of a sly but respectful synthesis of a variety of pop and country styles: whether they were closer to pop or closer to country is probably a toss-up. In 1987, everyone loved them. Their first single, "Crazy Over You," shot up to number four on the charts, and its accompanying Beatlesque video went into hot rotation on TNN and CMT just as music videos were becoming an important avenue to country exposure.

Everyone talked about Foster and Lloyd's influences, which Bill Lloyd described as "flattering, because we love mu-

sic. But I like to think that what we do is more than the sum of our influences. You don't sit down to write a song and say, 'Okay, today we're going to take side two of *Rubber Soul* and mix it with a little Everlys here, and a little Hank Williams here' . . . it's just what comes out. It's like squeezing a sponge. You write songs because you've absorbed a lot of personal information, a lot of musical information, then you squeeze the sponge and it comes out in a certain way."

Lloyd grew up in Bowling Green, where his father settled after retiring from the armed forces. With the characteristic rootlessness of the army brat, Lloyd doesn't credit that as a major shaping force in his musical development: "I don't think 'I grew up in this part of the country, therefore . . .' always works these days. Pop culture has so permeated all our lives that those regionalisms aren't necessarily true anymore." If you grew up in the sixties, you could hear the Beatles anywhere. Still, central Kentucky, the home of the Everly Brothers and the original members of Exile, is a place where rock and roll and bluegrass coexist easily, and Lloyd played with bluegrass virtuoso Sam Bush (of New Grass Revival and Emmylou Harris's Nash Ramblers) in local clubs.

"I came to country music through the country-rock synthesis that started with the Byrds. I listened to Poco, and the Eagles, and I thought it was neat that hippies were listening to country music. Country music had lost the kids for a long time. Rock and roll usurped the fun. Songs like Jimmy Dickens's 'I've Got a Hole in My Pocket' weren't being played anymore. From the late fifties through early seventies, the rock years, there was very much of an us-and-them attitude. A lot of young people weren't being turned on to any country music at all, except through hippie bands like Commander Cody and the Grateful Dead. Gradually, I got interested and started listening to the great old stuff. But I'm not one of those guys who grew up listening to the Opry every Saturday night."

Bill Lloyd has been working on eclectic projects since the duo split up. Radney Foster released a solidly commercial country album in late 1992 which moved him back into the spotlight.

Bill Lloyd's list of the greatest songs of all time: " 'I Can't Help It If I'm Still in Love With You.' Hank Williams is so direct, so straightforward, so well laid out . . . the guy was brilliant but he wasn't. The songs just came out of him. He was a primitive artist—the craftsmanship was innate, not learned. 'Bye Bye Love' for its sheer groove. 'Wichita Lineman' by Jim Webb—if you want to make a distinction between a great song and great record, I'd call that a great record. But it's a fine song, too. 'Here, There, and Everywhere' by the Beatles. 'Thunder Road' by Bruce Springsteen. And there's a lot to be said for all those songs that were written in cubicles—the Brill Building, Motown, or Nashville. There's a lot of genuine emotion in them."

Janie Frickie

b. 12/19/47, South Whitley, IN (*Jane Fricke—changed spelling of her last name so it could be pronounced phonetically*)

Style

All-purpose professional

Memorable songs

"It Ain't Easy Bein' Easy"

Awards

ACM—Female Vocalist 1983; CMA—Female Vocalist 1982–83; MCN—Most Promising Female Artist 1979, Female Artist 1983–84

Janie Frickie had a major reputation in the anonymous department of the country music industry before she had any reputation at all. As a backup singer, she contributed anonymous vocal duet lines to songs by Johnny Duncan and Tommy Cash and was credited, but still barely known, for her contribution to Charlie Rich's 1978 number one hit, "On My Knees." In Memphis, Dallas, and Los Angeles before she ever came to Nashville, the University of Indiana graduate had compiled a truckload of credits as a jingle and studio singer.

Studio singing is a demanding but anonymous art. Beginning with Porter and Dolly, Janie sang backup on hit records by Barbara Mandrell, Ronnie Milsap, Elvis, and others (including Dan Seals in his England Dan/John Ford Coley pop period). But that doesn't mean she stood behind them and did her whoo-hoos to their inspiring leads and grateful pats on the back. The featured artists had long since done their parts and gone back to their estates in the country by the time Janie got into the studio. The people whom she met—and impressed—in those days were the producers.

Billy Sherrill, most famous for his work with George Jones and Tammy Wynette, signed her to a Columbia Records contract, but didn't quite know what to do with her.

Janie's style was more than casually esoteric. Growing up in the Midwest in the sixties, her first major influence was Motown. In college, she sang folk, pop, and rock and roll; in the jingle business, she sang everything. "I'm used to working with singers like Tammy who have a certain style," Sherrill told her. "You have such a variety, it's hard to know what to do with you."

As a result, Janie recalls, her first two albums were "sort of experimental." On her third album, Jim Ed Norman took over as producer, and Frickie was on her way. "Don't Worry 'Bout Me Baby" became her first number one hit in 1982, the beginning of five years at the top of the charts, including a couple of Female Vocalist of the Year awards.

In 1986 she changed the spelling of her name to jibe with its correct pronunciation and charted her last number one, "Always Have Always Will." After that, she experienced a fairly precipitous falling off: these days, her major exposure is as a regular on the Statler Brothers' TNN variety show. Perhaps not coincidentally, this was the period that saw singers like Kathy Mattea burst into stardom, singers like Nanci Griffith and k. d. lang make their first appearances on the charts. Now, we're not talking about performers who have had, or ever will have, anywhere near the kind of chart success Janie Frickie achieved at her peak (with the possible exception of Mattea). But the late eighties were a time of striking new, personal styles—and perhaps tastes had moved away from the smooth professionalism that Frickie embodies.

The Gatlin Brothers

LARRY GATLIN
b. 5/2/48, Seminole, TX

STEVE GATLIN
b. 4/4/51, Olney, TX

RUDY GATLIN
b. 8/20/52, Olney, TX

Style

Vegas

Memorable songs

"Broken Lady" (Larry Gatlin), "I Just Wish You Were Someone I Love"

Awards

ACM—Single of the Year 1979 ("It's a Cheatin' Situation"), Male Vocalist 1979, Album of the Year 1979 (Straight Ahead); Grammy—Country Song 1979 ("Broken Lady"); MCN—Most Promising Male Artist 1977, Male Artist 1979, Band 1978, Songwriter 1978

Larry Gatlin went to the University of Houston on a football scholarship and majored in English. He then began a music career with the Imperials, a gospel harmony group that included backing up Elvis among its credits. He left the Imperials and moved to Nashville in 1972 to try a solo career, thanks to a vote of confidence from Dottie West. He had sent her a tape of his songs, and she responded by sending him an airline ticket to Nashville. He got his first recording contract with Monument Records in 1973 and had a few years of not quite catching on until he finally scored in 1976 with a solid hit, "Broken Lady," a song he wrote in fifteen minutes.

Meanwhile, young brothers Steve and Rudy had finished up their college educations at Texas Tech (Steve in elementary education, Rudy in business administration) and made their own move to Nashville, along with their sister LaDonna and her husband, Tim Johnson, where they auditioned unsuccessfully as a backup group to Charley Pride (Dave and Sugar got the gig), but were hired to back up Tammy Wynette.

But the brothers had always wanted to sing together, and when Larry hit with "Broken Lady," and a major career seemed like a real possibility, the brothers left Tammy and rejoined him.

Why not? They went back a long way together. When six-year-old Larry made his first public appearance, in the Cavalcade of Talent at Hardin-Simmons University in Abilene, Texas, Steve and Rudy wanted to join him onstage. The boys' mom thought that at ages four and two, they might have been a little too young, but she was talked out of that foolish idea, and the three of them made their stage debut together (they won).

The Gatlins have been a big group for the last fifteen years. As a touring group, they're one of the biggest, especially in that circuit which looks to Las Vegas as its summit. As a recording group, they've always been warm, but never hot-hot-hot. When you look at the Gatlins' chart record, you don't see any period of one top hit after another, like, say, George Strait or Alabama or Ricky Skaggs or Steve Wariner. No more than half the Gatlins' chart entries have gone to the Top Ten, and they've only had three number ones: "I Just Wish You Were Someone I Love," "All the Gold in California," and "Houston (Means I'm One Day Closer to You)."

Perhaps this shows that the Gatlins don't have as solid a following among the record-buying public as they do in Vegas. Perhaps it means that some people like them better than others.

One of those who likes them a lot—a whole lot—is Larry Gatlin. In a recent interview, Larry, who writes all the songs for the group, commented on how country music isn't what it used to be: "I don't see any new standards. You know, those great songs like 'Your Cheatin' Heart' or 'All the Gold in California.'"

Crystal Gayle

b. 1/9/51, Paintsville, KY (*Brenda Gail Webb*)

Style
Contemporary country

Memorable songs
"Don't It Make My Brown Eyes Blue"

Awards
ACM—New Female Vocalist 1975, Female Vocalist 1976–77, 1979; CMA—Female Vocalist 1977–78; Grammy—Country Vocal Performance—Female 1977 ("Don't It Make My Brown Eyes Blue"); MCN—Most Promising Female Vocalist 1975

These are the things you need to know about Crystal Gayle:

She's Loretta Lynn's sister, and her first professional experience was as a singer in her sister's traveling show (she joined it at age sixteen).

She's had eighteen number one records, but the only one anyone remembers is "Don't It Make My Brown Eyes Blue," a song that was originally written for Shirley "Goldfinger" Bassey and never intended to be a country song.

She has this hair that comes down to . . . but then, if you've ever seen Crystal Gayle, live or on TV, you know about that.

If you have seen Crystal on TV, perhaps you've seen her on a soap. Crystal's been musically connected with both day and nighttime soaps—she and Gary Morris recorded hit duets on the themes for "Dallas" and "Another World," the former going to number one in 1985, the latter to number four in 1987. Crystal appeared as a character on "Another World" for a while, too, playing herself—she comes to Bay City to appear on Felicia's TV show, a deranged killer starts stalking her, Cass tries to help her out but he's got Kathleen to worry about, while at the same time Donna is having trouble with Carl, and Jake is getting ready to leave the bad twin sister, Vicki, and take up with her good twin sister, Marley. . . .

Crystal toured China in 1979, making her the first country artist to appear in that country.

Crystal is an attractive, polished performer who'll go on knocking them dead on the Vegas–Atlantic City–Bob Hope Tour circuit for a long time, but she's probably over as a major recording star.

Vince Gill

b. 4/5/57, Norman, OK

Married to Janis Gill of Sweethearts of the Rodeo

Style

Consummate professional

Memorable songs

"Let Me Love You Tonight" (with Pure Prairie League), *"When I Call Your Name"*

Awards

ACM—New Male Vocalist 1984; CMA—Single of the Year 1990, Song of the Year 1991 ("When I Call Your Name"), Male Vocalist 1991; Grammy—Country Vocal Performance–Male 1990 ("When I Call Your Name"), 1992 ("I Still Believe In You"), Best Country Song, 1992 ("I Still Believe In You," w/John Barlow Jarvis); TNN/MCN—Single of the Year 1991, Instrumentalist 1991

It seems as though everyone in the country music was rooting for Vince Gill to make it to the career heights he finally achieved in 1990: a number one record, a platinum album, CMA Song of the Year, two Grammy nominations. Gill was the singer's singer, the pro's pro, the Guy Who Paid His Dues.

"I'm no overnight success," Vince Gill cheerfully admits. "You know, I am a lot different than Garth and Clint and Alan Jackson, and about ninety percent of the guys on the charts right now, because I have been recording for seven years in country music, with spotty success. So they are in a sense, overnight successes. And they may say, 'Yeah, but I played in bars for ten years'—well, everybody played in bars for ten years, that's just learning your trade. I would consider an artist whose first record goes platinum an overnight success."

Seven years in Nashville, as a solo artist and as perhaps the most sought-after session singer in town, are just a part of the story. Gill, who once had to choose between music and a career in professional golf (he scored a hole-in-one during a recent televised pro-am tournament), has racked up credits from bluegrass to rock, the latter as lead singer for Pure Prairie League, one of the better country-rock groups to spring up in the wake of the Byrds' *Sweetheart of the Rodeo*. He was also a member of the Cherry Bombs, a group put together by another cult figure turned superstar, Rodney Crowell.

Most male singers mention Merle or Hank or Lefty or George or Carl Perkins, or even Dan Fogelberg or Ray Charles, when you ask them about their chief influences. Gill, untypically, lists a couple of women: Emmylou Harris and Linda Ronstadt. Furthermore, he's confident enough to acknowledge without embarrassment, "I do find that I enjoy female singers more."

Gill is not ambivalent about his success. He's delighted by it. But he keeps it in a certain perspective at the same time: "I love to make records that every person would want to buy, but at the same time I've been very content with my contributions to music—and I'd say that ninety-five percent of the things I've done would definitely go unnoticed by the majority of people. But there aren't that many artists who have gotten to do all the things I've gotten to do.

"A lot of my heroes have ended up

being in a supporting-cast situation, so I treat each situation I'm in, whether it be singing harmony for Patty Loveless or playing a guitar solo for Dolly Parton or singing a lead vocal on my own album, as equally important. And if I start thinking I'm bigger than what's going on around me, then I can get slapped in the head. I felt that Don Rich was as important to the sound of Buck Owens's records as Buck Owens was—and I think Buck Owens will tell you the same thing. Rodney Crowell's songs were really important to Emmylou Harris's career, James Burton's guitar playing for Elvis, Albert Lee's guitar playing for Emmy. All these things are critical, and I always have the utmost respect for the artists who realize that. There are a lot of artists that don't realize that, and I hope I'm not one of them."

Vince Gill's list of the greatest songs of all time: "I Fall to Pieces," "Your Cheatin' Heart," "Yesterday," "Old Shep." "One record I'll never forget as a kid was 'Let It Be.' That was the first time I ever slow-danced with a girl, the first time I ever realized what all these sexual feelings were. I'll never forget that girl, and I'll never forget that dance—it was seventh or eighth grade."

Mickey Gilley

b. 3/9/36, Ferriday, LA

Style
Urban Cowboy with (a little) soul

Memorable songs
"Don't the Girls All Get Prettier at Closin' Time"

Awards
ACM—New Male Vocalist 1974, Male Vocalist 1976, Single of the Year 1976 ("Bring It on Home"), Album of the Year 1976 (Gilley's Smoking), Entertainer of the Year 1976, Club of the Year 1979–80, 1982–84; (Gilley's); Country Instrumental Performance 1980 ("Orange Blossom Special/Hoedown"–Gilley's "Urban Cowboy" Band), MCN—Most Promising Male Vocalist 1976

In 1956, the teenaged Mickey Gilley took off from his job as a garage mechanic to catch a concert by his cousin Jerry Lee Lewis, who was touring behind his new Sun Records contract and the regional success of his first record, "Crazy Arms."

It was a turning point in Gilley's life. Not the music—he'd heard his cousin before, had played together with him and their other cousin, Jimmy Swaggart. No, the moment of truth came "when I took him to the airport afterwards and he pulled out a big wad of hundred-dollar bills. It made me decide I was in the wrong business."

Gilley kept a close eye on the music business as a cash cow from then on in, and it's done well by him. After playing in Houston nightclubs for ten years, he finally opened his own club, Gilley's, in 1970, and the club, conceived on a Texas scale, became one of the great success stories in the entertainment business. "It's just a honky-tonk, but it looks as big as the MGM Grand Hotel or St. Patrick's Cathedral," wrote a Northerner who had discovered Gilley's and turned the club into a 1978 *Esquire* article. The article was entitled "The Ballad of the Urban Cowboy," and yes, it became the movie that was filmed in Gilley's and started the Urban

Cowboy phenomenon, whose glitzy excesses are now looked back on by traditional country fans the way social reformers look back at the greed-driven eighties.

Gilley contributed his remake of "Stand By Me" to the movie, and it went to number one on the charts in 1980. Gilley, of course, was no stranger to chart success by this time, but his recording career was more or less an accident. Like the Archies or the Teenage Mutant Ninja Turtles, Gilley's recording career was an incidental outgrowth of trying to sell a product—in this case, the nightclub. He had done TV commercials for Gilley's, and in 1974 he released a local single called "She Called Me Baby" as another promotion for the club. The flip side of the single was a song called "Room full of Roses," a remake of an old George Morgan hit from the fifties, and it was not a masterpiece of the recording arts. As Tom Roland describes it in *The Billboard Book of Number One Country Hits*:

> The single introduced Gilley with a piano style reminiscent of his cousin, Jerry Lee Lewis. . . . Convinced by others at the session that his imitation of the Killer was perfect for the tune, Gilley launched into the song once more . . . [he] momentarily got lost during the piano solo in the middle and somehow managed to come out of it in sync with the studio band. The steel guitar was also mixed louder than Gilley wanted and was treated with an excessive amount of "echo" to hide the fact that it was recorded out of tune. Gilley also muffed the lyrics at one point, switching the I's and you's around

in the first verse. "It really didn't make sense," he confesses, "but it was one of those things that had that particular sound that made it work."

It worked well enough that disc jockeys all over Houston started playing the Jerry Lee–wannabe side. And it worked well enough that Playboy Records, otherwise noted for being the only label ever to release a song celebrating a country girl's becoming a *Playboy* centerfold, picked up "Roomful of Roses" and released it nationally.

The song hit number one on the charts in June of 1974, the first of the series of Jerry Lee soundalike songs that made Gilley a fixture on the charts through the seventies and eighties and swelled the Gilley coffers even further. The year 1980 was the *Urban Cowboy* year, and the Gilley fortunes went through the roof, as his Houston nightclub became the epicenter of a national fad (Gilley's closed in 1989). In more recent years he's had success with songs like "Doo Wah Days," his last Top Ten hit (number six in 1986), which echoed the sentiments of Ronnie Milsap's "Lost in the Fifties Tonight."

And he's reopened Gilley's . . . this time in Branson.

Jimmie Dale Gilmore

Style
A pure tenor, a sort of cosmic Willie Nelson

Memorable songs
"Dallas," "White Freight Liner Blues"

Jimmie Dale Gilmore may be a reincarnation of David Carradine's Little Grasshopper, from the "King Fu" TV series: a true son of Texas who's also a wandering mystic visionary. Gilmore's mystic wandering took him from Lubbock (where his first group, with Joe Ely, was subsidized by Buddy Holly's father) to Austin (where he played at the grand opening of the Armadillo World Headquarters, the most legendary club of a legendary music scene) to Denver, where he gave up music for several years to pursue a study of oriental philosophy.

Gilmore's musical career has always been bound up with his fellow Texans Joe Fly and Butch Hancock. Their 1971 album as the Flatlanders had an underground (and unreleased) following for almost twenty years, until it was finally brought out in 1990 by Rounder Records as *More a Legend Than a Band*. In the interim, Ely had gone on to a career as an international cult figure, and Hancock to a career as a local cult figure and respected songwriter.

None of them entered the commercial mainstream of country music, including Gilmore, who returned to music around 1980. He came back to Austin ("The longest I've ever spent in Nashville is about a week and a half"), where he made two albums for Oakland's Hightone Records (the second of which was recorded in Nashville). The hottest single off either of them was "White Freight Liner Blues," which went to number 72 on the charts, but Gilmore is worth looking for. He's blessed with what may well be the most beautiful voice in country music, a clear, keening tenor that carries as much emotion on hard-driving numbers as it does on ballads. In 1991, he was one of seven artists, representing various styles of American music, presented by Elektra Records in its American Explorers series.

Jimmie Dale Gilmore's list of the greatest songs of all times: " 'I Was the One' by Lieber and Stoller—the Elvis song. That song summarizes a whole world of music for me." "Don't Think Twice, It's All Right"; "Mansion on the Hill"; "In My Life"; "Dust My Broom," the Elmore James version; "If You Were a Bluebird" by Butch Hancock.

Girls Next Door

DORIS KING
b. 2/13/57, Nashville TN

DIANE WILLIAMS
b. 8/9/59, Hahn AFB, Germany

CINDY NIXON
b. 8/3/58, Nashville, TN

TAMMY STEPHENS
b. 4/13/61, Arlington, TX

Style
Bland fifties

The fifties made a comeback in Nashville in the eighties, with such artists as Ronnie Milsap lost in them, the Judds reconstructing Elvis from a feminine perspective with "Don't Be Cruel," Eddie Rabbitt reprising Dion's "The Wanderer." What they and others had in common was a love for the tough, raw edge of early rock and roll, the sweet, soulful sound of urban rhythm and blues given a country interpretation.

Then there were the Girls Next Door, who seemed determined to re-create the blandest, most sterile sounds of the fifties, the chirpy harmonies of girl groups like the McGuire Sisters. But they put out two albums for the now-defunct MTM label and reached the Top Ten in 1986 with a remake of "Slow Boat to China."

Glaser Brothers

TOMPALL GLASER
b. 9/3/33, Spalding, NE

JIM GLASER
b. 12/16/37, Spalding, NE

CHUCK GLASER
b. 2/27/36, Spalding, NE

Style
Outlaw

Memorable songs
"Put Another Log on the Fire" (Tompall), *"You're Gettin' to Me Again"* (Jim)

Awards
ACM—New Male Vocalist 1983 (Jim); CMA—Vocal Group 1970, Album of the Year 1976 (Wanted—The Outlaws—Tompall w/ Willie Nelson, Waylon Jennings, Jessi Colter); MCN—Vocal Group 1967–68

You could make an argument for the theory that American social and political history has always come down to a battle between the cattle barons and the outlaws—with, for example, the outlaws raising a ruckus in the sixties and the cattle barons winning control back in the Reagan/Falwell eighties.

You could, but that's not our business here. We're concerned with the world of country music, and in the world of country music, there's no question but that this has been the battle, in one version or another.

In the eighties, we're told, morality and clean living made comebacks, and drinkin' and cheatin' and honky-tonkin' songs were O-U-T. But at the very time when a Nashville record company executive was telling us that country had grown far too sophisticated, and honky-tonks were passé, Dwight Yoakam was riding high on the charts with "Honky Tonk Man." And Travis Tritt, a wise-assed throwback, did pretty well in 1991 with "The Whiskey Ain't Working Anymore." Women were supposed to be strong and proud and codependent no more, but Highway 101 dealt with both drinkin' and destructive love in "Whiskey, If You Were a Woman."

The Glaser Brothers were part of a famous earlier generation of outlaws—the ones who rebelled against the cattle barons of the smooth and string-sweetened Nashville Sound, who went back to Luckenbach, Texas, with Waylon and Willie and the boys. Tompall Glaser was one of the contributors to the Waylon/Willie/Jessi Colter album, *The Outlaws,* which introduced a new word and a new old sound to country music.

Tompall was always the dominant Glaser brother, but Jim was the only member of the family to have a number one record: "'You're Gettin' to Me Again," in 1984.

These days, they're pretty much retired, although Tompall still does some occasional producing.

William Lee Golden

b. 1/12/35, Brewton, AL

Style
Still looking for a distinct solo voice

Golden spent the better part of two decades with the Oak Ridge Boys, then was bounced in 1987. When the Oaks lost Old Spanish Moss Face, they lost a lot of the group's visual distinctiveness; but the word was that Golden's increasing individualism and environmental purism led the others in the group to see him as neither the team player nor the Vegas-hotel player that they required.

Golden still lives in Brewton, in the old slave quarters of a two-hundred-year-old plantation he bought in 1980. The main house is occupied by his sons, Rusty and Chris, who perform as The Goldens. William Lee continues to attempt to establish himself as a solo performer.

Vern Gosdin

b. 8/5/34, Woodland, AL

Style

Chiseled in stone

Memorable songs

"Set 'em Up Joe," "Chiseled in Stone"

Awards

CMA—Song of the Year 1989 ("Chiseled in Stone")

Vern Gosdin's 1987 comeback was remarkable for all sorts of reasons, not the least of them being that he was fifty-three years old at a time when the youth movement was sweeping Nashville. But it was also a remarkable comeback in that (a) he'd never exactly been away, and (b) he'd never exactly arrived the first time, in spite of a number one record in 1984 and several Top Ten hits going back to the midseventies.

Gosdin came from a country family—the "Gosdin Family Gospel Show" was a staple of WVOK in Birmingham, Alabama, during the forties and fifties.

Vern and his brother Rex (who died in 1983) broke off from gospel and got into bluegrass, going on the road with a series of bands. They ended up in California, where they formed a bluegrass band called the Golden State Boys. The Golden State Boys later became the Hillmen, fronted by a younger instrumental whiz named Chris Hillman.

"Wouldn't it be nice if we knew then what we know now?" Gosdin reminisces. "I was just kickin' around and havin' a good time, and this guy Jim Dixon came to me with the idea for the Byrds. He gave me an album of Bob Dylan, with 'Mr. Tambourine Man' on it. And you know how Bob sang. I mean today we're kind of used to it, we can put up with it, but back then, I'd never heard nothin' like it before. And I just said, 'Man, there ain't no way I can get into this.' And I gave it back to him.

"That was the first mistake I made. The first of many. Man, there was a time when just about everything I did was wrong."

Out of the music business for ten years (he had his own glass and mirror company back in Georgia for a while), Gosdin returned in the midseventies with a demo of two songs, "Hangin' On" and "Yesterday's Gone." Emmylou Harris heard the demo and was so impressed with the quality of Gosdin's voice that she agreed to add harmony vocals to "Yesterday's Gone," which became Gosdin's first Top Ten hit on Elektra. Janie Frickie harmonized with him on "Never My Love," which also made the Top Ten, but after a few years Gosdin moved on, recording through the early eighties on a succession of independent labels: "I didn't know the difference between a big label and a small label. The first guy that came along and said, 'Vern, we sure would like to have you over at our label,' I'd go with them."

During this stage of his career, Gosdin racked up his first number one hit, "I Can Tell by the Way You Dance (You're Gonna Love Me Tonight,") for Compleat Records in 1984. This, and Jim Glaser's "You're Gettin' to Me Again," were the last indie label records to hit number one, as the Nashville music business became more and more corporate; it's difficult to imagine an independent doing it today.

So in 1987, when Gosdin signed with Columbia, he was a music business also-ran, a Nashville drifter who had not been off the charts since 1976, who had scored eleven Top Ten hits and a number one—the voice that wouldn't go away because he was just too good to ignore.

Chiseled in Stone, Gosdin's Columbia album, meant that finally Vern Gosdin had arrived. "Set 'em Up Joe" went to number one; "Chiseled in Stone" made the Top Ten and earned a CMA award.

At the same time, Vern's personal life was not keeping pace with his career. A divorce left him devastated, but in true country tradition, he incorporated it into his music. His next album, *Alone,* dug into the hurt of the divorce, and one of those songs, "I'm Still Crazy," went to number one. "That was probably a streak of luck for me in the long run, because I wrote honest songs, but I wouldn't want to get back in the same position to see if I could do it again."

Why is Gosdin making it so big now, when so many performers his age are considered yesterday's news?

"I don't know. But I think part of the reason is I'm writin' my own material. And I don't know if you know it or not, but a lot of artists, when they go into the studio to cut a song, they never heard it till they got into the studio.

"And some of these guys, they just got the wrong people pickin' songs for them. Janie Frickie had three number one records in a row, and then she decided to marry some guy at CBS Records, and he was gonna be her producer and manager all at the same time, and right to the bottom she went. I don't know, there's just something about human nature. Like if a guy comes in to me and says, 'Hey, my name's Randy Travis and this is my wife and she's managing me,' now that just turns me off. I didn't wanna have to talk to his wife about him. You can't argue with one of 'em because it's gonna make both of 'em mad at you."

In 1990, Gosdin underwent open-heart surgery ("I wrote one song about it, called 'Heart Don't Start Stoppin' on Me Now,' but I don't know who'd want to hear it"). But he recovered and continues to perform and record—including an odd greatest-hits package, *10 Years of Greatest Hits—Newly Recorded,* an event brought about because so many of Gosdin's hits were on independent labels.

Vern Gosdin's list of the greatest songs of all time: "Lovin' Her Was Easier Than Anything I'll Ever Do Again," "He Stopped Lovin' Her Today," "Hungry Eyes," "Angel Flying Too Close to the Ground," and a new song, Bob Seger's "Real Love."

Mark Gray

See EXILE.

Lee Greenwood

b. 10/27/42

Style
MOR

Memorable songs
"Ring on Her Finger, Time on Her Hands"

Awards
*ACM—New Male Vocalist 1983;
CMA—Song of the Year 1985 ("God Bless
the USA"), Male Vocalist 1983–84;
Grammy—Country Vocal
Performance—Male 1983 ("I.O.U.");
MCN—Male Artist 1983–84*

A lot of country artists, especially the slick variety, play Vegas after they've made it big in Nashville, but Lee Greenwood did it the other way around. He started out in Las Vegas as a dealer in the casinos, also keeping his musical wheels turning by playing saxophone and piano in various Vegas and Reno bands.

Discovered by Mel Tillis's bass player during a Vegas gig, Greenwood came to Nashville, where his husky voice and *Gentlemen's Quarterly* looks attracted attention. He recorded his first hit in 1981.

Greenwood is frequently compared to Kenny Rogers. But whereas Rogers presumably came by his limited but effective range naturally, Greenwood says he earned his. Long hours singing in smoky Vegas lounges, double-shifted with stints dealing at the tables, took about two octaves off his range and gave him that husky/sexy quality that has characterized him ever since.

In 1984, Greenwood recorded "God Bless the USA," his patriotic response to the 1983 downing of a South Korean jet-liner by a Soviet jet. Although the single never made it past number seven on the charts, it won him a CMA Award for Song of the Year, and a whole raft of patriotic awards, from the VFW to the American Legion to the Air Force to the Boy Scouts of America. In 1991, the Gulf War revived patriotism and the song, which was rereleased with a video.

Nanci Griffith

b. 7/6/54, Austin TX

Style
Literate, quirky

Memorable songs
"Lone Star State of Mind," "Love Wore a Halo"

The country charts, especially the country singles charts, reflect what's played on country radio, and while radio is somewhat democratic, responsive to the public taste of the majority, it's somewhat controlled as well. So what's the real story? Have the more adventurous artists of the eighties disappeared from the charts because they've been programmed out of existence by rigid program directors, or did they get their fair shake and were found wanting by the court of public opinion?

It's hard to say. "From a Distance" became a huge, Grammy-winning pop hit for Bette Midler, but it was first recorded by Nanci Griffith. Many still consider hers the definitive version (it was a number one hit in Ireland), and songwriter Julie Gold made a point of thanking Griffith when she picked up her Grammy. Would it have become a hit on country radio if it had been promoted more aggressively?

Well, in a recent Gallup Poll in the

United Kingdom, 43 percent of respondents liked country music, as compared to 36 percent for pop, 26 percent for rock, 17 percent for jazz. And on the British country music charts, you'll find that Diamond Rio, say, or Restless Heart or Lorrie Morgan haven't made much of an impact. In fact, the two hottest American acts of 1990 on their country charts (trailing only homegrown star Daniel O'Donnell) were Nanci Griffith and Steve Earle, with four albums each.

Raised in Texas on poetry as well as music ("My parents were Beat Generation people"), she began her career on the folkie circuit, eventually signing with the New England–based folk label Philo, and winning a Grammy nomination for Best Folk Album in 1984.

When her version of Pat Alger's "Once in a Very Blue Moon," off a Philo album, crept onto the bottom of the country charts in 1986, Nashville took notice of her and she was signed to MCA. Her first MCA release, "Lone Star State of Mind," by Alger and Fred Koller, went to Number 39—the highest country-chart position she was ever to reach.

Griffith's voice is a surprising combination of Texas-plains harshness and girlish sweetness. It's hard to adjust to at first, and perhaps it made demands that commercial-radio listeners weren't willing to meet, but it soon becomes addictive.

Her songwriting skills are among the best around. An aficionado of the great Southern short story writers such as Eudora Welty, Griffith's story songs are subtle and haunting. "Love Wore a Halo," told from the point of view of a young woman who has just bought a run-down resort hotel on the Jersey shore, relates the story of the older woman she's buying it from: an honest numbers runner who falls in love with a Seabee. Not the stuff of a three-minute pop song? Well, like they say, not until now. "Love Wore a Halo" fits it all in with ease.

Her "Love at the Five and Dime," Kathy Mattea's first hit, is another love song with an absorbing story line. Her own favorite from among her songs, "A Hard Life," is a moving plea for a generation of children the world has turned its back on.

MCA Records, which signed a number of the more adventurous acts in the late eighties, Griffith among them, has moved them all off their Nashville roster and is not even promoting them to country radio anymore. Since radio play these days is entirely a function of program directors and label promotion departments, that means none of these acts will get any airplay at all on a country station. There's no such thing as a local disc jockey falling in love with a song and breaking it him or herself.

With her 1991 release, *Late Night Grande Hotel,* Griffith pretty much abandoned a country approach altogether (not necessarily for the better). But she continues to be respected by her peers in Nashville and continues to have an impact as a songwriter. "Outbound Plane," which she wrote with Tom Russell, was a hit for Suzy Bogguss in 1991.

Rich Grissom

Style

Rugged

Memorable songs

"Hillbilly Boy With the Rock and Roll Blues"

Rich Grissom started out in music when he was a kid, leaving home to go on the road with the Champs. The Champs had hit it big with "Tequila"; Glen Campbell and Seals and Crofts had been with them, but by this time they were hanging on by their teeth, traveling the Northwest in an old station wagon. They broke up in a tiny town a million miles from anywhere, and Grissom went back to the farm and went straight for fifteen years, doing everything from cutting hair to driving a bulldozer.

Then he said the hell with it, moved to Nashville, got a contract with Mercury, and put out one damn good album in 1990 that didn't go anywhere. He's still under contract to Mercury as we swing into 1992, although as of this writing there's no second album.

If he doesn't make it in Nashville?

"Oh, shoot. I don't know. I might just go get my old pickup out of hock, fix it up good, and head for the Rocky Mountains or someplace, be a one-man band or something. I'm too far into this to get out now. It doesn't scare me. Shoot, man, I been broke down so many times, I can always find a way to climb back up, you know. I'm not a quitter."

Grissom's one of the guys we're rooting for. But if he doesn't make it, and we run into him someday in some little joint in the Rockies—hell, we'll grab a beer and listen to him.

Rich Grissom's list of the greatest songs of all time: "Born to Lose," "I Can't Stop Loving You," "Blue Christmas," "Take These Chains From My Heart," "Your Cheating Heart."

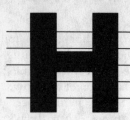

Merle Haggard

b. 4/6/37, Bakersfield, CA

Style

The Bakersfield Sound

Memorable songs

"Mama Tried," "Okie From Muskogee"

Awards

ACM—New Male Vocalist 1965, Male Vocalist 1966, 1969–70, 1972, 1974, 1981, Duet 1965–67 (w/ Bonnie Owens), Single of the Year, Album of the Year 1969, (Okie From Muskogee), Entertainer of the Year 1970, Touring Band 1969–72, 1974–75, 1981, 1987 (The Strangers); CMA—Male Vocalist 1970, Entertainer of the Year 1970, Vocal Duo 1983 (w/ Willie Nelson), Single of the Year, Album of the Year 1970, Album of the Year 1972; (Let Me Tell You About a Song); Grammy—Country Vocal Performance Male 1984 ("That's the Way Love Goes"); MCN—Male Artist 1967–68, Songwriter 1970, Band 1971–72 (The Strangers); TNN/MCN—Living Legend 1990

Not many country singers get thirteen-page biographies in *The New Yorker,* but Merle Haggard did, and no one was surprised. Words like *legend* adhere easily to Haggard. So does the word *outlaw.* Haggard hates it, but it probably fits him better than most of the singers who have attached it to themselves. Not only did he actually serve time, but for a long time, he and his band had a reputation for igniting assorted brawls, violence, and mayhem wherever they played. *Penthouse*'s Larry Linderman asked him if it was a bum rap.

"No, for a long time we were like the late Bob Wills band. Roy Nichols, my lead guitar player, says that Wills's music would make you either want to fuck or fight, and a helluva lot of both went on at any dance Bob played. We were like that, too. I don't know what it was, but our music would get everybody goin'. I remember one night in Amarillo, the owner of the dance hall we were playing picked us up when we got to town and told me, 'Merle, we've had this club for five years. We have a real fine reputation, and we never had a fight yet.' I said, 'Well, I hate to tell you this, but we'll fix that reputation right quick.' "

Dislocation and a sense of impermanence were Haggard's inheritance. His parents were Okies who moved to California to escape the dust bowl. Haggard's songs reflect the rootlessness of the trainman, the trucker, the fugitive. In the semi-autobiographical "Mama Tried," he says that his father gave him the dream of hopping a freight, of moving without destination. His mother desperately tried to keep young Merle straight and proper, but after his father's death, when Merle was nine, she lost control.

At fourteen, he was in a juvenile home, and by eighteen, he had escaped from four different reform schools, stolen cars, written bad checks, and finally tried armed robbery—unsuccessfully. At the age of twenty, he was in solitary confinement at San Quentin, with the celebrated condemned murderer Caryl Chessman in the next cell. When he sings, "Branded Man" or "Sing Me Back Home," evoking those days in prison when he prayed for death to end his pain, we hear the ache.

Music was the way out. While in prison, he schooled himself on Jimmie Rodgers, Bob Wills, Lefty Frizzell. Back in his home town of Bakersfield, California, he met a man named Jack McFadden, who had formed a booking agency for such local talent as Bonnie Owens (Buck's wife—later she would be Mrs. Haggard), Rose Maddox, Freddie Hart, Susan Raye.

His first hit, "All My Friends Are Gonna Be Strangers" (written by Liz Anderson, Lynn Anderson's mom), was on a local independent label in 1965. Picked up by Capitol, the label of fellow Bakersfield resident Buck Owens, he was a star right out of the starting gate, hitting the Top Ten with his second single, "Swinging Doors."

He had number one hits over the next few years with his own compositions: "The Fugitive," "Branded Man," "Sing Me Back Home," "The Legend of Bonnie and Clyde," "Mama Tried," "Hungry Eyes," "Working Man Blues." Then in 1969, the year of Woodstock, he made a quantum leap from country stardom to national notoriety with "Okie From Muskogee."

As Merle has told the story, "Me and the band were on a bus in Oklahoma when we passed a sign sayin' Muskogee one hundred miles, or something like that, and someone said, 'I bet they don't smoke marijuana in Muskogee.' I thought that was damn funny, and we started making up lines, and in about twenty minutes we had a song." Haggard rates the quality of the record as "very bad"—for musicianship and singing, "we weren't up to par." But its outspokenness struck a chord, and it was a monster hit.

To other country singers, Haggard is known as a lone wolf. He has an ongoing historical awareness that is matched by none of his contemporaries. He has recorded tributes to Jimmie Rodgers, the Carter Family, Bob Wills, and Elvis Presley. One of today's greatest bandleaders in any musical form, he has revived Western Swing, Cajun, and Dixieland jazz. The noted country music journalist Robert K. Oermann writes that Haggard "has continued to speak for America's working class. Despite Nashville's uptown tendencies, he has continued to write prolifically, whereas most performers who had been around as long have long since dried up as songwriters."

Haggard is very high on country music as an expression of America. "To me it's a way of life," he says, "and country music was my way of life before it became a profession. It's hard to explain, but it begins with the difference between the country music fan and a fan of some other kind of music. For lots of people music is something to create an atmosphere with or something to enjoy by yourself. Country music fans are different because they're not just satisfied to play their records, they've got to get everyone else in the neighborhood listening, too. I was like that myself as a kid. I liked the three guys who were big in 1950. Hank Williams, Bob Wills—who was going down in popularity at that time—and Lefty Frizzell. They were the top country artists in America, and whenever they came to my hometown of

Bakersfield, I'd get so excited I'd get a little crazy.

"I was in high school the first time Frizzell came to Bakersfield, and it was such an event for me that I got drunk the night before his appearance and stayed drunk all that night and the next day and wound up barely able to get to the dance."

The second time Frizzell came to Bakersfield, Haggard's friends talked him up, and Lefty invited him up to sing a song onstage—over the club owner's objections. As Haggard recalls, "Lefty refused to go on if I didn't sing, so he got his way, and I got to use his guitar and have his band play behind me. I sang Jimmie Rodger's 'Rough and Rowdy Ways.' It started my career, I guess."

It was an appropriate start for a rough and rowdy career. Haggard's mellowed considerably in recent years, but he still carries that attitude when he sings, and in recent compositions—for example, the prickly patriotism of "Me and Crippled Soldiers," and in remarks like this, from a recent interview: "Well, if it means anything, I was the guy that nice girls' parents wouldn't let their daughters go out with."

Tom T. Hall

b. 5/25/36, Olive Hill, KY

Style

Storyteller

Memorable songs

"The Year That Clayton Delaney Died," *"Old Dogs, Children, and Watermelon Wine"*

Awards

MCN—Most Promising Male Artist 1968

The army has provided a second chance to a lot of good old boys, and Tom T. Hall, one of country music's most literate and literary songwriters, was one of them. Although words were his early passion—he wrote his first song at the age of nine—the son of a Baptist minister/brickworker couldn't hack school the first time around, instead falling under the spell of such guitar pickers as local hero Clayton Delaney. He dropped out at age fifteen to work in a factory and perform some on a local radio station.

Korea intervened a couple of years later, and the radio band broke up, as guys kept getting drafted. Tom T. did his army service in Germany, where he went back to school and earned his high school diploma. Returning to the States, he entered Roanoke College in Salem, Virginia, where he studied writing and began writing songs in earnest, getting early cuts by Jimmy C. Newman, Bobby Bare, Burl Ives, and Dave Dudley. In 1964, he moved to Nashville.

Hall showed a flair for story songs early along, as shown by his first single, "I Washed My Face in the Morning Dew." But the stories about what he knew firsthand worked best. His first number one hit as a writer, "Harper Valley PTA," came from the confrontation between a woman in his hometown and the school board. And when he mined his own experience, it was even better: "A Week in a County Jail," his first number one, and "The Year That Clayton Delaney Died," a deeply moving tribute to a young boy's hero by a man now old enough to know that hero's limitations, but still in remembered awe of him.

Of course, one of the problems of fame is that you grow away from the life that provided all those experiences you've grown famous writing about. It happened to Hemingway, and it happened to Tom T. Hall. And when it happens, you may find yourself writing about loving little baby ducks and old pickup trucks.

Hall continues to record today, although his last hits were in the early eighties. But he's moved on to other interests—the life of a gentleman farmer and a figure in the Southern literary world.

Gus Hardin

b. 4/9/45, Tulsa, OK (Carol Ann Blankenship)

Awards
ACM—New Female Vocalist (1983)

A regional success in the Tulsa area, Gus Hardin scored in 1983 with her first record for RCA, "After the Last Good-bye." The label's brain trust were never able to duplicate her success until they teamed her with their megastar, Earl Thomas Conley, for what became the first in a series of successful boy/girl duets . . . for him.

Emmylou Harris

b. 4/2/47, Birmingham, AL

Style
Pure

Memorable songs
"Two More Bottles of Wine," "To Know Him Is to Love Him"

Awards
ACM—Album of the Year 1987 (Trio w/ Dolly Parton, Linda Ronstadt); CMA—Female Vocalist 1980, Vocal Event 1988 (Trio); Grammy—Country Vocal Performance Female 1976 (Elite Hotel), 1979 (Blue Kentucky Girl), 1984 ("In My Dreams"), Country Vocal Performance Duo or Group 1980 ("That Lovin' You Feelin' Again," w/ Roy Orbison), 1988 (Trio), (At the Ryman, w/ the Nash Ramblers); MCN—Vocal Collaboration 1988 (w/ Dolly Parton and Linda Ronstadt)

Like anyone else who thinks or feels, who loves country music or who loves what's best about American music or who simply loves style and grace and intelligence, we've naturally always been head over heels in love with Emmylou Harris.

We loved her as the young folkie who became the protégé of folk-rock pioneer Gram Parsons, and who took it upon herself to carry on Parsons's legacy. Parsons, as a member of the Byrds, brought country music to the sixties generation with *Sweetheart of the Rodeo;* then, when the Byrds went back to their rock-and-roll-star business, he founded the Flying Burrito Brothers and ultimately put out two country rock albums under his own name, *GP* and *Grievous Angel,* both of which featured Emmylou. Parsons loved country music with an aching passion, but it did not love him back, and it was up to Emmylou Harris to pick up his beacon and carry it, after he died in 1973.

We loved her as the new country star with Reprise Records in 1975 (not quite a country label—the *only* other artist signed to Reprise in 1975 was Frank Sinatra). Without compromising either musically or personally, she succeeded where Parsons had failed, hitting the Top Ten with "If I Could Only Win Your Love." Maybe the times were different, and artists like Parsons had paved the way; but they weren't that different. Somehow, people saw in

Emmylou something that they had (unfairly) missed in Parsons, and that they did not always require from singers who were packaged differently: humility, and a genuine respect for the integrity of the country tradition. A lot of country stations resisted Harris even so, but enough others gave her a chance, and the public responded.

At the same time, she was putting together her first Hot Band, one of the great touring bands in country music history. "I almost can't take credit for that," she says. "Gram put together the first band, and I just hired them. And then all I had to do was replace them one at a time."

She's too modest (we love her for that, too). The musicians—Bernie Leadon (from the Eagles), Hank DeVito (still an important Nashville musician/producer/songwriter), James Burton, Glen D. Hardin, and Emory Gordy (all of whom had played with Elvis; Gordy is now one of Nashville's leading producers, whose credits include Harris herself), and John Ware—had played in the studio with Parsons; it was Harris who made them a touring band, which is no small accomplishment. And the one-at-a-time replacements? Well, there was Rodney Crowell, for a start (Harris recalls that Rodney had also worked with Parsons); then Ricky Skaggs and Albert Lee. Vince Gill worked for her, though not as a Hot Band member; so did folk/bluegrass guitar great Tony Rice.

We loved her when she steered her vision of the greatness of country music into fields of bluegrass, with *Blue Kentucky Girl* and *Roses in the Snow,* into gospel with *Angel Band;* when she sought out material by great songwriters not represented enough in the country mainstream, such as John Hiatt, Butch Hancock, and Townes Van Zandt (hers is still our favorite version of "Pancho and Lefty"—sorry, Willie and Merle).

We heard the influence of her purity and integrity throughout *Trio,* her Dolly Parton/Linda Ronstadt collaboration. "It was definitely a product of the three of us," she says. "Actually, it sort of came more from Dolly's music, from her early music, her folk-mountain roots and that rolling style she writes in." But somehow—call us prejudiced, and we don't mean to take anything away from two other great singers—we heard Emmylou. Maybe it's because she's the only one of the three who has never had a lapse of taste, but for us she was the soul of the album, and its conscience.

Which was a word that came to mind when we spoke to her for this book. You've earned a reputation as the conscience of country music, we suggested.

"Oh, dear!" she exclaimed in a voice equal parts amused and aghast. "That doesn't sound like any fun at all."

And that did it. If there had been a shadow of doubt in our minds—which there wasn't—it would have been erased. We are, now and for all time, hopelessly in love with Emmylou Harris.

"The conscience. . . ? All I can say is, I've had a great time—being whatever it is that I am."

But she agreed to be conscience enough to talk about the state of country music in the nineties: "I think it's real healthy; there are obviously a lot of successful people out there who've listened to Merle Haggard and George Jones, and that's always good. I do think there is a lot more diversity of talent than is being played on the radio, and that makes me a little sad. I'd like to hear more of the older artists, Kitty Wells, Loretta Lynn, Buck

Owens. I'm still recovering from the demise of the O'Kanes. I think their albums stand out as some of the best work done in Nashville or anywhere else. Nanci Griffith, Steve Earle, Lyle Lovett, had to leave and be pop artists, and they're selling records. The Texas Tornadoes can't get arrested on the radio, and yet they're selling a lot more records than a lot of artists who are supposedly getting hits. My friends John Starling and Carl Jackson have put out an album that's nominated for a Grammy, and they couldn't even get a Nashville label. New artists like Jim Lauderdale . . . and there are probably dozens I haven't even heard yet because they can't get played, and I worry about who I'm not hearing. We could go on for hours; there's no answer for it. The conscience speaks."

In 1990, Emmylou dissolved the Hot Band and started a new group, the Nash Ramblers. That was a tough act to follow, but she did it—the Ramblers, led by New Grass Revival alumnus Sam Bush, are as dynamic an acoustic ensemble as the Hot Band was in its electric style. Her first album with the new group, *Live at the Ryman* (also a Nashville Network special), stretched the range of bluegrass-oriented acoustic music in new and astounding
directions, from Steve Earle's "Guitar Town" to Eddy Arnold's "Cattle Call."

Emmylou herself is one of those who don't get much radio play these days—"If you're doing something you're really excited about, you'd like it to get played on radio. But there's nothing I can do about it; I can't force radio to play me. And ultimately, you know, I am a live performer. So I go out and play for people, and it seems I've still got an audience. I only tour in the summer now because I have a child in school, but I'll always be out there performing, so I sort of create my own radio. Radio with people."

Emmylou Harris's list of the greatest songs of all time: "Hickory Wind," "Blue Eyes Cryin' in the Rain," "Like a Rolling Stone," "Kern River"—"I don't know if it's a great song or if Merle Haggard's performance of it is just so devastating, but I just fall apart every time I hear it."

John Hartford

b. 12/30/47, New York, NY

Style
Folkie

Memorable songs
"Gentle on My Mind"

Awards
ACM—Specialty Instrumentalist 1969 (banjo); Grammy—Folk Performance, Country Song 1967; ("Gentle on My Mind"), Ethnic or Traditional Recording 1976 (Mark Twang)

John Hartford hasn't had much of a career as a country music performer. He could probably have had one if he'd wanted to, but what he wanted was something else: namely, to be a riverboat captain, a trade there's not much call for these days. But with the money he made from "Gentle on My Mind" (the only song ever to be honored two years in a row as BMI's Most Performed Country Song of the Year) he was able to bring it off. Or maybe he couldn't have been that much of a success in country music. He has too much of a sense of humor.

Highway 101

CACTUS MOSER
b. 5/3/57, Montrose, CO

CURTIS STONE
b. 4/3/50, North Hollywood, CA

JACK DANIELS
b. 10/27/49, Choctaw, OK

NIKKI NELSON
b. 1/3/69, Topaz Lake, NV

Paulette Carlson left the group in 1990.

Style

First band fronted by female singer in country music

Memorable songs

*"Whiskey, If You Were a Woman,"
"Walkin', Talkin', Cryin', Barely Beatin'
Broken Heart"*

Awards

*ACM—Vocal Group 1987–88, Bass Player
1976, 1980–81, 1988 (Curtis Stone);
CMA—Vocal Group 1988–89*

Highway 101 presented themselves, when they made their debut in 1987, as a band in the tradition of Alabama (or more accurately, in the tradition of Restless Heart—they were a created band), with one major twist. They were the first country band with a woman singer.

They didn't exactly seem to be a band like Alabama, though. Right from the get-go, they struck us as a remarkable singer, Paulette Carlson, who for some reason had chosen to present herself with the semi-anonymity of a group name.

This, however, turned out not to be exactly the case. Not exactly, at all.

In the first place, the Minnesota-born Carlson was not a blinding new light on the Nashville scene, but a Music Row veteran who had been kicking around for the better part of a decade, unable to get her career off the ground. She'd even had a contract with RCA in 1983–84, but her recordings went nowhere.

In 1986, she engaged Chuck Morris, who also managed the Nitty Gritty Dirt Band, to guide her career. It was Morris who suggested that she become part of a band, and he helped put it together. They ultimately settled on LA studio drummer Cactus Moser, bassist Curtis Stone (son of West Coast country bandleader Cliffie Stone), and guitarist Jack Daniels.

Most created groups—especially groups made up of studio pros—are created because some producer has a sound in mind, but Highway 101 was a little different. Once the musicians were chosen and assembled, producer Paul Worley said, in effect, "Okay, guys, come up with a sound," and after a few false starts, they did: a high-energy, foot-stomping honky-tonk style. Their first release, "The Bed You Made for Me," cracked the Top Ten, and over the next three years, they produced three highly successful albums, and three number one singles: "Somewhere Tonight," "Cry Cry Cry," and "(Do You Love Me) Just Say Yes."

Then came the second place—the other exception to the theory that Highway 101 wasn't really a group, just Paulette Carlson and three guys named Joe. Paulette got married, had a baby, and left the group. (She released her first solo album in late 1991.) Highway 101 hired a new female singer, Nikki Nelson, and put another record on the charts. It wasn't as good as the first three. Nelson's conventional torch style was no substitute for Carlson's one-of-a-kind honky-tonk belting. But it did have that . . . group sound.

Tish Hinojosa

b. 12/6/55, San Antonio, TX

Style

Multicultural

Memorable song

"Something in the Rain"

Tish Hinojosa is the thirteenth child of a Mexican immigrant family, and her earliest recordings were for the Spanish language market—she had a couple of regional Latino hits as a teenager.

Like the Cajun/LA/Nashville recording artist Jo-El Sonnier, she had her own deeply felt cultural roots, but she grew up in a time when the mainstream musical culture was strong and alluring, and Tish began a pilgrimage through it, each stop adding a new layer to her musical coloring.

She started by playing the folkie coffeehouses in her native Texas, then moved to New Mexico, where she fell under the spell of progressive country artist Michael Martin Murphey. In the early eighties, she did a stint in Nashville, even releasing a semisuccessful single, "I'll Pull You Through."

Nashville wasn't quite what she wanted, though. "Incorporating elements of my ethnic heritage into my music was a problem, at least at that time. No one could see it as a natural part of my music." In 1985, she went back to New Mexico, and three years later completed a full circle back to Texas—this time to Austin, where she has remained.

Her first major label album, *Homeland,* came out in 1989 from A&M Records, and evoked critical comparisons to Joan Baez, Emmylou Harris, and Nanci Griffith. Her 1992 release, *Culture Swing,* on Rounder, according to Tish, "sums up the arc of the pendulum of my music. Though I deal with some Hispanic themes, I also include elements of folk, pop, Western swing, and everything in between."

Julio Iglesias

Style

Latin lover

Memorable songs

"To All the Girls I've Loved Before"

Awards

ACM—Single of the year 1984 ("To All the Girls I've Loved Before" w/ Willie Nelson); CMA—Vocal Duo 1984 (w/ Willie Nelson)

Willie Nelson claims—and why not believe him?—that he heard Julio Iglesias on the radio during a trip to London, liked his voice, and thought it would be nice to record with him. He didn't know, at the time, that Julio was the hottest-selling artist in the world.

It was one of the weirder ideas in country music, and it turned out to be one of the most successful—in 1984, it was number one on the country charts, number five on the pop charts. A 1988 duet with Willie, "Spanish Eyes," made the Top Ten, but Julio has not gone on to have a major country career.

J

Alan Jackson

b. 10/17/58, Newnan, GA

Style
Cowboy hat

Memorable songs
"Here in the Real World," "Chasin' That Neon Rainbow"

Awards
ACM—New Male Vocalist 1990; TNN/MCN—Star of Tomorrow 1991, Album of the Year 1991 (Here in the Real World)

You don't even need to see Alan Jackson to get a sense of his appeal. Just read along his fact sheet: Hair . . . blond; eyes . . . blue; height 6'4"; weight 180. What could be wrong?

And nothing is. Jackson is a genuine heartthrob. The blue eyes twinkle from underneath a white cowboy hat, the blond hair is enhanced by a mustache that manages to look endearingly bushy without being scruffy, and all with the sort of easy charm that probably can only come from being the baby brother to four older sisters. As Jackson told *Country America* writer Neil Pond, "Maybe I'm a little more sensitive to certain things than some men are. It could have something to do with growing up around girls . . . and being the baby, I probably got spoiled a little bit. All the girls looked after me."

Jackson's a one-woman man, though, married at twenty-one to Denise, his high school sweetheart, and recently a father.

Unlike so many future country stars who grow up with only music in their hearts from an early age, Jackson just sort of drifted into it through a friend, and it was more than a casual surprise when he informed Denise that he wanted to move to Nashville and try to make it in the music business.

"I never went to a concert till I was twenty and they opened up a country music park near my hometown," he told us. "You can listen to radio, or records, but it's nothing like seeing those people. That would get me so fired up . . . I'd say, 'Man, I'd love to be doing that.' Then I'd get back into the routine of making ends meet, and I'd say, 'No, that's way out of my reach.'

"But I had this real good friend in high school who used to say, 'I'm going to start flying these little private planes and get my license and try to be an airline pilot.' Now, where I was from a major airline pilot was a big deal—they made a hundred thousand dollars a year and had big houses and farms. So I just thought he was crazy, but four or five years later, he'd got his license and was copilot on a 737, so I decided to do what I really wanted to do, which was singing."

His first job in Nashville was in the mail room at the Nashville Network, and his first break came when Denise, a stewardess, ran into Glen Campbell in an airport and told him about her husband and his ambitions. Campbell told her to have Alan get in touch with his publishing company in Nashville, and that was the first door to open for him. He was signed as a writer and began the slow, four-year climb that finally led to recording offers from several of the major Nashville-based labels.

Jackson came along at an interesting time in the history of cowboy-hat acts, a movement that, hard as it is to believe now, took a while to gather momentum.

George Strait first saw the light of the Top Ten in 1981, but no one much saw the Future of Country Music in him. Cowboys in country were the slicked-up kind portrayed by Conway Twitty in "Tight-Fittin' Jeans," and nobody was thinking a whole lot about the traditional sound of country music.

Randy Travis broke the Top Ten in 1986. In 1985, there were fifty-one different number one records by thirty-seven different acts. Of those, only four had not been Top Ten acts in 1981. Those four were:

Exile (first hit 1983), not exactly a new act, although they were new to country.

The Judds (1984), the greatest girl group in country music, and the exception to the general pattern of stagnation.

Sawyer Brown (1985), *Star Search* novelties, not exactly from the heart of country, signed as Exile clones.

The Forester Sisters (1985), signed as Judds clones.

This is not a profile of a healthy industry. In five years, that's one vital new sound. And it was in 1985 that the *New York Times* ran an article that said country music was over.

In 1986, the *Times* did an about-face and welcomed country music back. Of course, New York is not where you'd check first to find out about the health of country music, and maybe it took the *Times* a couple of years to find out about the Judds, and a couple more to notice Ricky Skaggs and George Strait. But the big difference in 1986 was Randy Travis.

And if that didn't escape the *Times* in New York, it certainly didn't escape a generation of aspiring traditional singers. If Randy Travis could do it, maybe there'd be more.

But Nashville hadn't shaken off its sluggishness yet, and there was no hurry to sign handsome guys in cowboy hats. Ricky Van Shelton came along in 1987, and people started talking about "hat acts." The Oak Ridge Boys, representing the kind of act that had dominated country music over the previous decade, parodied them in their stage show—with a hat given to Joe Bonsall by Shelton. But Alan Jackson was still in the mail room at TNN.

Then in 1989, Clint Black hit the charts like a rocket. Five number ones off his first album, and nobody in any pop music genre had ever done that. Later in 1989, Garth Brooks came along.

By this time, it was clear that a new trend was happening. But for us, it was Alan Jackson's emergence that made us realize just how much of a trend it was. There were a whole bunch of talented, good-looking singers who owed a debt to Travis and Strait, and perhaps an even bigger debt to Haggard and Jones. And there was an audience for them—a younger audience than country music had attracted in some time.

That audience sent "Here in the Real World" to number one on the charts and followed it with "Wanted," "Blueblooded Woman'" and "Chasin' That Neon Rainbow." Jackson's second album, *Don't Rock the Jukebox,* increased his popularity even further, with the flat-out traditional message of its title song: "I wanna hear George Jones . . . my heart ain't ready for the Rolling Stones."

Jackson went out on tour in 1991 with Randy Travis, and as a result of the association, songs began appearing cowritten by the two heartthrobs—a new direction for Travis, who up until then had not been known as a songwriter.

We wondered about the difference between being a young Alan Jackson in 1991 and being a young George Jones in 1958.

"I suppose the main difference is that country music's on a much larger scale," Jackson theorized. "I think back then if you were a big star, you were still playing the honky-tonks and small state fairs.

"I don't think anybody's career is going to last as long as they used to. It's the same way in rock and roll—I don't know if there'll ever be another Elvis Presley. Everybody's so much more worldly now, there's so many more people coming to Nashville or LA or New York . . . it's a lot easier for people to get started, and so the competition's a lot tougher. Years ago, there were just a few people who stumbled into it or whatever.

"But I think most people like to cut back a little when they get older. I think a lot of people keep working because they have to, not because they're enjoying it as much. If George Jones had been a little more careful in a business sense, if he had all the money he'd made in music, instead of losing it in bad business deals, he might have quit twenty years ago."

As we move through the nineties, the cowboy-hat acts are the new orthodoxy in Nashville, and it can be said that they're crowding out other deserving, perhaps more innovative acts. Well, it's true that the cowboy-hat bandwagon has cut out a lot of the diversity and excitement that accompanied the first country new wave of the mideighties. And there were so many new acts signed to the major labels between 1989 and 1992 that people started grumbling about "flavor of the month," and the grumbling was often justified. But did anyone really want to go back to 1985?

Alan Jackson's list of the greatest songs of all time: " 'He Stopped Loving Her Today' is the classic country song of all time"; "Rose Colored Glasses" by John Conlee, "Are the Good Times Really Over for Good," "The Grand Tour," and "Farewell Party," by Gene Watson.

Waylon Jennings

b. 6/15/37, Littlefield, TX

Style
Lonesome, orn'ry, and mean

Memorable songs
"Honky Tonk Heroes," "Luckenbach, Texas," "My Heroes Have Always Been Cowboys"

Awards
ACM—Song/Single of the year 1985 ("Highwayman" w/ Willie Nelson, Kris Kristofferson); CMA—Male Vocalist 1975, Vocal Duo 1975 (w/ Willie Nelson), Single of the Year 1976 ("Good Hearted Woman" w/ Willie Nelson), Album of the Year 1976 (Wanted—The Outlaws w/ Willie Nelson, Tompall Glaser, Jessi Colter); Grammy —Country Vocal Performance–Duo or Group 1969 ("McArthur Park" w/ the Kimberleys), 1978 ("Mamas, Don't Let

*Your Babies Grow Up to be Cowboys" w/
Willie Nelson)*

Waylon's clean and sober now, and he's
pretty much off the road, with a theater in
Branson, Missouri—a place where it still is
hard to picture the old outlaw, but even
outlaws have to settle down sometime . . .
if the road doesn't kill them. It killed Jesse
James, but Frank James settled down, read
Shakespeare, supported socialism and the
cause of the working man, and finally died
in his sleep in 1915.

There was a time when Waylon virtually defined the road. Richie Albright,
Waylon's producer on many of his most
memorable recordings, and the drummer
in his band for years, remembers those
days: "I got away from the whole country
scene for a while in the sixties, and when I
came back, Waylon asked me to go back
to work with him. I said okay, and we got
into talking—I'd been playing with some
rock and roll groups, and we'd had roadies, and I started introducing these things
to Waylon—you know, there was no such
thing as a roadie until I came back into
country music in the seventies, and I just
told Waylon, there's a different way of doing it, and it's called rock and roll, man. If
you're going to do it, this is the way you
gotta do it.

"So we started doing that—you know,
a real organized, professional tour. And
then Waylon wanted to do his own producing, he wanted some creative control.
Actually, that's where the term *outlaw*
came from. We were bucking everything
in the system and going for it on our own
terms."

What kind of resistance did you get?
we wondered.

"Mainly resistance to what Waylon
wanted to cut, and how he wanted to cut

it. I remember Waylon saying to Chet Atkins, let's turn the kick drum up on this
thing, and Chet saying to Waylon, no, it'll
make the record skip."

Make the record skip? Frankly, this
blew our minds. Were they recording on
acetate? we asked Albright.

"No," he said. "That's just the way
they were thinking. Either nobody was
smart enough to EQ it right, or they just
didn't have the equipment—anyway, they
thought, if you turn up that bass drum,
that record's going to skip. Plus, they were
passing Waylon around to people like
Danny Davis to produce him, people who
didn't understand him at all. Chet had kind
of come to a bypass with him, or an im-
passe, where he just said, 'I don't know
what to do with him.' And you could kind
of understand it some ways, because Waylon was taking a lot of pills at the time, so
sometimes he'd be showing up for sessions
pretty wasted, and Chet kinda threw his
hands up. The upshot was that Waylon
got tired of being passed around, and he
got into this rebellion thing. So finally on
Honky Tonk Heroes, that's when they said,
take it, and we went in and did it—that
was us."

Honky Tonk Heroes, released in 1972,
was entirely made up of the compositions
of Billy Joe Shaver, an Austin-based songwriter whose tough, uncompromising
lyrics and hard-edged honky-tonk melodies perfectly fit the new image that Waylon was molding for himself, and it has
become a classic, with the title song, "Old
Five and Dimers," "Lonesome, Orn'ry
and Mean," "Black Rose," and others.

It was a new thing in country music:
an album that *mattered,* mattered beyond
country music, into the mainstream of
American music and the mainstream of
American consciousness.

Meanwhile, there was more to rebel against. "Waylon got screwed as bad as anyone ever did," Willie Nelson wrote in his autobiography, *Willie,* "because Waylon is a good old honest country boy who wants to trust people. Once Waylon put out a new album, went out on the road for about 180 days, came back to Nashville, and opened his new statement—and discovered he owed the company something like $31,000.

"He went in to get some money to pay his band, and they wound up signing him to a new, five-year contract at the oldest, lowest rate. The way they got him signed was by sending the contract-option pickup to Waylon Jennings at their own record company address. Then they signed the receipt for the option pickup themselves, and it was the same as if Waylon had signed it. After a short waiting period—which Waylon didn't know about—the contract automatically went into effect."

Richie Albright agrees, and he remembers how that all changed. "Waylon was down and out, man. He'd caught hepatitis, and the only thing that was supporting us during that time was the Indian reservations out in northern Arizona and New Mexico. We could go out there and work all we wanted to—we had fans out there, and we could work. He got hepatitis and he was down, and he went to RCA for some money, and they said they'd give him five thousand dollars if he re-signed. He was about to do it, and I said, hold it, why don't you talk to somebody. So I called Neil Reshen in New York—Neil was the lawyer for a lot of musicians, including Miles Davis at the time. He came down, and Waylon told him what he was about to do, and Neil said, 'They're fuckin' you, man, they're rakin' you. Here's what can be done.' So they talked, and then

Willie called and said, I'd like to meet him, too, so I called Neil, and Willie met him at the airport as he was leaving, and they talked there."

Reshen audited the record company's books, negotiated Waylon's contracts, put him on a solid business footing. And this is interesting stuff because, as strange as it seems, it's part of what made those guys outlaws—that they stood up for their legal rights against the cattle barons, the plantation owners who ran the country music business and had things their own way.

"Nowadays it's all different," Albright says, a little ruefully. "Guys come into town with a business plan. I met a songwriter the other day, and he said, pleased to meet you, Richie, and this is my manager, and this is my lawyer, and I said, great, who cuts your songs? and he said, well, I haven't had one cut yet."

None of the songs from *Honky Tonk Heroes* were chart hits, but it was a landmark album, and it marked the beginning of an extraordinary period of creative achievement for Jennings—an output of recordings that, like *Honky Tonk Heroes,* mattered; a body of work that defined an attitude that made a whole new audience care about country. Merle Haggard was doing it, too, but Haggard's aggressive jingoism was hard for some (not all) of the new young audience to swallow.

Waylon didn't write all his songs, and the ones he did write weren't always necessarily his best ones, but he made them his own—part of this new black-clad, bearded, outlaw persona, this rock and roll attitude applied to stone country music: "Rainy Day Woman" . . . "Are You Sure Hank Done It This Way" . . . "Luckenbach, Texas" . . . "My Heroes Have Always Been Cowboys" . . . "Good Hearted Woman" . . . "Mamas, Don't Let Your

Babies Grow Up to Be Cowboys." . . .

In 1975, the outlaw movement got more or less officialized with the release of *Wanted: The Outlaws,* a sampler album featuring Waylon, Willie, Tompall Glaser, and Waylon's wife, Jessi Colter. A true outlaw, Waylon rebelled against the outlaw movement itself with his 1978 release "Don't You Think This Outlaw Bit's Done Got out of Hand."

At the same time, Waylon was leading too much of a rock and roll lifestyle, fueled by too many drugs, and in 1988, as he moved into his fifties, he underwent triple-bypass heart surgery.

Fifty-something years old, beyond the wild touring and drug-abuse years, off the road. And Branson, Missouri, is not all that far from Clay County, where Frank James spent his last years, reading Shakespeare and championing the cause of the working man.

Michael Johnson

b. /45, Alamosa, AL

Style

Smooth

Memorable songs

"Give Me Wings"

Michael Johnson seems to drift in and out of country music. You never get the feeling he's totally committed to it as a career, much less a way of life, but enough people like his distinctive, folk-flavored voice that you can never count him out of the picture.

Johnson studied classical guitar in Spain during the sixties, and he returned to the U.S. to join the folkie/topical group the Chad Mitchell trio, which at that time was led by John Denver. He found his way to Nashville in 1985, where RCA signed him and paired him on duet with fast-fading Urban Cowboy–era songbird Sylvia. "I Love You by Heart" was her last Top Ten hit, his first.

After that, Johnson had a three-year string of solid hits, including two number ones: "Give Me Wings" in 1986 and "The Moon Is Over Her Shoulder" in 1987.

What stands in the way of Johnson's continued success in the country music business? "He doesn't want it enough," says one industry insider. "He'd rather go off to folkie clubs and play classical guitar. But don't count Michael Johnson out. He's not over yet."

David Lynn Jones

b. 1/15/50, Bexar, AR

Style

Intense, personal

Memorable songs

"Bonnie Jean (Little Sister)," "Living in the Promised Land"

David Lynn Jones lives in a place called Bexar, Arkansas, which isn't on most maps. It's a couple of hours from Branson, Missouri, where he doesn't usually play, and it's closer to Springfield, Missouri, than it is to Little Rock. Where is Bexar, exactly? It's about forty miles from Poplar Bluff, just like in the Porter Wagoner song. Porter is from the same part of the country; but we can't imagine David Lynn ever wearing a spangled nudie costume. Different era, different styles, different dreams. David Lynn gives off a strong aura of power, and a lot of that comes from his being rooted in a strong sense of place. The Joneses have lived on the same three or four hundred acres for three hundred years. David Lynn's father was the postmaster of Bexar.

David Lynn loves living there. His band members live within a few miles (except for one rebel who comes in from Texas to record). He has a wife and kids, and he rarely comes to Nashville.

When he does come to Nashville, he stays with his friend, drummer, and producer (for years with Waylon), Richie Albright. Lately, Richie has been producing David Lynn as well. Another outlaw?

David Lynn would say no. He's no outlaw; he's a solid citizen, solid as the granite mined near his hometown. But he knows something about the outlaw spirit, and he expressed it in his searing, heartfelt song about his sister, Bonnie Jean, who has to flash that outlaw spirit to make it in the man's world of long-distance trucking ("She knows how that lonesome highway feels / She's got a heart of gold and nerves of steel / Little sister rolls them eighteen wheels").

He's the father of three daughters: twenty-two, seven, and four. He's away from home more than he'd like to be, "and I miss my family. But I haven't had a sign from God that it's cruel to the kids."

His strongest musical influence comes from gospel; his mother was a Nazarene preacher, and he says, "There's always a moral in my songs," which have been recorded by Willie Nelson ("Living in the Promise Land"), Joe Cocker, Merle Haggard, and Lynn Anderson, among others.

When David Lynn decided to be a musician, he gathered his friends, they grabbed their instruments, and they got in a van and "drove till we came to a place where it looked like they needed musicians and asked if we could play. Sometimes we even got paid. We learned a lot out there with no mailing address. It makes you think about reality and home. We worked our asses off. I've always worked my ass off. As I said in a song, 'there's no easy way out.' When I think about how hard it is to do what I do . . . I'm a serious musician. I don't know any other way. I don't think about categories like country. I've played everything—blues, rock. I still think the Beatles are the best. Or are they? I don't think about it much anymore. I just want to produce music that means something."

Jones's first album for Mercury, *Hard Times on Easy Street*, was one of the most powerful albums we've ever heard, so personal and honest—even confessional—that listening to it took a lot out of a listener. His second album didn't quite have the same power, as he is the first to admit; it wasn't the record he wanted to make, and he left Mercury and moved over to Liberty where Jimmy Bowen has the reputation of letting artists be themselves.

George Jones

b. 9/12/31, Saratoga, TX

Style

Quintessential honky-tonk

Memorable songs

This is a little unfair, even though we made the rules ourselves: how can we limit ourselves to two, or three, or a handful of memorable songs for George Jones? But we'll take "He Stopped Loving Her Today," the song most often named by other artists in this book as among the greatest of all time, and our favorite of the Tammy duets, "Golden Ring."

Awards

CMA—Male Vocalist 1980–81, Music Video 1986 ("Who's Gonna Fill Their Shoes"); MCN—Male Artist 1981, Living Legend 1987. For "He Stopped Loving Her Today": Single of the year ACM, CMA 1980, MCN 1981: Grammy—Country Vocal Performance Male 1980

Even after several years of clean and sober living now, there are still more extravagant stories told about George Jones than any other country singer: the badass, the legendary drunk, the sum of his demons—outrageous, irresponsible, and charming. His wives (up until current wife Nancy, whom he married in 1983) have left him because of a combination of all of the above, including Tammy Wynette, who worshiped him. Tammy stayed with him for seven years, and together they recorded some of the best duets in country music history.

During those wild years (which comprised most of his career), promoters cringed in terror when they booked George Jones because often, he simply didn't show up. "They call me No-Show Jones," he sang in a duet with Merle Haggard, but his fans kept forgiving him and buying tickets to hear him.

"I sing white man's blues," Jones describes his music.

"Jones sings in an unearthly voice of after-hours bards, wee-hours drug abuse, and back-alley rendezvous," the *Nashville Tennessean*'s Robert K. Oermann once wrote. "He lives like Hank Williams did, in a world of titanic overindulgence and schizophrenic mood sweeps. He has squandered his ability and his money. And he *is a genius.*"

Just ask anybody who the best honky-tonk singer in the world is. Frank Sinatra, who has called Jones "the second-best male singer in America." Waylon Jennings, who ad-libbed at the fade-out of a duet, "I can't believe I'm singin' with George Jones." Mark Chesnutt, who, while his "Too Cold at Home" rode the top of the charts, could only talk abut the fact that George Jones liked it.

Jones was born in Depression-ravaged East Texas, where rural values were beginning their decline. Texas was becoming an oil and manufacturing state; city populations were zooming, farms were being abandoned. There are more horses in Ohio today than in Texas.

George's father was a factory worker and occasional truck driver. His mother went to church—relentlessly. Both parents were musical and viewed their talented son as a prospective preacher or gospel singer. They bought him his first guitar when he was nine; within months, he was performing.

They were less encouraging about his other passion, baseball (he once tried out for the Brooklyn Dodgers farm system and almost made it). "If I'd concentrated, I could have been a major leaguer," Jones had said. He joined the marines in order to play on a service baseball team, but the Korean War broke out, and he found himself carrying a rifle instead.

He returned to Texas and got a job as a housepainter, with no thought of a music career—"It was just something I did at night." Beaumont, where he lived, had a honky-tonk on every corner, and George hit them all, wearing his marine crew cut, a baggy tweed suit, and a gaudy tie. "I didn't look much like country music," he says now, "and it was hard times for country. Rock and roll was all around, and that's what my friends played.'' Jones sang "in every bar that had a Wurlitzer playing country.''

Jones lists Floyd Tillman, Ernest Tubb, Roy Acuff, and Bill Monroe as his early influences, and country music historian Bill Malone points out that if one listens closely, "the Acuff influence can be detected, especially in the phrasing of the high notes.''

A local recording entrepreneur, Pappy Dailey, heard Jones and convinced him to make a record on his Starday label. "Why Baby Why,'' in 1955, was his first chart hit; "White Lightning'' (written by J. P. "Big Bopper'' Richardson) was his first number one, in 1959. Actually, for a star as hugely popular over such a long period of years as Jones, he's had relatively few number one records.

Success was hard for Jones, a compulsive loner. He won few awards, never joined the Grand Ole Opry (he was the first *Billboard* Best Country Artist not to have been an Opry member). During a live performance of Jimmy Dean's TV show, a looped Jones had to be helped off the stage. "Destructive living is my middle name,'' he told reporter H. J. Ashborne.

In 1967, Jones met Tammy Wynette when the two played a package tour. Tammy was coming off a bad marriage, and George's wife had just gone back to Texas with the kids. They found each other, and their marriage was the stuff of gossip columns. Producer Billy Sherrill realized it was more than that—it was a natural duet pairing, and he was right. Their duet albums set a standard for the genre and remain consistent sellers to this day.

Their relationship wasn't as fortunate. George's drinking got completely out of hand. They lived in the country, far from the nearest bar, but Tammy couldn't control him. One night she confiscated the keys to his cars, but he took the power lawn mower and rode it fifteen miles to the nearest bar. Finally Tammy, who genuinely believed in Standing by Her Man, chose D-I-V-O-R-C-E.

The new, mellow George remains a top star. He owns a series of country clubs, called Possum Hollow, after his nickname. He travels internationally and has lived down the No-Show Jones image. His singing is always on the money; he sticks to honky-tonk—a tough, basic, roadhouse style with no orchestral embellishments and little compromise on the lyrics.

No one knows exactly how many albums Jones has made, or all the small labels he's recorded for. Estimates put the number of albums in the hundreds. Tammy Wynette says, "Most of us will lose our popularity. George may have problems, but he'll be played when all of us are forgotten. He is a genius, after all.''

The Judds

NAOMI JUDD
b. 1/11/46, Ashland, KY (*Diana Ellen Judd*)

WYNONNA JUDD
b. 5/30/64, Ashland, KY (*Christina Ciminella*)

Style
Family harmony

Memorable songs
"Mama, He's Crazy," "Grandpa (Tell Me 'Bout the Good Old Days)"

Awards
ACM—Vocal Duet 1984–90, Song of the Year 1984 ("Why Not Me");

CMA—Horizon Award 1984, Single of the Year 1985 ("Why Not Me"), Vocal Group 1985–87, Vocal Duo 1988–91; Grammy—Country Vocal Performance–Duo or Group 1984 ("Mama, He's Crazy"), 1985 ("Why Not Me"), 1986 ("Grandpa, Tell Me 'Bout the Good Old Days"), 1988 ("Give a Little Love"); MCN—Star of Tomorrow 1985, Vocal Duo 1985–89; TNN/MCN—Vocal Duo 1990–91

You can argue about who the greatest male harmony group of all time is. Maybe you like the Everly Brothers, or perhaps you'd rather go back further, to the Delmore Brothers or to Bill and Charlie Monroe. Whomever you choose, you're setting up a standard from the past by which all contemporary groups have to be judged.

But there's no question about the standard by which all female groups must be judged. The Judds attained that position hands down and had the field to themselves throughout the eighties, in image as well as musicianship. Their farewell concert, in December 1991, drew the biggest ratings in the history of pay-per-view TV concerts.

Their stage image was unique—a strange and unforgettable generation reversal that featured mother Naomi as a girlish, flirtatious prom queen, and daughter Wynonna, dressed like Johnny Cash in severe, dramatic black, holding center stage in a solid, responsible, almost maternal way.

"Y'all are the most immature audience I've ever seen," Wynonna would lecture a crowd after Naomi had whipped them into a frenzy of whooping and hollering with her antics. She'd pause a long moment for effect, then add, "My mama appreciates it."

Naomi Judd raised her two daughters between Kentucky and California. A tireless, ambitious, hardworking woman (she spent a number of years as an emergency room nurse, and that's not a job where you can get away with flirting like a prom queen), she had a lifelong dream about the bright lights and glamour of show business. When she discovered that her oldest daughter had a one-in-a-million voice, she moved the family to Nashville in 1979.

Naomi worked as a night-shift nurse at Williamson County Hospital and began working seriously with her fifteen-year-old daughter, making demo tapes, haunting Music Row, doing whatever she could to get their music listened to by the Nashville hitmakers.

Those were years of frayed nerves and tense confrontations. Wynonna and Naomi, thrown together far more intensely than is normal for a mother and daughter, were as temperamentally opposed to each other as a mother and daughter could be. For all of Naomi's drive and womanly wiles, she was nowhere near the singer that her daughter was. To the extent that anyone took the Judds seriously at all in those days, what they saw was a possible solo career for the still-developing teenager. Perhaps Naomi's biggest fight of all, in those days, was to keep herself in the act.

Finally, in 1983, when Wynonna was fresh out of high school, they got a live audition with RCA, and a contract.

Their first single, "Had a Dream," which had been a minor pop-chart hit for Elvis in 1976 (under the title "For the Heart"), was a minor country-chart hit for them.

The second was "Mama, He's Crazy," taken from a line of dialogue in a soap opera, and it broke through for them. Released in April 1984, by August it had climbed the charts to number one.

The Judds came along at a time when nothing much was going on in country music. The Urban Cowboy craze had crashed and burned, people had put away their sequined jeans and cowboy boots, and dumpsters behind bars and nightclubs all over the country were filled with mechanical bulls. No one was signing up new country acts. No one cared.

But the Judds made people start caring again. In 1985, they were nominated for a Grammy as Best New Artist—and that's not Best New Country Artist. Their albums consistently made the Billboard pop charts—and that was before the new methods of tabulating that brought country acts to chart prominence. In those days, only three country acts ever made a dent in the pop charts: Hank Williams, Jr., Randy Travis, and the Judds.

Naomi was right about the unique attraction of the mother-daughter duo. Wynonna was unquestionably the musical talent, and a major talent at that. But by herself, she would have been Tanya Tucker, she would have been Patty Loveless, she would have been Lacy J. Dalton. Now, Lord knows, that's not bad. But it's not the Judds.

The intensity and the difficulty of their relationship has always been a major part of the drama of their stage act. Every time you went to see the Judds, you always wondered if this would be the night when Wynonna, finally sick of Naomi's prancing and preening, knocked her off the stage with her guitar. And that, along with the great music, was part of why audiences turned out in droves to see them.

Their intense love/hate relationship, a larger-than-life passion play of every mother and daughter's melodrama, reached its culmination when the announcement, in 1990, that Naomi Judd was retiring from the act because of illness.

Naomi had contracted chronic active hepatitis, which is a terribly serious condition, possibly even life-threatening. The Judds embarked on a year-long farewell tour of music and sentiment, culminating in the December pay-per-view concert, which became the most-watched concert in the history of pay-per-view.

In 1992, Wynonna Judd began a new solo career, with a new record label, MCA, and one of the toughest jobs imaginable in show business—to compete with the legend of the Judds. On the basis of her first release, she's well on her way to creating her own solo legend.

Ray Kennedy

b. 5/13, Buffalo, NY

Style

Hasn't defined one yet

Although born in New York State, Ray Kennedy refined his songwriting talents in a cabin in the woods of Oregon, which he had drifted to in the midseventies, a college dropout with an idea that he wanted to make music. After a year with four walls and his guitar, he ventured out into the Pacific Northwest club circuit, mixing his own songs with popular oldies.

He took his act on the road to Nashville in 1980, where he sold songs to John Anderson, David Allan Coe, and Charley Pride, ran his own recording studio, did a little producing—your typical day's work in Nashville. In 1990 he finally got his shot with Atlantic Records and put out a creditable debut album and a good-naturedly raunchy hit song, "What a Way to Go."

Kentucky Headhunters

RICHARD YOUNG
b. 1/27/55, Glasgow, KY

FRED YOUNG
b. 7/8/58, Glasgow, KY

DOUG PHELPS
b. 12/15/60, Leachville, AR (*Calvin Douglas Phelps*)

RICKY LEE PHELPS
b. 10/8/53, Paragould, AR

GREG MARTIN
b. 3/31/53, Louisville, KY

Style

Wild

Memorable songs

"Dumas Walker," "Davy Crockett"

Awards

ACM—New Vocal Duet/Group 1989; CMA—Album of the Year 1990 (Pickin' on Nashville), *Vocal Group 1990–91; Grammy—Country Vocal Performance–Duo or Group ("Pickin' on Nashville") 1990 The Phelps brothers left the band in 1993.*

The Headhunters are wild, all right, but it's hard to figure out just why they're considered *that* wild. They play an exuberant, down-home brand of traditional, straight-ahead country and traditional, straight-ahead rock and roll. Fred Young bashes on the drums kinda hard, and Greg Martin pulls out some guitar licks that owe more to Jimmy Page than Lester Flatt, but that's all part of today's country music.

Maybe it's because they look so wild. But outside of drummer Fred Young's bald head and giant muttonchops, they don't look that different from a lot of other guys you might run into down on the farm, on the assembly line, or shooting pool at the local roadhouse. The way everyone looked in the early seventies (and actually, in our corner of upstate New York, most people still do). Ugly, perhaps, but not all that far-out.

And yet their down-home scruffiness is a wild look by Nashville's standards, and when they play off their ugliness in a parody of the Beatles' *A Hard Day's Night* sex-symbol sequence, in their video of "Oh, Lonesome Me," the effect is perversely charming.

As we said, lots of groups bring a lot of rock into country music today. Sawyer Brown, for example (although you wouldn't give odds to Sawyer Brown in a battle of the bands against the Headhunters, especially if the bands were allowed to use rusty razors). But what makes the Headhunters seem different, and seem wilder, is the material they choose: classic country songs such as Bill Monroe's "Walk Softly on This Heart of Mine," Don Gibson's "Oh, Lonesome Me," and of course "Davy Crockett." They don't trash these songs. They obviously love them, and they play them in the style that they love. Which is . . . well . . . wild.

The Young brothers and their cousin Greg Martin have been playing together since the midsixties. And while they give the impression that they hit the big time straight from the farm, they all have a his-

tory in commercial country music, including touring with the clean-cut eighties songbird Sylvia (Fred Young also played Patsy Cline's drummer in the movie *Sweet Dreams*). Richard Young was a staff writer for Acuff/Rose music, and Greg Martin was the lead guitarist in Ronnie McDowell's band from 1981–88.

Doug Phelps was McDowell's bass player over the same period, and Martin introduced him to the Youngs. In April of 1986, the four of them started getting together in Kentucky to jam at the old frame house on the Young family's Metcalfe County farm, which the Youngs' grandmother had given them as a "practice house." A few months later, Doug recommended that they invite his brother Ricky to sit in as a vocalist.

"When Ricky came up to sing," Fred Young remembers, "the room went neon. As much as his voice added a needed ingredient to the band, the fact that Doug and Ricky were playing together for the first time added fuel to the fire. In a matter of minutes, we went from two sets of brothers and a cousin to five brothers."

The Headhunters' first album, *Pickin' on Nashville,* came out in 1988 and became one of the first country albums of its era to make a major impact on the pop charts. Their stage act, while it draws enthusiastic country audiences (well, maybe not the Jim Reeves diehards), is an odd amalgam: a white-hot rock extravaganza, including songs made famous by Jimmy Page and Eric Clapton—and at the center of it Ricky Phelps, tall and skinny, dressed in overalls and work boots, carrying his microphone in a leather holster, dancing like a chorus boy from a road company version of *Li'l Abner*.

Their second album, *Electric Barnyard,* stretched from "Davy Crockett" to Norman Greenbaum's seventies pop hit "Spirit in the Sky." It won them a second straight CMA Award for Group of the Year.

Incidentally, if these guys are such roughy-tough, hell-raising rednecks, what are they doing down at Dumas Walker's with a six-pack of *light*?

The Kentucky Headhunters' list of the greatest songs of all time: "Honky Tonk Women" (Fred), "Imagine" (Richard), "Strawberry Fields Forever" (Doug), "Mississippi Queen" by Mountain (Ricky Lee), "God Only Knows" by the Beach Boys (Greg).

Sammy Kershaw

b. 2/24/58, Kaplan, LA
Style
Mainstream; a little too peppy to be a real neo-traditionalist

Memorable songs
"Cadillac Style"

One thing about Sammy Kershaw that makes you wonder whether today's country music might not be veering a little close for comfort to the show-biz mainstream: His past history includes, along with solid country credentials like carpenter and Cajun chef, a stint as a standup comic.

One thing about Sammy Kershaw that you have to like: Along with the usual influences like Hank and George, he lists the late Mel Street, a name too often left off the list of major contributors to the art of country music. Street, who took his own life at a tragically young age, left a searing legacy in just a few songs, most notably "Borrowed Angel."

Kershaw, a Louisiana native, broke into the big time in 1992 with "Cadillac Style," still his signature song. Although there are more popular songs that mention Cadillacs than every other brand of car put together, this one really caught the attention of the nationwide Gold Key Cadillac Dealers' Association.

Hal Ketchum

b. 4/9/53, Greenwich, NY

Style
Soul plus brain

Memorable songs
"Small Town Saturday Night"

You don't get much beyond the expected from most country performers' fact sheets, but Hal Ketchum's is nothing but surprises, starting with his favorite movie (*Sometimes a Great Notion,* by sixties cult hero Ken Kesey) and favorite book (*A Prayer for Owen Meany,* by highbrow novelist John Irving). His favorite restaurant is in New York's arty Greenwich Village, his favorite hobbies are painting and writing children's stories. You have to get down to favorite singer to find a conventional country interest (George Jones—and since he's the favorite singer of everyone who ever felt an honest emotion, this doesn't exactly redeem Ketchum as a good old boy). His favorite car is our all-time favorite as well, the Studebaker Golden Hawk. We don't know what this says about him.

His music says country. Critics have compared his storytelling ability to Tom T. Hall, and his voice is well equipped to search out the nuances in those songs. His grey-haired, lived-in good looks add to the overall impression of a guy who should wear well in a time of disposable artists.

Mark Knopfler

Style

Guitar wizard

Memorable songs

"Poor Boy Blues," "There'll Be Some Changes Made"

Awards

Grammy—Country Instrumental Performance 1985 ("Cosmic Square Dance" w/ Chet Atkins), 1990 ("So Soft Your Goodbye" w/ Chet Atkins), Country Vocal Collaboration 1990 ("Poor Boy Blues," w/ Chet Atkins)

Mark Knopfler is one of the great British rock and rollers of the seventies and eighties. As leader of the group Dire Straits, he is responsible for "Sultans of Swing," "Money for Nothing," "Walk of Life"—some of the most musical, listenable straight-ahead rock of recent memory.

Knopfler is also a country music lover, and he's shown it on records. He released an album with a pickup group of British rockers who called themselves the Notting Hillbillies. It wasn't exactly a first-rate album. As brilliant a songwriter as Knopfler is, he didn't quite capture the essence of country on the Notting Hillbilly songs. But as brilliant a guitarist as he is, he came up with an album that was almost worth buying just for the guitar licks alone.

Fortunately, country fans who wanted to hear Mark Knopfler's guitar had yet another alternative—his Grammy-winning collaborations with Chet Atkins, most notably on 1990's *Neck and Neck.*

Alison Krauss

b. 7/23/71, Decatur, IL

Style

Bluegrass

Memorable songs

"Two Highways," "I've Got That Old Feeling"

Awards

Grammy—Bluegrass Recording 1990 ("I've Got That Old Feeling"), Bluegrass Album 1992 (Everytime You Say Goodbye)

Here's a quick chronology of Alison Krauss's career:

Entered first fiddle contest, age eight; won first state fiddle contest, age ten; won first national fiddle contest, age twelve; first record contract, age fourteen; first Grammy nomination, age eighteen; first Grammy, age nineteen.

"I can't wait till people stop talking about my age," Krauss says.

Alison Krauss made her first four albums for the well-regarded independent Rounder Records. She became the new superstar of bluegrass. With her fourth album, *I've Got That Old Feeling,* she began to downplay her violin virtuosity and allow her vocals to take center stage.

The maturing teenager had developed a voice that people began to compare to the young Dolly Parton or Emmylou Harris. Two singles from *I've Got That Old*

Feeling, the title track and "Steel Rails," received heavy rotation on County Music Television, with the former becoming a CMT number one video hit. Krauss began to get serious offers from the major labels after the Grammy Award, but she opted to stay with Rounder for at least the time being, where she could continue to explore the bluegrass she loved, and where she could stick with her band, Union Station, which had added (with *Old Feeling*) a second young woman instrumentalist, banjo picker Alison Brown, a Harvard graduate who turned her back on Wall Street to play bluegrass professionally.

Two more notes about Alison Krauss. First, her success in general, and her performance of "Two Highways" in particular, are yet another tribute to how singularly important Ricky Skaggs is in the development of today's country music. "When Ricky Skaggs came on the scene, he was a breath of fresh air," Krauss told Elizabeth A. Brown of the *Christian Science Monitor*. "He made a huge impact on country music. He brought the acoustic instruments back in." And he was an inspiration to a lot of young musicians from Rodney Crowell to Alison Krauss, and he opened people's ears to the beauty and excitement of music made by real people playing real instruments.

Second, although she's not the first woman superpicker (Dolly Parton and Barbara Mandrell, to name two, got there ahead of her), she's in the forefront of creating an awareness of women as front-line musicians. Another first-rate young fiddler, Laurie Lewis, has recorded bluegrass for Chicago's independent Flying Fish Records, and an all-woman self-contained band, Wild Rose, has made some ripples in mainstream country. And this is just the beginning.

Kris Kristofferson

b. 6/22/36, Brownsville, TX

Style
Singer/songwriter

Memorable songs
"Me and Bobby McGee," "Help Me Make It Through the Night"

Awards
ACM—Song/Single of the Year 1970 ("For the Good Times"), 1985 ("Highwayman" w/ Waylon Jennings, Willie Nelson, Johnny Cash); CMA—Song of the Year 1970 ("Sunday Mornin' Comin' Down"), 1971 ("Help Me Make It Through the Night"); Grammy—Country Song 1971 ("Help Me Make It Through the Night"), Country Vocal Performance–Duo or Group 1973 ("From the Bottle to the Bottom" w/ Rita Coolidge), 1975 ("Lover Please" w/ Rita Coolidge); MCN—Songwriter 1972–73

There haven't been all that many Rhodes scholars pushing a broom and mop around Nashville's recording studios, but Kris Kristofferson did it, giving up a promising army career, including an offer to join the faculty at West Point, in order to do what's called "paying his dues," and in Kristofferson's case, that meant exactly what it said. He started on the ground floor (literally), while he worked hard at learning his craft of songwriting, which is different from any other kind of writing. Kristofferson had won short story contests in the prestigious intellectual journal *Atlantic Monthly*.

The apprenticeship was a long one, and Kristofferson was about to pack it in when his gift was recognized by another of country music's great songwriters, Roger

Miller, who became the first person to record "Me and Bobby McGee."

For all its intermittent bouts with hypocrisy, shallowness, and just plain rock-headness, Nashville loves talent, and Kristofferson's began to be recognized, often by solid, middle-of-the-road country performers such as Ray Price and the Statler Brothers.

Price was one of Kristofferson's early boosters, and Kristofferson repaid him—"For the Good Times" went to number one in 1970 and won Price a Grammy.

People started taking Kristofferson seriously, and once they began listening to his songs, his remarkable talent showed through. In a genre that's always been praised for songs that confront people's real problems honestly, Kristofferson was honest right through to the marrow. "For the Good Times" laid open the heart of a guy desperately hanging on to love that's slipping away; "Help Me Make It Through the Night" laid bare the need of a guy who'll do anything to stave off loneliness. That a song with a naked declaration of sexual need was recorded by a woman (Sammi Smith) made it, if anything, even more powerful. "Sunday Mornin' Comin' Down" caught the essence of loneliness as only someone who's led a hard life can know it.

Jazz immortal Miles Davis once reportedly expressed a fondness for country music. When asked why, he growled, "The stories, man. The stories." Country has always had the best stories, from ghostly trucker tales such as Red Sovine's "Phantom 309" to Tammy Wynette's heartbroken wife in "D-I-V-O-R-C-E" to Steve Earle's marijuana-growing Vietnam vet in "Copperhead Road." But perhaps no story embedded itself more deeply in the consciousness of a generation than Kris Kristofferson's tale of a girl who loved freedom more than she loved him, "Me and Bobby McGee."

"Me and Bobby McGee" was country, but it was bigger than country. It touched everyone. A partial list of artists who've recorded it would include Kristofferson, Roger Miller, the Grateful Dead, Gordon Lightfoot, Jerry Lee Lewis, and of course, Janis Joplin. Joplin's soulful cry that "freedom's just another word for nothing left to lose" made the song virtually an anthem of the sixties, and it moved Kristofferson out of country music (his only solo country hit was the spiritual "Why Me," number one in 1973).

The late sixties and early seventies were one of the great singer/songwriter eras—James Taylor, Lightfoot, Ian and Sylvia, Joni Mitchell—and Kristofferson fell into that category. His albums—targeted to the pop singer/songwriter audience rather than the country audience—contained one great song after another. "Darby's Castle" was a gothic tale of jealousy becoming a self-fulfilling prophecy; "Casey's Last Ride," a song that haunted us for years after we first heard it, was a sad urban love story; "The Silver Tongued Devil" created a Jekyll-and-Hyde womanizer that the singer was at a loss to understand.

Kristofferson's intelligence, strength, and natural ease brought him movie stardom, too, in such films as *Cisco Pike, Alice Doesn't Live Here Anymore, Pat Garrett and Billy the Kid,* and *A Star Is Born* (opposite Barbra Streisand).

The phenomenally successful "The Highwaymen" in 1985, with Waylon, Willie, and Johnny Cash, revived Kristofferson's country career, and the next year, he brought out a new solo album, the first in many years. True to the character of a man who has always followed his own muse, the album—released in the height of the Reagan superpatriot years—was a scorching political message, attacking American policy in Latin America and praising Jesse Jackson. It was consistently high-level, uncompromising work, but it did not tear up the country charts.

Kristofferson, Jennings, Nelson, and Cash released a second *Highwaymen* album in 1989.

L

k. d. lang

b. 11/2/61, Consort, Alberta, Canada

Style

*Musical—"torch and twang" (her phrase);
personal—Yoko Ono of the plains*

Memorable songs

*"Honky Tonk Angels' Medley," "Luck in
My Eyes"*

Award

*Grammy—Country Vocal Collaboration
1988 ("Crying" w/ Roy Orbison); Country
Vocal Performance–Female 1989 (Absolute
Torch and Twang), 1990 ("The Light In
Your Eyes")*

July 1990, a directive from the station
manager of KRVN, in Lexington, Nebraska: "Under no circumstances will anyone on this staff be allowed to play any
music by k. d. lang until such a time as she
publicly renounces her ties with People for
the Ethical Treatment of Animals and her
fanatic antimeat philosophy."

The boycott spread, in response to
lang's public denunciation of all meat eating and all meat eaters. It was the kiss of
death for k. d. lang in country music. And
that was *before* she came out of the closet as
an avowed lesbian. . . .

It was a little strange that lang was in
country music to start with. She didn't remotely fit the mold; she didn't even fit the
mold of the country music rebel.

She'd been a performance artist, and a
performance artist is . . . well, what they
do is . . . that is, the philosophy behind
performance art is . . . .

Well, a performance artist we knew
roller-skated nude through a moving train.
Another chained herself at the ankle to a
guy for a year. Why this was her performance art and not his, we aren't sure.

Anyway, whatever performance art is,
it's an urban, avant-garde phenomenon, a
celebration of the absurd, an art form cal-
culated to puzzle and intrigue the audience,
not to woo or seduce it.

So was it performance art when lang
performed her "Honky Tonk Angels'
Medley" on television with Kitty Wells,
Loretta Lynn, and Brenda Lee as her
backup singers—lang wearing baggy black
dancer's rehearsal clothes, and the other
three in Sweethearts of Country Music calico? Was it a put-on, a sardonic comment?
How were we supposed to react?

Well, there was one other joker in this
equation. k. d. lang had one of the most re-
markably moving, pure country voices of
the eighties. She sang this music better than
you could have imagined it was possible.

Lang's first U.S.-released album, *Angel With a Lariat,* was produced by Dave
Edmunds, a British rocker who is more
American than any native-born product by
virtue of his intense love for this country's
music. It featured polkas, two-steps, ballads, and up-tempo numbers, and it's a
gem. Her second, *Shadowland,* was produced by Owen Bradley, who was lured

out of retirement by the beauty of lang's voice. Bradley, who had worked with Patsy Cline, was a classic "woman's producer," lush and romantic, but always tasteful. With him, lang recorded such country ballads as Roger Miller's "Lock, Stock and Teardrops" and Harlan Howard's "I'm Down to My Last Cigarette," and Tin Pan Alley chestnuts like "Shadowland" and "Don't Let the Stars Get in Your Eyes."

With her third album, *Absolute Torch and Twang,* she made a promising start in a mainstream country direction, writing her own songs and producing herself.

Some promising start. When we approached lang's people for an interview for this book in 1991, we were told: "She doesn't want to have anything to do with country music, and she doesn't want to talk about country music." But it's country music's loss.

One last note: Would you believe her full name is Kathy Dawn Lang?

Tracy Lawrence

b. 1/27/68, Atlanta, TX
Style
Dedicated country

Memorable song
"Sticks and Stones"

May of 1991 should have been the best of times for Tracy Lawrence. Within a few months of arriving in Nashville, he had been signed to a recording contract by Atlantic Records; he had gone into the studio to make an album; and he was gearing himself for the promotional rounds that accompany the launching of a new act: showcases, press conferences, radio and TV appearances. Then he stepped into the middle of an armed robbery attempt, and was shot four times.

His life took top priority as his career went on hold. The album's release date was postponed as he recuperated. It was five months before he was strong enough to perform again.

Then perhaps because of, perhaps in spite of, the accident and its attendant publicity, his career took off. "Sticks and Stones," his first single, became one of the biggest successes of 1992. As an opening act for top-drawing acts like George Jones, Vince Gill, and Shenandoah, he began to draw a following of his own—a significant female one, owing in no small part to his Alan Jackson-like good looks.

Chris LeDoux

b. 10/2/48, Biloxi, MS
Style
Rodeo cowboy

Memorable songs
"Ridin' for a Fall"

There aren't many authentic folk musicians around these days, but Chris LeDoux would have to be one of them. He sings his life, and his life is rodeo. He spent fifteen years following the rodeo circuit, winning the world bareback bronco-riding title in 1976.

He started writing songs about cowboy life and rodeo life and singing them for his fellow riders, and gradually, as the bruises and broken bones of rodeo riding started to mount up, he turned to writing and singing more, while still following the rodeo circuit.

Eventually, he was following the same

circuit as a performer, selling tapes at rodeos (his parents ran the business end of it for him), getting some airplay ("There were a few stations that weren't tied to Top Forty"), and developing a legitimate grass-roots, cult reputation.

He numbered some pretty fair country singers in that cult following, as Chris himself found out one day when he was "driving to Casper, Wyoming, and this song comes on the radio I'd never heard before, this guy named Garth Brooks singing 'Much Too Young (To Feel This Damn Old).' I was thinking, 'Now that's a pretty good cowboy song,' and then that line came on and I almost ran off the road."

That line was "Listening to a worn-out tape of Chris LeDoux," and it warmed one cowboy's heart: "I'd been feeling like I was out there singing in the sagebrush and wondering if anyone was listening."

If Garth Brooks was listening, other people were going to start paying attention, too, and in 1991, LeDoux's brand of "western soul, sagebrush blues, cowboy folk, and rodeo rock 'n' roll" finally made it up from cult status to a major label.

Chris LeDoux's list of the greatest songs of all time: "Unanswered Prayers," "The Devil Went Down to Georgia," "A Country Boy Can Survive," "Big Iron," " '80s Ladies."

Brenda Lee

b. 12/11/44, Lithonia, GA *(Brenda Mae Tarpley)*
Style
Belter
Memorable songs
"I'm Sorry"

Brenda Lee's country influence is stronger than her actual career, although she did have a string of Top Ten hits in the late seventies. Her principal career was as "Little Miss Dynamite" in the fifties, a Dick Clark sensation whose voice was so much bigger than her four-foot-eleven-inch frame that an odd but persistent rumor arose that she was acutally a thirty-three-year-old midget.

Before she was a teenage rock 'n' roll star, though, she was a moppet country star, appearing on Red Foley's *Ozark Jubilee* when she was ten. And after her rock 'n' roll career wound down in the sixties, she came back, scoring her first country chart success in 1973 with Kris Kristofferson's "Nobody Wins."

By the mideighties, she had pretty much retired to become a legend, a role she filled in her 1989 guest shot on a k. d. lang album, joining Kitty Wells and Loretta Lynn to back up country music's first performance artist. In 1989 she also returned to a major label for the first time in five years, recording a new album for MCA, which was a good deal better than the reception it got from radio and the charts.

Robin Lee

b. 11/7, Nashville, TN
Style
Country/soft rock

It may be hard to grow up as a teenaged classical pianist in Nashville without getting bitten by the country music bug at some point, and Robin Lee didn't escape. While playing classical Sunday brunches at a Nashville restaurant, she started singing with a band in school and went straight into the demo business out of high school. She had a solid hit single, "Black Velvet," for Atlantic in 1990.

Jerry Lee Lewis

b. 9/29/35, Ferriday, LA

Style

The one he invented

Memorable songs

"Whole Lotta Shakin' Goin' On," "She Even Woke Me Up to Say Goodbye"

Awards

ACM—Keyboardist 1975; Grammy—Best Spoken Word or Non-Musical Recording 1986 (Interviews From the Class of '55 Recording Sessions w/ Carl Perkins, Roy Orbison, Johnny Cash, Sam Phillips, Rick Nelson & Chips Moman)

Like Waylon Jennings, Johnny Cash, and Vern Gosdin, Jerry Lee Lewis underwent open-heart surgery in the eighties—a watershed decade for a bunch of hard-living guys having to face up to serious evidence of their mortality.

Jerry Lee has had more than his share of mortality in recent years—a tempestuous, tragedy-streaked life. His three-year-old son and two of his wives met accidental deaths. He was arrested for firing a gun outside the gates of Graceland. He has collapsed and been hospitalized more than once.

And perhaps no one with more talent has ever surfaced in the fields of country or rock and roll.

Certainly Sam Phillips, who discovered Elvis, thought so: he always said that Jerry Lee Lewis had more pure talent than anyone he had ever seen in his life.

Jerry Lee's rock and roll career was ended by the disastrous publicity that surrounded the revelation that he had married his thirteen-year-old cousin, Myra Gale Brown. Country music took him back with the release of "Another Place, Another Time" in 1968, and he's been part of country music ever since.

The Killer had never fitted into any manageable niche. No label that's ever been put on a musical genre, from outlaw to progressive country—even rockabilly—could possibly hold him. He's had hits, including half a dozen country number ones, but even that seems irrelevant in a discussion of Jerry Lee Lewis.

What's worth mentioning, though, is this: Jerry Lee has made an amazing number of records, of an amazingly wide variety of songs—probably more recordings, in more genres, than even Willie Nelson. He's recorded everything from "Jailhouse Rock" to "Over the Rainbow." Many of them are available on small, obscure labels—no one but the most fanatical collector could possibly have all of them. And every song he has ever recorded, by the time he's through with it, sounds as though it could only have been recorded by Jerry Lee Lewis.

Patty Loveless

b. 1/4/57, Pikeville, KY (*Patricia Ramey*)

Style

Traditional with an edge; emotional resonance

Memorable songs

"Blue Side of Town," "Sounds of Loneliness"

Awards

*MCN—Star of Tomorrow 1989;
TNN/MCN—Female Artist 1990*

What is country music in the nineties? Where does it come from? Singer after singer will tell you some version of the same answer: traditional country (that is, the country music of the fifties with Hank Williams as its godfather) and rock and roll—"Hank and the Beatles." For Patty Loveless it was much the same story, except that her traditional godfathers were the Wilburn Brothers, and the rock and roll came from the heavy metal sounds of the seventies.

As a fourteen-year-old musical hopeful (she had barged into Porter Wagoner's office earlier the same year, and the story goes that she impressed him mightily), she attracted the attention of the Wilburn Brothers when she replaced a local opening act for a touring package show.

The Wilburns were a harmony duo from Hardy, Missouri. Along the lines of the Everly Brothers but without their sophistication, they nonetheless made some sweet music that was a staple of the charts in the fifties and into the sixties. They were past the peak of their careers then, but still an important touring and television act, and they were just losing their longtime girl singer, Loretta Lynn, to stardom. They hired Patty Ramey to replace her, and her early musical education was three years on the road as part of the Wilburn Brothers show—a sponsorship she repaid in 1989 when she produced a reissue of the Brothers' hits on MCA.

In 1975, Patty married Terry Lovelace, a sometime drummer with the act, and moved to North Carolina, where she drifted from country into hard rock, performing material by the Eagles, Bachman Turner Overdrive, Lynyrd Skynyrd, ZZ Top, Rossington Collins, Pat Benatar, even Led Zeppelin. For a hillbilly singer from Pikeville by way of the Wilburn Brothers, this was heady stuff: "When I finally got up onstage and started doing it, I was amazed that I could pull it off."

It was ten years before she played another country gig or even thought about country. Suddenly, she found audiences requesting songs she'd never heard of, and she had to go out and buy records by such new performers with names like Steve Wariner and the Judds. Shortly thereafter, her brother Roger called her from Nashville. His message: it's time to make your move—they're looking for new artists.

They were. She hit Nashville in April 1985, and she was signed to MCA by July. She kept her ex-husband's name, but changed the spelling so she wouldn't be confused with X-rated movie star Linda Lovelace.

Her first album had the critics exclaiming over her pure, traditional voice, but the rock and roll years had left a powerful mark on her. Patty showed flashes of an emotional intensity that owed more to Pat Benatar or Robert Plant of Led Zeppelin than to Loretta Lynn. The feeling you get from a country purist comes from close to home—the emotion that's found in a lonely room, or the bottom of a bottle. The feeling that Patty Loveless expresses owes as much to art as to the simple life. You're not surprised when you hear it from a rocker or an operatic diva, but coming from a country girl, it can make your hair stand on end.

She doesn't hit that nerve all the time, and she believes it's more likely to happen in a live performance. "I'm just finding this out about myself, that once I go ahead and lose myself in a song when I'm onstage, I'm really doing myself a real big favor. Because then—and it happens every once in a while—I get this feeing in my blood, that I'm really living this song. But other times I'll feel something distracts me, and I can't put one hundred percent into it.

"I love recording, too, but I feel I still haven't gotten that feeling down like I do onstage. But once the album is done, and I start rehearsing the songs with my band, and doing them onstage, a lot of people will come and see me and say, 'Wow, you sound better than your records.' And a lot of people may take it as an insult, but I don't. I feel you give them a record and they enjoy that, but when they come to the show and they like that even better—it makes me feel good about myself to be able to do it. When I listen to those records, I think I know I could have done that song much better, but it's done, it's pressed, you go on."

She hits it on record, too. Listen, for example, to "Sounds of Loneliness," from her first album, which adds a synthesizer to traditional instruments and achieves a startling union of country purity with rock intensity. Listen to "Blue Side of Town," from her third album, *Honky Tonk Angel.*

It's possible that Patty Loveless doesn't hit that emotional peak all the time because in her case it's so intense that no one could hit it all the time. It's also possible that when she misses, shallow material may be part of the problem. We feel that way about a song like "Timber (I'm Fallin' in Love)," but there are a lot who'd disagree. It was her first number one.

Patty Loveless's list of the greatest songs of all time: "Music is good therapy, and a whole lot cheaper. Sometimes when I'm really low, I'll go and put a record on, and it *helps me to pull myself out of falling into a deep depression. Some of the songs that have done that for me: 'Down So Low' by Linda Ronstadt; 'I Will Always Love You' by Dolly Parton—I just love the lyrics; 'Wheel in the Sky' by Journey; 'I Cried a River for Him' off Emmylou Harris's* Bluebird *album; 'Slow Healin' Heart' by Jim Rushing— Dolly Parton recorded it recently, but I had it on my first album, and it still does something special to me when I do it onstage with just an acoustic guitar."*

Lyle Lovett

b. 11/1/56, Klein, TX

Style

Idiosyncratic singer/songwriter with big band

Memorable songs

"God Will," "Farther Down the Line"

"Boy, you must be from Texas," Lyle Lovett was told by a Nashville executive on his first trip to Music City. "There are too many words in your songs."

But the words were glorious, original, poetic, and like nothing that anyone else was doing. Lovett was part of the Nashville Class of 1986/87 that included Steve Earle, the O'Kanes, Bobby Lee Springfield, k. d. lang, Foster and Lloyd, Nanci Griffith, New Grass Revival, and a handful of other artists who made audiences stop and rethink what country music was all about.

Lovett, who worked for his mother conducting high-level motivational seminars for businesspeople as a day job while he tried to get his music career off the ground, was in many ways the most striking of this bunch. Tall, angular, and topped off with a shock of hair that made him look like a cross between Jack Kerouac and Little Richard, he came from a musical place that was all his own.

Virtually every other country singer of the current era has roots in rock and roll, but there's no rock and roll at all in Lovett's music. It's an amalgam of honky-tonk and jazz ("That's right," we were told by Francine Reed, the vocalist in his band, "and if he ever puts any rock and roll in, we're leaving").

This has a precedent in country music—the Western Swing of Bob Wills and others. But Lovett, though his Texas roots certainly encompass Western Swing, is closer in spirit to the hipster jazz of the forties, and this sound reached its full flowering on his third album for MCA, *Lyle Lovett and His Large Band*. The Large Band was a mixture of hard-swinging white country guys from Nashville and black jazz musicians from Phoenix, Arizona, and they opened the album—as they open his live shows—with "Blues March," a composition by forties bebop legend Clifford Brown, followed by "Here I Am," a Tom Waitsian beatnik monologue with a Bob Wills–flavored chorus.

This is, in other words, a guy who is marching not only to his own drummer, but also his own bass player, his own arranger, his own road manager, his own jukebox. Country radio? Hah!

But he got it, at least at first. This was partly because 1986 was a little different. It was also because Lovett is steeped in a deep love for Americana, for Texas, for the cowboy myth, and for country music. It all came out together in his only Top Ten hit, "Cowboy Man," in which the cowboy myth and the Cinderella myth are intertwined.

That's a technique Lovett has always been drawn to—if one myth is the stuff dreams are made of, why not two or three

or more? In "If I Had a Boat," he's not content with just the boat as a symbol of freedom, he adds a pony as well—and dreams of riding the pony on his boat. He overlays that dream with more American dreams—Tonto, Roy Rogers.

"Give me a few songs for radio," is what record-label genius Jimmy Bowen tells his artists, and you can do what you want on the rest of the album. Bowen, who was president of MCA at the time Lovett released his first albums there (actually on Curb, distributed by MCA—Lovett didn't work directly with Bowen), should have been satisfied, more or less. Though "Cowboy Man" was Lovett's only Top Ten, he had a regular run on the Top Twenty between 1986 and 1988.

"Farther Down the Line," his first single, is a tour de force of imagery in which he compares a cowboy's unsuccessful rodeo bronc ride to a failed love affair. "God Will" may have offended some religious purists, but it blew away a legion of lovers of great songs. Who forgives the singer's lying, cheating girlfriend? "God does, but I don't / God will, but I won't / That's the difference between God and me."

"God Will" was a radio cut, but not "An Acceptable Level of Ecstasy," about institutionalized racism at a society wedding, nor "This Old Porch," written with Robert Earl Keen, one of those songs with too many words, but a beautiful, evocative piece of nostalgia.

His second album, *Pontiac,* also managed a couple of Top Twenty hits, but then the mood was changing, radio playlists were tightening, and by the *Large Band* album, Lovett was more or less officially pigeonholed as a cult figure.

We keep hoping a radio format will emerge that will be built around performers like Lyle Lovett, like the Texas Tornadoes, John Hiatt, Zachary Richard, Robert

Cray, Bonnie Raitt, Buddy Guy, Steve Earle. If that doesn't happen, you can always buy the CDs and look for them to show up at your local honky-tonk. In 1989, we saw Lovett share top billing with Tammy Wynette at a country music festival. Don't look for that to happen in 1993.

Loretta Lynn

b. 4/14/35, Butcher's Hollow, KY (*Loretta Webb*)

Style

Woman to woman

Memorable songs

"Coal Miner's Daughter," "Don't Come Home a-Drinkin' (With Lovin' on Your Mind)"

Awards

ACM—Female Vocalist 1971, 1973–75, Entertainer of the Year 1975, Artist of the Decade 1970s; CMA—Female Vocalist 1967, 1972–73, CMA Entertainer of the Year 1972; MCN—Female Artist 1967–78, 1980, Album of the Year 1976 (When the Tingle Becomes a Chill), Living Legend 1986, Touring Road Show 1974, Band 1975–77 (The Coalminers). With Conway Twitty: ACM Vocal Duet/Group 1971, 1974–76, Album of the Year 1975 (Feelings); CMA Vocal Duo 1972–75; Grammy—Country Vocal Performance–Duo or Group 1971 ("After the Fire Is Gone")

Women have traditionally been the primary consumers of country music, and for the most part, they have embraced, on record and in concert, performers that they also embrace in their fantasies: good looking muscle guys like Billy Ray Cyrus, smooth-voiced crooners like Eddy Arnold, sensitive macho men like Marty Robbins or Ricky Van Shelton, boyish charmers like Billy Dean, hunk-a-hunks o' burning love like Elvis. But there was another way of approaching women, and it seemed that no one caught onto it until Loretta Lynn came along: one woman talking to another, heart to heart.

It seemed so natural when Loretta did it that you wondered why no one had thought of it before; but Loretta didn't scope it out with focus groups and market surveys; she just did it. She wrote songs and sang them about her own life. She had problems with a no-good man ("Don't Come Home a-Drinkin' With Lovin' On Your Mind") and predatory women ("Fist City," "You Ain't Woman Enough To Take My Man"). She was a teenage mother and a grandmother by the time she was thirty-one, so she knew what "One's on the Way" felt like. When she began to get her consciousness raised by "The Pill," she sang about it with an authority that no political correctness could ever approach.

And she created an audience rapport that was like no other. As Joan Dew described it in her 1977 book, *Singers and Sweethearts,* "Loretta's fans . . . share an unprecedented, unbreakable bond with her. . . . They don't just love her, they worship her. This phenomenon cannot be fully appreciated unless one travels on the road with Loretta to the places where *her* people live—rural areas, factory towns, farm centers.

"At times her concerts take on the air of an evangelistic faith-healing meeting, with fans calling out her name and the songs they want to hear as fervently (and sometimes as reverently) as a sinner calling to the Lord.

"The outsider, who immediately feels like a stranger at a family reunion, observes it all with a mixture of awe and uneasiness.

It is spooky, and somehow sad, and yet terribly exciting."

That fan adoration which Joan Dew describes may be a part of country music's past. As the audience expands, as Nashville takes on the skillful and aggressive marketing techniques of LA and New York, as the music gets bigger, the stars may, paradoxically, be getting smaller.

How is that possible? Well, it depends on what you mean by big. Certainly, the athletes of a generation or so ago look like sharecroppers next to today's Six Million Dollar Men. But when Howie Morenz, the great Montreal Canadian hockey player of the forties, died, his body was laid in state in an open casket at center ice in the Montreal Forum. Can $5 million a year top that? Mordecai Richler, the Canadian novelist, went to pay his respects to Morenz. When he entered the Forum, the place was silent as a church, and Richler recalls wondering if he was the only person in Montreal who had bothered to turn out. When he came into the arena itself, he discovered that the place was packed to the rafters . . . but no one was making a sound. Everyone was sitting in reverent silence.

We're not among those who criticize today's stars for making what they can get, but . . . can $5 million a year top that? We don't think so. And we can't imagine any contemporary star receiving that kind of tribute after he/she is gone, except Loretta Lynn.

She is still one of the legends, one of the shining stars whom people think about when they think about country music, still so big that it's almost impossible to realize that as far as the recording and radio industry is concerned, she's been over for more than a decade. Her last number one hit ("Out of My Head and Back in My Bed") was in 1977, her last Top Ten in 1982.

Loretta's fragility has been well documented, and her fans know about her periods of hospitalization for exhaustion just as they know about her early and difficult marriage, her almost endless exile to the road and her tour bus because of the problems at home, her grandmotherhood at thirty-one; and most importantly, the way she changed the face of country music forever, and dramatically for the better.

Women virtually didn't exist in country music until Kitty Wells's "It Wasn't God Who Made Honky Tonk Angels" in 1952, and even after that, they were a novelty, the opening act on some male singer's show. Loretta Lynn changed all that. She wrote her own songs, she spoke to women directly and poetically. With Conway Twitty, she virtually invented the all-star duet pairing, now one of the staples of country recording.

And she created an audience that would never go away—an audience of women for women. Dolly Parton expanded that audience; so did Tammy Wynette. And all the women around today, from smart gals like Mary-Chapin Carpenter and Kathy Mattea to tough gals like Lacy J. Dalton and Tanya Tucker, to Loretta's natural heiress, Reba McEntire, are her inheritors.

Shelby Lynne

b. 10/22/68, Quantico, VA (*Shelby Lynn Moorer*)

Style

Emotional

Memorable song

"If I Could Bottle This Up" (*duet with George Jones*)

Awards

ACM—New Female Vocalist 1990

She hasn't yet made the mark that she's going to, but she's got a lot of time in front of her. Shelby Lynne started off incredibly young, appearing on "Nashville Now" in 1987 at the age of eighteen, and getting such a response that by the next morning, she had gotten four major label offers and a call from Billy Sherrill, producer of George Jones and Tammy Wynette in their glory years, offering to produce her.

Two years later at a Fan Fair appearance, according to Robert Oermann of the *Nashville Tennessean,* "Lynne won thousands of new fans. . . . In one of the most electrifying moments in Fan Fair history, she walked out from under the covered stage . . . and bravely sang in a driving rainstorm to a drenched and wildly applauding audience."

She took a hard route through life to her current success. She was thrown in jail in Texas on a trumped-up charge by her drunken and abusive father. After she had been returned to her mother's home in Alabama, her father came there with a gun. When her mother went out to try to shield her daughters, the father shot her dead, then committed suicide.

Expect Shelby Lynne to live up to her album title, *Tough All Over,* and stick around. She has a virtuoso style, an operatic coloratura talent in down-home pipes, the kind of distilled and channeled emotion that you hear in no other female singer today, with the possible exception of Patty Loveless.

Barbara Mandrell

b. 12/25/48, Houston, TX

Style

Vegas

Memorable songs

"Married but Not to Each Other,"
"Sleeping Single in a Double Bed"

Awards

ACM—New Female Vocalist 1971, Female Vocalist 1978, 1981, Entertainer of the Year 1980; CMA—Female Vocalist 1979, 1981, Entertainer of the Year 1980–81; Grammy—Inspirational Performance 1982 ("He Set My Life to Music"); MCN—Most Promising Female Artist 1976, Female Artist 1979, 1981–82, Musician 1981–82, Comedy Act 1981 (w/ Mandrell Sisters), Comedy TV Series 1981–82, Living Legend 1985; TNN/MCN—Minnie Pearl Award

When Barbara Mandrell recorded "I Was Country When Country Wasn't Cool" in 1981—the same year that she won her second consecutive CMA Entertainer of the Year Award, the same year that marked the crest of the Urban Cowboy wave, there were those who thought the lady might have been protesting too much. For those who liked their country music a little shaggy, a little rough-edged, a little more countrified, Barbara was neither country nor cool. But there was—and continues to be—a huge audience that clearly thought she was both.

And admire her brand of polished entertainment or not, there's no denying the lady's talent. And there's been no denying it for a long time, not since she was an eleven-year-old steel guitar prodigy in a Las Vegas revue.

Barbara Mandrell's profoundest influence, and the presiding genius behind her, is her father, Irby Mandrell. The senior Mandrell left his career as a police officer to shape her career, just as her husband, Ken Dudney, would later leave a career as a naval officer to support Barbara's show business aspirations. "Some people will call him a stage father," Barbara wrote in her autobiography, *Get to the Heart,* "which is often a derogatory term. . . . He wasn't a stage father. He was a father who raised his children to succeed. Our business just happened to be music."

Irby Mandrell's oldest child succeeded in business younger than most. An accomplished steel guitar and saxophone player by the time she was ten years old, she was booked onto a Las Vegas show at age eleven, on a bill with Joe and Rose Maphis, Tex Ritter, and Cowboy Copas. It was the beginning of a long love affair between the Mandrell family and Vegas, about which Barbara says in her autobiography: "We don't hold anything against the drinking and gambling. I know it's a pretty wild lifestyle in Las Vegas, but I try not to worry about other people's business or judge them. As a Christian, I have never felt out of place performing in Las Vegas."

On the advice of her father, Barbara added singing to her act and joined a package tour with Johnny Cash, Patsy Cline, and George Jones (for whom she also played steel guitar). After that, her father formed a group, the Mandrell Family Band, with himself on rhythm guitar and his wife (who learned music to support the family business) on bass. They played dates within range of the family home in Oceanside, California, particularly on military bases, establishing a milieu that has remained centrally important in Barbara's life: "I am very pro-military. Always have been . . . I'm a law and order person. A hawk. There's a strong side of me . . . the kind of business and military instincts we call 'masculine' for want of a better word. . . .

"As soon as I heard [the Beatles], I loved them immediately . . . but I thought their hair was ridiculous. Maybe it was because I was used to seeing marines at the bases on weekends, but to this day, I prefer short hair on a man. My theory is, if you're a man, look like a man. . . .

"I like masculine, military kind of guys, with relatively short hair. . . . Until he grew a mustache, I had a huge crush on Chad Everett. . . .

"Maybe because of his military background, Daddy was a firm believer in our looking like a unit. He'd say, 'What uniforms are you wearing? Are you going to change into civilian clothes right after the show?' Not costumes, but uniforms. Daddy figured when you say 'band,' you think of a marching band, and they're always in uniform. . . . From the beginning, we didn't wear blue jeans even while traveling."

Barbara Mandrell married a military man (who was also a musician—Ken Dud-

ney had been a drummer in the Mandrell Family Band), and she and the Family Band expanded their work at local military bases to include Vietnam, entertaining the troops. After that, for a few years, she retired to become a military wife, but show business called her back.

The Mandrells, father and daughter, began to put together a new Family Band, this one featuring her sister, fifteen-year-old Louise, replacing Mom on bass, and Irlene, barely thirteen, on drums. Barbara's first recordings for Columbia, between 1969 and 1971, centered on country remakes of soul classics (her first charted single was Otis Redding's "I've Been Loving You Too Long").

Her father's theory was that "I could get away with singing cheatin' songs because I was from such a wholesome background, with a good marriage, and I looked like I just came from church." That Las Vegas, military base–influenced balancing of what's wholesome and what's not is a consistent theme in Barbara Mandrell's life. She wouldn't presume to tell anyone not to gamble, but her live-and-let-live attitude doesn't go quite as far as telling people not to protest the war in Vietnam. She maintains a clean-cut, uniform-wearing image—she called her band the Do-Rites because "it suggested the image I wanted—no drinking around the show, no drugs at all, bright costumes, no jeans, no excessively long hair. A clean-cut look." And once you look clean-cut, then it's okay to sing about cheatin'.

There used to be a name for this sort of attitude, among those sixties types that Barbara Mandrell kept such a wary distance from, and it was hypocrisy. But who's to judge? There are discrepancies in everyone's attitudes, and maybe hypocrisy is just being inconsistent in the opposite way from your accuser.

Anyway, it worked. Mandrell's first big hit was the sexy suggestive "The Midnight Oil," which was followed by "Married but Not to Each Other."

Her first number one, "Sleeping Single in a Double Bed," came in 1978. Her second, a remake of Luther Ingram's "(If Loving You Is Wrong) I Don't Want to Be Right," put together all the ingredients of the Mandrell sound: a Vegas arrangement of a country rendition of a rhythm and blues song about cheatin'.

Barbara was on her way, and the next few years would be the zenith of her career: the two CMA Entertainer of the Year Awards, and the hit TV show with her sisters.

In 1984, she was in a head-on automobile accident, caused when another car, heading the wrong way down Tennessee's Highway 31, smashed into her Jaguar. The other driver was killed instantly, and Barbara suffered major head injuries. Even after she recovered from the physical effects of the accident, a complete psychological recovery was a long, slow, difficult process.

Today, however, Barbara Mandrell is a survivor of both that tragedy and the wreck of the Urban Cowboy style. She was still managing the occasional Top Ten hit well into the eighties, she still headlines in Vegas, and she still has TV stardom—nowadays on the Nashville Network.

Louise Mandrell

b. 7/13/54, Corpus Christi, TX

Style
Progressive country

Memorable songs
"I'm Not Through Loving You Yet"

Awards
MCN—Most Promising Female Artist 1981

In the Mandrell Sisters' TV act, Barbara was the bossy one, Irlene was the funny one, and Louise was the beautiful one. It was Barbara's show, of course, as it pretty much always had been, since Louise joined the Mandrell Family Band as a teenage bass player.

During the seventies, Louise was in and out of Barbara's orbit, marrying twice unsuccessfully, touring for a while with Merle Haggard. In 1977, she made a move to start her own career, putting together a band and touring and recording under her own name. In 1979, she married songwriter R. C. Bannon, who later became the music director for the Mandrell Sisters' TV show, and the two of them released a few duets. But it wasn't until after the TV show that her solo career took root, and she had a run of a couple of years on the charts.

Louise Mandrell may have deserved more success as a singer than she actually got—not that she hasn't done all right for herself as a personality. You could compare her style to Marie Osmond's—both of them are smoother and glitzier than today's tastes demand, but like Marie, Louise can surprise you with musicianship and emotional substance.

Like her sister, Louise is a lover of the military ("It's just as well they don't name me president—I'd give all the money to the military"). In 1991, Louise Mandrell headlined her own patriotic show at the Opryland theme park.

Mason Dixon

FRANK GILLIGAN
b. 11/2/55, Queens, NY

JERRY DENGLER
b. 5/29/55, Colorado Springs, CO

RICK HENDERSON
b. 5/29/53, Beaumont, TX

Style
Group folkie

Memorable songs
"When Karen Comes Around"

College guys from Lamar University in Beaumont, Texas, taking their name from the line that they came from both sides of, they scrambled around the lower echelons of the charts for most of the eighties on a couple of independent labels, before getting a shot at the brass ring with Capitol in 1988. They didn't catch on, at least their first time around. They were pretty good, though.

Kathy Mattea

b. 6/21/59, Cross Lanes, WV

Style
Crystalline

Memorable songs
"Goin' Gone," "Life as We Knew It"

Awards
ACM—Single/Song of the Year 1988 ("Eighteen Wheels and a Dozen Roses"), Song of the Year 1989 ("Where've You Been"), Female Vocalist 1989;

CMA—Single of the Year 1988, Female Vocalist 1989–90; Grammy—Country Vocal Performance–Female 1990 ("Where've You Been")

Kathy Mattea is the sort of entertainer people are thinking of when they talk about the new, college-educated face of country music, although actually it was George Strait, not Mattea, who stayed in college and got his degree, and who held a responsible managerial job before plunging into a music career. Mattea, an engineering and chemistry major at West Virginia University, dropped out at age nineteen, tied a mattress to her car, hung out a sign that said NASHVILLE OR BUST, and supported herself by waiting on tables and working as a tour guide at the Country Music Hall of Fame and Museum as she began a career as a demo singer that would be the first step in her rise to stardom.

But Mattea is a different kind of singer, and a different kind of personality. She *seems* like a college type, an intellectual, a—dare we say it?—folkie. Whereas a performer like Garth Brooks may make a new audience say, "Hey, there may be something to this country music after all," Mattea reaches out to the "I still hate country music, but . . ." audience.

Listen to some of her reviews. "Mattea's previous six albums are classifiable as folk-tinged country, this one [*Time Passes By*] is country-tinged folk . . . [she has] a quality that . . . asserts itself even more when she doesn't have to sing about trucks and trains" (Ralph Novak, *People*). Or this double-edged praise from the fashion magazine *Elle*, plucking Mattea out from its cosmopolitan condescension to country music: "Don't assume that Mattea deals strictly in impeccable taste. Certain rhymes (snore/floor, rain/pain) and themes ('Where've You Been' details a geriatric couple rekindling love in a hospital) may leave some with a dry mouth rather than moist eyes. But Mattea's assured vocals, which inevitably conjure the image of a clear mountain stream, are a cool salve to such excesses. Singing without vibrato or fashionable stylings—after all, fashion is timebound, and truth eternal—she shares a kinship with Suzanne Vega or Joan Baez."

We'll hold back from mentioning that Joan Baez's biggest hit rhymes "train/again," "feet/defeat," and "fell/well," or that while perhaps in the sophisticated *Elle* circles, no one ever gets old (or stays together), "Where've You Been" nevertheless takes on a theme that has not exactly been overexplored.

Mattea herself buys into this, to some extent. In 1991, as *Time Passes By* was ready for release, she told Deborah Kirk of *Interview*: "In the last few months, I've gone through a roller coaster of emotions about this new album. In the middle of making it I won the [CMA] Female Vocalist of the Year award. I go through euphoria, thinking how exhilarated I am to be taking this risk, and then this complete fear comes over me that it will be totally trashed. . . . But I'd rather do the kind of music I'm committed to, even if it reaches only ten people, than end up one of those performers who's fat and fifty, in spandex and false eyelashes, doing the same stuff year after year."

Time Passes By made the Top Ten album charts in 1991, although it was not the smash that her earlier albums had been and didn't do quite as well as her greatest-hits package, released at around the same time. But Mattea, whose first Mercury release came in 1983, and who first hit the Top Ten in 1986 with the Nanci Griffith–penned "Love at the Five and Dime," is one of the major success stories of the eighties, and one of the important events in the history of the changing role of women in country music.

Mattea made her early mark in Nashville as a demo singer, then eventually signed with Mercury, although it took her three years and two unsuccessful albums to find the style and material that would work for her.

"Love at the Five and Dime" was a bittersweet and delicately realized story song, and Mattea's voice—sweet and . . . yes, folk-tinged . . . and as pure in its own way as George Strait's—proved to be the ideal vehicle for it. "Goin' Gone," her first number one, had also been recorded by Griffith—and by the Forester Sisters, although their version was never released.

Mattea had demonstrated a simple yet intelligent approach to material that was original, yet basic and moving. "Eighteen Wheels and a Dozen Roses" fit that formula—if you could call it a formula. So did the remarkable "Life as We Knew It," written by Fred Koller and Walter Carter, "She Came From Fort Worth" by Koller and Pat Alger, and her crossover hit and signature song, "Where've You Been," cowritten by Don Henry and Mattea's husband, Jon Vezner.

As her career went on, though, perhaps influenced by all those she's-too-sensitive-to-be-country write-ups, she started to turn more toward New Age sensibility in her choice of songs. *Time Passes By* featured that new country concept, the codependent-no-more song. In "What Could Have Been" by Beth Nielsen Chapman, girl loses boy before she ever gets to tell him how she feels. So what does she do? Cry into the jukebox behind those sawdust doors and swinging floors? Or better yet, go into an irreversible decline and die?

Not a chance. She finds someone else with whom she can have a healthy relationship based on mutual respect, and she forgets all about the other guy.

Ah, yes. We're getting so healthy, it's sickening. She may be better off, but who cares about her? It's the listener who's important—and frankly, we're still better served with the all-out emotional release of "He Stopped Loving Her Today."

Her *Time Passes By* sound was heavily influenced by a trip to Scotland, and a meeting with Scottish folk musician Dougie MacLean. The album's instrumentation augments traditional country acoustic guitars and fiddles with bagpipes and autoharps. Mattea also recorded three songs for the acclaimed public television "Civil War" documentary series.

In 1992, Mattea's career was jeopardized by serious throat problems, but an operation appears to have been successful, and she's resumed singing.

McBride and the Ride

TERRY MCBRIDE
b. 9/16/58, Austin, TX

RAY HERNDON
b. 7/14/60, Scottsdale, AR

BILLY THOMAS
b. 10/24/53, Fort Myers, FL

Style
Smooth

Memorable songs
"Can I Count on You"

A decade ago, no one wanted to sign Alabama because the conventional wisdom said that groups don't make it in country. Now it's just the reverse. McBride and the Ride were put together by producer/MCA executive Tony Brown to pick up the slack at a point when, as Ride drummer Billy Thomas says, "Alabama was not quite as hot as they'd been, and labels started seeing a void. I think Tony Brown wanted a band for MCA, so he experimented with us. If we hadn't worked out, I think he would have gone for another."

However, Thomas says, Brown didn't start out with a particular sound in mind, then look for cookie-cutter parts to fill it. It was more a question of picking three guys from disparate backgrounds on instinct, throwing them into a room together, and saying, "See what you can come up with."

McBride and Herndon were country music professionals; Thomas was a converted rocker who had moved to country rock with Rick Nelson, then into country with Vince Gill and later Emmylou Harris. They hit it off; six weeks later they were in the studio, cutting their first album, and after that they had to start getting to know each other. "It's an ass backwards way to put a thing together, but it worked."

In spite of their bizarre beginnings, says Thomas, they feel like a band, and they're in it together for the long haul.

The McCarters

JENNIFER
b. 3/1/64, Sevierville, TN

LISA AND TERESA
twins, b. Sevierville, TN

Style
Depends on which album

Jennifer McCarter and her sisters, twins Lisa and Teresa, came from Dolly Parton's hometown, and they were actually one of the best sister harmony groups to come along at a time when a lot of them were being signed up (that was just before the labels discovered guys with cowboy hats). Their debut album on Warner Brothers yielded two Top Ten hits, "Timeless and True Love" and "The Gift." On their second album they billed themselves as Jennifer McCarter and the McCarter Sisters, scrapped their pure rural harmonies in favor of a contemporary country sound, and put out an album that nobody bought.

They seem to be continuing in that vein. One industry insider's prediction: "Jennifer McCarter will probably surface as a soloist, and her sisters will probably end up on a cooking show."

Charly McClain

b. 3/26/56, Jackson, TN

Style
MOR

Memorable songs
"Radio Heart"

Award
MCN—Most Promising Female Artist 1980

Looking back from the vantage point of a new decade, it's hard to remember Charly McClain clearly, although she had a nice voice and recorded several hits from the midseventies through the mideighties.

In 1984, she married Wayne Massey, former star of the soap opera "One Life to Live" turned unsuccessful country singer. Massey became her producer and used his drama coach skills to coax out her last number one hit, "Radio Heart." They also did a few duets.

Delbert McClinton

b. 11/4/40, Lubbock, TX

Style
Texas roots

Memorable songs
"Givin' It Up for Your Love," "Gonna Find a Good Woman (Gonna Find a Good Man)"

Delbert McClinton moved to Nashville in the mideighties, and gradually, he began turning up on "Nashville Now" and "Texas Connection" and some of the other Nashville Network shows. And we figured it's our book, we can include him if we want to, but his relationship to the country establishment, over the course of a long and impressive career, has been a nodding one at best.

Actually, we suggested to him, it might be said that the main justification for including you in a book on country music is that you're white.

"Well," he said, chuckling, "country music is my birthright. I grew up in West Texas, and that should qualify me. Although I should qualify that by saying I don't think my music is anything in particular. It's a combination, it's American music. It's a combination of everything I loved growing up, and each kind of music hit me like a sledgehammer when I started hearing it.

"I grew up on country music in Lubbock in the forties, and then in Fort Worth. I listened to Little Jimmy Dickens and Hank Williams and Patti Page, and an awful lot of Bob Wills.

"I moved to Fort Worth in 1951, and then in the early fifties I started listening to the doo-wop singers: the Turbans, the

Lamplighters, the Penguins . . . you see that old stuff advertised on TV now, on CD reissues, and I'm tickled to death because it's such great music. Anyway, back in '52 I started to get into the doo-wop and R and B vocal groups big time. Then rockabilly came along. . . .

"These days, I don't listen to much radio. To tell the truth, I hate what they play on the radio. But there's still a lot of great music being made. That's why I moved to Nashville, because I wanted to sharpen up my songwriting, and the writers' community here is probably the best in the world.

"Sometimes I feel like I'm not paying enough attention to what's going on—all of a sudden Garth Brooks is the biggest thing in the world, and I still didn't know who he was. And I'm still not sure I do. I mean, I'm happy for him, more power to him, but I don't see where it's coming from."

McClinton brought some credentials with him to Nashville, songwriting and others, going back to his first R&B/rockabilly single in 1960 (as Mac Clinton). His first brush with the big time was as the harmonica player on Bruce Channel's 1962 hit, "Hey Baby." Touring Europe with Channel, he taught a young musician named John Lennon some harmonica licks—the ones that Lennon used on the Beatles' "Love Me Do."

McClinton's songs have been recorded by Emmylou Harris ("Two More Bottles of Wine," number one in 1978), the Blues Brothers, and others. His "Givin' It Up for Your Love" was a Top Ten pop hit in 1980.

Delbert had bad problems during the late seventies and early eighties, with the IRS, the bottle, drugs, divorce . . . he pulled himself together, with the help of his current love (and manager) Wendy Goldstein, and that was when he decided to make a new start in life in Nashville.

Today, McClinton speaks with a truly amazing enthusiasm about writing and performing—the enthusiasm of youth, which is not bad for a guy over fifty. "I suppose I'm still a cult figure. I hate that word, but a lot of great performers have been cult figures. I've had a wonderful career, and I still feel like a young guy who hasn't made it yet, but knows he will. And when I realize I still have that passion, it's like . . . wow. And it can always happen, as long as your heart is really in it."

In 1991, Delbert McClinton won a Grammy nomination for his duet with Bonnie Raitt, "Gonna Find a Good Woman (Gonna Find a Good Man)."

Delbert McClinton's list of the greatest songs of all time: "At Last" by Etta James; "Faded Love"; anything by Jimmy Reed; "I Wanna Be Around" by Tony Bennett.

Mel McDaniel

b. 9/6/42, Checotah, OK

Style
Ordinary

Memorable songs
"Baby's Got Her Blue Jeans On"

Frank Sullivan, who pitched for the Red Sox in the fifties and sixties, once summed up his status with the words, "I'm in the twilight of a mediocre career."

Somehow, this quote brings Mel McDaniel to mind. A long time on the scene, a lot of records on the charts, relatively few big hits—out of thirty-eight chart entries, spanning thirteen years, only nine of them made the Top Ten. And his only number one, "Baby's Got Her Blue Jeans On" (1984), was one of those songs best described as a classic mediocrity, the kind of song that's not really much good, but has an irritating catchiness that makes it linger in the mind much longer than you really want it to. Like "Jingle Bell Rock."

McDaniel first moved to Nashville from Oklahoma in the early seventies, but he wasn't quite ready for the big time yet, so he made the decision that many young hopefuls have made: to take his act out of town and work on it. In McDaniel's case, that meant way out of town . . . Alaska.

He returned to Nashville and signed with Capitol, getting his first charted single in 1976, and his first Top Ten ("Louisiana Saturday Night") five years later. His last Top Ten was "Real Good Feel Good Song" in 1988, and shortly after, Capitol dropped him. McDaniel is now recording for an independent label.

Ronnie McDowell

b. 3/26/50, Fountain Head, TN

Style
Elvis

Memorable songs
"The King Is Gone"

Ronnie McDowell has been around for over a decade; he's had two number one hits ("Older Women" in 1981 and "You're Gonna Ruin My Bad Reputation" in 1983) and a whole bunch of Top Ten songs. Although he's most closely associated with the stagnant years of the early eighties, and he's probably not a hot-hot name in the

nineties, he's still hanging on, and a lot of other performers of his musical generation can't make that statement.

Still, for all of that workmanlike, varied career that hundreds of thousands of hopeful performers would envy, Ronnie McDowell's name is inextricably intertwined with that of another: Elvis.

McDowell's ticket into the big time was a tribute song he wrote in 1977, when Elvis died. "The King Is Gone" made number thirteen on both the pop and country charts.

Later, McDowell was chosen to sing for Kurt Russell in the 1979 TV movie *Elvis*. And in 1990, as his career needed a shot in the arm, McDowell recorded an early Elvis album cut, "Paralyzed."

Reba McEntire

b. 3/28/54, Chockie, OK

Style
Cowgirl pure traditional (with some variations)

Memorable songs
"You Lie," "For My Broken Heart"

Awards
ACM—Female Vocalist 1984–87, 1990, Video 1986 ("Whoever's in New England"); CMA—Female Vocalist 1984–87, Entertainer of the Year 1986; Grammy—Country Vocal Performance–Female 1986 ("Whoever's in New England"); MCN—Female Artist 1985–89, Video 1987 ("Whoever's in New England"); TNN—Female Vocalist 1988–89; TNN/MCN—Female Artist 1991

There are two distinct halves to the Reba McEntire story, one an upbeat success story, the other the aftermath of devastation. The point of demarcation was March 16, 1991, when she and her band had just finished playing a private show for IBM in San Diego. They left the city on tour-chartered planes, one of them carrying tour manager Jim Henry and eight band members. The next morning, Reba's husband/manager Narvel Blackstock broke the news to her: the plane had crashed into a mountain, and everyone on board had been killed.

Her album and single, *For My Broken Heart,* released late in that same year, is her tribute to those who died in the crash. Talking about it and singing about it are therapy for her, she told Larry King on his CNN cable network show, shortly after the album's release: "The whole album is about the pain that people go through daily —not necessarily a plane crash. And it did help me to go out and sing about it."

Reba was born into a rodeo family. Her grandfather had been a rodeo rider. As a teenager she competed in rodeos as a barrel rider, while at the same time she was singing on the rodeo circuit with her brother Pake and sister Susie, as the Singing McEntires.

In 1974, she sang the national anthem at the National Rodeo Finals in Oklahoma and caught the attention of Red Steagall, a stockbreeder who was himself enjoying a respectable country music career in the seventies ("Lone Star Beer and Bob Wills Music" was his biggest hit). Steagall arranged for her to cut a demo tape in Nashville, and Mercury/Polygram heard it and signed her up.

Reba, newly married to rodeo champ Charlie Battles, began the process of being turned into something she wasn't. In the era of the Urban Cowboy, no one knew what to do with a real cowgirl. For the first six years of her career, she cut a bunch of records that only reached—not to be unkind—a Red Steagall plateau of success, and she fought a pitched battle to be allowed to use her own, traditional style.

She finally broke through in 1982 with her first number one hit, "Can't Even Get the Blues."

But the conflict over what she should be singing continued when she switched labels to MCA in 1984. She was initially teamed with producer Harold Shedd, whose big success had come with Alabama, and who wanted to take Reba in a pop direction, complete with strings. She won most of the battles and scored a couple more number ones, but she really came into her own with her next album, *Have I Got a Deal for You.* Jimmy Bowen, then head of MCA, took over the producing reins, along with his well-known philosophy that artists should coproduce themselves. Reba found the fullest expression, to that date, of her natural voice and talent with "Whoever's in New England," the song that won her her first Grammy—and which, curiously enough, she refuses to interpret as a cheatin' song.

"Little Rock," "What Am I Gonna Do About You," and "One Promise Too Late" all hit number one off the same album.

From that point on, she has moved to the head of the pack and stayed there. Like the Judds, she has found an audience for her traditional style that goes way beyond the traditional country audience.

It was around this time—1987—that her marriage to Battles ended, and she moved from Oklahoma to Nashville. She and her manager, Narvel Blackstock, were married in 1989; their son, Shelby Steven, was born in February 1990.

After making her point that she would

do things her own way, Reba started backing out of an unswerving commitment to traditional country, recording such songs as the Aretha Franklin/Otis Redding classic, "Respect." She didn't pursue that line, thankfully, but she did try other new things, including stretching her vocal range in her 1990 album, *Rumor Has It,* to encompass new emotional possibilities.

Also in 1990, Reba made her big-screen debut, in a sci-fi thriller called *Tremors.* She would later costar with Kenny Rogers in his TV movie *The Luck of the Draw: The Gambler Returns.*

Then, the tragedy.

Reba was devastated, but she had to go on. She took two and a half weeks off, then performed on Hollywood's Academy Awards show, where she sang Shel Silverstein's Oscar-nominated "I'm Checkin' Out (Of This Heartbreak Hotel)".

After that, it was time to get back to work. "Gary Smith, who works for Dolly Parton, helped us find a new band," she told Larry King. "They're a great bunch of people. They had a tough job, not only to fill their shoes because they're great musicians, but to have to go into that atmosphere where they knew everyone was missing [the guys who were gone].

"I never was mad at God. He's the big boy, He's the boss, and whatever He says goes. If He wanted Jim and the guys to be doing something else, that's His business. I believe they're better off where they are now."

Reba's 1988 album release was entitled simply *Reba*—a fullfillment of an early ambition she had cherished ever since seeing Dolly Parton's album *Dolly*—to be so well-known that one name would suffice.

Mike Jahn, who used to write about pop music for the formal *New York Times,* once told us about covering a Bo Diddley concert and finally rebelling against the *Times* style code when told that he'd have to refer to "Mr. Diddley." We ran into the same problem in 1986, when we reviewed *Have I Got a Deal for You* for a newspaper with the same rules of style.

"Sorry, but you just can't say 'Ms. McEntire,' we told our unrelenting editor. It's 'Reba.' "

Roger Miller

b. 1/2/36, Fort Worth, TX

d. 10/25/92

Style
Idiosyncratic songwriter

Memorable songs
"King of the Road," "Dang Me"

Awards
ACM—Songwriter 1965, Man of the Year 1965, Single of the Year 1968 ("Little Green Apples"), Pioneer Award 1987; Grammy—New Country Artist 1964, Country Single, Song, Recording and Vocal Performance Male 1964 ("Dang Me"), Country Album 1964 (Dang Me/Chug-a-Lug), Contemporary (R&R) Single, Contemporary (R&R) Vocal Performance Male, Country Single, Country Vocal Performance Male, Country Song 1965 ("King of the Road"), Country Album 1965 (The Return of Roger Miller). Miller's domination of the '64 and '65 Grammys led to a revision of the rules for awards eligibility.

When Roger Miller died on October 25, 1992, the music world lost a droll and gifted guy who is not likely to be replaced. Miller was one of a kind: In fact, you had to wonder if anyone who claimed to be as eccentric as Roger Miller claimed he was could really be all that eccentric—or was it just part of a carefully orchestrated PR campaign?

In Miller's case, the image was so engaging, and the talent was so prodigious, who could possibly have cared? If a guy can define himself as the "Jekyll and Hammerstein" of songwriting, your best bet is to let him do it, and just sit back and enjoy.

Miller came to Nashville in the fifties as a songwriter and very early on made an impression with such songs as "Invitation to the Blues" for Ray Price, "Billy Bayou" for Jim Reeves, and "Big Harlan Taylor" for George Jones. He had his own first hit in 1960 with "(In the Summertime) You Don't Want My Love." After that he went to work as a drummer in Faron Young's band for a couple of years, but then broke out in his own right in 1964, when he had his first number one hit ("Dang Me"). "Dang Me" was a Top Ten hit on the pop charts, too, but Miller's real breakthrough into megastardom came a year later, with the country classic "King of the Road," which has been described to us by various journeyman singers who work the honky-tonks as "the one song that everyone always knows."

Miller became a personality, a frequent guest on TV talk shows and a regular on the Merv Griffin show. In 1966, he had his own TV show, but it didn't work out too well. Our recollection of it is of Miller picking his ear with his little finger and trying too hard to appear aw-shucks folksy.

Miller's career as a maker of hit records was actually short-lived. His last Top Ten was "Little Green Apples," a cover of a pop hit for O. C. Smith, reportedly written by Bobby Russell after someone bet him he couldn't find a rhyme for "Indianapolis."

Miller moved on to conquer other worlds, including the unlikely one of motel management (maybe not so unlikely—remember "Rooms to let, fifty cents"?). His King of the Road Motel in Nashville became a legendary Music City address, and for a while its lounge featured an up-and-coming young piano player named Ronnie Milsap.

Equally unlikely for a country singer/writer was an offer to write the score for a Broadway show. Miller turned down New York producer Rocco Landesman at first, but finally consented to read the book Landesman intended to use as the basis for the play—Mark Twain's *Huckleberry Finn*. Miller, says Otto Kitsinger in his notes to the Roger Miller retrospective album on Germany's Bear Family label, "was overcome by the way Twain's language and imagery paralleled his own rural upbringing. 'I was amazed to find that it was written in the same everyday conversation that I grew up talking. And since I write the way I talk, I realized, my gosh, I could really do this.' "

The musical, *Big River*, won seven Tony Awards on Broadway, including Best Musical. Miller also wrote the score for Walt Disney's animated version of *Robin Hood*.

Buddy Killen, the head of Tree Music, Miller's publisher, says of his songwriting (in Kitsinger's Bear Family notes): "Roger never did write a lot of volume. Up until he finally hit, he wrote about 125 or 135 songs at most, and I got every one of them recorded. I don't think there was one song that we never got recorded. That's pretty phenomenal. I don't know of any other writer who's got that."

And Miller on himself: "I just want to be remembered for what I did, a writer who tried to be creative and tried to further his own music by experimenting. I always took a great deal of pride in being original. When somebody said, 'My God, where did that come from?' that was the big payoff for me."

We muse from time to time, in this book, on legendary stars whose styles are *not* being appropriated by any of the young traditionalists. Roger Miller would be on that list, but for a very good reason: Who else could possibly do what he did?

Ronnie Milsap

b. 1/16/46, Robbinsville, NC

Style

MOR

Memorable songs

"A Legend in My Time," "Lost in the Fifties Tonight (In the Still of the Night)"

Awards

ACM—Male Vocalist 1982, Keyboard Player 1987, Song of the Year 1985 ("Lost in the Fifties/In the Still of the Night"); CMA—Male Vocalist 1974, 1976–77; Album of the Year 1975 (A Legend in My Time), 1977 (Live), 1978 (It Was Almost Like a Song), 1986 (Lost in the Fifties Tonight), Entertainer of the Year 1977; Grammy—Country Vocal Performance–Male 1974 ("Please Don't Tell Me How the Story Ends"), 1976 ("I'm a Stand by My Woman Man"), 1981 ("There's No Gettin' Over Me"), 1985 ("Lost in the Fifties Tonight/In the Still of the Night"–single), 1986 (Lost in the Fifties Tonight–album), Country Vocal Performance–Duet 1987 ("Make No Mistake, She's Mine" w/ Kenny Rogers); MCN—Most Promising Male Artist 1975

Ronnie Milsap is a skilled professional entertainer who has devoted his life to honing those skills, working hard at developing his talent, and adjusting it to fit the demands of a changing market. If Milsap had not been a country entertainer, he could as easily have been a cabaret act, singing "I've Got You Under My Skin" and "New York, New York." He could have been an arranger/bandleader for a "Tonight"-type TV show. He could have fashioned a career on the smooth end of rhythm and blues—and in fact, his first successes as a recording artist were as an R&B performer on Scepter Records, best known as the label of the Shirelles ("Dedicated to the One I Love," "Will You Still Love Me Tomorrow"). In short, he's had all the qualifications of a performer superbly talented but without a deep commitment to any particular kind of music.

The one circumstance you can't imagine, however, is Milsap not being an entertainer. But Ronnie, actually, can imagine it. He was born blind in a deeply rural, poverty-ridden section of the Smoky Mountains in North Carolina. It was a painful, abusive early life that Ronnie has described in detail in his autobiography, *Almost Like a Song*. But at the age of six, he was sent away to the Governor Morehead School for the Blind in Raleigh. "It seems almost crazy to say it," he says now, "but in some ways it's almost a blessing that I was born blind. I was totally taken out of the environment that my father's family and all the generations before me had been in. If I'd been born sighted in western North Carolina and gone through the public school system there, I certainly wouldn't be doing what I'm doing now."

Milsap got early classical music training at Morehead, and a solid education as well—after two years of junior college, he was offered a scholarship to study law at Atlanta's Emory University, but chose instead to make his commitment to music, playing piano in a number of rock and rhythm and blues bands in Atlanta and then Memphis during the sixties, doing studio work on recordings by artists like Petula Clark and Dionne Warwick. He even played piano on Elvis Presley's "Kentucky Rain."

Moving to Nashville in 1972, Milsap got a gig playing piano and singing at the King of the Road Motel, a highly popular mainstream Nashville night spot of that time owned by Roger Miller, where he was heard and discovered by Charley Pride. Pride's company took over his management and got him a deal with RCA as a country singer.

Although Milsap's earliest North Carolina memories were of country music, and he had played some country along with some of everything else in his Nashville and Memphis days, this was his first serious work in the country field, and Tom Collins, his longtime producer, went all out to give him a country sound. He first hit the charts in 1973 with "I Hate You," which made the Top Ten, and he had his first number one the next year with "Pure Love," a song written by Eddie Rabbitt. "Pure Love" was first offered to Pride, but he decided to pass on it in favor of his protégé.

"I suppose it would be easier for them to categorize my music and put it in a convenient little slot if I could do the same thing, year after year," Milsap has said. "But I just can't stay in one place. What I've done throughout the years is try to find new things, new sounds, that keep my interest up. Besides, this business is always changing, and I've always believed that if you're going to be a leader rather than a follower, you've got to take chances."

Generally, when a guy talks like that, the direction he's leading in is toward the middle of the road. And generally, that makes sense. One unvarying characteristic of a long career in the music business is that the guy who's having the career will get older rather than younger. And the raw edge of stylistic expression is generally the property of the younger self. Elvis moved from "Good Rockin' Tonight" to "My Way," Steve Winwood from "Gimme Some Lovin' " to "Higher Love."

Ronnie Milsap, as he passed thirty, went to the smoother-edged pop sounds of "It Was Almost Like a Song" and launched a crossover career that saw him place that song at number sixteen on the pop charts (it was number one country), and a number of succeeding releases in the pop midranks, with "There's No Gettin' Over Me" (1981) peaking at number five.

In 1985, Milsap's brand of MOR-pop-country disappeared from the pop charts completely in favor of a harder, younger, urban sound. Milsap moved back toward straight country with "She Keeps the Home Fires Burning," then discovered a new and even more retro direction—the doo-wop ballads of the fifties. "Lost in the Fifties Tonight" hit number one in 1985, and he has returned to that vein with the Tune Weavers' "Happy Happy Birthday Baby" and the Skyliners' "Since I Don't Have You."

Bill Monroe

b. 9/13/11, Rosine, KY

Style

Bluegrass

Memorable songs

"Molly and Tenbrooks," "Uncle Pen," "Blue Moon of Kentucky"

Awards

Grammy—Bluegrass Recording 1988 (Southern Flavor); MCN—Bluegrass Act 1980–81. Hall of Fame 1970

If there was to be only one immortal named in the pantheon of country music, you couldn't go wrong if you named Bill Monroe.

Bill and his brother Charlie Monroe put together their first group in 1928 and not long after got their first national radio exposure on "National Barn Dance" from WLS in Chicago. "Before long," as Billy Altman wrote in his notes to RCA's *Are You From Dixie? Great Country Brother Acts of the Thirties,* "their rough and tumble blend of mountain harmonies and breakneck instrumental workouts had garnered them a significant following. . . . In 1935, the brothers moved back to the Southeast, where they spent the last three years of their partnership delighting regional audiences with their radio shows and, eventually, Bluebird recordings. (The Monroes, it should be noted, almost had to be dragged into the recording studio by RCA's Eli Oberstein. Knowing how little money most other artists made from record sales—standard royalties in the thirties for country artists ranged from half a cent to a penny a record—the Monroes were dubious about the benefits of recording. It wasn't until Oberstein made them recognize that records could bring them into new markets where they could generate more live work, and thus command higher performance fees, that they agreed to sign.)

It's generally agreed that the birth of what we know as recorded country music came on August 4, 1927, when a record producer named Ralph Peer, who worked for the Victor Talking Machine Company, recorded both Jimmie Rodgers, "the Singing Brakeman," and the Carter Family, in a hotel room in Bristol, Tennessee. Rodgers got $50 per song. His records have sold in the millions over the years and are now available on remastered CDs. Peer recorded a number of "mountain musicians" in those Bristol sessions, but the most important—the ones who started a new genre of music—were Rodgers and the Carter Family. Rodgers had promised Peer that he knew lots of old folk songs, but the truth was, he knew virtually nothing but Tin Pan Alley standards, so he and his sister-in-law had to start writing some original material. The singer/songwriter, the cornerstone of modern country music, was born.

During the thirties, country music continued to develop an audience. In 1938, when Bill and Charlie Monroe parted company, each was able to form his own band. Bill called his the Bluegrass Boys, and the name became generic—especially after 1945, when Monroe added banjo virtuoso Earl Scruggs, and Scruggs added the concept of using the banjo as a lead instrument to Monroe's guitar-and-mandolin sound. Scruggs and guitarist Lester Flatt left Monroe in 1945 to form their own band, the Foggy Mountain Boys, but their music, and the music of everyone who has followed in their wake, is forever called bluegrass.

Jimmie Rodgers died in 1933 and has since been inducted into not only the Country Music but also the Rock and Roll Hall of Fame. Mother Maybelle, last of the first-generation Carter Family, died in 1978. Her daughters Anita, Helen, and June (Mrs. Johnny Cash) carry on the family tradition, performing as the Carter Family. June's daughter Carlene Carter, on her way to a country music comeback in

1990, performed for a while with the family group.

Flatt and Scruggs disbanded in 1969, and Lester Flatt died in 1979. Earl Scruggs's restless musical genius, and his desire to work with his sons, led him to move on from bluegrass to other musical forms with the Earl Scruggs Revue. He had success, but never the same impact as he had with his Flatt and Scruggs bluegrass recordings. He's now mostly retired; his son Randy is a successful Nashville producer.

But Bill Monroe keeps going. He's had health problems, but as the nineties rolled around, he was still playing bluegrass, still recording bluegrass, and he had lost none of that wonderful tenor voice and virtuoso mandolin style that defined one of America's most important musical styles.

Lorrie Morgan

b. 6/27/59, Nashville, TN (*Loretta Lynn Morgan—but it's just a coincidence*)

Style

Torchy

Memorable songs

"Out of Your Shoes"

Awards

CMA—Vocal Event 1990 (w/ Keith Whitley)

Lorrie Morgan's life is a model for the nineties, a story straight out of Oprah or Sally Jessy: twenty-eight years in the shadow of one powerful man after another, then finally stepping forward to take charge of her life and her career.

The daughter of George Morgan, an Opry regular and country star of the fifties (his "Candy Kisses" went to number one in 1949), Lorrie grew up backstage and made her first appearance on the Opry at age thirteen.

George Morgan was a typical country star of his generation—four years of solid chart activity, a few sporadic hits over the next few years, then two decades of playing the Opry and touring, playing "Candy Kisses" and "Roomful of Roses" to an audience that was aging right along with him. He was still on the road when he died in 1975.

Lorrie had been touring with her father for about a decade by that time, as the cute little girl, and then the cute ingenue, on the George Morgan Show. This is good experience in many ways, but it's not necessarily the best route to forging a distinctive personal style. After Morgan died, she continued touring with his band, but it wasn't the same, and things started to fall apart. "I drove thousands of miles with just me and my mom or me and one musician," she recalls. "There were times when I couldn't get through a show without literally crying because the band was so bad."

Later, she was hired by George Jones as his girl singer, opening the show, singing backup and a couple of duets with Jones.

In 1985, she signed her first major-label record deal and became the youngest member of the Grand Ole Opry. The following year, she married Keith Whitley, whom she'd met backstage at the Opry.

Lorrie's career took a backseat to Whitley's for the next few years as he suddenly exploded as one of country music's bright new stars. But Whitley was a troubled soul, a destructive drinker, and he died in 1989 of an alcohol overdose—ironically, just as Morgan's solo career was starting to happen again. In 1988, she had signed a new contract with RCA, and her first single, "Trainwreck of Emotion," was released that winter.

During 1989, "Out of Your Shoes" went to number one for Morgan— whether it was spurred on by the publicity surrounding Keith Whitley's death is hard to say, but there were two more hit singles off that album, and another successful album, *Something in Red,* in 1991.

"It's true that at different points in my life I was defined in terms of those men, and I was proud of it at the time," Morgan says. "I was proud to be George Morgan's daughter. If he'd been a creep, maybe I'd feel different. But he was a wonderful man and I was proud to be his daughter. I was also proud to sing with one of my idols, George Jones. At that point in my career that was a great title for me. And then being in love with Keith, I was proud to be his wife. You know, Keith wasn't a powerful star when I married him—he lived in a little one-bedroom filthy apartment down on Music Row and didn't have any money and was barely gettin' by. Keith's power came in the year after I married him, which we were both real proud of and thankful for, but I've always gone for love, not power. And even today, if he were still here, it wouldn't bother me at all if someone said, 'This is Keith Whitley's wife,' because that and the others were titles that I was proud of.

"Keith was the first man I ever really loved in my life, and I woke up one morning and he was gone. After he passed away, I didn't even know if I wanted to face the day. Maybe if I hadn't had the children, I just would have withered away. But I knew there were bills to be paid, and I was the sole provider."

Morgan has paid tribute in song to each of the men in her life. "I'm Completely Satisfied With You," in 1979, was an electronic duet with her late father. "A Picture of Me (Without You)" is her remake of a George Jones classic. ("A last-minute decision," she recalls. "We were in the studio, ready to wrap up the album, and Norro Wilson, who'd cowritten the song, dropped by and said by the way, have you ever thought of . . . and he ran and got a copy of it while we were on our lunch break, and we just did it.") Her duet with Keith Whitley, "Till a Tear Becomes a Rose," with her voice dubbed onto a demo tape of Keith's and released after his death, became a CMA award winner in 1990.

Lorrie Morgan's list of the greatest songs of all time: "Misty," "Miami My Amy," "Autumn Leaves," "Unforgettable"—"I'd love to do an album of pop ballads sometime, but we don't think the time is right at this state of my career"—"That's Where I Wanna Take Our Love and Settle Down," an album cut of Keith's.

Gary Morris

b. 12/7/48, Forth Worth, TX

Style
Well, there aren't that many country singers who have sung grand opera on the New York stage.

Memorable songs
"Wind Beneath My Wings"

Awards
ACM—Song of the Year 1983 ("Wind Beneath My Wings")

Can a guy who's starred in a Broadway musical (*Les Misérables*), not to mention an opera (*La Bohème*, at New York City's Public Theater), not to mention playing a recurring character on "The Colbys," a spin-off series from TV's glitzier-than-glitz "Dynasty," really still be country?

Maybe not. Morris, who was previously associated with the slicked-up, contemporary country style anyway, is sounding more and more like Robert Goulet on his post-Broadway albums. "I'm not going to bat my brains anymore about country music and the industry and where I fit into it," he told *USA Today* in 1988, in one of his *Les Mis* promotional interviews.

Well, what the hey. The guy has his career going, and if country music programmers and audiences decide to ease him off to the side, it will frankly not be as great a loss to the country tradition as some other performers who've been shunted out of the picture for being too hard-edged or too hard to pigeonhole.

Morris came to Broadway in a fairly haphazard way. He was not only untrained as a classical singer, he had never even heard of *La Bohème*'s composer Giacomo Puccini when he landed the role in 1984 opposite Linda Ronstadt, around whom the production was being built. He landed the *Les Mis* role, the most coveted part on Broadway at that time, when he dropped into the William Morris Agency in New York to let executives there know that he was interested in trying something different.

He came to Nashville in much the same way. He performed in shows for the 1976 Jimmy Carter presidential campaign, and when President Carter invited him to perform at the White House, he had one of the most visible audition stages ever offered to a performer.

Morris began his career as a charted country artist in 1980 and in 1983 recorded "The Wind Beneath My Wings." It wasn't his biggest hit, only reaching number three on the country charts, but it's gone on to become his most famous song, thanks to its association with the space program. He's had four number one singles on his own, and two huge TV tie-in hits with Crystal Gayle, "Makin' Up for Lost Time (The 'Dallas' Lovers' Song)" and "Another World," the theme for the popular daytime soap opera.

Michael Martin Murphey

b. 3/14/45, Dallas, TX

Style

Cowboy

Memorable songs

"Wildfire," "Wild Ripplin' Waters"

Awards

ACM—New Male Vocalist 1982

Michael Martin Murphey celebrates two central experiences in his work: the satisfactions of home, hearth, and family in his 1987 album, *Americana,* which featured the number one hit "A Long Line of Love," and such songs as "Talkin' to the Wrong Man," a duet with his son, Ryan; and the lure of the open range.

The home and hearth songs are affecting, if a little too sweet. The open-range songs are just about the definitive songs in this genre, from his own compositions such as "Wildfire" to his faithful and deeply personal interpretations of such cowboy classics as "Home on the Range," "When the Work's All Done This Fall,"

"Old Chisholm Trail," and our personal favorite, "Wild Ripplin' Water." All of those came from his 1990 release, *Cowboy Songs,* which also includes a magnificent new song, "Cowboy Pride," by the Canadian master songwriter of the Western experience, Ian Tyson, and a moving version of a song you generally think of as rousing, rather than moving. The song is "Yellow Rose of Texas," and in his informative liner notes, Jim Bob Tinsley gives its little-known history: "Dating from the era of the Texas Revolution is this song about Texas heroine Emily D. West, a mulatto slave bound to Col. James Morgan, whose plantation bordered the San Jacinto River. The defeat of the Mexican army was directly connected with Gen. Santa Anna's preoccupation with this domestic girl."

Murphey grew up in Texas but migrated to Los Angeles in the sixties, where he went to UCLA and started a career as a pop singer/songwriter. His own band, the Lewis and Clark expedition, had minor chart success in the midsixties, and his songs were recorded by such groups as the Nitty Gritty Dirt Band (in their LA hippie days) and even the Monkees. His biggest success in that era was a concept album, *The Ballad of Calico,* which he wrote for Kenny Rogers.

His own career really came alive after he moved back to Texas in 1971. He scored his first hit the following year with "Geronimo's Cadillac," a song that was adopted by the Native American civil rights movement as an anthem. In 1975 he had his biggest pop successes, "Wildfire" and "Carolina in the Pines."

Murphey now lives in the Taos, New Mexico, where he maintains an interest in the environment and in Western history, both from the cowboy and Native American point of view. His annual West Fest, held in Copper Mountain, Colorado, celebrates this segment of Americana, with arts, crafts, and folk tales as well as music.

Anne Murray

b. 10/20/46, Springhill, Nova Scotia, Canada

Style

Pop

Memorable songs

"Snowbird," "Just Another Woman in Love"

Springhill, Nova Scotia, is best known for the folk song about a mine disaster (sung by both Pete Seeger and Canadian Gordon Lightfoot). It is also the birthplace of a couple of legends of early country music, Hank Snow and Wilf "Montana Slim" Carter, neither of whom Anne Murray listened to in her formative years ("My first influences were the wonderful pop singers of the fifties, like Rosemary Clooney and Jo Stafford").

And it's the birthplace of Anne Murray, once called by the *Toronto Daily Star* "as much as anything we have in Canada that can be considered a national shrine."

If so, she's the only shrine that's as wholesome as a fresh-picked apple, with a straightforward, no-holds-barred kind of attitude (she once told Prime Minister and Mrs. Trudeau that looking wholesome doesn't make her a goody-goody, and that under her conservative clothes she's "a mass of hickeys").

There's not much "Hee Haw" about Anne Murray. She's an honors graduate of the University of New Brunswick, and her ambition was to teach physical education. "I really wanted to be a hockey player, but that wasn't in the cards for a girl." She considers herself the world's foremost hockey fan, and there's a permanent seat with her name engraved on it at Maple Leaf Stadium in Toronto.

Murray minored in classical music in college. On a summer break, "desperate for funds to buy a car," she auditioned for a Canadian TV show, "Sing Along Jamboree." Their producer insisted she cut a record. "I thought he was crazy. Around the bonfire, I was pretty good—but to think about being a recording artist was something for people in Hollywood."

Nonetheless, she cut a record. A visiting Capitol Records producer heard it, and her monster hit, "Snowbird," was released on Capitol the next year. Its light, airy melody was on everyone's lips. It scored on both country and pop charts in America, Canada, and England. It provided her with two potential markets—and for a long time, she walked that tightrope. Onstage, she makes it clear to audiences that she refuses to be tied down to any genre, and she proves it by singing across the spectrum. A proud Canadian, she has always tried to make a point of introducing Canadian songwriters on her albums.

Recently, Anne severed a twenty-year association with Capitol—with mutual respect, she says. She fits in a touring schedule around school-age kids, but she's still much in demand.

Nancy Griffith

Lyle Lovett

K. T. Olsin

Lorrie Morgan

Patty Loveless

Gary Gershoff/Retna Ltd.

George Jones and Elvis Costello

Robert Mathieu/Retna Ltd.

Beth Gwinn/Retna Ltd.

Joe Diffie and Doug Stone

Beth Gwinn/Retna Ltd.

Pam Tillis

Ricky Van Shelton

Beth Gwinn/Retna Ltd.

Beth Gwinn/Retna Ltd.

Lisa Hartman and Clint Black

Dwight Yoakum

Larry Busacca/Retna Ltd.

Beth Gwinn/Retna Ltd.

John Carter Cash, June Carter Cash, Johnny Cash, Rosanne Cash, and Rodney Crowell

John Anderson

Billy Ray Cyrus

Travis Tritt

Alan Jackson

Randy Travis

Carl Perkins

Garth Brooks

Reba McEntire

Beth Gwinn/Retna Ltd.

Kentucky Headhunters

Gary Gershoff/Retna Ltd.

Alabama with disc jockey Lee Arnold

Ricky Scaggs

David Redfern/Retna Ltd.

Suzy Bogguss

Beth Gwinn/Retna Ltd.

Vince Gill

Rodney Crowell

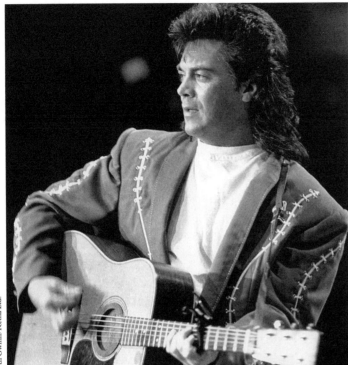

Marty Stuart

Steve Earle

Tanya Tucker

Willie Nelson

b. 4/30/33, Fort Worth, TX

Style

Bob Wills meets Frank Sinatra, Opry meets Woodstock

Memorable songs

"Blue Eyes Crying in the Rain," "On the Road Again"

Awards

ACM—Entertainer of the Year 1979, Album, Single of the Year 1982 (Always on My Mind), Single of the Year 1984 ("To All the Girls I've Loved Before" w/ Julio Iglesias), Song/Single of the Year 1985 ("Highwayman"); CMA—Album, Single of the Year 1982 (Always on My Mind), Vocal Duo 1976 (w/ Waylon Jennings), 1983 (w/ Merle Haggard), 1984 (w/ Julio Iglesias), Single of the Year 1976 ("Good Hearted Woman" w/ Waylon Jennings), Album of the Year 1976 (Wanted—The Outlaws w/ Waylon Jennings, Jessi Colter, Tompall Glaser), Entertainer of the Year 1979; Grammy—Country Vocal Performance–Male 1975 ("Blue Eyes Crying in the Rain"), 1978 ("Georgia on My Mind"), 1982 ("Always on My Mind"), Country Vocal Performance–Duo or Group 1978 ("Mamas, Don't Let Your Babies Grow Up to Be Cowboys" w/ Waylon Jennings), Country Song 1980 ("On the Road Again")

When we began reviewing country music on a regular basis for a newspaper, sometime in the eighties, our editor said, "Look, you don't have to review every Willie Nelson album that comes out."

But we did. It's true there have been a lot of them. But we reviewed Willie singing with Lefty, and Willie singing with Roger Miller, and Willie singing with Webb Pierce, and with Merle and Waylon and Ray Charles and Julio Iglesias and Ray Price and David Allan Coe and Brenda Lee and Kris Kristofferson and Johnny Cash and Leon Russell (Nelson holds the *Billboard* chart record for most duet partners with twenty, according to Joel Whitburn), and we reviewed Willie singing such standards as "It's a Wonderful World" and his own compositions such as "On the Road Again" and the works of such great modern songwriters as Townes Van Zandt's "Pancho and Lefty" and Steve Goodman's "City of New Orleans."

What the hell, we said in our defense at one point, Willie may be overdoing it a touch, and we're not saying every cut on every album was an inspired selection or an inspired rendition, but like everyone else, he won't be around forever. Someday that wonderful voice will be gone, and will people then look back and say, "Hot damn, I wish there were a few less Willie Nelson albums"?

We don't think so. Does anyone wish the Marx Brothers hadn't made *The Big Store* or *A Night in Casablanca*? They may not have been very good movies, but the

Marx Brothers won't be making any more, and they do have a few golden moments. Which Miles Davis albums would you unrecord, which Sherlock Holmes stories would you unwrite, which Picasso drawings would you erase?

The resistance to Nelson's career is legendary. He first came to Nashville in 1960 and began to make a name for himself as a songwriter. A name, but not necessarily a fortune. He sold all the rights to one early song, "Family Bible," for $50, and another, "Night Life," for $150. "Family Bible" was a hit for both Claude Gray and George Jones; "Night Life," recorded many times and still a staple of Willie's live shows, was first cut by Ray Price. A decade later, Price would be one of the first to record a Kris Kristofferson song.

Nelson made some money on Patsy Cline's version of "Crazy" and Faron Young's "Hello Walls." Crew-cut like George Jones and billed as "Little Willie Nelson," he had a Top Ten hit in 1962 with a song called "Touch Me," but after that, his career sank into a treadmill to oblivion. Nelson was difficult, and they're not always comfortable with difficult in Nashville. They can sometimes deal with difficult to handle (George Jones comes to mind), but not with difficult to categorize. "Nearly everybody realized how good Willie was," says Tompall Glaser (in *Willie,* by Nelson and Bud Shrake), "but the people who ran the music business in Nashville would just keep saying, 'Well, I don't know if Willie is country or not. Is Willie country? Because if he ain't country, then the music he plays won't get played on the country music stations. If he don't get played on the country music stations, then he won't make money for us. And if he don't make money for us, the hell with Willie Nelson. Who needs him?'

"It was such a major concern—are you country enough for Nashville? If you didn't fit in, if you didn't do their idea of country material, whether it suited your sound or not, then you weren't worth a dime."

The sound in Nashville back then, of course, was the Nashville Sound, sweetened with strings, skillfully produced to soothe rather than to challenge.

Finally, frustrated, Nelson went back to Texas, where his legend continued to grow, even if his record sales didn't. In 1973, he held his first Fourth of July picnic in Dripping Springs, Texas, and for the first time, brought an audience of hippies and rockers together with a country crowd. Willie was hip, although as yet it was only the hip avant-garde who knew it.

Some of the leading players in that hip avant-garde sat in on Willie's 1973 session for Atlantic Records, players such as Leon Russell, David Bromberg, and Doug Sahm (later of the Texas Tornadoes). That session became the *Shotgun Willie* album, and while it didn't yield any hits either, people were writing about it and talking about it.

Then Atlantic closed up its country division, and Willie's career was stalled again. He got one more chance with Columbia in 1974, where, as Tom Roland writes in *The Billboard Book of Number One Country Hits,* "he was given 'creative control.'

"He had no idea what do with that control, though, until a drive from Colorado to Texas. He and his wife, Connie, formulated a concept album about a preacher in the Old West based around the song 'Red Headed Stranger,' which Willie had first heard while working as a disc jockey in the midfifties. The album mixed older songs with several Willie wrote to tie the story together, and he cut it in three days for $20,000. . . . Columbia was less than pleased with the results.

" 'They thought it wasn't finished,' Willie told Frederick Burger in *Billboard*. 'They thought it was underproduced, too sparse, all those things. Even though they didn't like it, they had already paid me a bunch of money for it, so they had to release it under my contract. And since they had put money into it, they had to promote it.' "

Red Headed Stranger yielded Nelson's first number one hit, "Blue Eyes Crying in the Rain." More than that, it made him—and the music and lifestyle that he represented—important.

Willie Nelson is so thoroughly the honest voice of America—tough, sincere, straightforward—that it's hard today to imagine a time when the country music industry had to catch up with him. But that was how it was, and that's what happened with *Red Headed Stranger*. And with the release of *Wanted—the Outlaws*, cofeaturing Waylon Jennings and Tompall Glaser in 1976, everyone in the world knew who Willie Nelson was.

His Willie Nelson Picnics became gigantic, the Opry and Woodstock rolled into one, Texas-style. Willie became a successful actor—and a good one, holding his own with Robert Redford in *The Electric Horseman* and James Caan in *Thief* (an unusual, masterful performance as an old jailbird).

When he cut *Stardust,* an album of Tin Pan Alley standards, in 1978, he moved beyond country music legend to all-purpose American icon. From there it was an easy step to beloved elder statesman, able even to unite world cultures with his Julio Iglesias duets.

Beloved by everyone, it seemed, but the Internal Revenue Service. In 1991, they came knocking on the door of the man who had created Farm Aid to save the American farmer from, among other things, the IRS-driven auctioneers. He was stripped of nearly everything he owned for back taxes, and his next album, called *The IRS Tapes,* was dedicated to squaring himself with the government.

New Grass Revival

SAM BUSH
b. Bowling Green, KY

JOHN COWAN
b. Louisville, KY

BELA FLECK
b. New York, NY

PAT FLYNN
b. Redondo Beach, CA

Style

New grass

Memorable songs

"Friday Night in America," "I'm Down"

In 1991, New Grass Revival broke up after seventeen years. Banjo virtuoso Bela Fleck wanted to play other kinds of music, and the group decided to pack it in rather than replace him. But in their heyday, after Fleck and Pat Flynn joined the group in 1981, they were the hottest band in contemporary bluegrass, one of the hottest bands in all of bluegrass. They worked steadily—over two hundred dates a year. "We were a pretty healthy little small business," John Cowan tells us. At their peak, they took in . . .

"Forty to sixty grand a year, which is pretty healthy for guys playin' music on the road. We never had a bus—that just burns your money up. We took an old bread truck and converted it and traveled in that. Before that, we had some really lean years."

This is the economics of one of the best—and one of the most recognized—bands on the fringes of stardom, which is something to think about when you wonder why it is that those precious few entertainment and sports figures who make it to the top tend to want all the money they can negotiate for.

"But I'm proud of the work we did," Cowan says. "And I'm proud of the fact that I shared the same stage with . . . that I actually played with guys like Bill Monroe, Doc Watson, the Osborne Brothers. I feel so fortunate to have been exposed to that."

We talk about current stars—good, talented singers whose work we both admire—who don't have that connection with the country tradition, some of whom don't know exactly who Bob Wills is. "I'm not really bemoaning that," Cowan says. "It just seems kind of strange to me that there are so many people in this business who just have no sense of their history. It's like if you're a successful architect, I don't think you could really do anything to advance your profession without knowing who Frank Lloyd Wright was. Does this bother you at all?"

Yes, we have to admit. It does.

New Grass Revival was founded by Sam Bush, a long-haired sixties hippie from Bowling Green, Kentucky, who was an extraordinary instrumental prodigy (mandolin and fiddle) and a passionate lover of bluegrass. Bush wanted to combine traditional bluegrass styles with his generation's music—Jefferson Airplane, Leon Russell, Eric Clapton. Their first album, Cowan says, "kind of took the bluegrass world by storm. It had 'Prince of Peace' by Eric Clapton on it. They used an electric bass, which was, you know, oooooh! Plus these guys were all dope-smokin' hippie radical leftist pigs."

Adding Cowan to the group didn't make them more traditional. John was a rocker, totally unfamiliar with bluegrass—he joined the group because it beat working at the local car wash, and he became the Robert Plant, the Roger Daltrey, of bluegrass. The group toured with Leon Russell, but as weird as they were, they were basically a bluegrass group.

The older bluegrass musicians hated them at first. "We looked like Charles Manson, and we were screwing with their music. They thought of us as like the Sex Pistols or something. They thought we were dealing drugs to the audience, which of course we weren't. Bill Monroe wouldn't appear onstage with us. Over the years, that changed. Young people started going to the traditional bluegrass festivals, the alternative bluegrass festivals started springing up with us and Earl Scruggs Review and Nitty Gritty Dirt Band. And gradually, we all started getting together in the same festivals—the best of the traditionalists and the best of the weirdos."

Cowan has a few regrets about breaking up the group—"When we finally signed on with a major label, with Capitol, and we made some really good records that might have been commercial, Capitol was one of the worst labels in Nashville, completely impotent in terms of what they could do with radio. I still wonder what might have happened if we'd stayed on the label after Jimmy Bowen took over. But it was, okay, Bela's leaving, what are we going to do now? Hire a drummer and sound like Restless Heart? We decided it was time to move on to other things."

Sam Bush is now a member of Emmylou Harris's Nash Ramblers. Bela Fleck is playing his own music, somewhere between bluegrass, jazz fusion, and New Age. Pat Flynn is teaching guitar, going back to school, and helping to care for his first child. John Cowan was taken the invaluable lessons of New Grass back to rock and roll, in a group he's formed with kids twenty years younger than he is, trying to bring the love and brotherhood/sisterhood values of the sixties to a contemporary rock scene he sees as distressingly macho and intolerant.

John Cowan's list of the greatest songs of all time: "Lovesick Blues," "Wayfaring Stranger," by Bill Monroe, "Dark As a Dungeon," by Merle Travis, Bob Dylan's "All Along the Watchtower" as performed by Jimi Hendrix.

Juice Newton

b. 2/18/52, Lakehurst, NJ (*Judy Kay Newton*)

Style
Pop

Memorable songs
"Queen of Hearts," "The Sweetest Thing"

Awards
ACM—New Female Vocalist 1981; Grammy—Country Vocal Performance–Female 1982 ("Break It to Me Gently")

Like Kathy Baillie or Mary-Chapin Carpenter, Juice Newton is a Jersey girl. Like them, she didn't come from a country background or a country-music-loving family, she never set out to sing country music, but she found that whatever she was singing, people thought it was country.

Raised in Virginia Beach, Virginia, Juice went to California at age twenty-two to pursue a singing career. With her boyfriend, Otha Young, she started a band called Silver Spur, which played the Los Angeles club circuit and released a couple of unsuccessful albums on RCA.

Using Vince Gill's definition of an overnight success (see entry), Newton was certainly no overnight success. She signed with RCA in 1975, and her first single, "Love Is a Word," barely tickled the bottom of the charts in '76. After that, she went three years with no recognition at all.

Dropping the Silver Spur moniker and signing with Capitol, she had a few minor hits in 1979 and '80, still nothing to build a career on. Then recognition finally hit big with a remake of "Angel of the Morning," which had been a pop hit for Merilee Rush. It was a pop and country hit for Newton, and in '81 and '82 she had a flurry of major success on both charts: "Angel of the Morning," "Queen of Hearts," "The Sweetest Thing (I've Ever Known)" (her first number one), and "Love's Been a Little Bit Hard on Me." Except for "The Sweetest Thing," those were all stronger in the pop than the country market.

After that, Juice faded as a pop star, but perhaps for country audiences, the stigma was there, and while she continued to have hit records through the eighties, she hasn't had that consistent success—one hit after another—except for a period of about a year and a half in 1985–86.

And you don't hear her talked about the way they talk about other artists with tremendous talent who've paid their dues, such as Vince Gill or Rodney Crowell. Maybe it's because that kind of admiration is reserved for guys. Maybe it's because she has—undeservedly—an Urban Cowboy stigma, with all those pop hits during That Era.

The Nitty Gritty Dirt Band

JEFF HANNA
b. 7/10/47, Detroit, MI

JIMMY FADDEN
b. 3/9, Long Beach, CA

JIMMY IBBOTSON
b. 1/21, PA

ROB CARPENTER
b. 12/26, Philadelphia, PA

Style

Country rock

Memorable songs:

"Dance Little Jean," "Fishin' in the Dark"

Awards:

*CMA—Album of the Year 1989 (*Will the Circle Be Unbroken, Vol. II*); Grammy —Country Vocal Performance–Duo or Group (*Will the Circle Be Unbroken, Vol. II*) 1989, Bluegrass Recording ("The Valley Road" w/ Bruce Hornsby) 1989*

We asked Jeff Hanna about his 1971 history-making *Will the Circle Be Unbroken* album, in which the Nitty Gritty Dirt Band, then a bunch of scruffy hippies from California, did a series of duets with such country music legends as the Carter Family and Roy Acuff. We asked him how

things have changed in the intervening twenty years between that album and their 1991 release, *Will the Circle Be Unbroken,* Vol. II. Then we sat back and listened.

"Country rock wasn't part of the mainstream then. All sorts of hybrid things have come out of Nashville since then, the New Grass sound that New Grass Revival played a strong role in, the legitimization of country rock by bands like Alabama. There were always vocal quartets and stuff in country music, but they created a place for self-contained bands. Now you hear them on country radio every day.

"When we cut the first album there was more of a generational and cultural gap, and there were all kinds of fences to scoot over. When we did the second, most of those barriers were down.

"In recent years, the role of big-arrangement, pop-sounding records has diminished, which I think is a healthy trend. The traditional movement is healthy, as long as it doesn't become some sort of cloning process.

"But I don't really think that's happening. For every act that plays it safe, I see really exciting acts breaking through—Rodney Crowell, Vince Gill, Marty Stuart. These are all people who've been waiting in the wings, for as much as fifteen years in Rodney's case. To country music's credit, it's been one of the most flexible formats in radio in the past few years.

"Still, the healthiest kind of radio to me is on these alternative stations that'll play Mary-Chapin Carpenter, us, Rosanne Cash, John Hiatt, Stevie Ray Vaughan— that reminds me of the radio I grew up listening to in the sixties, when radio actually meant something. I sound like some crotchety old guy, don't I? Like my dad telling stories about walking ten miles to school through the snow.

"When we were around southern California during the birth of country rock—Poco, the Flying Burrito Brothers, Linda Ronstadt, and the guys who eventually became the Eagles—my heroes were Buddy Holly and Eddie Cochran and Little Richard and Chuck Berry, and of course early Elvis and Jerry Lee. I used to think, wouldn't it have been great to have been there. And now there are kids who say the same to me about hanging out in a bar with Neil Young—it's kind of strange, you know? But I think that the healthiest thing in music is change, and I think there's a lot of that going on right now. I've met most of these young guys and I think they're legit. I don't think these guys are sitting around saying, 'I want to be the next Clint Black.' They may be getting their chance because they remind industry people of . . . you know, it's ironic, guys in the industry aren't sitting around saying, 'Who's going to be the next George Jones?' They're saying, 'Who's going to be the next Garth?' And next year it'll be, 'Who's going to be the next Mark Chesnutt?' But there's plenty of great music—it's the marketing that's a little suspect to me.

"On that first album we were wondering what we were doing there. We were in there with legends, but they weren't acting like legends. They were just regular, warm, generous people, and everyone was having a ball. As far as age goes, we were like New Kids on the Block when we cut that record—we were incredibly young by country music standards. I think the legends got a kick out of us—these long-haired, bearded hippie types from southern California who loved this music and knew something about it. Because it wasn't a manipulated deal—we really loved that stuff, and we brought enthusiasm to it. And people from all ages and all walks of life have told me that's the first country music album they ever bought. That—and the scene in LA in the late sixties—are nice bits of history to have been part of."

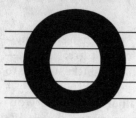

Oak Ridge Boys

DUANE ALLEN
b. 4/29/43, Taylortown, TX

JOE BONSALL
b. 5/18/48, Philadelphia, PA

RICHARD STERBAN
b. 4/24/43, Camden, NJ

STEVE SANDERS
b. 9/17/52, Richland, GA

William Lee Golden joined the group in 1965, left it in 1987.

Style

Slick harmony, originally gospel

Memorable songs

"Elvira," "American Made"

Awards

ACM—Vocal Duet/Group 1978; Album of the Year 1978 (Y'All Come Back Saloon), Single of the Year 1981 ("Elvira"); CMA—Vocal Group 1978, Single of the Year 1981 ("Elvira"), Instrumental Group 1978, 1986 (Oak Ridge Boys Band); Grammy—Gospel Performance Other Than Soul Gospel 1970 ("Talk About the Good Times"), Gospel Performance 1974 ("The Baptism of Jesse Taylor"), Gospel Performance, Traditional 1977 ("Just a Little Talk With Jesus"), Country Vocal Performance-Duo or Group 1981 ("Elvira"); MCN—Band 1979 (Oak Ridge Boys Band), TNN—Vocal Group 1988–89

The Oak Ridge Boys have the longest history of any current act in country music, though not with their current personnel. This most sophisticated of contemporary country groups began in 1945 as a hillbilly and hillbilly gospel act called Wally Fowler and his Georgia Clodhoppers. One of the Clodhoppers' earliest and, as it turned out, most reliable gigs was the top-secret, top-security government plant in Oak Ridge, Tennessee—the plant in which the first atomic bombs were being built. The group quickly became the most popular of the acts brought in to entertain the workers and eventually took its identification from the plant, changing its name to the Oak Ridge Quartet.

The group joined the Grand Ole Opry in 1945, but at the same time they were starting to phase out country in favor of a total commitment to gospel. Through numerous personnel changes—including the complete disbanding and reconstruction of the group in 1946 and 1956—they became, and remain, one of the most popular gospel groups of all time.

The current version of the Oaks dates from 1965, when William Lee Golden joined the group, and 1966, when Duane Allen came on board. Between the two of them, they defined the future of the Oak Ridge Boys—Golden the visionary, and Allen the rock-solid organizing force who held the group together even when times were desperate.

Throughout the late sixties and into the seventies, the Oaks' reputation in gospel grew, and so did a storm of controversy around them. The gospel world had its rigid fashion code of marcelled hair and string ties and overlapping shirt collars: as a parody of Townes Van Zandt's "Pancho and Lefty" put it:

Pancho was a Baptist boy
His home was down in Tennessee
He wore his collar outside his coat
For all the honest world to see

The Oak Ridge Boys wore turtlenecks and bell-bottoms and long hair; they had a drummer in their band playing a beat that sounded suspiciously like that rock and roll Southern preachers had been warning their flocks about for so long. While their commitment was still to gospel, they found themselves getting more and more resistance from the gospel community. As Joe Bonsall, who joined the group in 1973 (following Richard Sterban, who came on board in 1972), recalls it, the Oaks gradually found themselves getting more and more discouraged by the hypocrisy of the gospel business, and its criticism of them because they brought their gospel message to secular venues.

Finally, at William Lee Golden's urging, they made the break and moved from gospel to country.

But Golden's vision was a difficult, painful time before its realization, and for a few years the group was held together by Duane Allen's leadership—and Johnny Cash's support, both moral and financial. A 1975 record contract with Columbia yielded nothing, and they were soon dropped.

ABC/Dot (which later became MCA) took a chance on the Oaks in 1977, and it paid off. Their first single, "Y'All Come Back Saloon," made number three on the country charts, and by 1978 they had their first number one, "I'll Be True to You."

It was the eighties, though, that saw the massive breakthrough for the Oak Ridge Boys. They came into 1980 with two number one singles, Rodney Crowell's "Leavin' Louisiana in the Broad Daylight" and "Trying to Love Two Women." Then in 1981, they were pitched a song that had been around for fifteen years and had been cut by a number of acts, including Rodney Crowell in the days when he couldn't get anyone to listen to him. Kenny Rogers and the First Edition had it on a pop album, and the song's writer, Dallas Frazier, had also put out a pop version of the song he had been inspired to write one afternoon as he drove down Elvira Street in Nashville, Tennessee.

"Elvira" was a sensation. Almost cartoonishly catchy, it created a sort of synthesis of barbershop, gospel, and doo-wop harmonies, with an extravagantly rolling bass part and an exuberantly rocking sense of humor. On its way to platinum, it hit number five on the pop charts and of course number one on the country charts.

At around the same time, William Lee Golden was undergoing a transformation of his own. Always one to march to a different drummer, Golden awoke to a new spiritual understanding that included forsaking the taking of scissors to any part of his hair.

The Oaks have always prided themselves on their individualism. They don't dress alike onstage, they maintain their separate images and personalities; to an outsider, the hairy William Lee was a refreshing counterpoint to the clean-cut looks of the other three. But Golden apparently became increasingly difficult to deal with in a group situation, and in 1987, the rest of the Oaks fired him.

As befits a group that has lasted for close to half a century, considerably longer than many sports franchises, the Oak Ridge Boys have a sort of farm system. Richard Sterban and Joe Bonsall came from a gospel group that was managed by the Oak Ridge Boys organization, in part as a source for young talent. Steve Sanders, who replaced Golden, had been the rhythm guitar player in the Oaks' band when the group tapped him. Sanders, even though he came along when the Oak Ridge Boys had been out of gospel music for years, has a gospel background like his colleagues.

In the nineties, the Oak Ridge Boys are committed to continuing their own brand of gospel-tinged pop harmonies. Their concession to the new style is a song called "Cowboy Hat" that they do in their stage act, using a hat given to Joe Bonsall by Ricky Van Shelton.

Though they've gotten out of gospel, the Oak Ridge Boys still give service. From 1985 to 1988, they were honorary chairmen of the National Committee for the Prevention of Child Abuse, and they now serve on its board of directors.

The Oak Ridge Boys' list of the greatest songs of all time: Duane Allen—"MacArthur Park," Joe Bonsall—"Maria," Steve Sanders—"Crazy," Richard Sterban—"You Needed Me."

Mark O'Connor

b. Seattle, WA

Style
Virtuoso

From child prodigy to slouch-hatted fixture on TNN's "American Music Shop," Mark O'Connor has come to be the most prominent symbol of Nashville's new generation of virtuosos, in a city that's always been known for turning out some of the best musicians in the world.

Like Chet Atkins, who has said that O'Connor "is one of the few musicians I'd pay money to see," Mark has made his mark in a wide variety of musical fields, from pop (James Taylor's *Never Die Young*) to jazz (Michael Brecker's Grammy-winning *Don't Try This at Home*), but country is his home turf.

He made his first major mark in Nashville with his landmark solos on the Nitty Gritty Dirt Band's "The High Horse," then Michael Martin Murphey's "The Fiddling Man," where his three-minute fade impressed Murphey and the producers so much that they kept the entire solo on the album cut. Since then, he has played fiddle, mandolin, and mandola on hundreds of records.

O'Connor's advice to parents: "You have to force the issue of practice when a child is young, up to about the age of eleven, because a child must just not quit. Just don't push kids into playing in embarrassing situations. When I was growing up, my parents took me to fiddle contests, but told me that I never had to play if I didn't want to. And I'll tell you there were a lot of parents there who were very pushy with their kids, and there were a lot of prodigies playing that you don't hear about anymore."

In 1991, O'Connor's *The New Nashville Cats* album, featuring such guest artists as Vince Gill and Ricky Skaggs, went a long way toward reestablishing instrumental music as a popular country genre.

The O'Kanes

KIERAN KANE
b. 10/7/49, Queens, NY

JAMIE O'HARA
b. 8/18, Toledo, OH

Style

Minimalist close harmony

Memorable songs

"Can't Stop My Heart From Lovin' You,"
"Daddies Need to Grow Up Too"

Awards

Grammy—Country Song 1986 ("Grandpa, Tell Me 'Bout the Good Old Days"—Jamie O'Hara) Album Package 1988 ("Tired of the Runnin")

The O'Kanes moved from songwriters who had never worked together to a writing and performing duet in 1986 and had a run that lasted through 1990. They were the first male duet since the Everly Brothers to come up with a genuinely new sound, which featured deceptively simple, spare arrangements and subtle, delicately interlaced harmonies, in which the lead and harmony lines are traded back and forth between two strikingly distinctive voices at scrupulously planned intervals, unquestionably the result of an almost mathematical sifting out of possibilities, culminating in the meticulous juxtaposition of precise melodic and phonemic pattern syntheses. So how did the O'Kanes work out those harmonies, exactly?

"Very casually," Kieran Kane told us in an interview before their breakup. "It's really a matter of who thinks he can sing whatever part at that particular moment."

And the switching of lead and harmony lines within a song?

"Well, yes, we switch parts a lot," he agreed. "Sometimes we'll switch three times in the same song. We work that out just by threading through it, and if it seems like one or the other of us can get a better effect, we'll just switch, until sometimes it's hard for me to tell, listening to it back, who's singing what."

Kieran Kane began as a folk rocker from Queens, New York; Jamie O'Hara was a football hero from Ohio. They met as contract songwriters for Nashville's Tree Publishing, where O'Hara wrote "Grandpa (Tell Me 'Bout the Good Old Days)" for the Judds, and Alabama recorded Kane's "Let's Have a Party." Kane credits the generosity of a veteran songwriter for his first success: "T. G. Sheppard was going into the studio with one of my songs, and Curly Putman [writer of 'He Stopped Loving Her Today' and 'Green Green Grass of Home'], who was also with Tree, had just finished a song that was perfect for T.G. He brought it straight over to the studio. But when he got there, they were just about to start recording my song—the last number on the album. So he just took his song, stuck it back in his pocket, and walked out without saying a word."

Kane and O'Hara worked alongside each other for a few years without paying the slightest attention to each other. Finally, more or less by chance, they got together for a writing session and stumbled on a new sound. They took it down to a writer's night at Nashville's famed Bluebird Cafe, where the audience promptly walked out on them.

Undaunted, they kept crafting their sound and in 1986 brought it before the general public in a breathtaking debut album for Columbia Records.

171

Subsequent albums didn't quite capture the same lightning, and after losing their deal with Columbia, the guys decided to pack it in.

K. T. Oslin

b. 5/15/41, Crossett, AR

Style

Woman of a certain age

Memorable songs

"80's Ladies," "I Ain't Never Gonna Love No One but Cornell Crawford"

Awards

ACM—New Female Vocalist 1987, Video 1987 ("80's Ladies"), Female Vocalist 1988, Album of the Year 1988 (This Woman); CMA—Female Vocalist 1988, Song of the Year 1988 ("80's Ladies"); Grammy—Country Vocal Performance —Female 1987 ("80's Ladies"), 1988 ("Hold Me"), Country Song '88 ("Hold Me")

In 1987, when good-looking guys in cowboy hats seemed to have no trouble at all breaking into country music with smash-hit debut albums, a middle-aged woman from New York, who wore white gloves and boxy tailored suits that looked as though they came from Best & Co., or some other long-defunct department store, saw her debut album go gold (ultimately, it was to go platinum). And no woman had accomplished that since 1973, when Anne Murray did it with *Snowbird*.

K. T. Oslin's breakthrough song was a tour de force called "80's Ladies," which spoke straight to the hearts of that generation of women who were girls in the fif-

ties, stone rockers in the sixties, and who lost that provocative but unspecified "more than our names" in the seventies.

Well, we know those women. We've known them since the fifties, when they were girls of budding beauty like nothing we had ever seen before in our lives, and we were gawky, tongued-tied, and overcome with awestruck fascination in their presence. Of course, over the past quarter century, they've grown, and so have we— we've grown older, more worldly, more sophisticated, and . . . come to think of it, we still feel the same awestruck fascination.

K. T. Oslin knew them, too, from a different perspective than ours, and they knew her, and what she was saying. They responded to "80's Ladies," and they responded even more strongly to subsequent releases, sending several to number one. One of those, "Hold Me," was an even more poignant examination of the souls of middle-aged women—and middle-aged men, too. In it, a husband and wife both come to the verge of leaving each other, then fight to regain their lost closeness.

Oslin had been living in New York, trying to hang onto a not-quite-successful career on the Broadway stage, but like most New Yorkers, she was from out of town: born in Arkansas, raised in Alabama and Texas. In fact, during her college years, she formed one-third of a folk trio with Guy Clark.

She auditioned for a touring production of *Hello, Dolly!* starring Carol Channing, in 1966, and ended up moving into the Broadway production of the same play, starring Betty Grable, the following year. In the course of the next couple of decades in New York, she appeared in productions of *West Side Story* and *Promises,*

Promises, then settled into a career of commercial and studio backup singing.

Meanwhile, she had taken up writing songs. She wrote her first one in the mid-seventies, inspired by a message scrawled on a ladies' room wall: "I ain't never gonna love no one but Cornell Crawford" (the song eventually made it onto her third album, *Love in a Small Town*). She got her first shot at a record deal in 1981. She had one pretty good song she wanted to put on the album, about three ladies entering what was then the brand-new decade of the eighties—one smart, one pretty, and one a borderline fool. But the label rejected it, and the album didn't hit.

Meanwhile, others were starting to notice that Oslin had something special to say about women's lives and feelings in the eighties. Gail Davies, Rodney Crowell, Judy Rodman, Dottie West, and the Judds all recorded Oslin songs.

In 1986, Oslin went to Nashville and paid for a showcase, which was heard by producer Harold Shedd and RCA executive Joe Galante. It led to a record deal, and since the eighties weren't quite over, that song about the three girls was still relevant.

Becoming an overnight success at forty-five is a heady thing, but it has its problems, too. "I think younger women enjoy [the road] more than older women, and men enjoy it more than women," she told Patrick Carr in a *Country Music* interview. And she's in the older woman category, she has to admit, a fact that was recently brought home to her when a magazine called with a request: "They wanted a newcomer to interview an old-timer. When they first called me about it, I thought, 'Oh, great! They want me to interview, like, Tammy or Loretta! But then the lady said, 'No, you're the old-timer.' "

The magazine wanted Shelby Lynne to interview Oslin. "That really floors me, you know? An old-timer after two years!"

In the same interview, Oslin offered this opinion on women in today's country music: "I'm not sure that women will ever have the power careers that men have in country music. . . . In country music, the women are the consumers. They buy the records. They call the radio station and request the songs. They buy the concert tickets. . . . So you have to appeal to women. The easiest way to do that is to be a cute guy singing a nice love song that they want to hear."

Marie Osmond

b. 10/13/59, Ogden, UT (*Olive Marie Osmond*)

Style
Slick but emotional

Awards
CMA—Vocal Duo 1986 w/ Dan Seals

Marie Osmond treads a delicate stylistic line between Patsy Cline and Karen Carpenter. That's a chasm, not a delicate stylistic line, you say? Well, Ms. Osmond sure makes it seem that way.

If there was ever a bland, bubble-gum, Vegas lounge act on wheels, it was the various permutations of the Osmond family act. Marie came along on the heels of her brothers' success; "Paper Roses," which she made at age thirteen, was a dumb, cutesy-kid novelty, of the kind that occasionally finds its way to the top of the charts even though you can never find anyone who'll admit to liking it except your Aunt Fannie, and you know she doesn't buy records.

After that, Aunt Fannie watched that cute Marie and that cute Donnie on TV from 1976 to 1978, and after that, no one cared about that cute Marie anymore.

She made a couple of unsuccessful comeback attempts; then finally, in 1985, her duet with Dan Seals, "Meet Me in Montana," broke through for her—all the way to number one, and the CMA Award for Vocal Duet of the Year.

Marie Osmond is still not one of the monsters of country music, but she's established herself as a respectable star. She is what she is. She's never going to get the Vegas out of her style altogether, but she surprised a lot of people—including us—when she turned out to be musically sound, emotionally grounded, and in her own way, country.

Paul Overstreet

b. 3/17/55, Van Cleave, MS

Style
Sincere, Christian

Memorable Songs
"I Won't Take Less Than Your Love," "Daddy's Come Around"

Awards
ACM—Songwriter 1986 ("On the Other Hand"), 1987 ("Forever and Ever, Amen"); CMA—Song of the Year 1986 ("On the Other Hand"), 1987 ("Forever and Ever, Amen"); Grammy—Country Song 1987 ("Forever and Ever, Amen")

Paul Overstreet is an absolutely extraordinary songwriter. Here's a guy who's a singer himself—as part of the trio Schuyler, Knobloch, Overstreet, and then as a solo act—and he's still got songs enough to pass around: songs like "Same Ole Me" for George Jones, "One Love at a Time" and "My Arms Stay Open All Night" for Tanya Tucker, "I Fell in Love Again Last Night" for the Forester Sisters, "A Long Line of Love" for Michael Martin Murphey, "When You Say Nothing at All" for Keith Whitley, "Houston Solution" for Ronnie Milsap, "Love Can Build a Bridge" for the Judds, and for Randy Travis, a heavy-hitting lineup: "1982," "On the Other Hand," "Diggin' Up Bones," "Forever and Ever, Amen," "Deeper Than the Holler." He was named BMI's Songwriter of the Year in 1987, 1988, 1989, and 1990.

It's amazing that it took a guy with that kind of talent nearly ten years to notch his first hit, but it did. He came to Nashville in 1973, and "Same Ole Me" hit the charts in 1982. In the interim, he did what people do: played in a lot of clubs, drank in a lot of clubs. When he got his first big payoff for "Same Ole Me," he "bought a lot of wine and booze and drugs and a new car," he told the *Chicago Tribune*'s Jack Hurst. "But while I was spending it, I felt something wrong, that I didn't have something I was supposed to have in my life."

He found part of that something in 1984, when he married his second wife, Julie (he had previously been briefly married to Dolly Parton's sister Frieda), and the rest on January 1, 1985, when he gave up drinking permanently and made the decision to devote himself to God and his family.

About Overstreet's 1990 album, *Heroes*, we said in our *Middletown* (NY) *Times-Herald-Record* review:

"Paul Overstreet has his priorities absolutely clear in his mind: devotion to God and marital love will solve everything.

"It makes for a simple and happy life. In 'Billy Can't Read,' thanks to the devotion of the family he devoted his life to, Billy becomes literate, to the point where he can read everything from cereal boxes to the Bible, though one suspects he may have passed on *The Satanic Verses*. In 'She Supports Her Man,' a loving and grateful husband endures the taunts of less enlightened guys during the rough times when he can't find a job and his wife has to work, and it pays off in a lifetime of happiness. Nice work if you can get it.

"You might figure that this album is too saccharine and simplistic to appeal to an old cynic, and you might be wrong. We don't know if we could survive a weekend marriage encounter with the Overstreets, but the guy is touched with artistry as well as sincerity. He gets inside his world of sweetness and illuminates it with a songwriter's touch, and a sure instinct for the truth as he sees it."

Buck Owens

b. 8/12/29, Sherman, TX *(Alvis Edgar Owens)*

Style

The Bakersfield Sound, which he and Merle Haggard created: butt-kicking, rednecked California honky-tonk.

Memorable songs

"Tiger by the Tail," "Streets of Bakersfield"

Awards

ACM—Male Vocalist 1965, Touring Band 1965–68, (The Buckaroos), Pioneer Award 1988; CMA—Instrumental Group 1967–68; MCN—Band 1967–70, Instrumentalist 1975–76, Founder's Award (1980), Vocal Collaboration 1988 (w/ Dwight Yoakam)

Buck Owens walked away from country music around 1980, figuring there was no place for him in it anymore. This is like Lyndon Johnson walking away from Texas politics or John Paul Jones deciding there was no place for him in the Navy anymore. Along with George Jones, Merle Haggard, and Marty Robbins, Owens defined what country music was in the sixties. His Carnegie Hall concert in 1966 did more than any other event to bring country music to the mainstream (the Cash and Campbell TV shows and "Okie From Muskogee" all came later). Although he was unreservedly and unconditionally country, rocker John Fogerty of Creedence Clearwater Revival paid tribute to him in "Looking Out My Back Door ('Listenin' to Buck Owens')."

Owens stuck around with "Hee Haw" for a few years after he retired from touring and recording (and that was sort of like John Paul Jones taking over the *Love Boat*), but the Urban Cowboy era, the soupy arrangements and the genuflection of Nashville before the altar of such as Olivia Newton-John, had gotten to be too much for him.

Further, the death of his right-hand man, Don Rich, in 1974, was a devastating blow. Rich, the Buckaroos' lead guitar and fiddle player, had been with him since 1958, and when he died in a motorcycle accident, Owens "went through the motions from '74 to '79," as he told the *Washington Post's* Richard Harrington. "It was like a haze—maybe that's what the mind and body do for problems you cannot consciously handle. I was in shock and I think in that time I had a nervous breakdown. I don't know what else it could have been.

I'm not even a drinker, but hell, I got drunk. I got married [to the fiddle player who replaced Rich; three days later, they were divorced]. All that was a direct result of losing Don Rich. I'd never thought of being without Don. . . . I thought he'd always be there, to sing with me, to play with me."

In fact, Owens had pretty much lost all interest in the whole country music world. He had retreated to Bakersfield, California, the town he had made legendary as the capital of West Coast country—so much so that a recent album of young hard-core, hard-assed honky-tonk traditionalists from Los Angeles entitled their compilation album *A Town South of Bakersfield*. He was running his real estate and radio empire.

Then, one day in 1987, a guy dropped by his Bakersfield office. No, he didn't have an appointment, but he was a big fan of Buck's. Buck decided to see him. The young guy's name was Dwight Yoakam, and Yoakam was there to try to talk Owens into giving it another shot.

Things have changed, Yoakam told Buck. There's a new era in country music, new young guys who grew up idolizing you and Merle and Hank and Lefty. We're throwing out all the glitz and phoniness

and going back to the music you made. Owens liked Yoakam, and his enthusiasm was contagious. The old pro let himself be talked out of retirement for that night, anyway, to go out and make a guest appearance with his young admirer.

It was a risk. Owens had not even been considering a comeback; neither he nor Yoakam knew if he could still cut it onstage. But Yoakam's band knew all the classic Owens material and arrangements, and when Owens hit the stage, as Yoakam recalls, "it was like pinch yourself. He sounded just like Buck Owens."

Owens's new career took off with a tremendous bang: "The Streets of Bakersfield," done as a duet with Dwight Yoakam, was a number one hit in 1988. Other duets followed, including a remake of his old hit "Act Naturally," with the other guy who had made it a signature song—Beatle Ringo Starr. He also remade "Cryin' Time" with Emmylou Harris and released two new solo albums, *Hot Dog!* and *Kickin' In*.

Now in his sixties, Owens has no real interest in a full-scale, heavy touring schedule. Although immensely gratified by the response his comeback generated, he announced his retirement in November 1991 after a show at Billy Bob's in Texas.

Lee Roy Parnell

b. 12/21/56, Abilene, TX

Style

Rockin'

Memorable Songs

"Oughta Be a Law"

Lee Roy Parnell, one of many young stars who got discovered playing a showcase at Nashville's legendary Bluebird Cafe, on his music (from an interview in *CountryAmerica*): "People ask me to describe my musical style, and I end up talking about growing up in Texas and what can happen musically to you there. There was Buddy Holly and the open-string sound, which is western Texas. Then you've got southeastern Texas, with a great New Orleans–style rhythm and blues. My dad never listened to anything but Western Swing [Bob Wills was a close family friend]. My mom was really into Sam Cooke. I guess you could say I was always really into roots music, whatever it was. If it was real rootsy, I liked it. My own music has elements of blues, old rock 'n' roll, Western Swing, and of course, country—because my background and demeanor is such that it couldn't be anything else."

Of his 1990 debut album on Arista, an immediate favorite with the critics, *USA Today*'s David Zimmerman wrote, "Lee Roy Parnell is different from the try-too-hard earnestness of many current country music singers. He actually sounds like he's having fun."

Dolly Parton

b. 1/19/46, Sevier County, TN

Style

Sometimes Hollywood, sometimes mountain balladeer

Memorable songs

"Coat of Many Colors," "The Bargain Store"

Awards

ACM—Entertainer of the Year 1977, Female Vocalist 1980, Vocal Duet 1983 (w/ Kenny Rogers), Single of the Year 1983 ("Islands in the Stream" w/ Kenny Rogers), Album of the Year 1987 (Trio, w/ Emmylou Harris and Linda Ronstadt); CMA—Vocal Group 1968 (w/ Porter Wagoner); Vocal Duo 1970–71 (w/ Porter Wagoner), Female Vocalist 1975–76, Entertainer of the Year 1978, Vocal Event 1988 (Trio); Grammy—Country Vocal Performance–Female 1978 ("Here You Come Again"), 1981 ("9 to 5"), Country Song 1981, Country Vocal Performance, Duo or Group 1987, Album of the Year 1987 (Trio); MCN—Most Promising Female Artist 1968, Vocal Duet 1968–70 (w/ Porter Wagoner), 1984 (w/ Kenny Rogers), Vocal Collaboration 1987 (w/ Emmylou Harris and Linda Ronstadt)

One way or another, she's going to drive you nuts. She's the most extravagant success story of our time in country music, but whoever you are, and whatever your tastes are, she's bound to have done *something* that you think is absolutely tasteless and wretched.

Certainly, her last attempt at a network TV variety show didn't please much of anyone, even after ABC lavished a record $44-million contract on her. Dolly seemed to be trying to deliver an entire $44 million worth of cuteness, at the expense of—among other things—musicianship. What we remember mostly about the series were the duets with guest artists. One of the great duet singers of our time, teamed up with the likes of Porter Wagoner, Kenny Rogers, Emmylou Harris, and Linda Ronstadt, Dolly mugged and simpered and upstaged her way through numbers with guests like Merle Haggard, who deserved better.

And besides that . . . but hold it a minute. Why are we trashing Dolly? Why are we being so negative about America's sweetheart, everyone's favorite big-busted blonde? Were we really going to mention *Rhinestone,* the disastrous vanity production in which she costarred with Sylvester Stallone, rather than, for example, her easy, charming portrayal of the beauty parlor owner in *Steel Magnolias,* where she more than held her own with such high-powered actresses as Julia Roberts and Shirley MacLaine?

Like we said. She drives us nuts. Frankly, it would be easier to dismiss her like Paul McCartney, just another youthful genius turned lightweight, middle-aged pop entertainer, another artist who turned her back on her roots, went Hollywood, and has never recaptured the magic.

A lot of people felt she'd recaptured that magic with her 1989 album, *White Limozeen,* her return to straight country, with Ricky Skaggs producing. But we didn't. "Why'd You Come Here Looking Like That? "—one of the two number ones off the album—reminded us, in conception and execution, of "Love's Gonna Get You," far and away the worst record Ricky Skaggs ever made.

Dolly felt that she'd recaptured the magic, and furthermore, she appears to have this maddening attitude that she can recapture it, or anything else, anytime she wants to.

What about all those years in which she, as Stephen Holden of the *New York Times* put it, "steadily squandered her talents on vapid, commercial pop ditties"?

What about them? Dolly's basic attitude seems to be the same as Ollie North's about the Iran-contra affair: "Never happened."

Or if it did, it happened behind her back, while she wasn't looking. "For quite a while, my heart wasn't in a lot of the music I was doing," she told Patrick Carr in *Country Music.*

You mean, Carr asked, you've "been pretty much showing up at the recording studio and singing what other people told you to sing?"

"Yes, basically. I don't mean that I haven't taken my singing or myself seriously, but yes, I've been wanting to just get on into the studio and get out.

"You see, it's been really hard to prove to the people I've been working with on other things that country music is okay. It's like, you have to prove to these people that country music's where it's at before they'll get behind you doing it. . . .

"Take my manager, Sandy Gallin . . . he thinks I can do just anything and everything—but he's never had a true love for what I do best. He's never understood [country music] or had any respect for it . . . [neither have] a lot of the other businesspeople who are involved with me. So . . . you do what you have to do. You go through all these moves that they recommend. You do all those things they suggest. . . . What I've been doing is setting myself up as an entertainer, so I'm allowed to do all those other things like movies and TV if I want to. They're like my hobbies, you know, but my music is my life."

This is all fairly hard to swallow, but you can probably believe it if you'll also believe Dolly's assertion that she got run out of Nashville "because I couldn't make a living with songs like 'Coat of Many Colors' and all that other stuff I really love," when in fact Dolly was a huge star, sending one record after another to the top of the charts, at the time she left Nashville.

According to her 1979 biographer, Alanna Nash, Dolly "has been known to say one thing one day and the exact opposite the next"; she told Nash, back then, that her music had always been pop, but Nashville had stifled her and not let her express the real Dolly.

Parton's Hollywood career took off in 1980 with the release of *9 to 5,* a feminist comedy in which she costarred with Jane Fonda and Lily Tomlin. The movie was a success, with a lot of people, critics included, crediting Dolly for stealing it out from under her two powerful costars. She also wrote the movie's title song, featuring archly clever images such as "pour myself a cup of ambition." "9 to 5" became her only number one pop hit, as well as hitting the top of the country charts.

Until *Steel Magnolias,* there wasn't much else memorable in Parton's movie career. *Rhinestone* was one bomb; *Best Little Whorehouse in Texas* was another. There wasn't much memorable in her recording career, either, although she continued to have hits. Dolly was well on her way to becoming the Zsa Zsa Gabor of the eighties.

None of this would be enough to drive anyone particularly nuts if it weren't for one thing: Dolly Parton really is an extraordinary talent; she really is more than a Blue Ridge Mountain Charo.

And she proved that she hadn't lost that talent with her 1991 album, *Eagle When She Flies.* The title song was a sensitive feminist anthem, and her duet with Ricky Van Shelton, "Rockin' Years," showed that she could move into the new country scene with as much ease and confidence as she's moved everywhere else.

And, of course, there was her 1986 partnership with Linda Ronstadt and Emmylou Harris for the critically acclaimed, award-winning, and audience-pleasing *Trio.* In many ways, the controlling sensibility of the album was the purity and intelligence of Emmylou Harris, but in other important ways the wild, untrammeled talent of Dolly Parton showed through (Emmylou says that the album was built around Dolly).

All three women have said that they'd love to do it again, but the chances were that their schedules would never permit it. But, come on. Schedules aren't that inflexible, and if Emilio Estevez, Lou Diamond Phillips, and all those guys could find room in their schedules to do another *Young Guns,* you've got to figure Emmylou, Linda, and Dolly could do another *Trio.* If they really wanted to.

J. P. Pennington

See EXILE.

In a 1988 review of an Exile album in the *Middletown* (NY) *Times-Herald-Record*, we wrote; "J. P. Pennington is possessed of one of the better voices in Nashville—smoky, soulful, authoritative. It makes a listener wonder what he'd sound like in a more interesting context—a less obvious sound, songs with more originality."

"But, hey, he writes the songs himself."

Carl Perkins

b. 4/9/32, Tiptonville, TN

Style

Rockabilly

Memorable songs

"Blue Suede Shoes," "Boppin' the Blues"

Awards

ACM—Career Achievement 1986; Grammy—Best Spoken Word or Non-Musical Recording 1986 (Interviews From the Class of '55 Recording Sessions w/ Jerry Lee Lewis, Roy Orbison, Johnny Cash, Sam Phillips, Rick Nelson & Chips Moman)

By the time you read these words, don't bother to look for us. We'll be gone. We will have left home, hitchhiked down to Tennessee, wrapped ourselves up in a blanket, and placed ourselves in a basket on Carl Perkins's doorstep with a note imploring him to adopt us.

We fell in love with Carl Perkins back in 1956, when we first heard "Blue Suede Shoes," our favorite song then, our favorite song now. And our feelings were only strengthened when we talked to Perkins recently from his farm home in Tennessee, catching him between well-earned relaxation and a burst of creativity—"I just wrote a new thing this morning," Perkins told us. "Came in the den here and grabbed my li'l ole guitar, and bop! There it was."

Carl Perkins, for all the monumentality of his achievement in music—including induction into the Rock and Roll Hall of Fame—is a modest man who's generally tended to play a supporting role to more flamboyant names. Even with "Blue Suede Shoes," his only number one hit, he was overshadowed by Elvis Presley. A serious auto accident derailed Perkins's career when he was at his hottest, and he never recovered the lost momentum.

He was one of the Million Dollar Quartet (Elvis, Jerry Lee Lewis, Johnny Cash, and Perkins), who spent a few afternoons fooling around in the studio, but most of the tapes remain lost.

The Beatles loved Carl and recorded two of his songs, "Honey, Don't" and "Everybody's Trying to Be My Baby."

From 1965 to 1975, he played guitar for Johnny Cash and wrote Cash's number one hit "Daddy Sang Bass."

In the late eighties, he was associated with the Judds, touring with them, writing and playing guitar for them. He co-wrote their 1989 number one hit, "Let Me Tell You About Love."

The generation that Perkins represented, the one that he called "The Class of '55" on the song he recorded for the album of the same name, changed the face of country music even as they were creating rock and roll. Elvis was the first, and the story is well-known. Sam Phillips, president of Sun Records, who was recording black rhythm and blues singers as well as country performers in his Memphis studio, realized that the quintessential sound of the American soul would be the one that brought those two sounds together. "If I could find a white singer who has that Negro sound, that Negro feel," he said at the time, "I could make a million dollars."

Elvis was the first, but there were other Southern white boys who grew up—such as Hank Williams—loving and absorbing the music of the black South. Carl Perkins was one of them. Jerry Lee Lewis, the man whom Phillips called the most purely talented performer he had ever discovered, was another. Roy Orbison was there, too, but his career was to blossom later.

A lot of country purists hated it, but the new sound wasn't going away. Two sons of a Kentucky folksinger, Don and Phil Everly, put a new twist on the mountain harmonies they had grown up with and created a harmony sound that is still the standard against which every male harmony act is measured. A Rhino Records release, *All They Had to Do Was Dream,* featuring outtakes from their original 1957 sessions for Cadence Records, gives an insight into just what the Everlys accomplished. The earlier, rejected takes have wonderful harmonies, but they're just a shade more conventional—nothing that hadn't been done before by the Delmore Brothers in the thirties and forties or wasn't being done at that time by the Louvin Brothers.

The son of a Hollywood bandleader and a cast member of a family TV show, Ricky Nelson added to the visibility of the new sound. And a number of more traditional country singers made the pop charts in the wake of the Sun Records revolution: Sonny James with "Young Love," Marty Robbins with "A White Sport Coat" and later "El Paso," Ferlin Husky with "Gone," Bobby Helms with "Fraulein" and the all-too-immortal "Jingle Bell Rock."

Something happened to Carl Perkins over the thirty-something years between "Blue Suede Shoes" and the nineties. He turned from a jug-eared country boy into a distinguished country gentleman, with incredible presence and the looks of a down-home Cesar Romero.

He never stopped rocking, though. A little-heard 1989 release, *Born to Rock,* on Jimmy Bowen's short-lived Uni label, was as good a collection of rockabilly songs and rockabilly performances as you're likely to hear.

"All it takes to make me happy," Carl Perkins says, "is to be drivin' down the street in some li'l ole town and stop at a light and see some old boy in the car next to me kinda grinnin' and tappin' his hand on the steering wheel. I know he's listenin' to something hot."

Could be he's listening to a li'l ole Carl Perkins tune.

Pirates of the Mississippi

RICH ALVES
b. 5/25/53, Pleasanton, CA

BILL McCORVEY
b. 7/4/59, Montgomery, AL

JIMMY LOWE
b. 8/2/55, Nashville, TN

DEAN TOWNSON
b. 4/2/59, St. Petersburg, FL

PAT SEVERS
b. 11/10/52, Camden, SC

Style
Honky-tonk rockers

Memorable songs

"Feed Jake," "Honky Tonk Blues"

Awards

ACM—New Vocal Duet/Group 1990

They say rock is where the big money is, but according to Jimmy Lowe of the Pirates of the Mississippi, he and the other Pirates "graduated from rock 'n' roll garage bands to country music when we saw how much more lucrative country music is as opposed to rock.

"That means as a working musician, not necessarily a top act," he explains. "Because unless you're in some really big touring act in the rock business, the gigs are few and far between, and people just don't appreciate you the way they do in country, and you just don't make enough bucks. A friend of mine talked me into it. We'd played in rock bands together, and now he was making all this money playing country, and he saw how I was struggling to play with a rock 'n' roll band and ending up with maybe ten bucks a night. He said, 'Jimmy, you've got to get into this country thing, 'cause it's a lot more fun to play and it makes a lot more money.' And that was the magic word.

"It took me a couple of years to really learn how to play country—my favorite drummer of all time was John Bonham of Led Zeppelin, although I love country drummers like Kenny Malone, and Russ Kunkel, who played a lot with Linda Ronstadt, and Larrie Londin.

"When you're playing drums in a country band, it's the sound of the band as a whole that really counts, and you have to remember that anything you play either adds to it or takes away from it—as opposed to a rock or heavy metal band, where it's almost like a drum solo with band accompaniment. Playing country, you have to learn how to get rid of the drum rolls and all the fancy footwork and settle down into a good groove, so that the other pickers can do their thing.

"A country drummer needs to have a catalog of unusual licks in his head, so you whip out an appropriate one at a moment's notice, and it sounds fresh, and it fits the song. It took me a while to appreciate country music as music, but after a year or two you learn to really love it. But I'll still cut loose and play some rock stuff when we're onstage."

The Pirates were signed to Jimmy Bowen's Universal label around the same time that the Kentucky Headhunters were starting—"actually, we cut our album before the Headhunters did," says Jimmy Lowe, "but theirs was released first, and I think they definitely opened some doors for us.

"We went into the best state-of-the-arts studio in Nashville, forty-eight-track digital with all these isolation booths, like being at NASA. When we heard the playback, it was so sterile it scared us. It didn't sound like the Pirates at all. So we decided to take a chance and went down to this funky old studio downtown and cut ten tracks in one day and took the result over to Mr. Bowen, and he said, 'Well, damn, boys—you could have saved me a lot of money!' "

The funky downtown tape was the one that got released. It included their rocking remake of Hank Williams, Sr.'s "Honky Tonk Blues" and their entry into the hall of classic dog songs, "Feed Jake."

Jimmy Lowe's list of the greatest songs of all time: "Georgia on My Mind," "Free Bird," "Good Hearted Woman," "He Stopped Lovin' Her Today."

Charley Pride

b. 3/18/38, Sledge, MS

Style

Straight-ahead country; heavy Hank, Sr., influence

Memorable songs

"Is Anybody Goin' to San Antone," "Kiss an Angel Good Mornin' "

Awards

CMA—Male Vocalist 1971–72, Entertainer of the Year 1971; Grammy—Sacred Performance 1971 ("Did You Think to Pray"), Gospel Performance (Other Than Soul Gospel) 1971 ("Let Me Live"), Country Vocal Performance—Male 1972 (Charley Pride Sings Heart Songs); MCN—Male Artist 1969–73

Charley Pride made history as the first black star in country music, the first black performer to take a song to number one, and much more than that. Pride has sold more country records for RCA Victor than any other artist they've ever had on the label, with the single exception of Elvis Presley. And when you think about that, consider that RCA has historically been the premier label in country music, the label of Waylon Jennings, Eddy Arnold, and Dolly Parton in their glory years. Pride's had twenty-nine number one hits, and only Conway Twitty, Merle Haggard, and Ronnie Milsap have had more (chart figures from Joel Whitburn's *Top Country Singles*).

There are number one hits and number one hits, a lot of them instantly forgettable. Chances are, though, you'll remember a lot of Charley Pride's: "All I Have to Offer You (Is Me)," "(I'm So) Afraid of Losing You Again," "Is Anybody Going to San Antone," "I Wonder Could I Live Here Anymore," "I Can't Believe That You've Stopped Loving Me," "I'd Rather Love You," "I'm Just Me," "Kiss an Angel Good Mornin'," "It's Gonna Take a Little Bit Longer," "She's Too Good to Be True," "A Shoulder to Cry On," "Don't Fight the Feeling of Love," "Amazing Love," "Then Who Am I," "Hope You're Feelin' Me (Like I'm Feelin' You)," "My Eyes Can Only See As Far As You," "She's Just an Old Love Turned Memory," "I'll Be Leaving Alone," "More to Me," "Someone Loves You Honey," "Where Do I Put Her Memory," "You're My Jamaica," "Honky Tonky Blues," "You Win Again," "Never Been So Loved (In All My Life)," "Mountain of Love," "You're So Good When You're Bad," "Why Baby Why," "Night Games."

"Night Games" came in 1983. In 1986 Pride left RCA. "A bunch of us exited the label then—myself and Waylon and Dolly and others. I asked for an early release from my contract—I didn't actually expect them to give it to me, but they did. I felt—and it turned out to be right—that they were looking to get rid of the more established artists and get newer blood and compete with MTV. Which they've certainly accomplished—look at the success of Garth Brooks alone. But I wonder if they may not be losing the longevity that country music has been known for over the years—establishing someone who's going to be an Eddy Arnold or . . ."

Or a Charley Pride, we suggested.

"Or a Merle Haggard. This is not coming from a point of view of complaining, just someone who's observed a lot. It's like George Jones says, 'Who's gonna fill their shoes?" The difference is, when I came along, my records were played on the radio alongside the artists who pioneered the way for me, like Ernest Tubb and Eddy Arnold and Marty Robbins, right up the line to Johnny Cash.

"I guess a lot of people will look at a guy who's a certain age and say, 'Well, he's no longer productive,' and there's no way I can agree with that. I think my voice is actually better now, more relaxed. I'm out there onstage—I still tour worldwide, just got back from Australia—and I know what kind of response I get, not just from the older fans but from the Garth Brooks listeners, too. And they come up after the show and ask me where's my new record.

"I'm telling you, give me any one of the good songs that any one of the new people have, I don't care who it is, and we go in and produce it and let me put my spin on it, and if it gets played over the radio, I guarantee it will sell."

After leaving RCA, Pride signed with an independent label, 16th Avenue, and had some success, including a 1987 top ten hit, "Shouldn't It Be Easier Than This?" But it was the wrong time for an ambitious independent label in Nashville; 16th Avenue folded, and Pride has been without a label ever since.

That's tough in the nineties. As Pride says, "It used to be that you could drive by and stop at a country station in Texas or Louisiana or wherever, and you might not be on a big label, but you might have a good voice and a good song, and the program director would listen to it and say, 'Well, let's give it a spin and see what people think.' But that don't hold anymore. It's determined by how much money a label is spending on you."

He's right. Back in the sixties, a young Loretta Lynn could drive around the South with a station wagon full of 45s, visiting radio stations. Today, "they wouldn't even let her in the door," says Allen Butler of Arista Records.

And if it were a legend, like Charley Pride? "They'd let him in the door, of course, because he's Charley Pride. But they wouldn't play his record."

Before we took leave of Pride, we had to ask him one more question:

You didn't just open a crack in the color line in country music; you completely smashed it open. You became a major star, and yet no one has followed you. Why not?

"I don't know. I really don't. But I think, coupled with the [music business] situation that's going on right now, there might be the possibility that someone's saying, do we really need another Charley Pride? Or, for that matter, do we need Charley Pride?"

Charley Pride's list of the greatest songs of all time: "Love Is a Many Splendored Thing," "Please Help Me I'm Falling," "For the Good Times" . . . "You know, if you asked me the greatest singers, I could just name 'em, bing, bing, bing. Sam Cooke, Nat King Cole, Brook Benton, Perry Como. I love ballad singers. I love gospel—Mahalia Jackson, the Chuckwagon Gang, the Louvin Brothers, the Five Blind Boys of Mississippi, the Dixie Hummingbirds. And the blues —B. B. King, Muddy Waters, Sonny Boy Williamson, Etta James, Elmore James.

"Country is what I heard the most growing up, and I'm blessed with a voice for country music, but I love all that other music. In my own studio, though, I've gone in and tried out some experimental stuff—a Brook Benton thing, a B. B. King thing."

John Prine

b. 10/10/46, Maywood, IL

Style

Folk

Memorable songs

"Hello in There," "Dear Abby," "Picture Show"

We're thinking of setting up our own awards show, for performers who attract love and admiration with a fervency that's way out of proportion to the amount of fame they have with the general public.

We plan on calling them the Culties. They'd go to actors like Harry Dean Stanton, singers like Marcia Ball or Jonelle Mosser. And naturally, there'd be a Cultie Hall of Fame.

And the first inductee, plus Lifetime Achievement Award recipient, would be John Prine. Since his debut album in the late sixties, with songs like "Sam Stone," about a Vietnam vet strung out on heroin, to recent work like the devilish "Let's Talk Dirty in Hawaiian" (with Fred Koller), Prine has been out there, a wandering troubadour with no band, just his guitar, a gritty voice, his humor, and his insight.

He lives in Nashville now, writes songs, and inspires new generations of songwriters and young folks who hear a different drummer. His 1992 album, *The Missing Years,* may not quite have moved him beyond cult status, but it won him the biggest sales of his career.

Eddie Rabbitt

b. 11/27/44, Brooklyn, NY

Style

Country

Memorable songs

"Drivin' My Life Away," "I Love a Rainy Night"

Awards

ACM—New Male Vocalist 1977; MCN—Songwriter 1979

Style . . . "country"? Not very descriptive, perhaps? But wait a second.

"I came to Nashville from New Jersey in 1968," says Eddie Rabbitt. "I'd been playing country bars in northern New Jersey for a few years before that—lying about my age, to tell the truth. I'd had twelve number one hits before 'I Love a Rainy Night' had that huge pop success. [Note: Twelve Top Ten hits on the Billboard chart; only six of them made it to number one. But this is pointless quibbling, isn't it? Six number one hits, twelve Top Ten hits in five years is a remarkable accomplishment—and this is before his greatest success.] But a lot of people think I just started out with 'Rainy Night,' and I was some kind of pop singer who just latched onto country.

"Hey, I'm glad 'Rainy Night' was a big hit. You do the best you can, and you get it out there, and you hope it does well, but it does sort of hurt me to always see myself described as a pop-country singer. I'd at least like it to be country-pop."

Okay, we said, country-pop it is.

"Wellll . . . I'd really rather you just made it 'country.' "

Though he sprang from the same roots as Bruce Springsteen, Rabbitt was never a rock-and-roller, and his teenage sojourns across the Hudson River to try to sell songs in the Brill Building, which had been the mecca for such pop songsmiths as Carole King and Neil Sedaka, taught him two things: "First, there's not a great understanding of country in the mahogany dusty offices of New York, and second, how to walk around with tapes in my pocket."

Rabbitt recalls taking a Greyhound to Nashville in 1968, where he began hanging out with a group of young songwriters that included Kris Kristofferson and Billy Swan. His first success was a Roy Drusky album cut, then a Top Forty single for Billy Grammer called "Bottles." (Incidentally, cold numbers and memories are at odds here: "Bottles" made the charts in 1966, and Rabbitt's first Top Ten as writer, Bobby Lewis's, "Love Me and Make It All Better," was 1967.) He was signed for $37.50 a week as a staff writer for Elvis Presley's Nashville publishing company, and when Elvis recorded "Kentucky Rain" (number 31 country and number 16 pop in 1970), his career was moving.

In the early seventies, David Malloy, then a backup engineer at Ray Stevens's studio, "used to let me sneak in after everyone was gone, about eleven or twelve o'clock at night, and put songs down on some of the used twenty-four-track tape. Around 1974 we went in one night and put down a couple of songs with just guitar and vocals, then next night we had Chips Moman come in and put a bass line down on it, and another night we had Kenny Malone put some drums on it, and a couple other guitar players, and we made a record by putting on pieces every other night of the week when no one was around to charge us."

These tracks garnered Rabbitt a contract with Elektra Records and began an association with Malloy that was to last several years and a carload of hits. And if Jersey boy Rabbitt was all country, second-generation Nashville producer Malloy was a strong crossover advocate whose goal, he told Tim Roland in *The Billboard Book of Number One Country Hits*, was to "make pop records that could be acceptable to country radio."

The Rabbitt/Malloy vision bore immediate fruit, as Eddie hit the charts in '74 and clicked with his first number one ("Drinkin' My Baby Off My Mind") in '76. He roared into the eighties on a string of hits, including some decent crossover action, that reached high-octane status with "Drivin'" and "Rainy Night" in 1980. His crossover career tailed off in 1983, but he remains a top country music attraction.

Eddie and his wife, Janine, lived through a personal tragedy in 1985: the death of their son, Timmy, who had been born with a severe birth defect. A second son, Tommy, was born in 1986, and Eddie is a devoted family man ("I think I got more lovable," he joked when we asked him about how he came to move beyond drinkin' and cheatin' and truck drivin' songs), and he interrupted our interview

to affectionately chide his son for hanging over the stair railing.

Speaking of "Rainy Night," one question we had always wanted to ask Eddie: How could he see the moon on that rainy night?

"It's one of those nights," he says, not missing a beat. "The dark clouds were just passing by, and they opened up, and that moon kinda cranked in there. I never thought about that. But somebody asked me the other day, 'How did the road in "Rocky Mountain Music" change from an old dirt road to a gravel road?' and I realized she was right—in the first line it's an old dirt road, and in the last it's a gravel road. I said, Progress. They fixed up the old dirt road—do you think those people were hicks? They put gravel down after a few years."

Eddie Rabbitt's list of the greatest songs of all time: Harlan Howard's "You Took Her Off My Hands, Now Take Her Off My Mind"; "Crazy Arms," "Friends in Low Places"—"I think that's one of the few songs of right now that's destined to be a classic"; George Jones's "Open Pit Mine" (we've forgotten the song, so Eddie sings a couple of bars, immediately giving an uncanny impression of George Jones).

Eddy Raven

b. 8/19/44, Lafayette, LA (*Edward Garvin Futch*)

Style
MOR

Memorable songs
"Right Hand Man"

Ever notice how when you hear a word you've never heard before, suddenly you'll hear six more people using it that same day? Ever notice how sometimes a theme, or an image, will suddenly take over country music, and you'll start hearing it everywhere? A few years ago, we started making a list of songs with lines about somebody thinking that somebody hung the moon, but it started to get depressingly long.

But the really striking example, the one that came along in the mid-eighties, was the sudden onslaught of hand songs.

The hand songs were about synecdoche (wait and see if you hear six people using that word today). Synecdoche means "a figure of speech by which the part is put for the whole or the whole for a part, the special for the general or the general for the special, as in 'a fleet of ten *sail*' (for *ships*)," according to Webster. In this case *hand,* specifically the hand that had a finger that you might or might not find a wedding ring on, or put a wedding ring on. Except in the case of "Daddy's Hands" (Holly Dunn), which symbolized hard work and sacrifice. (Actually, "Daddy's Hands" may be less an eighties hand song than a precursor of the great onslaught of nineties daddy songs.)

Randy Travis had back luck because the girl he had eyes for had all sorts of good qualities on one hand, but on the other hand she had a wedding band. George Jones was a little luckier—he got to put the ring on the right left hand this time. Eddy Raven had to be a right-hand man because he couldn't be a left-hand man—that is, the guy who got to put the ring on the left hand.

This is actually as close as Eddy Raven gets to being mentioned in the same breath with George Jones or Randy Travis. A Nashville journeyman, he moved to town from Cajun country in 1970 and had a solid string of Top Ten

hits, including four number ones, between 1984 and 1988.

Even though he has that exotic Louisiana background (including a stint as a moonshine runner), there's not much Cajun shading to Raven's style. Actually, he reminds us a little of Eddie Rabbitt.

Mike Reid

b. 5/24/47, Altoona, PA

Style
MOR

Memorable songs
"Walk on Faith," "Lost in the Fifties Tonight" (*as writer*)

Awards
ACM—Songwriter 1985 ("Lost in the Fifties/In the Still of the Night"); Grammy—Country Song 1983 ("Stranger in My House")

Mike Reid has a great story: all-American football player at Penn State, number one draft pick by the Cincinnati Bengals, Rookie of the Year, All-Pro defensive tackle—and during the off-season, a guest soloist with the Cincinnati, Dallas, San Antonio, and Utah symphony orchestras ("I didn't embarrass myself, but I had no illusions—I was invited to perform because I was a football player"). And after three years in the NFL, Reid quit—still an All-Pro—and went on the road as a performer, eventually moving to Nashville in 1980 to become a songwriter.

He turned out to be a pretty good one. He caught on quickly with Ronnie Milsap, for whom he wrote several songs, while also providing hits for Tanya Tucker, Don Williams, Lorrie Morgan, the Judds, and

Alabama—an All-Pro lineup by anyone's reckoning.

In 1990, he moved on to the next phase of his career, with the release—to good, if not superstar, response—of his first album on Columbia. As a singer, Reid is more a lineman than a quarterback—workmanlike and dependable, but not what you'd call nimble.

Restless Heart

LARRY STEWART
b. 3/2/59, Paducah, KY

JOHN DITTRICH
b. 4/7/51, Union, NJ

PAUL GREGG
b. 12/3/54

GREG JENNINGS
b. 10/2/54, Oklahoma City, OK

DAVE INNIS
b. 4/9/59, Bartlesville, OK

Equally, if not more, important to the group is its founder and original producer, Tim DuBois.

In 1992, Larry Stewart left the group to pursue a solo career.

Style
Country-pop

Memorable songs
"Wheels"

Awards
ACM—Vocal Group 1989

All sorts of influences go into developing the various sounds of an era, some of them too close for comfort, and sometimes too close to be acknowledged. The Beatles are safely in the ranks of musical immortals, and the new young country groups, especially the ones with strong pop leanings, will all tell you they listened to the Beatles.

The Beatles learned their vocal harmonies from the Everly Brothers and the great street-corner harmony groups of the fifties: the Moonglows, the Cadillacs, the Cleftones, etc. John Lennon and Paul McCartney wrote an important chapter to the story of the group sound in popular music in the sixties; so did Simon and Garfunkel, the Beach Boys, Crosby, Stills, and Nash, the Mamas and the Papas.

The group harmony sound in the seventies was largely defined on the West Coast by country-rock groups such as the Eagles, and on the East Coast by the upstate New York group Orleans, who had such hits as "Still the One" and "Dance With Me."

As we were preparing this book, a pop musician friend asked us one day, "Who's this Restless Heart group? I heard them on the radio the other day, and I thought I was listening to Orleans."

We thought about it, sat down, and listened to Restless Heart again and decided he was right. We talked to some Nashville insiders, who said, yeah, back in 1985, when both groups got their record contracts, the word on Music Row was that one of them would make it—there was only room for one.

Restless Heart was the one. They were a group of highly professional studio musicians who had been put together by producer Tim DuBois. Created sound or not, it was a sound that struck some kind of chord with country audiences: Restless Heart ran off a string of six straight number one hits between 1986 and 1988.

Riders in the Sky

RANGER DOUG (*Douglas B. Green*)
b. 3/20/46, Great Lakes Naval Base, IL

WOODY PAUL (*Paul Woodrow Chrisman*)
b. 8/23/49, Nashville, TN

TOO SLIM (*Fred LaBour*)
b. 6/3/48, Grand Rapids, MI

Style
Cowboy music and comedy

Memorable album
The Cowboy Way, *the best country comedy album of all time.*

If an act is at least partly the sum of its influences, consider Riders in the Sky's influences, as listed by Ranger Doug: Roy Rogers, Gene Autry, the Sons of the Pioneers, the Smothers Brothers, Spike Jones, Tommy Dorsey, the Beatles, Elton Britt (the classic yodeling C&W star of the forties)—and, he adds, fiddler Woody Paul was, for a while, deeply into bebop, the style of modern jazz pioneered by Charlie Parker and Dizzy Gillespie.

What does it all add up to? A group of "needlessly overeducated guys" (all have college degrees, with Woody Paul boasting a Ph.D. in nuclear engineering from MIT) who got together to play cowboy music, then found that once they got onstage, they couldn't stop clowning.

They have an unsettling degree of intellectualism for a country act: their first seven albums were on Rounder Records, an independent label out of Cambridge, Massachusetts, that caters to the highbrow crowd, and their long-running radio program, "Riders Radio Theater," plays on National Public Radio.

But they're pure of heart as cowboy singers in the classic mold of the Sons of the Pioneers, and their humor is as goofy as it is intellectual. In fact, their goofiness and their purity of heart have won them a chance at network television, in what is surely the perfect spot for them: a Saturday-morning kiddie show.

Ranger Doug's choice as the all-time greatest song: "The Cowboy's Lament."

Judy Rodman

b. 5/23/51, Riverside, CA

Style
Warm

Memorable Songs
"Girls Ride Horses Too," "I'll Be Your Baby Tonight"

Awards
ACM—New Female Vocalist 1985

Why do some careers flourish and others flounder? Judy Rodman, a singer of warmth and sensitivity and professionalism, was signed to a contract by MTM records, the Nashville recording arm of Mary Tyler Moore's show business empire. Rodman made a couple of albums for MTM and notched one number one single, "Until I Met You."

An accomplished studio musician, Rodman sang multitracked backup vocals to her own lead and created a lovely textured sound, especially on her hit remake of Bob Dylan's "I'll Be Your Baby Tonight."

Then, in early 1989, MTM folded. The label had two female singing stars,

Judy Rodman and Holly Dunn. Dunn, who unquestionably deserved it, was picked up by Warner Brothers, and her career has soared. Rodman, who also deserved success, could not find another label.

Kenny Rogers

b. 8/21/38, Houston, TX

Style
Workmanlike

Memorable songs
"The Gambler," "Lucille"

Awards
ACM—Single of the Year 1977 ("Lucille"), Album of the Year 1977 (Kenny Rogers), Male Vocalist 1977–78, Entertainer of the Year 1978, Single of the Year 1983 ("Islands in the Stream" w/ Dolly Parton), Vocal Duet 1983 (w/ Dolly Parton); CMA—Single of the Year 1977 ("Lucille"), Album of the Year 1979 (The Gambler), Male Vocalist 1979, Vocal Duo 1978–79 (w/ Dottie West); Grammy—Country Vocal Performance–Male 1977 ("Lucille"), 1979 ("The Gambler"), Country Vocal Performance–Duet 1987 ("Make No Mistake, She's Mine" w/ Ronnie Milsap); MCN—Male Artist 1979, Duet 1979 (w/ Dottie West), 1984 (w/ Dolly Parton), Single of the Year 1979 ("The Gambler")

Scene: the Nashville airport on a hot Saturday afternoon. A middle-aged, prosperous-looking man, his wife, and three children are running to catch a plane. As they get to the gate—which is being held open for them—the man stops and goes over to a familiar figure in a white Stetson hat and tan corduroy jacket. The wife screams at her husband, "Joe, what the hell are you doing? We'll miss the plane." The husband ignores her, reaching out to shake the hand of the seated man. "Hell nothing, Mary Jane," he then calls over his shoulder. "This is Kenny Rogers. I ain't gonna miss shakin' hands with him."

It would be an understatement to say that Kenny Rogers is at the summit of his popularity. What's amazing is how long that summit has lasted, and what a wide range it has covered. His TV shows, no matter what the reviews, get high ratings. His concerts are packed, and not only with country music fans. As one reviewer said, "No wonder Rogers has so many fans. He's been in so many branches of music." Or, as Rogers puts it, "crossover is my middle name."

But while crossover to most singers means country to pop, Rogers started in the opposite direction; in fact, he's criss-crossed. In 1957, he appeared on Dick Clark's "American Bandstand" with a group called The Scholars; he's played in two modern-jazz groups, the Bobby Doyle Trio and the Kirby Stone Four. "I have a nose for what's happening," Rogers says.

In the early sixties, realizing that folk music was the new choice of many listeners, he crossed over and joined the New Christy Minstrels. "It was a monetary step down," he says, "but I felt it was a professional step up and would do something towards my future career."

As folk waned, Rogers and three other Minstrels left to form a psychedelic rock group, the First Edition. "In those days I wore skintight suits and a beard [he still has the beard, but it's grayer] and was très hip." Their first release was a song by

Mickey Newbury: "I Just Dropped In To See What Condition My Condition Was In." The song topped the *Billboard* charts for ten weeks (although Rogers declines to sing it today).

During the nine years of the First Edition, the group had four gold albums and nine gold singles (including Mel Tillis's "Ruby, Don't Take Your Love to Town").

Rogers claims that he's always leaned toward country, and that the First Edition was rooted in the country tradition. *Entertainment Weekly* reviewer Alanna Nash says that "in retrospect, it appears that the First Edition played a not too small but largely unheralded role in helping bridge the gap between country and rock."

All bands have their day, as Rogers acknowledges, and eventually the First Edition's sales dried up. Perceiving an upsurge of interest in country—Rogers has always been the first to admit that he looks on music as "a business, strictly a business"—he decided to try his hand as a solo country artist, with a style that Alanna Nash describes as "a little contemporary folk, a little pasteurized country, a little half-baked rock and roll, a few string-swathed love songs and ballads, and lots of good-natured congeniality."

None of which was quite enough to put him back on top without the right song, which he got in 1977, when he bumped into Waylon Jennings. Kenny was down, and Waylon tried to help—"I've got a song for you. I was going to do it, but you need it more than me." Rogers skimmed the words, the story goes, and shook his head. "Not my style. I'm looking for something upbeat."

"Take my advice, buddy," Waylon insisted. "Cut it."

Rogers did, and "Lucille" became the top song of the year, number one on the country charts, number five on the pop charts. And he'd learned something. The "story song" was perfectly suited for his pleasantly raspy voice. In 1979, he found another one—a song that had languished in obscurity twice before, when Bobby Bare and Johnny Cash had tried it. "The Gambler" did well by Kenny Rogers, though: a number one record, a string of successful TV movies, even a football team (the USFL Houston Gamblers, co-owned by Rogers).

In 1981, Rogers told Alanna Nash he didn't expect his success to last, but he seems to have made one of his few career misjudgments there. Today, this prudent businessman of music makes an estimated $10 million a year, owns a $5-million mansion in Georgia, plus a share of the Golden Nugget in Las Vegas, a $600,000 yacht, office buildings in Nashville, a fleet of cars including a yellow Rolls-Royce, and he hangs out in some fairly impressive company. When Anwar Sadat and Menachem Begin signed their historic peace agreement, Kenny Rogers was there to entertain them.

Roy Rogers

b. 11/5/12, Cincinnati, OH (*Leonard Slye*)

Style

Cowboy

Memorable songs

"Happy Trails"

Who is the only performer to have been inducted into the Country Music Hall of Fame twice? That's right, it's Roy Rogers—once on his own, and once as a member of the Sons of the Pioneers.

Wyatt Earp was an authentic Western hero, an important lawman in Dodge City, Kansas, and Tombstone, Arizona, the victor of the gunfight at the OK Corral (which, incidentally, was a battle between Democrats and Republicans). But the reason he became a larger-than-life legend (his brother Virgil was certainly the more important figure in Tombstone) was that he lived so gosh-darned long—into the 1920s, so that he got to tell his story to John Ford and the other moviemakers who created the Western legend.

Roy Rogers was an authentic Western movie star (an authentic inauthentic Western hero?), and one of the giants of a limited but deeply appealing genre. Certainly a bigger star than Buck Jones or Allan "Rocky" Lane, say. But what makes him the King of the Cowboys, the idol of every contemporary singer who's ever drawn on a pair of cowboy boots? Partly that he had a fair amount of charisma in his prime. Partly that he's still around, so that if you want to pay tribute to a real or imagined era in which everyone knew who the good guys were, all you have to do is look over your shoulder and there's the King of the Cowboys, riding down the trail.

In 1991, Roy made a comeback on the recording scene, cutting an album of duets with current stars like K. T. Oslin, Restless Heart, and Clint Black. Rumor has it that Rogers's return to the studio may have been motivated, at least in part, by the need to beef up the image (if not the sandwiches) of his fast food restaurants—it seems most of the young people who are the target audience for fast food had zero name recognition for the old King of the Cowboys. Now, anyone who's seen his appearance or his hit video on TNN knows who he is—he's that old guy who looks like Clint Black.

Linda Ronstadt

b. 7/15/46, Tucson, AZ

Style
Incredibly versatile

Memorable songs
"Blue Bayou," "To Know Him Is to Love Him"

Awards
ACM—New Female Vocalist 1974, Album of the Year 1987 (Trio, w/ Emmylou Harris and Dolly Parton); CMA—Vocal Event 1988 (Trio); Grammy—Country Vocal Performance–Female 1975 ("I Can't Help It If I'm Still in Love With You"), Pop Vocal Performance–Female 1976 ("Hasten Down the Wind"), Country Vocal Performance –Duo or Group 1987 (Trio), Mexican/ American Performance 1988 (Canciónes de Mi Padre), Song of the Year 1987 ("Somewhere Out There" w/ James Ingram), Pop Vocal Performance–Duo or Group 1990 ("All My Life" w/ Aaron Neville); MCN—Vocal Collaboration 1988 (w/ Dolly Parton and Emmylou Harris)

Linda Ronstadt's career has spanned such a range of musical styles that it almost defies credibility. Folk, pop, rock, Latin, light opera, big band. And oh, by the way, country. Given the fact that the country music fraternity can sometimes get a little bit suspicious of outsiders even from the pop/folk world, to say nothing of the worlds of big band music and light opera, it might be surprising that Ronstadt has been so accepted in country.

But such is the emotional persuasiveness of Linda Ronstadt's voice, she seems to be able to wander in and out of country music at will, and almost without even trying. Other artists have had songs that hit the country charts and the pop charts at the same time, but Ronstadt, on two different occasions, has hit the country charts with songs that were the B sides of huge pop records. Her remake of Hank Williams's "I Can't Help It If I'm Still in Love With You," which had come out on the flip of her number one pop hit "You're No Good," went to number two on the country charts in 1974, and the following year country radio, and country audiences, picked up "Love Is a Rose," which had been released as the flip side of "Heat Wave."

After that, it almost got to be a habit. While songs like "Blue Bayou" and Buddy Holly's "It's So Easy" charted both pop and country, other numbers went the flip route. "I Never Will Marry" was the flip side of her 1978 pop cover of the Rolling Stones' "Tumbling Dice"; her 1979 remake of Elvis's "Love Me Tender" turned over to "Just One Look" on the pop charts; 1980's "Rambler Gambler" was "How Do I Make You"; and her 1982 country duet with John David Souther, "Sometimes You Just Can't Win," was the flip of pop hit "Get Closer."

Then there were the totally noncountry numbers by the Remake Queen of the seventies that found favor with country audiences: the various Buddy Holly songs, Smokey Robinson and the Miracles' "Tracks of My Tears," Chuck Berry's "Back in the U.S.A.," and "Poor Poor Pitiful Me," by the surreal West Coast literary rocker Warren Zevon.

The more you look at Linda Ronstadt's career, the more you can't escape the conclusion that it is one of the most amazing careers in American popular music. But in terms of her contribution to country in particular, the highlight, both commercially and critically, was her contribution to the 1987 album *Trio*.

Ronstadt's country ties were strengthened, early on, by her well-publicized friendships with two great ladies of country, Dolly Parton and Emmylou Harris. Emmylou sang harmony on "I Can't Help It If I'm Still in Love With You," and when the three of them got together, it was love at first sight. All they could talk about was how much they wanted to sing together. But talking about it apparently proved a good deal easier than doing it, given the demands of conflicting careers—and worse, the contractual confusion created by labels and lawyers. Linda and Emmylou had a hit duet in 1976, "The Sweetest Gift," Dolly backed up Linda on "I Never Will Marry," Dolly and Emmylou did a few tracks together, and the three of them sang together on Dolly's ill-fated TV variety show, but it was not until 1987 that they were finally able to realize their dream.

Trio, their one and only album together, was that rarity of rarities—a true collaboration between three distinctive, individual personalities. It is one of the most beautiful and artistically challenging country albums ever made, and its critical success was matched by commercial success. Four singles from it went to the Top Ten, and one, a remake of Phil Spector's "To Know Him Is to Love Him," hit number one.

The supergroup was a hot item in pop music of the late sixties and early seventies. The idea originally came from jazz, where individual stars such as Charlie Parker, Dizzy Gillespie, Thelonious Monk, or Miles Davis would get together in various temporary combinations. Pop music groups, on the other hand, were entities: the Platters, the Beach Boys, the Temptations. A featured performer—Frankie Lymon, Buddy Holly, Diana Ross—might leave the group and start a solo career. But you didn't see a Beatle, a Rolling Stone, and a Beach Boy getting together with Otis Redding to form a group to make an album or two.

Then, as pop musicians grew more sophisticated and started to take themselves more seriously, the idea of jamming together like jazz musicians started to appeal to them. A guy from the Byrds, on the West Coast, got together with a guy from Buffalo Springfield, on the East Coast, and a guy from the Hollies, from England—Crosby, Stills, and Nash.

The same thing is starting to happen in country music. Of course, duets have always been a country staple. But in 1991, Mark O'Connor, Vince Gill, and Ricky Skaggs got together on O'Connor's album as the New Nashville Cats. And they say the Nashville supergroup could be the trend of the nineties. But you could say that these three women, from different backgrounds and with different careers, were the first country supergroup.

Billy Joe Royal

b. 4/3/42, Valdosta, GA

Style
Dick Clark comes to Nashville

Memorable Songs
"Down in the Boondocks," "Burned Like a Rocket"

Billy Joe Royal took the pop world by storm with "Down in the Boondocks" in 1965 and his last Top Twenty pop single,

"Cherry Hill Park," in 1969. And while a lot of singers have moved from Top Ten pop singles to Top Ten country singles, I don't recall anyone else who took twenty years in between.

It wasn't twenty years of total obscurity. In 1970, playing a gig at New York's trendiest disco, Arthur, he met Liberace's manager, who told the Georgia boy he could book him into Las Vegas. "At that time Elvis had just come out of retirement to do Vegas," Royal recalls, "and for some reason I decided I just had to work Vegas. So he got me an engagement at the Flamingo Hotel, and I did good, so I got a five-year contract with the Flamingo for sixteen weeks a year. Then the Sahara in Lake Tahoe offered me the same deal. So financially I was still doing okay, but record-wise I was doing nothing."

All right . . . let's leave Billy Joe's career stranded in the Golden Desert and flash back to a boy growing up in south Georgia in the fifties, where the local radio stations "would play three or four formats during the day. You'd get a country thing during the afternoon, and then black gospel—I loved that stuff. It was a sundown station—when the sun went down, the station went off—so then at night, you'd get rhythm and blues on WLAC in Nashville. And, man, that's what I really love. It just stirred my soul when I heard it back then."

Billy Joe made his professional debut in 1959 on "Georgia Jubilee" in Atlanta, a country show that was then falling heavily under the rockabilly influence of Elvis and Conway Twitty. From Atlanta, the next career move was . . . back home. He was still in high school. But the "Jubilee" appearance had made him a hometown hero, and he began putting on his own rock and roll shows in the local theater.

Then it was a circuit of local clubs and theaters, and then back to Atlanta, this time to a downtown strip joint, where Royal just jumped up onstage, started singing, and got hired. "I was there a couple of weeks and then a guy came through from Savannah, Georgia, who—this is the best thing that ever happened to me—owned a club called the Bamboo Ranch in Savannah. So I moved down there with him, and this guy was so crazy, but God love him, he'd book big names, R and B or country, and he didn't really know anything about music, so one time, and this is no joke, he booked Bo Diddley and Jim Reeves on the same show. I thought, 'Somebody's gonna die here tonight,' but they both went over great. By that time Joe South had come down to work with me, so we talked this guy into booking people we wanted to see—Roy Orbison, Sam Cooke."

Royal and South used the Bamboo Club as their headquarters, cutting demos and taking them around to radio stations. Finally they clicked with South's "Down in the Boondocks," and suddenly Royal was getting phone calls from Dick Clark.

"Ninety one-nighters in ninety cities," Billy Joe recalls. "We came home in a box. It was kind of neat because I was kind of young—I don't know if I could do it now. Tom Jones was on that tour, Peter and Gordon, the Shirelles, the Drifters, Mel Carter, Ronnie Dove, Brian Hyland, the Jive Five, Jackie de Shannon. We did that for ninety days, and anybody can be nice for five or ten minutes, but after ninety days you really have to get to know those people. The friendships I made back then I still have."

The Dick Clark TV series "Where the Action Is" followed. Royal was making good money—"not like today, when even country music now is probably ten times bigger than pop was back then. And if you had a good manager—which I did, Bill Lowry looked after me like he was my father—you could save money because there was nothing to spend it on. So when you got through with a tour, you had a nice little nest egg."

Back to Vegas, where Royal was playing the big hotels, riding a high-flying record career, and figuring none of it was ever going to end. But suddenly nobody was listening to the new records. He left Columbia, signed with Mike Curb at MGM (whose big act at the time was the Osmonds), then moved to Scepter . . . but nothing worked for him.

Maybe it was the wrong material?

Royal doesn't disagree: "I'm from the South and I love soul music, and all of a sudden I was cutting this real vanilla kind of stuff. But I thought they knew what they were doing, you know? So then about '76, things really came tumbling down. No record label, and the economy was bad, so the Vegas deals fell apart."

Broke and discouraged, Royal moved back to Georgia, where he worked for a while with producer "Chips" Moman—a pal from the old days who had produced Waylon Jennings and Willie Nelson—still without success. Finally, listening to country radio, he started hearing some oddly familiar voices: Bill Medley of the Righteous Brothers . . . B. J. Thomas . . . Kenny Rogers . . . even Fats Domino. "And some of those records they were playing sounded like the same stuff I was doing in the sixties. So I thought, 'What if you go to Nashville and *don't* sell out? You can't sing country music, so don't even try. Just do what you can do. Back then—and this is just ten years ago—you could still go out to every radio station, go do the national anthem at a ball game, work a free day at a radio station—anything I could do to get them to play the record. And the timing was right, too, because it was pretty much the same acts over and over in country—the only act I could see that had broken in in the last four or five years was the Judds. I don't know if I'd have the nerve to try it today."

Royal kicked around Nashville for a few years, paying the struggling-artist dues all over again, until he found a song called "Burned Like a Rocket." He decided that if there was one song he would bet his future on, this was the song. He released it on Bill Lowry's Southern Tracks label and devoted himself to promoting it. "Burned Like a Rocket," picked up by Atlantic Records' new country division, made it to number ten on the country charts in January of 1986—and then came the *Challenger* disaster, and suddenly the title's connotations became too painful, and overnight, radio stations stopped playing it.

But Billy Joe Royal was back, and a string of Top Ten records has followed, including a remake of Aaron Neville's classic, "Tell It Like It Is," about which Royal says: "Steve Popovich, who ran Polygram in Nashville at the time, kept telling me I should record it, and I kept saying, 'I wouldn't touch it.' But he kept after me, so finally I just gave it a shot. I had no idea it'd be a single. I'm glad he talked me into it because it did well, but it was never my idea. Aaron Neville— that's his song. But I love the blues. I love soul music, I love gospel music, but I also love country music. And I like the guys like Roy Orbison and Gene Pitney. What I do is a combination of all those influences, I guess."

Billy Joe Royal's list of the greatest songs of all time: "Running Scared" by Roy Orbison, "In the Still of the Night" by the Five Satins, "Someday We'll Be Together Again" by the Supremes, "The Thrill Is Gone" by B. B. King, "I Got a Woman" by Ray Charles.

Sawyer Brown

MARK MILLER
b. 10/25/58, Dayton, OH

BOBBY RANDALL
b. Midland, MI

GREGG "HOBIE" HUBBARD
b. 10/4/60, Apopka, FL

JIM SCHOLTEN
b. 4/18/52, Midland, MI

"CURLEY" JOE SMYTH
b. 9/6/57, Westbrook, ME

Cameron Duncan replaced Bobby Randall in 1993.

Style

Celebrity spokesmodel

Memorable songs

"Betty's Bein' Bad"

Awards

CMA—Horizon Award 1985

Sawyer Brown was one of many pop-influenced, self-contained groups that came along in the wake of Alabama, and like Alabama, the group named itself after Southern geography: Savanna. They soon renamed themselves after a street corner in Nashville, but that didn't exactly mean the guys were takin' it to the streets.

Quite the contrary. They were takin' it to TV—Ed McMahon's "Star Search,"

not the rootsiest of venues. They won "Star Search"'s first prize in 1984: $100,000 and a recording contract, and that made them the right group at the right time: 1985, when the group sound was peaking, when Alabama sent three songs to number one, and Exile hit with two. Sawyer Brown sent three songs to the Top Ten that year, including their only chart-topper, "Step That Step."

They've never re-achieved quite that level of sustained success, but they've been a solid chart and touring act through the eighties. In fact, like the classic Southern and Midwestern rock bands, Sawyer Brown have built a solid base on the road, and they use that core audience as a sounding board for new material. Hobie Hubbard describes their 1991 album, *Buick,* as being "like a greatest-hits album, even though it was all new songs—we'd been playing them in front of our fans for such a long time." The new country market of the nineties has Sawyer Brown (like Exile and other rock-styled groups) moving more toward straight country, but their crowd-pleasing road act has always leaned toward high energy and the heavy metal trappings of lights and smoke machines, and the flamboyant costumes and stage performance of lead singer Mark Miller. Well, they certainly aren't the only act in the music business who use a lot of smoke and lights to distract attention from musical blandness, which Lord knows was their hallmark for years.

But an odd thing happened to Sawyer

Brown as they began to go back to those roots no one thought they had. They turned out to have a real feel for straight-ahead music. We're not quite prepared to say we've changed our attitude toward them, but we're keeping an eye on them.

John Schneider

b. 4/8/54, Mt. Kisco, NY

Style

Stylish outlaw

Memorable songs

"I've Been Around Long Enough to Know"

Awards

MCN—Star of Tomorrow

Schneider was the Duke of Hazzard who could sing, but it took an end-around play by producer/mastermind Jimmy Bowen to prove it.

Schneider had used his Duke notoriety to get one country/Top Forty crossover hit, a remake of Elvis Presley's "It's Now or Never," but that was a one-shot, a novelty for the kiddie crowd, and no one took the idea of a John Schneider musical career seriously.

When Schneider signed with MCA, Bowen used a daring ploy to break through the stereotype. He sent copies of "I've Been Around Long Enough to Know" to key country radio stations with no artist's name at all listed on the record.

It worked. The programmers liked the song, they liked the singer on his own merits (several thought it was George Strait), and they agreed to add "I've Been Around Long Enough to Know" to their playlists.

"The Dukes of Hazzard," it turned out, did not scratch the surface of Schneider's talent. A writer/director/actor, he played the role of a country star with flair. He grew a scruffy beard, he hung out with Waylon and Willie, and he made some creditable records, including three more that went to number one.

Eventually, Schneider moved on. In 1990, he opened on Broadway as the star of the successful musical *Grand Hotel*.

Dan Seals

b. 2/8/48, McCamey, TX

Style
MOR

Memorable songs

"You Still Move Me"

Awards

CMA—Single of the Year 1986 ("Bop"), Vocal Duo 1986 (w/ Marie Osmond)

What's a guy named England Dan, the guy best known for the smooth 1976 pop hit "I'd Really Like to See You Tonight," doing in Nashville? What's the brother of folk-popper Jim Seals (Seals and Crofts) doing recording country music? Another one of those carpetbaggers, maybe?

Uh-uh, says Seals. He may have taken some detours, but he was always country, raised in Texas by a father who played with Ernest Tubb. Young Dan joined the family band when he was four years old, playing stand-up bass (now, there's an image to conjure with—those big old stand-up basses have to look pretty formidable next to a four-year old). He heard nothing but country until he was ten, when the family moved to Dallas and he got his first taste of rhythm and blues.

He was hearing some rock and roll about that time, too. His brother Jim, and Jim's partner, Dash Crofts, had joined a group called the Champs, soon to become immortal for recording the all-time party-band hit, "Tequila."

As a teenager in Dallas, Dan joined bands that played everything—"so we could get those gigs in Lions Clubs and stuff, you just played whatever was out"—until a group he formed with John Ford Coley called Southwest FOB, a Dallas version of "a West Coast pop-art experimental band," scored a minor hit with a song called "A Smell of Incense."

Southwest FOB foundered, and Seals and Coley found themselves doing a folk duo out on the West Coast, and Seals picked up the stage name "England Dan," given to him by his brother for no apparent reason. They had a 1973 hit in Japan, but otherwise were going nowhere, until they came up with "I'd Really Like to See You Tonight." It seemed like a pop possibility, but as Dan recalls, he told producer Kyle Lehning, " 'You know, I don't understand this pop music. I don't know how to sing this song.' He said, 'I can tell that by the demo, man. Let's go to Nashville and work on it.' So we came back to Nashville where he lived. And started recording in Hendersonville. Then all of a sudden we sold two million copies and went from a folk duo, acoustic guitar and banjo, to a pop act."

"Really Like to See You" was Seals's biggest pop hit, and as his career slowed down, he also found himself making music he was less and less interested in. "I've come to realize," he says, "that the reason for our success was material rather than talent—and Kyle had a way of moving us

from a folk sound to a contemporary—what you'd now call a contemporary country sound. Even right now, if England Dan–John Ford Coley came out, they would be played on country radio as were Kenny Rogers, Anne Murray, and many others."

The downslope of Seals's pop career was a series of pale carbon copies of "Really Like to See You," and "one day I just said, 'Kyle, I can't do this onstage. I don't want to do this scene.' He said, 'Give me a call when you know what you want to do.' So I went and I wrote some songs with Rafe Van Hoy, and then I went back and said, 'Kyle, I want to do a country thing. That's really where I was raised, that's really where I feel good.' I felt like I had come home in a way with the decision. But I thought it would be eight or ten years before anyone would take me seriously. My first three releases didn't do too well. Then they put out a song I wrote by myself called 'God Must Be a Cowboy.' It was my first Top Ten, and it was the beginning of my acceptance by the country audience."

Seals has still flickered in and out of commitment to the heart of country (but not it seems, from the hearts of his country fans). Two of his biggest hits were "Meet Me in Montana," a duet with Marie Osmond, who was in one of her country periods at the time, and "Bop," more a techno-pop dance number than a country tune. "You Still Move Me," on the other hand, is a sensitive song about love and temptation, deeply in the country tradition.

A devoted family man, Seals lives outside Nashville with his wife, Andy, their two children, and his two sons by a former marriage. Like many country performers, Seals is deeply religious. Unlike most of his fellows, though, he and his wife are converts to the Eastern Baha'i faith.

Dan Seals's list of the greatest songs of all time: "Your Cheating Heart," "I'm So Lonesome I Could Cry," "El Paso," "You Are My Sunshine."

Ricky Van Shelton

b. 1/2/52, Grit, VA

Style
Sexy, honest

Memorable songs
"Wild-Eyed Dream," "From a Jack to a King"

Awards
ACM—New Male Vocalist 1987; CMA—Horizon Award 1988, Male Vocalist 1989; MCN—Star of Tomorrow 1988, Male Artist 1989, Single of the Year 1989 ("I'll Leave This World Loving You"), Video 1989, Album of the Year 1989 (Loving Proof); TNN—Favorite Newcomer 1988, Male Vocalist 1989, Single of the Year 1989, Video 1989; TNN/MCN—Male Artist 1990–91, Entertainer of the Year 1990–91

It's not "Van Shelton," the way that Grace Van Owen from "L.A. Law" is "Ms. Van Owen," although everyone pronounces it as though it were. His last name is Shelton, his middle name is Van.

That's a mistake anyone could make. We recall making another one, perhaps not quite so understandable or forgivable, when we reviewed Mr. Shelton's first album, *Wild-Eyed Dream,* and said that this guy Van Shelton was a burning rockabilly,

and that if he knew what was good for him, he'd stick to the burners and forget the ballad stuff that intruded here or there on the album, like "Life Turned Her That Way."

Yes, we began to have second thoughts when "Life Turned Her That Way" went to number one on the charts. But we realized the enormity of our mistake a year later, when we went to interview Shelton backstage at a summer music festival in upstate New York and saw Ricky performing live in front of an audience that had a sizable component of women. This was a guy who just had to be himself, and he radiated sex appeal.

We'd just begun this book then, and Mr. V . . . Shelton was the first name on our list of interviewees. We set it up with his PR office in Nashville. Yes, Ricky will be up in your part of the mountains; yes, there should be no problem setting up an interview. Ricky's out on the road now, we'll get word to him. But come the morning of the show, and the hoped-for interview, and they hadn't been able to reach him on the road. You can go up and try, they suggested. Tell his manager you talked to us.

Fat chance. But we gave it a try. Asked around backstage, found Mike Campbell, the manager. We're supposed to have an interview with Ricky, we know they never got in touch with you, if it's not convenient, we'll understand. . . .

No, not at all, no problem. I'll just check with Ricky.

And there was no problem. Hey, we decided, these guys are great. Putting this book together is going to be a snap.

And, as we went on, we discovered that most of these guys are great, and as gracious and accommodating as their schedules allow. But it was never to be quite that easy again.

We talked to Ricky on his tour bus, in back of the tent, and as we got onto the bus, we got our next object lesson in Ricky's sex appeal: a cordon of women, from teenagers to grandmothers, squealing with excitement at *us,* just for getting on the bus.

How does Ricky feel about this Rickymania?

A shy grin. "I'm a little uncomfortable with it. I'm glad I'm as successful onstage, that people like what I do, but I honestly wish when I come offstage, I could just be normal."

We weren't talking to a Rickymaniac, that was for sure. Just a guy who grinned when we confessed we had once dismissed his ballad singing and said, yes, actually, he'd been singing "Statue of a Fool" for a long time now. Just a guy who cared a lot about music, about the same kind of music we cared about.

"Hank Williams and the Beatles." That's who he listened to growing up, but not in that order. A small-town kid from south-central Virginia in the fifties and sixties, he started out singing gospel music in church at the age of three ("You trace anybody's musical heritage far enough back, you're gonna find gospel in ninety percent of them. They learn to sing with conviction, and how to put emotion into a song"). Then, a few years down the road, he fell in love with rock 'n' roll.

His older brother, Ronnie, a country/bluegrass mandolin player, asked Ricky to join his group, but rock 'n' roll Ricky was having none of it, until Ronnie upped the ante: "Sing with my group and I'll let you drive my Ford Fairlane."

Well, a car is a car, and if you have to sing "Walkin' the Floor Over You" to get

it, who wouldn't? Funny thing was, Ricky soon found himself liking country music even more than he liked the Fairlane.

In 1984, Ricky's wife, Bettye, landed a job in Nashville, and they made the big move. Bettye got him his first break in the music business, too, when she got a demo tape to Nashville journalist Jerry Thompson, the husband of one of her coworkers. Thompson sent the tape on to a friend at CBS records, who liked it well enough to twist the arm of producer Steve Buckingham and get him to a Shelton showcase. "They liked the rockabilly stuff best, too," he reassured us. Within two weeks, Ricky was in the studio, cutting the songs for *Wild-Eyed Dream.*

Shelton is a songwriter of no mean ability, but when he turns to other writers, he frequently—more frequently than any other contemporary Nashville star—turns to old songs. "Life Turned Her That Way" was a hit for Mel Tillis; Ned Miller took "From a Jack to a King" to number two in 1963; "I'll Leave This World Loving You" first hit the charts for Wayne Kemp in 1980; "Statue of a Fool" has been recorded several times since Jack Greene took it to number one in 1969 (Righteous Brother Bill Medley took one shot at it).

Sometimes Shelton creates the definitive version of a song. Songwriter Kemp was never able to do more than dent the public consciousness as a performer, and the '63 success of "From a Jack to a King" owed more to the quality of the song than to Miller's insipid performance. Frankly, we'll take Ricky over Tillis and Greene, too.

Other times, he'll recycle a song that's indelibly associated with another artist: "Pretty Woman," "Cryin' Time," "Great Balls of Fire." These have all become highlights of his stage show, and if they've led critics to dismiss him as conservative—hey, we live in conservationist, recycling times. And so far, no audience has rebelled at hearing a great singer like Ricky Van Shelton perform great songs that work for his style.

We left the Shelton bus to the squeals of teenagers and grandmothers and went back into the real world of performers who won't give interviews on the road, or won't give interviews at home, or are doing a series of phoners a week from Thursday and can fit you in from 1:10 to 1:35. Not that we're complaining, but . . . .

Thanks, Ricky Van.

Shenandoah

MARTY RAYBON
b. 12/8/59, Sanford, FL

MIKE MCGUIRE
b. 12/28/58, Haleyville, AL

RALPH EZELL
b. 6/26/53, Union, MS

STAN THORN
b. 3/16/59, Kenosha, WI

JIM SEALES
b. 3/20/54, Hamilton, AL

Style

Hard-working, blue-collar band

Memorable songs

"The Church on Cumberland Road,"
"Sunday in the South"

Awards

ACM—Vocal Group 1990;
TNN—Favorite Newcomer 1989

In 1990, Shenandoah began to distance themselves from the post-Alabama groups that had come onto the country music scene in the eighties.

They distanced themselves literally, spending more than three hundred nights on the road in 1989, and earning a reputation as the hardest-working band in the business. And with three consecutive number one records, they definitely began to give notice that they might have something extra.

Shenandoah was different. The earlier groups of the eighties, such as Exile and Sawyer Brown, had followed the Alabama formula of tastes-great, less-filling, pop-based slickness. They were followed by the experimentalists, such as the O'Kanes or Foster and Lloyd, whose goals were to create entirely new sounds. They succeeded, and they drew an audience, but not enough of a mass audience to satisfy their labels, and they fell by the wayside.

Desert Rose Band revived and extended the classic California country-rock sounds that leader Chris Hillman had pioneered with the Byrds and the Flying Burrito Brothers. Highway 101 offered another variant of West Coast country rock, with a great girl singer from Minnesota. Nobody had heard of the Kentucky Headhunters yet, but it did appear that the signs were right for a new kind of country group.

Shenandoah didn't get that message right away. Their first album was the old-style, pop-flavored sound that was beginning to get tired and certainly sounded tired from them, new group or no. The audience responded with massive disinterest, and the album went nowhere.

The members of the band, listening to what they'd put out, tended to agree with the public. They were blue-collar guys. Marty Raybon had worked for eight years as a bricklayer alongside his father, while at the same time playing in his father's bluegrass band. Like any other bunch of working bar-band guys from the South, they'd played everything—country, rock, soul covers—and what they liked was basic, down-home music.

They found that the public liked it, too. The songs from *The Road Not Taken*, their second album, which was also the road they hadn't taken the first time around, drew an instant response, and the group's nonstop, tireless touring didn't hurt, either. And their rootsy, basic sound had a retro effect, too, as existing groups such as Sawyer Brown started to tone down the glitz and strive for a more country sound.

At the height of its popularity in 1991, the group was almost destroyed by legal problems, as groups from Kentucky, Nevada, and Massachusetts sued them, claiming that they had prior claim on the name Shenandoah—a name that the group had not picked for themselves.

Actually, "we did pick the name," Raybon told Jack Hurst of the *Chicago Tribune*, "but we were given a choice [by Sony Music and producer Rick Hall] between the Rhythm Rangers and Shenandoah—which would you have picked?"

The name they wanted at that time was Diamond Rio. Alas, it's too late for that now.

Embroiled in legal problems and caught up in bankruptcy proceedings, they couldn't even afford to go out to Los Angeles in April 1991 for the Academy of Country Music Awards show. They watched it on TV from their tour bus in Corpus Christi, Texas, as they waited to go onstage to play a concert.

As the group entered 1992, however, they were finally rescued from their troubles by that most uncountry of champi-

ons, a lawyer—their attorney/manager, William Carter. They began the new year with a new recording contract and the hope that they hadn't lost too much momentum.

Marty Raybon's list of the greatest songs of all time: "The Grand Tour," "Walkin' on the Fightin' Side of Me," "The Year That Clayton Delaney Died," "When a Man Loves a Woman" by Percy Sledge.

T. G. Sheppard

b. 7/20/42, Humboldt, TN (*William Browder*)

Style

Contemporary, flexible. T. G. will sing about drinkin' and good-timin', but he's not afraid to embrace mom and apple pie, either. He's covered an eclectic assortment of pop tunes and done duets with Clint Eastwood and Judy Collins.

Memorable songs

"Devil in the Bottle," "Last Cheater's Waltz"

Awards

MCN—Most Promising Male Artist 1975

It's a remarkable American success story that T. G. Sheppard pulled himself up from the life of a fifteen-year-old runaway, sleeping in doorways, living under bridges, going to bed hungry, to become a vice president of RCA Victor. It's even more remarkable that he did all that *before* becoming an entertainer.

"Having a business career in music—record producer, publisher, songwriter, promotion man, sales, finally vice president of RCA—gave me a full understanding of that side of things, which has helped me a lot in my career as a performer," Sheppard told us. And, in fact, he makes no bones about having a keen eye for the business end of the music business.

"A lot of my musical decisions are governed by the marketplace," he says. "There's a business side to every artist's career. A lot of artists don't recognize that when they're starting out, if you want to be around for a while, you have to keep your ear to the ground. You have to watch what's happening on radio, where trends are going. You might want to go one way, but music may be going in another direction, and you don't want to get left behind or jeopardize your career by getting too far out into left field. Thirty-five percent of your career should be governed by the marketplace, sixty-five percent should be in your ballpark."

Sheppard exploded onto the charts in 1975 with a number one hit, "Devil in the Bottle," but it was the Urban Cowboy days of the late seventies and early eighties that sent his career into orbit, with eleven chart-toppers in four years. "That period was a phenomenon," he remembers. "We had a lot of crossover hits—but everyone was crossing over then, Mickey Gilley, Charlie Daniels, Eddie Rabbitt."

Unlike some stars looking back on their heydays, Sheppard remembers correctly. All the guys he mentioned had pop hits during that period. T. G. himself had four. The highest ranked, "I Loved 'Em Every One," went to number 37.

Sheppard, like any good businessman, is looking ahead. He's still putting out hits, but he's dispassionate enough to know that doesn't last forever, and he's scouting out possibilities in the media. "I've always thought I would let my music run its course, and then go into TV," he told us, and he's preparing for it by taking such

gigs as guest host for Ralph Emery on "Nashville Now."

But he's not ready to hang it up yet. "We're dealing in a business where age is not really a factor, as opposed to pop music. And it's a little easier to take the touring life, too. A rock and roll band will go out and play every night for thirty days, and then not do anything for six months. In country music, we're consistently touring. But until it gets to the summertime, when state fairs and outdoor parks open up, our touring consists of Fridays, Saturdays, and Sundays. You leave on Thursday and get back on Monday, so it gives you Tuesday and Wednesday at home. An artist at forty-six who's stayed healthy and dedicated to his trade can still compete."

T. G. Sheppard's list of the greatest songs of all time: "Sunday Morning Coming Down" by Kris Kristofferson, "New York, New York" by Frank Sinatra, "Theme From A Summer Place" by Percy Faith, "In the Mood" by Glenn Miller, "The Gambler" by Kenny Rogers.

If you consider a greatest-songs list as a kind of musical self-portrait, you can see it at work in T. G.'s case: one foot in the nitty gritty, another (larger) foot in the smooth and pretty.

Ricky Skaggs

b. 7/18/54, Cordell, KY

Style
Rooted in bluegrass

Memorable songs
"Heartbroke," "Country Boy," "Walkin' in Jerusalem Just Like John"

Awards

ACM—New Male Vocalist 1981, Specialty Instrument (mandolin) 1984, 1987, Touring Band 1982–85, 1990; CMA—Horizon Award, Male Vocalist 1982, Entertainer of the Year 1985, Instrumental Group 1983–85, Vocal Duo 1987 (w/ Sharon White); Grammy—Country Instrumental Performance 1973 ("Fireball"—as part of J. D. Crowe and the New South), 1984 ("Wheel Hoss"), 1986 ("Raisin' the Dickens"); MCN—Star of Tomorrow 1983, Bluegrass Act 1982–84, Instrumental Artist 1982–89; TNN/MCN—Instrumentalist 1990

It was 1982, and like a lot of former country music fans, we weren't listening to much country music anymore. When we turned on a country station, we were likely to hear Barbara Mandrell singing about being country when country wasn't cool, and if that was how it was, we kinda wished it would go back to being uncool again. But the truth was, we couldn't have turned on country stations very often even if we'd wanted to. In our part of upstate New York, there weren't any country stations anymore. Urban Cowboy craze or no, they'd all gone off the air. There was a bar in New Paltz that had a mechanical bull for a while, but they didn't play any country music.

You could still catch the Sutton family occasionally, playing bluegrass at one small bar or another, and they had a few Hank Williams tunes on the jukebox at Dottie's Rock Cliff House in High Falls. They had a few new country songs, too, but nobody ever played them.

We were shooting pool one lazy afternoon at the Rock Cliff when somebody put a quarter in the jukebox, and a singer with a wonderful high, lonesome voice started keening a classic Flatt and Scruggs lament, "Crying My Heart Out Over You," with an incredibly together band backing him up—bluegrass, but like no bluegrass we'd ever heard.

"What is that?" we asked of the bar in general.

"That's Ricky Skaggs," said Ken Cluen over his shoulder.

"He's an old-timer, right? Just someone we somehow never heard before?"

"No, he's new. Brand-new."

Okay, we decided then and there. Country music is back. Time to start listening to it again.

There are two theories about how a new artistic direction happens. One is that it's inevitable—you can only listen to Urban Cowboy glossiness for so long, and then you automatically start pining for a traditional sound, and Ricky Skaggs just happened to be in the right place at the right time.

Ricky himself goes along with this theory: "People give me an awful lot of credit for starting the resurgence. It's hard for me to accept that. . . . Maybe anyone could have done it had they thought of doing it. I don't know. I set out to create a more traditional, back-to-basics kind of sound . . . the mandolin, fiddle, banjo, and steel guitars that had really been lost by the wayside. It was something I felt like the fans wanted, and it was certainly something I wanted."

It's hard for us to accept *that*. The alternate theory, which we subscribe to, is that nothing is inevitable. People start listening to a new sound when, and only when, a great artist comes along and reshapes their ears. No one was waiting for Stravinsky at the turn of the century, Charlie Parker in the forties, Hank Williams or Little Richard in the fifties, Bob Dylan or the Beatles in the sixties. And Ricky Skaggs wasn't created by a sudden mainstream demand for traditional, bluegrass-based music. If Skaggs hadn't been the great artist he was, if he'd just been very good, he'd be playing tiny folk and bluegrass festivals today, and there would have been no Dwight Yoakam, no O'Kanes, no Lyle Lovett, no Holly Dunn, no Desert Rose Band.

Skaggs described his musical roots to *Musician* magazine in January 1990: "My dad bought me a mandolin when I was five years old and showed me the basic G, C, and D chords with two fingers—the Mel Bay style. Much of my influences came through radio. We had an old 78 crank record player, so I would listen to a lot of Flatt and Scruggs and Bill Monroe and the Stanley Brothers on 78s, and I'd slow them down to learn the licks. . . . But a lot of the stuff I grew up listening to was on WCKY in Cincinnati, a fifty-thousand-watt AM station that just blasted all over the country. I heard Buck Owens . . . and then George Jones, Ray Price, and that early big-band, 'Cherokee Cowboy' swing sound—that real tight *integrity* sound. There was some really great music coming out then, because there was a lot of competition . . . you really had to have a great band.

"In '63, I heard the Beatles and the Stones and the Hollies and I realized that there was a much bigger world out there musically. It wasn't that I wanted to quit my roots and what I was doing, but it made me listen to other things, and that was one of the best things that could ever have happened to me. If I had just kept my ears closed and my eyes open in country, that's as far as I ever would have gotten. Instead, the wells are just full of different things that I can draw from."

In 1970, Skaggs and his friend Keith Whitley joined Ralph Stanley and the Clinch Mountain Boys, one of the great traditional bluegrass groups. In 1973,

burnt out by the touring grind that had occupied virtually his entire adolescence, Skaggs left music and moved to Washington, DC, where he took a job in a boiler room. During this period, he told *Musician,* "a friend gave me a double-album set of Django Reinhardt, and I started listening to Stephane Grappelli's violin. . . . I was learning all kinds of swing stuff from Grappelli, and of course that rhythm stuff from Django—that swing feel. It made me see where much of that Western Swing stuff had come from."

In 1974, Skaggs brought his expanding musical awareness to celebrated "newgrass" Country Gentlemen, then to J. D. Crowe and the New South, then his own group, Boone Creek.

His jump into the big time came in 1977, when he joined Emmylou Harris's Hot Band. He stayed with Emmylou for three years, writing many of the arrangements for her 1980 album, *Roses in the Snow* (which won Harris the CMA Award for Female Vocalist of the Year).

After that, he moved to Nashville full-time to pursue a solo career. He did some fiddle playing for a traditional family harmony group, the Whites, and in 1981 married Sharon White. They have four children.

He signed with Epic Records in 1981. No one, not even his own label, considered this an epic event, no more than anyone was impressed by MCA's signing, at around the same time, of a young cowboy named George Strait. But Skaggs's first single off the album, Flatt and Scruggs's "Don't Get Above Your Raisin'," was a solid hit. "You May See Me Walkin' " made the Top Ten, and "Cryin' My Heart Out Over You," Skaggs's third release, hit number one.

Skaggs's period of greatest chart success came between 1981 and 1986, when he placed ten songs at number one. In the next few years, he seemed to drift into compromises with the very pop sounds that he had blasted country music away from in 1981, with un-Ricky-like songs such as "Love's Gonna Get Ya Someday."

The Skaggs family faced a devastating near-tragedy during this period. In 1986, a crazed gunman in a pickup truck fired through the window of Sharon's car, hitting their son Andrew in the face. Andrew was hospitalized in critical condition, but he survived. During this time, the family, always devout, turned even more deeply toward religion. Earlier that year, for the *Love's Gonna Get Ya!* album, Skaggs had made his most brilliant spiritual recording, a soul-stirring bluegrass version of "Walkin' in Jerusalem Just Like John."

In 1989, looking for a comeback of his own, Skaggs produced Dolly Parton's country comeback album, *White Limozeen.* One of the songs he chose for her, "Lovin' Only Me," was turned down by Parton, and Skaggs ended up using it on his *Kentucky Thunder* album. The song went to number one.

Billy and Terry Smith

BILLY SMITH
b. 11/11/56, Reidsville, NC

TERRY SMITH
b. 6/15/60, Reidsville, NC

Style
Progressive bluegrass

Memorable songs
"Blues Stay Away From Me"

"Blues Stay Away From Me," the first single off Billy and Terry Smith's 1990 de-but album on Epic, got a lot of play on CMT video network, but that turned out not to be enough to get the duo into major radio rotation in most markets, or onto the upper levels of the charts.

They deserved more. They were one of the brightest new acts of 1990, and their blend of traditional bluegrass harmonies over country rock/bluegrass instrumentals was as unique as their upbringing. They spent most of their preteen and teenage years working on Bill Monroe's farm, where the greatest bluegrass music of all time became as natural a part of their lives as haying or "What's for dinner?"

Billy Smith remembers an afternoon when they were thirteen and fourteen. They had taken the truck down to the general store to pick up some supplies. Monroe was at the store, and he handed Billy something wrapped up in tissue paper and asked him to take it home.

Back in the truck, the inquisitive kids unwrapped the paper and found Monroe's false teeth. "Suddenly it struck me," Billy remembers, "and I said to Terry, 'Can you imagine all the great music that's passed through these teeth?' And I started working them like a ventriloquist's dummy and singing, 'Blue moon of Kentucky . . .'"

The year 1993 saw the brothers signed to a new label, RCA, and readying a hot new album for a 1994 release.

Jo-el Sonnier

b. 10/2/46, Rayne, LA

Style
Cajun to mainstream

Memorable songs
"Tear-Stained Letter," "Louisiana"

In Jo-el Sonnier's Nashville albums (he's been a regional recording star since early childhood), his deep, rich voice extends its mastery over a variety of musical styles from Cajun to R&B to mainstream country; but his home and his heart are still in native Louisiana. When we talked to him on the telephone from his home in Bogalusa, words cascaded out of him the way his music does: from the heart, and full of the lilt of his native Louisiana, the names and the places and rhythms.

His childhood: "The school was not my forte. Music was. I did it at first to help my mom and my dad because I seen them in those fields with their hands in the dirt, picking that cotton, and I just said, 'You know, there's got to be another way of living.' The first time the accordion was on my lap, I was about three years old. Each night I would go to bed and pray with my accordion beside me, and then I'd play the accordion, and then my mama would come in and take the accordion away from my hand, and she'd wrap me up and I'd go to sleep. Every night I'd play my accordion 'cause we didn't have no TVs in those days, no electricity. I remember the day when electricity came in. It was a pretty wild deal. I kept pulling the string up and down on the light cord. And I went from there to a club down in Crowley, Louisiana, when I was seven, which is where I first sat in, you know, and got to play with a lot of the old legends. My father took me to a dance once and asked the bandleader, 'Can my little boy sit in for one song?' I found out later that it was the great Iry LeJeune."

At eight, Jo-el entered his first statewide contest and finished third. The winner was one of the greatest of all Cajun accordion players, Nathan Abshire. Six years later, Jo-el was the state champion.

On his influences: "Jimmy C. Newman would come to our little part of Lou-isiana and sit in many times at the Midway Club down in Breaux Bridge, Louisiana, and I idolized him very much. I always said, 'Now, that's what I want to be.' I never knew what the Grand Ole Opry was till 1966, which ought to tell you something. But when I was seven years old or eight years old, I got to see George Jones. He was the first country artist I ever witnessed onstage, and I remember him so clearly, with his flattop. I loved Clifton Chenier. I may have been the only white musician ever to play with him onstage, although black and white musicians in southwestern Louisiana were always very close."

Moving beyond southwest Louisiana: "I knew I had to step out and take that chance in life, wherever it took me. I didn't know where I was going. I got a call back in 1972 to do a folk festival. I didn't know what a folk festival was till I got there." But when the college students at the festival responded enthusiastically, the festival's director encouraged him to keep branching out. "I didn't know what I was doing, but I went back home and kissed Mom and Dad and said, 'I don't know where I'm going, but I'm motivated to do this,' and it was a very, very hurting thing. But I knew I had done everything I possibly could in those little parish towns, and I had to move on."

He arrived in Los Angeles, and his wife, Jamie (who died in 1989), got him entered in an amateur night at the Palomino Club, where they had never heard anything like him. He was billed as the first Cajun rock and roll star, but meanwhile, he was learning a new world of music, in his unique way, "by writing out the words of the songs of each artist that I loved and respected. George Jones, Buck Owens, Merle Haggard, Ray Price, Ray Charles. I wrote these songs on paper, and as I wrote them, I digested the feeling as they sung it on record, but when I sang them, they came to me in a different deliverance."

Jo-el came to Nashville in 1974, where he worked regularly as a session musician and released a few sides for Mercury. It was his 1987 album for RCA, *Come On Joe,* that established him as a strong new voice in country music.

Jo-el on his late wife, the former Jamie Talbert from Bogalusa: "The loss of my wife was very hard on me. It was just like trying to pick my heart up from the floor. And for a year I was not good for nobody. But through prayers and friends, they started building me up and that love came through, and I'm back to health again, the pain is much easier but it doesn't go away. She was my music then, she is my music now."

On his music: "Since I was a little boy, my dream was to bring it to a worldwide audience, and without diluting it. I saw Nathan Abshire a week before he died, and he told me, 'Jo-el, you're the chosen one.' Tears came to my eyes"—his voice breaks as he talks over the telephone. "He told me, 'Don't let them take advantage of our music and don't let them dilute it, but take it to new places.' "

Jo-el Sonnier's list of the greatest songs of all time: "I Can't Stop Loving You," "Today I Started Loving You Again," "Sitting on the Dock of the Bay," "He Stopped Loving Her Today." "The Willie Nelson song . . . it was written by my friend who helped me write a song about my wife. . . . What's that song? . . . Oh, yes, 'You Were Always on My Mind.' "

We couldn't help feeling that Jamie Talbert from Bogalusa was very close to Jo-el's mind as he chose the list.

Southern Pacific

JOHN MCFEE

STU COOK

KEITH KNUDSEN

KURT HOWELL

DAVID JENKINS

Style

Country-rock

Memorable songs

"New Shade of Blue"

Southern Pacific was a Los Angeles group, made up of ex-rockers, but they had an authentic country feel, and they made some good music. They included two ex–Doobie Brothers (McFee and Knudsen), and ex–Creedence Clearwater Revivalist (Cook), and an ex–Pablo Cruiser (Jenkins).

The California country-rock sound, pioneered by the Byrds and the Flying Burrito Brothers, then brought to its summit of popularity by the Eagles and Linda Ronstadt, has always been a sort of unacknowledged relative of Nashville country, the big-city cousin who puts on too many highfalutin airs, but in the more tolerant mideighties, Southern Pacific gained ungrudging acceptance.

Their first hit, "Thing About You" (1985), featured the guest vocals of Emmylou Harris. They reached their peak of popularity in 1988–89 with such songs as "New Shade of Blue" and "Honey I Dare You." A lot of new groups came along at that time, and there are only room for so many. Southern Pacific did better than, say, Zaca Creek, but they were eclipsed by Shenandoah and the Kentucky Headhunters.

Southern Pacific broke up when Kurt Howell left for a solo career; Cook, McFee, and Knudsen, the group's original nucleus, planned to stay together and create a new ensemble with a new name and a new sound.

The Statler Brothers

DON S. REID
b. 6/5/45, Staunton, VA

HAROLD W. REID
b. 8/21/39, Augusta County, VA

PHILIP E. BAISLEY
b. 8/8/39, Augusta County, VA

JIMMY FORTUNE
b. 3/1/55, Newport News, VA

Lew DeWitt, one of the original Statler Brothers and the writer of "Flowers on the Wall," died August 15, 1990, at the age of fifty-two.

Style
Feels like barbershop harmony but sounds more like the Jordanaires; small-town Americana.

Memorable songs
"Flowers on the Wall," "The Class of '57" (nominated by novelist Kurt Vonnegut to be our national anthem "for a while")

Awards
ACM—Vocal Duet/Group 1972, 1977; CMA—Vocal Group 1972–80, 1984; Grammy—New Country Artist 1965,

Contemporary (R&R) Performance Group 1965, Country Vocal Performance–Duo or Group 1972 ("Class of '57"); MCN—Vocal Group 1971–82, Comedy Act 1980, 1982–85, Entertainer of the Year 1985–87, Single of the Year 1984, Video 1985 ("Elizabeth"), Single of the Year, Video 1986 ("My Only Love"), Video 1988 ("Maple Street Memories"), Album of the Year 1979 (Entertainers On and Off the Record), 1980 (The Originals), 1981 (Tenth Anniversary), 1985 (Atlanta Blue), 1986 (Pardners in Rhythm), TV Special 1984–85 ("Another Evening With the Statler Brothers"), 1987 ("The Statlers' Christmas Present"); TNN/MCN—Vocal Group 1990–91, Single of the Year 1990 ("More Than a Name on a Wall")

Don Reid is a man of surprisingly eclectic tastes for a guy from a group whose style is so closely identified with the front-porch swing, the white picket fence, and a set of values personified by Randolph Scott. Irving Berlin, yes: the Statlers could be described as the Irving Berlins of country music. But Kris Kristofferson, the wandering visionary bohemian poet, the Walt Whitman of country music?

"Absolutely," says Reid. "That's what's so great about country music—there are so many different styles and points of view that can not only coexist but embrace each other." The Statlers were one of the early country acts to record Kristofferson's songs.

But they didn't make their reputation as interpreters of the Kris Kristofferson songbook. They are makers of little movies in song about middle America, and those little movies, at their best, are made in the style of John Ford. They are lovingly evocative of a time and place that may really exist nowhere except in the mind, but exists so clearly there that you could almost reach out and touch it.

That evocation is strongest when their vision of America admits a little complexity and opens itself to some of the ragged edges of life, as in "The Class of '57," which includes some failures and even a suicide, but shows an underlying warmth toward the human comedy. It's less effective when they dive headlong into sentimentality about this country of the mind, as in their 1987 album, *Maple Street Memories*.

Harold Reid puts it this way: "A song is the most transitional thing that's ever been invented. Nothing else can take you from one place and point in time to another quicker than a song can. For that reason, we are always extra careful not to violate the trust that the fans have in us, extra careful not to go overboard, or play any mind games with people by taking them someplace where they don't want to go. We always try to make it positive."

The Statlers—it's not quite true that none of them are brothers, but it's most definitely the case that none is named Statler—come by their feeling for middle America from their heritage, which is the Shenandoah Valley community of Staunton, Virginia, and their present-day lifestyle, which is the same thing. They all still live in or around Staunton, and they even have their offices in the building that was their old elementary school. Some may think this carries staying close to your roots to a bizarre extreme, but it works for the Statlers. As Don Reid puts it, "When most people write about the past, they have to rely on their memories. But we have it all here right with us. My office is in the same room I went to in the seventh grade. Just down the hall is the gymnasium where we won our first local talent contest. Every day, we walk through the same doors we used to walk through to go to school."

It seems odd, considering how completely the Statler Brothers embrace that old-fashioned country image, but they began as pop stars, shooting up to number four on the pop charts in 1965 with their first single, "Flowers on the Wall." Maybe they're right—there was a time when America was a kinder, gentler place.

The Statlers have won three Grammy Awards, including one for pop vocal group of the year in 1965, a year in which both the Beatles and the Supremes were at the peaks of their careers. They've been named the Country Music Association's Vocal Group of the year ten times, which is a record no other group has matched, including Alabama. Currently, they're the stars of their own variety series on the Nashville Network.

Don Reid's list of the greatest songs of all time: "White Christmas," "Help Me Make It Through the Night," and anything else by Irving Berlin or Kris Kristofferson.

Ray Stevens

b. 1/24/39, Clarkdale, GA (*Ray Ragsdale*)

Style

Comedy

Memorable songs

"Gitarzan," "Would Jesus Wear a Rolex," "The Streak"

Awards

Grammy—Contemporary Country Vocal Performance–Male 1970 ("Everything Is Beautiful"), Arrangement Accompanying

Vocalists 1975 ("Misty");
MCN—Comedian 1988–89;
TNN/MCN—Comedian 1990–91

Ray Stevens is a Nashville institution by this time, and in a branch of the entertainment industry that's not always responsive to innovation or risk-taking and is not always comfortable with cleverness, it's hard to imagine being a Nashville institution as humorist, and also being funny. But Ray Stevens is pretty funny a lot of the time.

A streak of malice helps any humorist, and Stevens has that. He doesn't mind skewering televangelists such as Jim Bakker, in "Would Jesus Wear a Rolex." A streak of zaniness doesn't hurt, and "Gitarzan" was so far out of left field, it's hard to figure out *where* it came from. A streak of musical sophistication is useful to a musical humorist, and the classically trained Stevens had enough of that to transform the jazz standard "Misty" into a bluegrass romp (although Stevens denies any sophistication in what he does). A "streak" can sometimes be enough all by itself—it was for Stevens in 1974, when the seventies fad provided him with a country number one and a pop number one.

Stevens started his recording career while still in high school, but nothing really hit for him until he "decided to do something really strange to attract radio attention. I made a record in 1960 called 'Sergeant Preston of the Yukon,' with lots of sound effects—dogs barking and wind blowing—and it did well until King Features, who owned the show, sent us a letter telling us to cease and desist." But Stevens realized that comedy worked, and he kept at it. "Ahab the Arab," in 1962, was his first hit.

Stevens got a shot at TV stardom in 1970 when Andy Williams hired him as his summer replacement. "Everything Is Beautiful," written as a theme for the TV show, went to number one and became his biggest straight hit.

"But then I slid back," he says, chuckling. "Once the public gloms on to an image, that's pretty much it. But actually, I think that comedy is harder to write and produce than straight music. And you have more longevity as a comedy act."

In 1990, Stevens opened his own theater in Branson, and these days he spends six months a year there.

Gary Stewart

b. 5/28/45, Letcher County, KY
Style
Honky-tonk
Memorable songs
"She's Actin' Single (I'm Drinkin' Doubles)"

Gary Stewart lived out his own legend a little too fully, and it cut short the career of one of the wildest honky-tonkers of recent memory. He burst on the scene in the early seventies with a raw, rasping voice and a go-for-broke style that echoed the rock and blues artists he credited as his influences: the Allman Brothers, Fats Domino, Jimmy Reed, Ritchie Valens, Don Gibson.

His biggest hits were "Drinkin' Thing," "Out of Hand," and "She's Actin' Single (I'm Drinkin' Doubles)." After that, he never cracked the Top Ten again, and although he remained signed to RCA Records through 1982, a drug problem and a raft of personal problems, including the suicide of his son, dragged him further and further down.

But no one who ever heard Gary Stewart at his peak of performance was ever quite able to forget him. *Billboard* columnist Gerry Wood, who has heard it all, once wrote: "Gary Stewart just may be the best singer in the history of country music." So it was good news to a lot of fans when Stewart began recording again in 1988 for Oakland's feisty independent Hightone label, which has also rereleased his classic 1974 album.

Doug Stone

b. 6/19/56, Newnan, GA

Style

Merle Haggard–influenced pure country

Memorable songs

"I'd Be Better Off (In a Pine Box)"

In the spring of 1990, members of the country music press got a cassette with a picture of a dinosaur on the front, and the words "Entering the Stone Age." Nothing else to identify it. On the cassette was a song called "I'd Be Better Off (In a Pine Box)," and a few bars each from some other songs.

We put it on. Good stuff, we thought. Another solid performance by Merle Haggard, and typically strong Hag material.

Then . . . just a second, there. The guy does sound sort of like Merle Haggard, but he's much too young. Good, though. Real good. We thought it through a little more. Okay, this has to be a new artist, and his name must be Stone, and we'll be hearing more from him.

We are right on all counts, particularly the one about hearing more from him. "Pine Box" was released not long after that

and went straight up the charts, as did Stone's next single and first number one, "Fourteen Minutes Old." Doug Stone had arrived as one of the New Traditionalist Class of 1990, a powerful, if sometimes interchangeable, bunch of new voices. And if they all reminded you of someone else—if Mark Chesnutt was, for example, the new George Jones, then Doug Stone was the new Merle Haggard.

All of this is more than a little unkind. It's not Doug Stone's fault that country radio programmers have a herd mentality; it's not Alan Jackson's or Mark Chesnutt's or Joe Diffie's. And if these guys, and guys like them, are sometimes marketed as the flavor of the month, they're not the flavor of the month in their own hearts or minds. Doug Stone didn't model himself to fit into a currently fashionable mold. This is the guy he is, and this is the singer he is.

His background is in many ways a traditional country background, but it's his: Newnan, Georgia, was the "right place for a kid to grow up—it had the woods that you could roam in, and a big old barn you could play in. Daddy built us a go-cart, and he took a 1950 panel truck, cut the back half of it off, and put it up in an oak tree in the backyard, and that was our tree hut."

Like so many successful men in every field, Stone had that classic combination: a daddy who taught him to work, and a mama who taught him to dream. "Daddy was a mechanic, and he taught me diesel mechanics. I had a band when I was fifteen, but really my first band was me and Mama. Mama was an aspiring singer, a great singer, but she never made it—she came in the wrong era. She's still the inspiration behind me, and my greatest critic."

In an odd way, Stone discovered himself. "I was working this second-shift job," he recalls, "and the way I relaxed when I got home was to get in my little home studio, put on my headphones, and listen to music. I dozed off one night with the headphones on and woke up with this song playing in my ears. I didn't recognize it for about five seconds. I was going, 'Who is that? I really like this guy!' And then it hit me: 'That's me!' and I got cold chills all over me. It was like waking up with someone else's ears, and that's the first time I really knew I could sing."

Later he would get the mentor, the person who believed in him. Phyllis Bennett was an aspiring personal manager who had once turned down the chance to manage Alabama and had spent the next decade trying to make up for that mistake—to find another act that she believed in as much as Alabama. "She came into the VFW in Newnan one night to hear us play and decided that I was the guy. That was in 1987, and I'd turned thirty, and I was starting to think, 'If I don't do something soon, I'm going to be too old to do this.' She came back about a year later with a personal management contract and said sign this, and I'll see what I can do for you."

Stone thought it over and decided that since the contract only tied him up for a year, he'd take a chance. He hasn't regretted it. Bennett got his tapes to Bob Montgomery, then head honcho at Epic Records; a live audition, just Doug and his guitar in Montgomery's office, sealed the deal.

If there is a flavor-of-the-month mentality to the industry, and if the new voices of the nineties are all in a knockout competition with each other for just a few rungs on the ladder, you'd never know it by Doug Stone. At the time we interviewed him for this book and asked him for his five-greatest-songs list, he told us about a song that "hasn't hit the airways yet, but it's going to be a great song—that's 'Almost Home' by Joe Diffie. When I first got my contract, I got a lot of demos that Joe Diffie sang on, and finally one day I called CBS and said, 'Look, I don't want you to throw me off the label, but why don't you sign that guy?' His vocals just blew me away."

Doug Stone's list of the greatest songs of all time: "Tell It Like It Is," "He Stopped Loving Her Today," Shenandoah's "The Church on Cumberland Road" and "Mama Knows," "Almost Home."

George Strait

b. 5/18/52, Pearsall, TX

Style

New Traditional

Memorable songs

"Does Fort Worth Ever Cross Your Mind," "All My Exes Live in Texas"

Awards

ACM—Album of the Year 1985 (Does Fort Worth Ever Cross Your Mind), *also coproducer w/ Jimmy Bowen, Male Vocalist 1984–85, 1988, Entertainer of the Year 1989; CMA—Album of the Year 1985* (Does Fort Worth Ever Cross Your Mind), *Male Vocalist 1985–86, Entertainer of the Year 1989–90; MCN—Male Artist 1986*

For a guy who's as important as he is in the country music industry . . . for a guy who's changed the face of country music to the extent that he has . . . for a guy who's been as popular, and as beloved, to his fans as George Strait, people have always been free enough with the advice on how to change him.

Starting, incredibly enough, with the advice he was given when his first album was coming out, and the smart guys in Nashville were working up an image for him: lose the cowboy hat, kid. No one wears 'em anymore. It just don't work.

Later, as the era he created was in full sail, and new stars such as Dwight Yoakam took the stage with frayed Levi's jeans under their cowboy hats, Strait was belittled as the Perma-Prest cowboy. Critics said that no real honky-tonk hero would wear Strait's starched, pressed jeans and button-down shirts. Strait responds to this in the same way he responds to any other suggestion that he change.

"I don't know what some people expect me to look like," he told the *Houston Chronicle*. "Do they want me to wear dirty clothes, like I just came from the garage? I like to look at least like I've cleaned up for the show. I just wear what I like. Of course, I don't have any tailor for my jeans, and the shirts are just regular old store-bought deals." Which you can do, if you're built like George Strait.

Critics have noted that Strait basically follows the same formula, album after album: a no-frills delivery, some simple, affecting ballads, some straight-ahead, fiddle-and-guitar-powered Texas honky-tonk swing. Come to think of it, what could possibly be wrong with that? And yet other long-lasting acts, such as Hank Williams, Jr., Willie Nelson, Reba McEntire, or Alabama, have kept their careers going by tinkering, changing, adjusting.

"What am I supposed to do?" asks Strait. "Sing rock or what?"

But none of this criticism is very serious. No one doesn't like George Strait. He's not like Alabama, a fan favorite but rejected by the critics. On the contrary. Country music critics are a traditionalist bunch, and overwhelmingly, they love George, and they've always loved George. His recorded work, Bob Allen wrote in *Country Music* magazine, has "been a chain without so much as a single weak link. Each new album has seemed to solidify and build upon the obvious strengths of the ones before, strengths summed up in Strait's no-nonsense approach, his power and emotion as a country vocal interpreter, and his almost unerring sixth sense for picking great material."

And for his fans, a Strait concert is an occasion. They come up to the edge of the stage and present cowboy hats for him to autograph (he always obliges), or long-stemmed red roses as a tribute, or ladies' panties as . . . as . . . hey, maybe that Perma-Prest look really does work.

Strait came from what he recalled (to Bob Allen) as "not exactly a country music background." His father, a junior high school math teacher, "didn't even have a record player, and when he listened to the radio, it was generally the news or the cow market reports, or something like that. If a song did happen to come on, I never paid too much attention to what it was."

Strait fooled around with a couple of garage bands in high school, but it was never serious, not until he joined the army and began singing in a country band put together by the commander of his base in Hawaii. Back home in Texas, he studied for a degree in agricultural engineering at Southwest Texas State and put together the band that became his Ace in the Hole Band.

By this time, he was serious about music, but he was using his agricultural education, too, managing a cattle ranch by day and singing at night. It was a tough schedule for a family man (Strait had married his high school sweetheart, Norma, right out of high school), but he kept at it, making periodic trips to Nashville to try to interest a record label.

In the late seventies, no one was buying a country purist from Texas, and in 1980, Strait finally decided to pack it in and make his living in the cattle business.

But finally, Nashville was listening. Erv Woolsey, who had once owned a San Marcos, Texas, nightclub where Strait performed, was now working for MCA/Nashville, and he landed George a contract. Woolsey now manages Strait.

Strait's first album, *Strait Country,* was released in 1981, and the first single off it, "Unwound," made the Top Ten. After a small setback with his next release, "Down and Out," he bounced back in 1982 with "If You're Thinking You Want a Stranger (There's One Coming Home)" (number three) and hit his first number one with "Fool Hearted Memory," from a forgettable film called *The Soldier,* in which Strait made his film debut.

If you want to follow a perfectly structured career in the music business, look at George Strait's history as a charted artist. Using Joel Whitburn's *Top Country Singles 1944–1988* (Record Research, Inc.), we see this list of hits (almost all number ones) and the dates when they debuted on the charts:

6/19/82	"Fool Hearted Memory"
10/9/82	"Marina Del Rey"
2/12/83	"Amarillo by Morning"
6/11/83	"A Fire I Can't Put Out"
10/8/83	"You Look So Good in Love"
2/11/84	"Right or Wrong"

6/2/84	"Let's Fall to Pieces Together"
9/29/84	"Does Fort Worth Ever Cross Your Mind"
2/2/85	"The Cowboy Rides Again"
6/1/85	"The Fireman"
9/21/85	"The Chair"
1/18/86	"You're Something Special to Me"
5/17/86	"Nobody in His Right Mind Would've Left Her"
9/13/86	"It Ain't Cool to Be Crazy About You"
1/17/87	"Ocean Front Property"
5/2/87	"All My Exes Live in Texas"
8/22/87	"Am I Blue"
2/6/88	"Famous Last Words of a Fool"
5/21/88	"Baby Blue"
9/17/88	"If You Ain't Lovin' "

You could set your watch by it. Every four months, three Top Ten singles a year. It's the mark of an act secure at the top; you see it in the Judds, in Randy Travis. Five or six a year means someone's nervous, tinkering, trying to find the right song; miss a turn and it means you're having problems—producer problems, label problems, life problems. Keep it going for ten years, as Strait has, and you're a phenomenon—and Strait managed it even through scrapping a two-thirds-finished album in 1983, changing producers (Blake Mevis, his first producer, wanted him to move more toward a pop sound), and starting all over again.

"I never dreamed I could be as successful as I have been," Strait told Bob Allen. "When I first signed with MCA records, and I went to their offices in Nashville, I remember lookin' at all those gold records on the wall. . . . I asked Erv, my manager, 'Hey, Erv, you think I'll ever have one of those?' "

He's had a couple. And at a recent

charity auction, one of Strait's trademark white cowboy hats went for $6,500.

Marty Stuart

b. 9/30/58, Philadelphia, MS

Style

Hillbilly

Memorable songs

"Hillbilly Rock"

Awards

Grammy—Country Vocal Collaboration 1992 ("The Whiskey Ain't Workin'," w/ Travis Tritt)

"**I**m a hillbilly," says Marty Stuart, "and I'm proud of it. I'm proud of the word. That's why I'm so glad that 'Hillbilly Rock' became such a big hit. I wanted to restore that word *hillbilly* to its rightful place in our music."

What kind of a hillbilly is Marty Stuart? The best kind. A protégé of Lester Flatt and Johnny Cash, he's the kind of hillbilly who honors his elders, and the great country artists who came before him. He's the kind of hillbilly who's in love with the country tradition, even the faintly ridiculous parts of it—his stage costumes are old Porter Wagoner band uniforms, lovingly reclaimed from secondhand shops.

He's not a hillbilly from the Ozarks, though. He's from Philadelphia, Mississippi, a town that became infamous back in the sixties when three civil rights workers—one black, two white—were murdered there. We wondered if Stuart was old enough to remember that.

"I remember," he told us. "I did a con-

cert back home not long ago, and some of those guys—the ones who were involved—were in the audience, and it gave me a really strange feeling. I remember my father lifting me up onto his shoulders so I could see Martin Luther King leading a march. I remember all those church guys with their guns and baseball bats and two-by-fours, and I remember not being able to understand what any of that had to do with the church or Our Lord.

"I love my mother very much, for everything she did for me in my life, but one thing that I love her the most for is that she taught me it was wrong to hate."

Sweethearts of the Rodeo

KRISTINE ARNOLD (*Kristine Oliver*)
b. 11/28/56, Torrance, CA

JANIS GILL (*Janis Oliver*)
b. 3/1/54, Torrance, CA

Style

Sister harmony, often applied to unlikely material

Memorable songs

"Midnight Girl/Sunset Town"

The Oliver sisters grew up in Manhattan Beach, California, otherwise known as one of the surfing towns mentioned in the Beach Boys' "Surfin' USA," so it's not surprising that they named themselves after the Byrds' classic album that pioneered the sound of West Coast country rock. They started out playing country and bluegrass music in high school just to be different—all their friends were forming rock and surf music bands. "The funny thing is," Janis remembers, "that after a while we realized that we thoroughly enjoyed it.''

There is, of course, a strong country music circuit in California, although not exactly in Manhattan Beach, and the sisters soon found themselves a part of it, playing bluegrass clubs up and down the coast, and trying to break into the music business in that Town South of Bakersfield, Los Angeles.

They didn't get much out of the music business in California except husbands. Kristine married a songwriter, and Janis married an aspiring guitar player/singer named Vince Gill.

When Vince moved to Nashville, Janis, then retired from the music business, went with him. Nashville snapped her out of retirement, and she convinced Kristine to join her and give their career one more shot. After winning a national talent contest sponsored by Wrangler Jeans, they were signed to a Columbia recording contract.

Signed in the wake of the Judds' huge success, when female harmony groups suddenly became a hot item in trend-hungry Nashville, the Sweethearts found their own niche. They are the tough girls on the block, the Shangri-las of country. Lean and cowgirl stylish and razor-sharp, you'll never mistake them for mincing suburban housewives like the Girls Next Door; you'll never find them swinging on a porch swing in white eyelet trim like the Forester Sisters or the McCarters; you'll certainly never find them playing second fiddle to their mother, like Wynonna Judd.

For much of their career, unfortu-nately, they've been more hard-edged style than substance. They've chosen some interesting and unusual material. Their first hit was "Hey, Doll Baby," a fifties hit for the Clovers, a pioneer rhythm and blues group, also covered memorably by the Everly Brothers. They've recorded exciting nontraditional contemporary material such as John (Orleans) Hall's "The Chosen Few," and they had a hit in 1988 with the Beatles' "I Feel Fine," but it wasn't clear that they'd added anything in the way of interpretation to these fine songs. They do seem to be getting better, though, and their 1990 album, *Buffalo Zone,* got some impressive critical praise.

Sylvia

b. 12/9/56, Kokomo, IN (*Sylvia Allen*)

Style

Urban Cowboy

Memorable songs

"Nobody"

Awards

ACM—Female Vocalist 1982

Sylvia was in case you thought that just one Crystal Gayle wasn't enough to go around, and the only solution was to come up with another one. She had quite a vogue in the early eighties, with two number one hits, including one ("Nobody") that's still a favorite of the late-night TV anthologies with names like *Country Magic* or *Golden MOR Moments.*

T

Les Taylor

b. 1965, Killen, AL

See EXILE.

Texas Tornadoes

DOUG SAHM
b. 11/6/41, San Antonio, TX

FREDDY FENDER (*Baldemar Huerta*)
b. 6/4/37, San Benito, TX

AUGIE MEYERS

FLACO JIMENEZ

Style

Tex-mex

Memorable songs

"Dinero," "Is Anybody Goin' to San Antone"

Awards

ACM—New Male Vocalist 1975 (Freddy Fender, "Before the Next Teardrop Falls"); Grammy—Mexican/American Performance 1986 (Flaco Jimenez, "Ay Te Deo en San Antonio"), 1990 (Soy de San Luis)

"You've heard of the New Kids on the Block?" Doug Sahm says. "Well, we're the old farts in the neighborhood." All four of the Texas Tornadoes are grandfathers, and all four of them have had long and honorable careers in the music business. Sahm and Augie Meyers were members of the Sir Douglas Quintet, a group of Texans whose, "She's About a Mover," during the height of the British invasion, was such a perfect imitation of a British imitation of Texas rhythm and blues that most audiences thought they were British. Flaco Jimenez was the master of the *conjunto* accordion, the Tex-Mex border sound that has become such an integral thread in the tapestry of American music. Freddy Fender had been in popular music forever, a rock and roll balladeer in the fifties, then one of the most powerful country ballad singers of the seventies. Brought together as the Texas Tornadoes in 1989, they surprised everyone, including themselves.

"Even amongst ourselves," Freddy Fender says, "I don't think any of us have actually gotten to the bottom of how the Tornadoes came about. Doug Sahm claims it was all his dream, and he did have an album out once with another group called the Texas Tornadoes, but as far as him having a concept of what the Tornadoes are now, I don't know." Fender joined the group more or less by accident. He was looking for a solo deal with Warner Brothers, and he went to play a showcase in San Francisco on the same bill with Sahm and Meyers. After the show, his manager told him, "They want you together or not at all."

"Even when we started, I was a doubting Thomas. I was still into Freddy Fender makin' it on his own, and who were these three characters? We were playing smoky rooms, and I'd played at Carnegie Hall, you know? But all of a sudden, I found myself doin' a lot of interviews, I was doin' TNN, and then I saw the record goin' up the charts, and I said, there's got to be somethin' to this, because the charts go not by radio play, but by sales. For the first year of the Tornadoes, I was thinking about getting out and doing something on my own, but then we got the Grammy Award, and this year we've been nominated for a Grammy again, and I finally said, well, it's happened. We do have something. And now I am completely in full confidence that we can make a good living here for the rest of our lives. It's just amazing, because musically I was in doubt of what we had. It's funny, you know, how success can be staring you in the face and you don't see it."

Musically, the mixture is sensational, one of our very favorite sounds. The combination of a rocking ethnic band and a sweet-voiced ballad singer had worked for the Neville Brothers, and it works here, with Freddy as the Aaron Neville of the Tornadoes.

"Of course, I'm older than Aaron, and I was in the music business before Aaron," says Fender. "But of all the singers in the world, I would rather be compared with him, 'cause he sings like an angel. Actually, I'd compare my style with the older singers—the Ink Spots, the Platters. You know, when it comes to country radio, we don't get played much. We get a lot of Mexican American play, and college radio plays the hell out of us. But as for country radio, we're nowhere, and anyone who plays us does so at the risk of the program director getting on his ass. Our manager asked one program director, 'Why don't you play "Is Anybody Goin' to San Antone"?' and he said, 'We can't play that. It doesn't sound like Garth Brooks or Clint Black.' Well, why the hell would I want to sound like them? I'm happy the way I sound. I'd like to hear Garth Brooks or Clint Black sing 'Secret Love.'

"We've proved what we can do. We're flexible. We're rhythm and blues guys, and rock and roll, but we can play anything—I had a lot of success in country music, and I'm grateful to it. But it's like painting, you know? A lot of people were shocked at the brushstrokes of van Gogh or Picasso. But shit, that's what art is, man. Either you buy it or you don't. And people bought us. They bought Lyle Lovett, too, and radio will not play him. Or that girl, k. d. lang, and she has a beautiful voice.

"I think one of the reasons we got nominated for a Grammy is that there are a lot of Grammy voters outside Nashville. Nashville is great, man, and they give us a little opening every now and then and I appreciate that, but they're not gonna change.

"But there's more than Nashville. We're number one in Holland. And Australia, because we play there. Willie Nelson, great as he is, might have trouble getting arrested in Canberra or Perth or Sydney or New South Wales, but they love Charley Pride and Kenny Rogers and George Hamilton IV—you don't hear much from him here, but he's one of the strongest acts in Australia and New Zealand. We played Utrecht, Holland, three years ago, on the same bill with Randy Travis, and they gave us a much bigger hand. Not because he's not good— he's great. But you have to plow the field before you can harvest it."

Freddy Fender's list of the greatest songs of all time: "Stardust," "Dream"—the old one, not the Everly Brothers song—"Dream, when you're feelin' blue . . .", "Twilight Time," "Secret Love," "I Just Called to Say I Love You."

Mel Tillis

b. 8/8/32, Pahokee, FL

Style

Smooth singin' from a stutterin' boy

Memorable songs

"Detroit City" (as writer), "I Believe in You"

Awards

CMA—Entertainer of the Year 1976; MCN—Comedy act 1973–78

A huge segment of the country music audience (at least those over forty-years old) thrives on songs about the past. Many country songs yearn for better days. No song evokes "going home" more then "Detroit City," written by Mel Tillis and Danny Dill. It depicts the plight of a Southerner who left home to find work in a Northern factory and now longs to return to his family and his friends.

Times change, and maybe a future country songwriter will create a lament by a guy who's moved to Houston to earn a living and now dreams of the winters in Dearborn or Milwaukee. But "Detroit City'" stands as an anthem for many dislocated people; and in the same way, Tillis's adopted hometown of Branson, Missouri, stands as a new symbol for the old Nashville.

This hardscrabble Missouri town—even its mayor concedes that it's in the middle of nowhere—attracts over 2 million tourists a year, even though the only way to get there is over a two-lane highway that's backed up for miles during the summer. Those tourists wait in line for hours to get to the five-mile strip of neon, glitz, and instant buildings that house motels, miniature golf courses (indoor and outdoor), and especially, theaters—there are half again as many theater seats in Branson as there are on Broadway.

The draw is big-time country music shows—enough to pack the ever-increasing number of theaters every afternoon and evening with such stars as Mickey Gilley, Conway Twitty, Waylon Jennings, Roy Clark, and other veterans. Branson is working on attracting more current stars, but the staple diet is the oldies who own the theaters. "You go to Nashville," says Mel Tillis, "and you see the stars' homes. You come to Branson, you see the stars."

"Down-home hospitality keeps the audiences coming," *Time* magazine reported. "Patrons can meet the stars' families in theater lobbies: Tillis's wife, for one, sells candy."

Tillis explains why a lot of the older Nashville stars are coming to Branson. "We don't have to spend two hundred nights a year going to the audiences. Here, the audiences come to us. Night after night. Day after day. It's wonderful, and the fishing is terrific."

Country music careers are two-tiered affairs—radio and chart stardom, and real stardom. Mel Tillis may not be on a major label anymore; he may not be getting new records played on the radio. But Tillis, or Waylon Jennings or Loretta Lynn, can probably still draw a larger concert audience than Doug Stone or Patty Loveless or Joe Diffie.

Nevertheless, the money from record sales isn't there, and the overhead is greater because the audience expects a bigger show, and unless you're Loretta Lynn and addicted to it, all that touring can start to wear you down. So the second half of a career can be trying to an artist's enthusiasm. That's why Branson is such a godsend to so many of these performers.

Tillis is as well known for his stuttering as his singing, and because of that, a lot of his friends laughed at the idea of a singing career for him, but as he has put it, "I never stutter when I'm singing. Never did. Singing is where I'm always calm, and always happiest."

He doesn't stutter when writing, either. To date, he's published almost a thousand songs. "Detroit City" alone has been recorded by over one hundred singers, including Burl Ives, Tom Jones, and Dean Martin. The "bloody Asian war" in "Ruby, Don't Take Your Love to Town" was the Korean War, but the song became a Vietnam-era hit for Kenny Rogers.

"I've spent my life on the road," Tillis says. "It's time for my daughter Pam to bring the family name to the four corners of the world, I guess." (Pam Tillis, after a career in rock, has returned to country and stardom.) He has sold his house in Nashville and plans to remain in Branson, where he can sing, fish, and have a home life.

He worries a little about Branson turning into a kind of entertainment Las Vegas. But most of the city fathers see the town as a family attraction, and almost every show has a flag-waving segment (Louise Mandrell is bringing her patriotic spectacular here), and a song about the good old days. There are several gospel shows, and Tillis and other stars always include gospel in their own sets. Branson's primary audience, unsurprisingly enough, tends to be a little long in the tooth.

Prices are right in Branson. Motel rooms average $40 a night, and there are six thousand campsites in town. Most of the performers sit on the stage and pose for pictures with the fans—even the shy Tillis gets into the folksy Branson spirit.

"We're an all-American city," Tillis says.

And as with every all-American activity these days, it contains a touch of Japan. One of the biggest draws in Branson is Japanese fiddler Shoji Tabuichi, the Wayne Newton of Branson—that is to say, one of the biggest draws in town, but it's hard to imagine him exporting his popularity. "He's a damn good fisherman, too," says Tillis.

Pam Tillis

b. 7/24/57, Plant City, FL

Style
Rock-shaded traditional

Memorable songs
"Melancholy Child"

Around the midseventies, Conway Twitty's daughters made unsuccessful attempts to follow in their father's footsteps, but a few years later, Rosanne Cash broke through to second-generation stardom, while her half sister, Carlene Carter, opted for a rock career. Cool self-interest might have drawn Pam Tillis in Rosanne's path rather than Carlene's, but the need to distance herself from father Mel drove her to a series of unsuccessful attempts to storm rock's bastions, while at the same time she was showing her country talents as a songwriter, placing songs with such acts as Conway Twitty, the Forester Sisters, Ricky Van Shelton, and Juice Newton. Finally, in 1991, she made the commitment to country with a new album, *Put Yourself in My Place,* on Arista Records, and a number one single, "Don't Tell Me What to Do."

Embracing country meant embracing her roots, a hard thing for her to do. "People have a lot of preconceived notions about having a star like Mel Tillis for a father," she told us in a conversation just before the release of what was to become her breakthrough album, *Put Yourself in My Place.* "They ask me what it was like, but they don't want to hear; in their minds they've already decided. So I generally just smile and agree when they say 'He's wonderful' and 'He's great' and all those things because those are all true things, but they're not the whole story. The truth of it is that country music of the fifties and sixties was about being on the road three hundred days a year, and that makes it real hard to get to know your kid—not to sound like a sob story, but it took a big toll on our family. My dad and I have an understanding, but we don't really know each other. I think what my dad didn't give to his family he gave to others, like a public service: he's given a lot of pleasure and joy to other people, and I can't argue with that. But there's only so much of a person to go around, and unfortunately it was his family that suffered.

"As a songwriter all these years, I've kept busy as heck just staying here in town, and as a single mom [Pam was recently remarried, to songwriter Bob DiPiero] it's been Ben and me together, and we've had a different kind of relationship than my father and I had, and I've been thankful for that. Recently I played a date with Michael Martin Murphey in Canada, and he had his son in the band, and that made me think. If I start doing a lot of touring, I'd like to take my son with me as much as I can. My dad told me recently, 'If you can balance a career and family better than I could, more power to you.'

"My dad grew up during the Depression in rural Florida, where he worked in the fields and everyone went to bed with the chickens, and Dad would sit up in the dark and listen to the Grand Ole Opry. I grew up in suburban Nashville with a new Cadillac every year, listening to Southern rock: the Allman Brothers, Leon Russell, Bonnie Raitt, Janis Joplin. I loved the Rolling Stones and Led Zeppelin and Daddy hated it—you know, 'Turn that shit off, it's terrible.'

"But it was—and this is real weird, because so many people in Nashville hated this stuff—it was when people like Leon Russell and Elvis Costello and Dave Edmunds started cutting country albums, I started to go, 'Wait a minute. That's cool. I've been missing it.' So I started teaching myself about country roots, going down to the Country Music Foundation, asking [Nashville journalist] Bob Oermann, learning about guys like Ernest Tubb and Bob Wills. And then I organized an evening here in town called Twang Night, a bunch of young people like myself. We put together this fantastic band, fiddles, stand-up bass, and we did all songs from the forties and fifties. Delmore Brothers, Johnny and Jack, Kitty Wells. Real cool stuff. People loved it. It was important for me to do . . . Pam Tillis's tribute to her own roots.

"Recently my father told me, 'You know, you've never taken one piece of advice that I've given you.' Well, he thinks that, but I've learned a lot more from him than he realizes. Or I don't think I'd still be here.''

Aaron Tippin

b. 7/3/58, Pensacola, FL

Style

Muscular

Memorable songs

"You've Got to Stand for Something"

Everybody has to be discovered by somebody, but most country stars don't get discovered by Bob Hope's wife. That's okay—most country stars aren't licensed commercial pilots or competitive bodybuilders, either.

Tippin got his pilot's license at the age of fifteen and played music as a sideline while he flew corporate planes and studied to get his transport rating, to fly big commercial jets. He had to give up his dream of an aviation career during the early eighties, when "the energy crunch came, and the big airlines started furloughing pilots, and I saw the writing on the wall." At that same time, depressed and discouraged by a divorce, he was "about to give up music completely, go get me a job at the mill, and live out the rest of my life in South Carolina."

He finally took a shot at Nashville in 1987, first as a staff songwriter and finally, after the brain trust of RCA heard him singing on his own demos, as a recording artist.

His first single, "You've Got to Stand for Something," came out just as Gulf War patriotism had the American public look-

ing for patriotic anthems. One person who heard Tippin's song and responded to it was Mrs. Hope. She urged her husband to sign Aaron up for his tour and TV special, and a new star was born.

Randy Travis

b. 5/4/59, Marshville, NC (*Randy Traywick*)

Style

Traditional

Memorable songs

"Diggin' Up Bones," "Forever and Ever, Amen"

Awards

ACM—New Male Vocalist 1985, Male Vocalist 1986, 1987, Song/Single of the Year 1986 ("On the Other Hand"), 1987 ("Forever and Ever, Amen"), Album of the Year 1986 (Storms of Life); CMA—Horizon Award 1986, Male Vocalist 1987, 1988, Album of the Year, 1987 (Always and Forever), Single of the Year 1987; Grammy—Country Vocal Performance–Male 1987, (Always and Forever), 1988 (Old 8x10); MCN—Star of Tomorrow 1987, Single of the Year 1986, 1987, Album of the Year 1987 (Storms of Life), 1988 (Always and Forever), Male Artist 1987–88, Entertainer of the Year 1988–89; TNN—Album of the Year 1988 (Always and Forever), 1989 (Old 8x10), Song of the Year 1988 ("Forever and Ever, Amen"), Male Vocalist 1988, Entertainer of the Year 1988–89

Nobody is more traditional, for a young guy, than Randy Travis—and at the same time, no one has a more distinctive style. Of all the young traditionalists, Randy

Travis is the only one who's not a young George or a young Hank or a young Lefty or a young Merle: he has a vocal quality all his own. While Garth Brooks has gotten a bit more publicity in his first year than Travis did, as of 1991 *every* album Randy had ever made (including, around Christmas, his Christmas album) was still on the charts, from *Storms of Life,* his first album and the first country debut album ever to go platinum. George Bush, whose campaign slogan about a thousand points of light ended up as a Travis song, travels with a Randy tape close at hand.

Life wasn't always this good for Randy Traywick. He grew up on his father's turkey farm in North Carolina. He hated school—and turkeys, too. The one thing he had in common with the fowl was a love for the Merle Haggard, Lefty Frizzell, Roy Rogers, and Hank Williams tapes that his father played to calm the birds.

Randy dropped out of school at thirteen to play music. By fifteen, he was playing the local honky-tonks, with his father as chaperon. There were fights in those places. Critic Dave Hickey has defined honky-tonks as "places where white folks go to kill other white folks." Travis says it was good training: "If you can hold the attention of hard-drinking and hard-talking crowds, you learn stage presence."

Randy learned more. A driven, angry kid, he spent his teens drinking and getting in progressively more serious scrapes with the law. In his midteens, he was "dropping acid and Quaaludes, speed, whatever I could get my hands on." Yes, even in rural North Carolina.

"I destroyed my health," Travis told Jack Hurst of the *Chicago Tribune.* "I was a very old, very sick seventeen-year-old. Almost a diabetic and sick most of the time."

His parents took him to a shrink, who diagnosed him as hopeless.

God, Randy says, led him to an amateur night in a Charlotte nightclub owned by a woman named Lib Hatcher. "I was standing at a table holding some papers when Randy started singing," Lib recalls. "I dropped the papers. He was something special."

Travis went on singing at Lib Hatcher's club, and when he was arrested shortly thereafter for breaking and entering, she had him released in her custody, and he moved in with Lib and her husband.

Hatcher's husband didn't like the arrangement and ordered Lib to get rid of the kid and sell the club. Instead, she walked out on him and never talked to him again, "until the divorce, of course."

With Lib as his manager, Randy had "someone I could talk to, and just knowing her helped me straighten out." She moved the two of them to Nashville, where she got a job as manager of a local club called the Nashville Palace and installed Randy as a short-order cook and part-time singer. For Travis, "it was the first time audiences ever sat and listened to the music. It was nothing like the honky-tonks. I thought their silence was because they hated me."

He had reason to think that. Except for George Strait, no one sang traditional country music in those days. Martha Sharp, a vice president at Warner Brothers, wanted to sign him, but "I knew I'd get a lot of guff from my associates. Everyone thought that anyone as country as Randy couldn't sell a record."

She signed him anyway, in 1985. His third single, "1982," released at the end of the year, broke through to the Top Ten; then Warner rereleased "On the Other Hand," which had bombed out just a few months earlier, and it went to number one, the beginning of a nonstop string of successes. These days, no single ever stays at number one on the charts for more than a week; Travis's "Forever and Ever, Amen" held the top spot for three weeks.

Critics, even big-city critics, love Travis as much as fans do. Jazz critic Nat Hentoff, not a country fan, wrote in the *Wall Street Journal:* "He sings conversationally. There is no straining for dramatic effect. The people in the stories tell of what's going on inside them, and Mr. Travis becomes each of them so convincingly that their natural presence and cadences make for natural drama."

In *The New York Times,* Steven Holden wrote that "Mr. Travis possesses a once-in-a-generation country twang that seems to quiver perpetually on the edge of an emotional precipice, while maintaining a secure technical footing." And in *The New Yorker,* which rarely mentions country music at all, Mark Moses wrote: "As in most masterly country singing, Travis's voice is all about the quiet, painful acknowledgement of limits; the constrained ripple he gives to the end of a phrase betrays a struggle to maintain his reserve."

Travis was the first of the new country singers (well, unless you count Hank Williams, Jr.) to make a serious dent on the pop charts, but he's not about to cross over. He feels that pop audiences should come to him. Frequently painfully shy, he's capable of losing his reserve when the subject of country music comes up: "Country singers sing with emotion and soul. They sing songs that people can easily relate to. The songs are good and simple. It's authentic. They live their music. It's in their souls. That's the way I've always wanted to sound."

Today, a healthy Travis has not had a drink in some years. He works out four days a week in a gym. He rides horses. Lib Hatcher has continued to manage his business affairs. She is several years older than Randy, and for years the two of them denied that there was anything more than a business arrangement between the two of them. Randy never had any other romantic involvements in his life, so perhaps inevitably, a sleazy tabloid put out rumors for a while that he was gay. He denied the rumors; and in 1991, he and Lib Hatcher were married.

In a statement to the press over the issue of the gay rumors, Travis had the last word on his career: "It could have been worse. They could have said I wasn't country."

Travis Tritt

b. 2/8/63, Marietta, GA

Style

Redneck

Memorable songs

"Here's a Quarter (Call Someone Who Cares)," "Anymore"

Awards

CMA—Horizon Award 1991; Grammy—Country Vocal Collaboration 1992 ("The Whiskey Ain't Working'," w/ Marty Stuart)

When Travis Tritt's second album, *It's All About to Change,* came out in 1991, a lot of things were about to change—including, Tritt believes, people's opinion of him. "It really just kicked things into another dimension," he told the *Chicago Tribune's* Jack Hurst. "I don't know if people didn't take me seriously on the album because they thought I was trying to mix too many styles, or maybe because 'Country Club' was labeled as a novelty tune by many people.

"I don't know what it was, but with this album people seem to have changed their opinion. They seem to be starting to take us seriously and realize there's substance to what we're doing."

Well, there may be something to that. "Country Club" was a breezy, wise-assed redneck anthem about a guy who puts a snob in his place by proclaiming that he, too, is a member of a country club because "country music is what I love." When it came out, we hated it instantly, and not because we labeled it as a novelty. We're great lovers of good novelty songs, from Steve Goodman's "You Never Even Called Me by My Name" to Ray Stevens's "Gourmet Restaurant" to John Prine and Fred Koller's "Let's Talk Dirty in Hawaiian" to Riders in the Sky. No, we perceived "Country Club" as what we've called a *classic mediocrity*, a song that's not very good but has something terminally catchy about it, so that it hangs on forever and drives everyone crazy.

We didn't care much for "Put Some Drive in Your Country," either, and we were building up quite a healthy aversion for Tritt. In fact, we refused to acknowledge any merit to "Here's a Quarter," which is actually a great song. We only gradually began to be turned around by the moving video of "Anymore," set in a VA hospital.

Finally, we came around to the realization that the guy wasn't going away, and that he was a fresh and distinctive new style and approach in country music.

Tritt takes Hank Williams, Jr., as his starting point, rather than Jones/Haggard like so many of his contemporaries. That breezy, wise-assed redneck attitude has been developed into something refreshing, and it gives his songs the edge that makes a difference.

Tritt joined forces with Marty Stuart at a 1991 Fan Fair appearance in Nashville, singing Stuart's "The Whiskey Ain't Workin' Anymore," and the chemistry between the two was solid enough that they've made plans to do more work together. "We see it as the Waylon and Willie of the nineties," Tritt told Hurst. "At the time Waylon and Willie first started doing things together, their music wasn't trendy stuff that was considered to be mainstream. They pretty much grabbed people by the ear and dragged them over into the next era.

"In a lot of ways, I think Marty and I are doing that, too."

Travis Tritt's list of the greatest songs of all time: "He Stopped Loving Her Today," "I Walk the Line," "Together Again" by Emmylou Harris, "Mama Tried," "Easy Lovin' " by Freddie Hart.

Tanya Tucker

b. 10/10/58, Seminole, TX

Style

Passionate

Memorable songs

"Delta Dawn,""Strong Enough to Bend"

Awards

ACM—New Female Vocalist 1972; CMA—Female Vocalist 1991; MCN—Most Promising Female Artist 1973

Bobby Bare once said that "in country music we want wet eyes, not wet crotches."

Beau Tucker, Tanya's father, undoubtedly would agree with that dictum. But Webb Pierce, a quiet man who rarely commented on anything, was moved to say, as he watched button-cute little Tanya, standing onstage wearing bobby socks and starched petticoats, belting out the worldly-wise, Faulknerian saga of "Delta Dawn" with a voice that throbbed with experience she could not possibly have had: "That's too provocative for country music. That little girl is sure lucky her daddy is always at her side."

In her early days, Tanya was often called "the Lolita of country music." Her earliest hits were about a waif being adopted by a hooker ("In the bed of Rose's where I learned to love a man"), or about going with an enraged father to a Georgia motel to shoot her mother and her mother's lover ("Blood Red and Goin' Down").

"I never did sing kiddie hits," Tanya says. "I always loved hard country ballads and I still do. I am not really into rock and roll. Rock may be good to dance to for kids, but you can dance to country, too."

Tanya's been making the charts, with up and down periods (in an up-and-down life), for over twenty years. "I keep punching," she says. In 1988 she received CMA nominations for Female Vocalist and Vocal Event of the Year (with Paul Davis and Paul Overstreet).

In 1991, twenty years after she began her career, she won the Female Vocalist award, but she couldn't be present to accept it: she was giving birth to a second out-of-wedlock child, daughter Presley Tanita. Tanya won't give the name of the father of both, but the supermarket scandal sheets credit a not-too-famous young actor who lives in Hollywood. In the old days, having two fatherless kids would have ruined a female singer's career in Nashville, but today's Music City is as hip as any other entertainment center.

Tanya's older sister, LaCosta Tucker, was originally groomed to be the singer in the family. Their father, Beau Tucker, was a construction gypsy and country music fan. They moved around a lot, mostly in Arizona. When Tanya was eight, she went to Beau and asked if he'd like to hear her sing. After Tanya sang "Your Cheatin' Heart," a surprised Beau added her to his talent roster and set about making his daughters stars.

Beau's construction business took him to Monument Valley, where Robert Redford was making *Jeremiah Johnson*. The movie's scouts liked Tanya's horse and wanted to rent it, but Tanya wouldn't let the horse go unless she went with it, so she made her movie debut in a cameo role (she recently returned in front of the cameras, in a much-praised dramatic role in TV's "Shannon's Deal").

After "one hundred and sixty-four turndowns," Beau Tucker got a demo tape to producer Billy Sherrill, who signed her up and gave her an upbeat song that fitted the style of a thirteen-year-old, and that Sherrill guaranteed would be a hit for her: "The Happiest Girl in the Whole U.S.A."

"It's not for me," Tanya said, and she turned out to be right. The little girl with the sultry voice was meant for grittier material: "Delta Dawn," "Would You Lay With Me in a Field of Stone," "Lizzie and the Rainman."

It was harder for her to work out becoming an adult woman in her private life. She made headlines with romances with Don Johnson, Andy Gibb, boxer Gerry Cooney, and with a fiery, unsuccessful engagement to Glen Campbell, an episode neither of them will talk about today. Their two duets did not fare well on the charts.

Tanya was never exactly a has-been, but her career from 1976 to 1986 was spotty. She was booed at the Grand Ole Opry for appearing in black leather and singing Elvis. She had a few hits, the best of them being "Texas (When I Die)."

In 1986, she switched labels to Capitol and returned to her career with a new fervor. "Just Another Love," number one in 1986, was just the beginning. In 1991, the top five female singers on the *Billboard* country charts included four newcomers and Tanya. She's well liked, she's given credit for all she's done in country music, and she's respected as a veteran who's seen a lot, done a lot, endured a lot.

In the light of her grizzled-veteran status, here's a trivia question for you: What do new stars Mary Chapin-Carpenter, Rob Crosby, Holly Dunn, Ronnie Dunn, Martin Delray, Steve Earle, Nanci Griffith, Patty Loveless, Lee Roy Parnell, Ricky Van Shelton, Doug Stone, and Pam Tillis, not to mention three Kentucky Headhunters, three Restless Hearts, and three Shenandoahs, have in common? They're all older than Tanya Tucker.

Conway Twitty

b. 9/31/33, Friars Point, MS (*Harold Jenkins*)
d. 6/5/93

Style

Sexy, authoritative

Memorable songs

"You've Never Seen This Far Before," "I'd Love to Lay You Down"

Awards

ACM—Male Vocalist 1975; MCN—Male Artist 1974–77, Single of the Year 1970 ("Hello Darlin' "), 1974 ("You've Never Been This Far Before"), TV Special 1983 ("On the Mississippi"), Living Legend 1988

With Loretta Lynn: ACM—Vocal Duet/Group 1971, 1974–76, Album of the Year 1975 (Feelings); CMA—Vocal Duo 1972–75; Grammy—Country Vocal Performance–Duo or Group 1970 ("After the Fire Is Gone"); MCN—Vocal Duet 1971–76, 1980–81

Harold Jenkins was born in Friars Point, Mississippi, in the heart of the Delta country that produced America's great blues heritage. He was raised in Helena, Arkansas, a town not far from Memphis, Tennessee.

Jenkins was one of those Southern guys who grew up in the late forties and early fifties playing the guitar and listening to Roy Acuff and Hank Williams, but not seriously thinking about a recording career. His dream was baseball. He was offered a contract by the Philadelphia Phillies, and when he went into the army in the midfifties, he had every intention of pursuing a baseball career when he got out.

But when he got back to the United States and civilian life after a year in Japan, something happened to him that was happening to a lot of those guitar-playing Southern guys, and that something came out of Sun studios in Memphis.

Elvis. Carl Perkins. Jerry Lee. Elvis's R&B-drenched "Mystery Train" was a regional hit when Jenkins got back home. There was a new sound in Southern music, and Harold Jenkins wanted to be part of it.

Told that he needed a new name that would attract attention, Jenkins picked two towns off a map of his native Southland—Conway, Arkansas, and Twitty, Texas. As Conway Twitty, he recorded his own composition, "It's Only Make Believe," for MGM Records in 1958. Then, when nobody responded right away, he decided to give up music and go back to his father-in-law's farm in Arkansas. He was driving a tractor when he heard that "It's Only Make Believe" had become the hottest-selling song in Columbus, Ohio.

Conway Twitty had a run of four years as a pop idol, but it was never where his heart was. Even while he was touring as a rock and roll act, he was writing country songs (in fact, "Hello Darlin'," a song that was to become one of the biggest country hits, was written during this period). Ray Price had a country hit with a Twitty song in 1962.

Unlike many pop stars who try country as a last resort, Conway had always wanted to sing country—in fact, he ultimately walked out in the middle of a pop engagement, declaring that from that point on, he would sink or swim as a country singer.

He released his first country sides for Decca in 1966, but those were still the years in which country pedigree was as important as talent, and it took a couple of years before the country audiences really began to accept him. In 1968 he had his first hit, "The Image of Me."

Twitty developed as a country singer. He grew up, from teen idol to man. His mature voice was deep, resonant, sincere, and sexy as all get out. More and more, he became associated with mature love songs, and it was perhaps a natural progression for him to move into very mature love songs.

One of the oddest moves of Conway Twitty's pop star career had been his title song for a B movie starring Tuesday Weld and Mamie Van Doren, *Sex Kittens Go to College*. In later years, in a voice that came

straight from the college of hard-lived experience, Conway was to score some of his hugest hits and gain some of his greatest fame (or notoriety) by singing some extremely sexy material, and the first of these adult songs, in 1973, was "You've Never Been This Far Before."

No song had ever gone that far before. The singer addressed a married woman who was about to sleep with someone other than her husband for the first time. The language was explicit, or at least it seemed that way: among other things, Conway sang about his fingers touching forbidden places. The beat was insistent and sexual, and Conway's voice was as mature and reassuring as it was sexy and enticing. If you were a woman who'd been in the sheltered environment of a marriage, even an unhappy one, and you were ready to make a move to reclaim your sense of yourself, you'd want Conway there with you. "I record all my songs for women," Conway says, and you know that's the truth.

Of course, the public relations business being what it is, everyone denied that it was really about infidelity. Those forbidden places were merely her hands (she was so repressed). She'd already left her husband, and this was just her first date as a single woman. But nobody believed it, any more than anyone believes the official line that Garth Brooks's "Friends in Low Places" is really an antidrinking song, and "You've Never Been This Far Before" became a huge hit, in spite of—or perhaps because of—the refusal of several major country stations to play it. And it became Twitty's first pop chart success in twelve years.

In "Linda on My Mind," Conway lies in bed with one woman, fantasizing about another. In "Tight Fittin' Jeans" he's a rough and ready guy who gives a night of fantasy fulfillment to a rich married woman who's never had a real man before. In "I'd Love to Lay You Down". . .

Conway Twitty has had over forty number one hits, not all of them sexy. But the sexy ones are the ones you remember him for.

Twitty had a second major career, as a duet singer with Loretta Lynn, in a ten-year run of hits from "After the Fire Is Gone" in 1971 through "I Still Believe in Waltzes" in 1981. They were the greatest of the superstar duos and won the CMA's Duo of the Year award four times. Their best song together was the exquisitely painful "As Soon As I Hang Up the Phone" in 1974, in which a guy named Conway jilts a woman named Loretta over the telephone. It was a risky career move because it gave a face to the woman he may have been lying with when he had Linda on his mind, and the face was that of the most beloved woman in country music.

Twitty also released a duet with his daughter Joni, a minor success. Both his daughters are performers, and his wife, Dee Henry, manages his career.

Conway Twitty became one of Nashville's major entrepreneurs with his theme park, Twitty City, and a variety of other business and real estate holdings, including a part ownership of Nashville's minor league baseball team, the Sounds. In recent years, he has refocused himself, selling off all his business interests that aren't directly related to music: "I'm getting it down to me and my music, and I don't have to worry about anything else. I don't have to do anything but put it in the bank, and I know how to count, so I don't need all those accounting firms and attorneys. I feel so much better now, so much better."

Today's young retro country singers talk about (and echo, in their singing) Hank and Lefty, Merle Haggard and George Jones. You don't, for whatever reason, hear any young Conway Twittys, but he is arguably as strong a stylist as any of them.

Conway Twitty died suddenly of an aneurysm on June 5, 1993, leaving a great legacy. Today's young retro country singers talk about (and echo, in their own singing) Hank and Lefty, Merle Haggard and George Jones. You don't, for whatever reason, hear any young Conway Twittys, but he was arguably as strong a stylist as any of them.

Jerry Jeff Walker

b. 3/14/42, Oneonta, NY (*Paul Crosby*)

Style

Laid-back

Memorable songs

"Mr. Bojangles," "Up Against the Wall, Redneck Mother"

In 1991, Jerry Jeff Walker made it into the mainstream, which he had not particularly been courting over a quarter-century career. He was named the host of TNN's weekly "The Texas Connection," and his self-produced, casually recorded, independently released album, *Navajo Rug,* made a more than respectable showing on the charts.

Did this mean that the Lost Gonzo was finally ready for the big time, and a major-label deal?

"No," Walker unequivocally told the *Los Angeles Times.* He was not ready, he made it clear, for "roadies and light shows and a lot of antagonistic people. No thanks, I've done that. I like it fine now, and I'm doing fine."

Jerry Jeff's big time was the late sixties, when a song of almost unparalleled beauty and emotional depth, "Mr. Bojangles," brought him fame, a recording contract, and access to perhaps too much of the wild life of the sixties and seventies, first in New York and then in Austin, and of course, Luckenbach, Texas ("Hank Williams pain songs and Jerry Jeff's train songs"). He was in danger of being one of those legendary self-destructive burnouts, until with the help of his wife and manager, Susan, he pulled himself together in the eighties.

He was never unproductive, though. *Navajo Rug* is his twenty-first album. And he expressed, as well as anyone we've ever heard, what makes a good record (in a 1989 interview with Susan Barton in *Sing Out!* magazine): "Records have to have a life of their own, like a party or an event captured on vinyl. I've always said, 'What's the song say?' After you pull the bass track off and the drum track off and the piano track off and the click track off, what does the song sound like? I still basically work that way."

Steve Wariner

b. 12/25/54, Noblesville, IN

Style

Musicianly

Memorable songs

"You Can Dream of Me," "Small Town Girl"

Steve Wariner is a big star who hasn't really made a huge impact. He's had seven number one hits; people like him; he has tremendous musical skills both as a singer and as a guitarist; he has even been heard by millions more people than have heard a lot of other country stars with higher profiles (he did the theme for the hit TV show "Who's the Boss?"); and yet the public at large is probably less aware of him than of many other less successful singers.

Well, fame is a bunch of things: image and notoriety and sometimes just being in the right place at the right time.

Wariner has had a solid, hardworking career. As a high school student, he went to work playing bass for Dottie West's band; altogether, he put in about seven years as a working musician, including stints with West and Bob Luman, before he finally got his shot at a solo recording career.

He had a couple of Top Ten hits and his first number one, "All Roads Lead to You," in 1980–81, then spent a few more years scuffling around the middle of the charts before finally hitting his stride in 1985 with a string of number ones.

Wariner has made a successful duet with Glen Campbell, with whom he has often been compared, and he's made a popular and successful Christmas album (perhaps there's a natural affinity—Steve Noel Wariner was born on December 25). They say that in today's restless, businesslike, hit-driven country world, there won't be any more long careers; and if that's so, maybe Steve Wariner's salad days are behind him. On the other hand, they say that today's charts are song-driven, not star-driven, so it's probably always a mistake to count a really good musician out too quickly.

Gene Watson

b. 10/11/43, Palestine, TX (*Gary Gene Watson*)

Style
Honky-tonk

Memorable songs
"Paper Rosie," "This Dream's on Me"

Gene Watson's been a working professional for thirty years, and he's been having hit songs since 1975. His gruff, honky-tonk, blues-based style seems as though it's always been around and maybe always will be, although he's only had one number one record ("Fourteen Carat Mind," in 1981).

As a country performer, Watson spends "sixty to seventy-five percent of my life on the road. That won't kill you if you take care of yourself. I've been married to the same woman, Maggie, for thirty years." Watson takes care of himself by not living in Nashville. When he gets off the road, he goes back home to Houston, Texas, and his first love: auto body work. "When I get off the road, I get as far away from music as I can. I go back to working on my cars and trucks, and I get away from it completely. That gives me a freshness I need to get recharged. I own a little place with my brother, and when I'm out on the road, he has the radio going, but when I come in the door, he knows it's time to turn it off. Sometimes I'll listen to an easy-listening or oldies station when I'm out in my pickup, but that's all.

"I've got a car sittin' in my shop right now—well, actually, it's two cars. One was burned in front and the other was totaled out behind. So what I did was, I cut 'em in two and put 'em together. And you'd never know it by lookin' at this car. It's probably stronger now than it was before it—before they were wrecked. That's because I'm a critical person, and because I know what I'm doing.

"If you'll stop and think about it, when a car gets hit, say it gets hit from behind, you don't start working on the side of it. You start straightening it from behind; you try to re-create that accident in reverse. That's how you fix a car."

Could the same theory apply to music? we wondered.

"No. Music's just the opposite, or at least it should be. A lot of people have tried to stay on top by re-creatin' the same effect, but I'm not interested in that. Once you hear a song, you've heard it. Once you see a movie, you've seen it.

"The one thing about it that I don't like is what I consider the manufacturing of an artist or a song or a feeling. You can't manufacture a feeling. You can take an artist who's not a good singer at all and put him in the studio, and given enough time, you can make him sound as good as you want him to sound. With the digital equipment they've got now, they can literally take a song word for word and make it absolutely perfect. But the feeling's either there or it's not, and if it's not, it's going to tell on you, it's going to jump up and bite you, because the minute you hit the stage, they're going to know the truth. And that's where I think country music is going to go through a weeding-out process, of the throwaway artist. Alan Jackson and I were talking about that last night. I think he's going to be around for a long time, and I'll tell you why. He can walk into the studio and sing you a song. He don't have to spend no hour in there. He goes in and sings the song, and if you don't get it on tape, that's your fault. But he can also walk out on a stage and sing it live. In my songs, I'll sacrifice a little perfection for the feeling. Red Sovine told me once, and I'll always remember this, 'If the song deserves a tear, then cry. You've got to believe in what you're doing before you can sell it to somebody else.'"

Kevin Welch

b. 8/17/55, Long Beach, CA

Style
New outlaw

Welch is a successful songwriter, with Moe Bandy's "Till I'm Too Old to Die Young" to his credit, and cuts recorded by Don Williams, the Judds, Ricky Skaggs, and others. As a singer/songwriter, the material he saves for himself is tough, uncompromising, and hard-edged. He draws comparisons to Tom Waits, John Prine, Randy Newman, Steve Earle.

He's a huge favorite in clubs, from Nashville's Bluebird to New York's Bottom Line, for his fiery delivery and cutting-edge material. But he hasn't broken through on country radio, and it could be that the powers that be in Nashville are a little afraid of him. What we're talking about here, folks, has all the earmarks of a cult artist.

Keith Whitley

b. 7/1/55, Sandy Hook, KY

d. 5/9/89, Nashville, TN

Style
Bluegrass-tinged traditional

Memorable songs
"Don't Close Your Eyes," "I'm No Stranger to the Rain"

Awards
CMA—Single of the Year 1989 ("I'm No Stranger to the Rain"), Vocal Event 1990 (w/ Lorrie Morgan)

Keith Whitley's career was short, sweet, and painful. It's impossible to write about him without focusing in on the painful part, the part that finds him dead at thirty-three, in his Nashville home, with a blood alcohol level of .477. In Tennessee, .10 is the legal standard for intoxicated; a lethal level is .30.

"I've lost so many friends," Ricky Skaggs told mourners at his funeral. "If any of you have a drinking problem or a drug problem or an emotional problem, please go get help. There's one person who can help: Jesus. Keith would say the same thing."

"None of us are strangers to the rain," said the Reverend Pat Kibby, who conducted the funeral service.

And certainly Whitley was not. He knew about pain, and the demons that bedevil a human life, and that knowledge was always present in his songs. Journalist Barbara Green writes that on the day he recorded Lefty Frizzell's "I Never Go Around Mirrors," Whitley "took a special route to the studio. On his way, he stopped at the cemetery where Frizzell is buried, visited the grave, and sang 'I Never Go Around Mirrors' to the spirit of the man who wrote it. Whitley went on to the studio and recorded the song with extraordinary feeling. When he finished singing it, there wasn't a dry eye in the place."

You want to get away from it, to write about something else, but you keep coming back to it. During his last recording session, Keith recorded a song called "I've Done Everything Hank Did But Die."

Whitley began his career in a bluegrass group with Ricky Skaggs. He moved to Nashville in 1983, put out his first album for RCA in 1984. It was a promising start, and he went back into the studio to record a second album.

But he wasn't satisfied with it, and with the blessing of RCA executive Joe Galante, he scrapped it and started over. The new album, Don't Close Your Eyes, was his breakthrough to stardom, and more than that, the breakthrough to his mature style as a country artist of major importance.

"Every time I'd get close to something happening, I'd get drunk," Whitley told Music City News in a July 1988 interview, during a period when he had achieved what proved to be only a temporary holding action against alcohol. "I wanted a career worse than anything in the world. But I was scared to have it. Somehow or another, I told myself that if I didn't do it, it wouldn't be as bad as doing it and failing.

"I have heard from the time I was a little kid how great I was, what a great singer I was. But I don't think I ever believed any of it."

In 1984, Keith's brother died in a motorcycle accident; in 1987, his father died. Don't Close Your Eyes had an emotional immediacy, a sense that this was the real Keith Whitley, which he had not captured on record before; and this was no accident. Of the ten songs on the album, seven of them were nailed on the first take.

In 1986, Keith and Lorrie Morgan were married, and friends hoped it was the beginning of a new life for Keith. In 1987, their first child, Jesse, was born, and Keith adopted Lorrie's daughter, Morgan.

In 1989, Keith and producer Garth Fundis went back into the studio to record another album, I Wonder Do You Think of Me. They were still on the creative high that they had achieved with Don't Close Your Eyes, and they knew they had another important piece of work. Keith was on his way to the top.

On May 8, 1989, Lorrie Morgan left

town to do a concert in Alaska. During a stopover in Seattle, she got the news that Keith had died.

"It's not easy for me to stand here and talk about my friend," Ricky Skaggs said at the funeral. "I loved him so much. We loved music and we loved our families and we loved each other."

Roger Whittaker

b. 3/22/36, Nairobi, Kenya

Style
MOR

Maybe he'll become a major force on the country scene. Then again, maybe so will Zamfir, Peter Lemongello, and Nana Mouskouri. On the other hand, look at Julio Iglesias.

Don Williams

b. 5/27/39, Floydada, TX

Style
Straight ahead

Memorable songs
"I Believe in You," "Old Coyote Town"

Awards
ACM—New Male Vocalist 1978, Single of the Year 1978 ("Tulsa Time");
CMA—Male Vocalist 1978, Album of the Year 1981 (I Believe in You);
MCN—Most Promising Male Artist 1978

Most of what you get of Don Williams, you get from his music. He's not much for public relations, not much for interviews,

and when he does talk, he tends to play it safe. "Matters of the heart are the spiritual core of a song—that's what it's all about." "I care about the average voice of the average worker dealing with their average everyday problems. If I have ever tried to address a certain group of people, it would have to be that average person who's trying to work and deal with their relationships—that silent majority out there." "I don't like to write or choose songs with specific situations in mind, but my wife is, without a doubt, my biggest inspiration."

Don and Joy Williams have been married for thirty years, and he's been a big star for nearly twenty—a worldwide star. In England, he was recently voted Country Music Artist of the Decade. His records are best-sellers throughout Europe, and Europe has not always been considered the most receptive ground for country music. You wouldn't look to Africa for country music audiences, either, but Williams draws huge amounts of fan mail from Nigeria, and he has been named All-Time Favorite Artist by music fans in the Ivory Coast.

You wouldn't expect country music's quiet man to have come from the rock world, but Williams's first musical career was with the Pozo-Seco Singers, a Texas folk-rock trio he founded in the midsixties. They had a couple of minor hits on the pop charts and moved to Nashville in 1967, where they stayed together for four years, even though the pop music wells had dried up for them (ironically, *pozo seco* translates as "dry well"). In 1971, Williams went off on his own.

He began working for the legendary "Cowboy" Jack Clement, a producer whose career has spanned the entire history of modern country music. (He started out at Sun Records in Memphis, engineering Jerry Lee Lewis's first sessions among others, and he is still active, a maverick producer with a golden touch.) Williams worked as a songwriter and song plugger for Clement's publishing company, and eventually as a singer for Clement's independent label, JMI Records.

One of his first singles for JMI was "Amanda," in 1973, which got some airplay for him, but eventually became a monster hit for Waylon Jennings. The following year he had his first Top Ten hit, "We Should Be Together."

Williams signed with Dot (which merged with ABC, which ultimately merged with MCA) on the strength of "We Should Be Together." His first Dot release, "I Wouldn't Want to Live If You Didn't Love Me," became his first number one hit.

Since then, Don Williams has become an institution, through "You're My Best Friend," "Tulsa Time," "Good Old Boys Like Me," "I Believe in You," through his later RCA albums, *One Good Well* and *True Love,* on which he paid tribute to his folk roots by covering Harry Belafonte's Hit "Jamaica Farewell." *Esquire* magazine has called him "the Gary Cooper of American music." Over the years, he has acquired a battered hat that's somewhere between a cowboy hat and a fedora, a gray-streaked beard, and a loyal following of fans who just love his voice.

Because that's what there is to love about Don Williams. In spite of some acting success (*W.W. and the Dixie Dancekings, Smokey and the Bandit II*), he's not a flamboyant stage personality. His songs are, with a few notable exceptions, nothing out of the ordinary. He doesn't do videos.

But his voice is out of that incredible tradition of male singers that only country music breeds: singers like George Jones, Randy Travis, John Anderson, Keith Whitley. Singers with masculine yet vulnerable voices, with such an immediate, affecting simplicity that you don't even notice—or don't care, if you do notice—that they are first-rate musicians. If Don Williams wasn't such a good singer, he wouldn't have lasted so long.

Hank Williams, Jr.

b. 5/26/49, Shreveport, LA

Style

Southern rock

Memorable songs

"Family Tradition," "All My Rowdy Friends Have Settled Down"

Awards

ACM—Video 1985 ("All My Rowdy Friends Are Coming Over Tonight"), 1987 ("My Name Is Bocephus"), 1988 ("Young Country"), 1990 ("There's a Tear in My Beer"), Entertainer of the Year 1986–88; CMA—Video 1985, 1989 ("There's a Tear in My Beer"), Album of the Year 1988 (Born to Boogie), Vocal Collaboration 1989 ("There's a Tear in My Beer"), Entertainer of the Year 1987–88; Grammy—Country Vocal Collaboration 1990 ("There's a Tear in My Beer"); MCN—Most Promising Male Artist 1980; TNN/MCN—Video 1990, Vocal Collaboration 1990

When he was only eight years old, Hank Williams, Jr., played his first professional show, and he hasn't stopped since. Between the ages of eight and fourteen, he played about fifty shows a year. At the age of fourteen, he did his first "Ed Sullivan Show," sang the sound track for the Hank, Sr., movie bio with George Hamilton, and made a number of TV appearances on the "Jimmy Dean Show."

The producers—and the audiences—weren't interested in what songs he wanted to sing. They wanted Hank, Sr.'s songs, and little Hank, the "Bocephus" of his father's monologues, gave 'em what they wanted. He learned to play six instruments, all of them taught to him by virtuosos. Earl Scruggs taught him banjo. Fats Domino came up from New Orleans to teach him piano. And backstage at the Grand Ole Opry, Red Foley would pat his head fondly and say, "You're nothin' but a ghost, son, a ghost of your daddy." His mother, Miss Audrey, would smile at Foley and nod agreement.

"I traveled with all the big acts," Hank told writer John Eskow. "I didn't have any friends my own age. I'd tour the honky-tonk circuit with wild men like Johnny Cash and Jerry Lee." He described how he'd watch Cash drop cherry bombs down hotel toilets and leave booby traps for the maids, how he'd run errands for musicians as they sat around getting stoned. "Then," Eskow writes, "he'd go back to Nashville and sit in class with the other third-graders."

By the time Hank, Jr., was sixteen, MGM (also his father's label) had him overdubbing duets with Hank, Sr. He was already drinking heavily. "I had a nonstop bender during my twenties," he has said. "It was the whole country music syndrome. I got to where I didn't have any more hangovers—I just woke up drunk, went to sleep drunk."

He appeared in a Hollywood movie, *A Time to Sing,* with Ed Begley, Sr. He was billed as "the son of Hank Williams."

One can imagine Hank's troubles. With a myth for a father, and a classic stage mother, "I was caught in a classic squeeze play. I snapped in 1973.

"I was still having to do shows as Daddy," he told *New Times* magazine. "I'd sit home listening to Chuck Berry and Fats Domino, thinking of musical concepts myself, but I'd still have to play those lonesome concepts of Hank's, and they were hittin' pretty close to home. Marriage bustin' up. I was supposed to be a big success, but where were the friends? Where were the lovers? I guess it all ganged up on me. So I tried the checkout route."

"Getting Over You" wasn't Hank, Jr.'s biggest hit, but it was an accurate description of his motive for an attempted suicide. His friends did show up in time and had his stomach pumped. Hank says that the song was about his first wife, but associates suggest that it could well have been a message to his father (if so, it was one of many he would write and sing over the years).

Hank resisted therapy. He was a man trained to be a macho loner. But there was one doctor in Nashville with whom he'd gone hunting, and Hank relented. "It was pretty much life or death at that time. I learned that I was trapped," Hank says. "Depressed." The deadly triangle was his mother (often described as a hard-drinking, obsessed woman, who resisted Hank's creative impulses), his manager (who saw a good thing in making Hank a carbon copy of his legendary father), and the Nashville community, which "conspired in keeping me a ghost."

The doctor insisted that Hank move. He did, to Cullman, Alabama (his father's home state). "I started having some fun. I realized that self-pity is bullcrap. Pain is something you get to leaning on. I fell into the trap of thinking I had to suffer to create. Finally I realized, hell, I don't need it that bad. No matter how good the songs that might come out of it, nothing's worth that kind of pain."

On August 7, 1975, Hank finished a landmark country rock album: *Hank Williams, Jr., and Friends:* "I think it signaled the emergence from my father's shadow." To celebrate, Hank planned a climbing expedition in Montana, in search of mountain goats.

Starting back down the mountain, Hank lost his footing and got caught in a snow slide.

Hank told *New Times* that it was like falling out of an airplane. "I just froze inside, no feeling. Just shock. And I thought, 'You're dead. You're just gonna splatter on the rocks.' "

The guide said that it was like watching a guy coming off a ski jump. Hank tumbled over spiny rocks, until he hit a boulder, face first, "that split my face in half. It started right at the top of the hairline, split me right exactly between the eyes, down the left side of my nose—and stopped at the chin, though that was broken, too. I woke up in a hospital room."

Johnny Cash was in the room when he awoke. "Don't let me catch you buzzin' for that Demerol when you don't need it, 'cause it's real good, ain't it?" Cash told him.

Shortly after Hank, Jr., got out of the hospital, his jaw wired and "looking like a monster, one eye screwed way off to the side," his mother died.

The press reported that Hank, Jr., looked "like death himself" at the funeral, as the Reverend Bob Harrington, "the Bourbon Street preacher," leaned over Miss Audrey's open casket and crooned, "Hey, Good Lookin'."

Hank was alive, but some of his ghosts had been laid to rest. After extensive physical therapy and reconstructive plastic surgery, he came back to performing, and having looked death in the face, he was ready to do it his way, and nothing but. He started playing the music he was to describe years later in "Young Country": "We like old Waylon / And we like Van Halen . . . We like our country / Mixed with some rhythm and blues." If audiences booed and walked out on him for playing rock and roll, for not playing "Cold, Cold Heart," he stayed and played for the handful that were left.

And slowly, the audiences started coming around. "The biggest star in popular music—any kind of popular music—is going to be Hank Williams, Jr.," Michael Bane told us. "Hank Williams, Jr.?" we asked Bane, who would later cowrite Hank's autobiography, *Living Proof.* "Isn't he that guy who sings his father's songs?"

But Bane was pretty close to right.

Hank sang raw, outlaw rock (the Bobby Fuller Four's "I Fought the Law"). He sang about the hard life ("Whiskey Bent and Hell Bound") and survivalism ("A Country Boy Can Survive"). He sang about his rowdy friends settling down, and his friends getting rowdy all over again and coming over tonight (accompanied by a spectacular video of the biggest party since Hugh Hefner settled down). He sang about his father, over and over again, from "Family Tradition" to "Hey, operator, give me Cloud Number Nine / Tell Hank, Sr., that Junior's on the line"—but they were *his* songs. He even came back to his father's songs again, scoring hits with "Honky Tonkin' " and a guest-star version of "Mind Your Own Business," which included, in addition to the usual suspects (Willie Nelson, Reba McEntire, and Tom Petty), a unique guest: big-bucks televangelist the Reverend Ike.

Hank's major collaboration with his father was an electronic duet on a forgotten Hank, Sr., song called "There's a Tear in My Beer." Well, electronic duets are nothing new; electronic duets between Hank Williams, father and son, were nothing new. But this was a song that had never been released: a demo of it, recorded on cheap acetate, was found in an attic forty years later.

And Hank, Jr., not only recorded the duet, he did a video of it—a real first in the world of electronic duets, and something of a technological marvel. Hank, Jr., was inserted into an old film of Hank, Sr.—not so difficult in itself, but Hank was singing "Hey, Good Lookin'." Another mouth, lip-synching "Tear in My Beer," was superimposed over Hank's mouth, and the whole film was slowed down until his guitar strumming matched the new song's slower tempo. The result won Hank, Jr., his seventh video award, making him pretty much the king of this relatively new field.

Jason D. Williams

Style

Unique (see below)

Memorable songs

"St. James Infirmary," "Dueling Pianos"

If you can find Williams's RCA album in a remainder bin, snap it up, because you'll never hear anything like it again. Even if he ever gets a chance to release another album, no one will ever again have the commercial lunacy or the artistic good judgment to let him do something so flamboyantly commercially unclassifiable.

Williams, who allows that, because he was adopted, he cannot absolutely swear that he is not the illegitimate son of Jerry Lee Lewis, plays the piano in a style that's a cross between Jerry Lee and Vladimir Horowitz and gives a stage show that's unrivaled since the heyday of the Killer, but with dizzying range. In an industry that tends not to reward originality, he's an original.

Kelly Willis

Style

Bluesy

Memorable songs

"Sincerely (Too Late to Turn Back Now)"

Kelly Willis, in her early twenties, was tabbed as the next crossover star, but crossover to what? Bonnie Raitt aside, there's no call for rootsy white country soul wailers in the pop world these days.

As we wrote in the *Middletown* (NY) *Times-Herald-Record* about her 1991 album, *Bang Bang*: "Kelly Willis is another one of those artists who's being groomed for that great country crossover market that doesn't exist, and won't exist as long as the audience that's outgrown Vanilla Ice and New Kids on the Block keeps reaching backward for Jim Croce and Grace Slick and the Doors, instead of exploring whether there's anyone new who's any good.

"Personally, we avoided the Doors' movie on the grounds that we don't believe First Amendment protection should be extended to singing 'Light My Fire' in a crowded theater. And we go on listening to good singers like Butch Hancock and Jonelle Mosser and Kelly Willis—and reporting that Willis's second album is a worthy step in her growth as a bluesy country rocker—who takes chances with cutting-edge songwriters like Steve Earle, Robert Earle Keen, Joe Ely, and Jim Lauderdale.''

Or, as *Rolling Stone* put it: "By applying a rich, libidinal delivery even to songs of heartbreak, Kelly Willis comes closer than most to Patsy Cline's true spirit.''

Willis can be heard on the sound track of the feminist action flick *Thelma and Louise* and seen on the screen in 1992's *Bob Roberts*.

Tom Wopat

b. 9/9/50, Lodi, WI

Style

Duke! Duke! Duke! Duke of Hazzard! Duke! Duke . . .

The Duke of Hazzard who couldn't sing. Well, what were you expecting? Lightning to strike twice in the same place? Anyway, Wopat turned out to be no John Schneider, even though he had a few different chances with a few different labels. Maybe he should have gotten Boss Hogg to manage his career.

Wopat, however, ultimately didn't need country. He made a successful career for himself on the stage.

Michelle Wright

Style

Canadian country/soul

In 1990, for the first time, Michelle Wright won the Canadian Country Music Association Award for Female Vocalist of the Year, an honor that had pretty much belonged to k. d. lang theretofore.

She's been compared to lang, K. T. Oslin, Lacy J. Dalton, Carly Simon, Barbara Mandrell, and Bonnie Raitt. This doesn't exactly mean that she doesn't have a style of her own, and probably in Canada, she doesn't need to be identified by all these comparisons.

Tammy Wynette

b. 5/5/42, Itawamba County, MS (*Virginia Wynette Pugh*)

Style

"A teardrop in every note"

Memorable songs

"D-I-V-O-R-C-E," "Stand By Your Man," "Golden Ring" (with George Jones)

Awards

ACM—Female Vocalist 1969; CMA—Female Vocalist 1968–70; Grammy—Country Solo Vocal Performance Female 1967 ("I Don't Wanna Play House"), 1969 ("Stand By Your Man"); MCN—Most Promising Female Artist 1967; TNN/MCN—Living Legend 1991

In 1990, in one of the most bizarrely conceived double bills of all time, we saw Tammy Wynette and Lyle Lovett coheadlining the same show. We held out a fond, faint hope that they'd get together and do a duet on the song that they've both recorded, "Stand By Your Man." But . . . not in a million years.

As we sat down to write this entry, we

happened to catch, via cable, the 1970 movie *Five Easy Pieces,* the Jack Nicholson vehicle that prominently featured Tammy's songs on the sound track. We were reminded all over again of just how much Tammy Wynette defined that era, with an extraordinary body of songs abut real women in painful real-life situations: "Apartment Number 9," "D-I-V-O-R-C-E," "I Don't Wanna Play House," "Stand By Your Man." Feminists put down "Stand By Your Man" at the time, but it has endured. Sometimes it *is* hard to be a woman, and nothing that's happened in the world in the past twenty years has changed that, just as personal loyalty has gone on being a virtue. "Stand By Your Man" is credited with being the biggest-selling single in the history of country music.

What may not be as widely known is how good Tammy Wynette still is, and not just at singing the old songs. In 1989, a year that saw huge hits from the Judds, Reba McEntire, K. T. Oslin, Rosanne Cash, Kathy Mattea, Patty Loveless, Holly Dunn, not to mention Dolly Parton's skillfully managed country comeback, when we made up our year-end ten-best list (for the *Middletown* (NY) *Times-Herald-Record*), we put an album by Tammy at the top of the list.

The album was called *Next to You,* and it was a gem. It included songs from a broad range of viewpoints, including that of an innocent teenage child bride ("When a Girl Becomes a Wife"), no mean feat for a woman close to fifty, but she pulled it off. "If You Let Him Drive You Crazy (He Will)" presented a mother forced to deal with her teenage daughter's sexuality—it's painful for her, and she wishes it weren't happening, but she has to accept it. On the other hand, in "Thank the Cow-boy for the Ride," she's an elderly woman looking back at a lifetime with the man who began as her childhood sweetheart; the song strongly implies a teenage premarital sexual initiation for the two of them.

A 1990 album, *Heart Over Mind,* was another solid effort.

The Tammy Wynette story is well known—her 1979 autobiography (entitled, of course, *Stand By Your Man*) was made into a TV movie in 1981, starring Annette O'Toole as Tammy and Tim McIntyre as George Jones. Born into extreme poverty on the Mississippi-Alabama border, Wynette grew up chopping cotton and fantasizing about one day singing duets with George Jones. After going through beauty school and becoming a licensed beautician (she still keeps her license up to date, as a reminder of the fickleness of fame), she moved to Nashville in 1966, so naive that when a producer asked her for a demo tape, she didn't know what he meant.

She was discovered by Billy Sherrill, George Jones's producer. In one of the most famous of all show business unions, she married her girlhood idol, George Jones, in 1968. They were married for seven hectic years, made some memorable duets, and were finally divorced in 1975. Tammy married her present husband/manager, George Richey, in 1978, but she and Jones are still close and have recorded and performed together.

Ironically, Tammy says today, it was not until years after her divorce that she came to understand Jones's problem, when a painful stomach operation left her addicted to pain pills for a time.

In the past few years, Tammy surprised show biz experts who figured that she was yesterday's news by selling out

243

performances at the Bottom Line in New York City and the Roxy in Los Angeles.

As always, she had her critics, such as the *New York Post*'s Gene Santoro: "Each musical ingredient, from pedal steel swells to weepy violin, was . . . totally predictable. Virtually every lyric dealt with the sorrows (and occasionally joys) of being a woman in love. . . . Her idea of independence is for a woman to start attracting a new man as soon as her old one moves out. It's a narrow emotional range whose dated simplicities probably help explain why Wynette needs to make this comeback tour."

Tammy Wynette's critics are full of shit. And you can tell them we said so.

Or you can quote eighties rocker Patty Smyth: "Honesty is always hip, and Tammy's voice comes from an emotionally honest place everyone can relate to."

Y

Trisha Yearwood

b. 6/27/59, Nashville, TN

Style
Hot but subtle

Memorable songs
"She's in Love With the Boy," "Like We Never Had a Broken Heart"

They say the new breed of country singers is set apart from the old guard by their college education, which means they're not so likely to be taken advantage of. If that's so, Trisha Yearwood is a particularly good example of the rule: she took her degree in music business from Nashville's Belmont College and did her college internship on Music Row, at the now-defunct MTM records.

Like marketing major Garth Brooks (who sings harmony on her debut album), Yearwood is equipped to play a key role in the management of her career, and she's doing just that. After the huge success of her debut album, as she told *CMA Closeup,* she and her new manager worked out "a plan for the next five years. We sat down and seriously talked . . . looking at tour options and everything. I want to really put a show together, not just go out and sing and see what happens. . . . It's really important for me to start thinking about the next step in my career."

But Trisha Yearwood did not get a number one record by having good business skills, any more than Garth Brooks did. She's the Grace Kelly of country music, preppy cool on the surface, smoldering just underneath. It's that quality that enables her to get away with Merle Haggard's "I Think I'll Just Stay Here and Drink," which she does in her live show, or the sexy "Like We Never Had a Broken Heart."

Dwight Yoakam

b. 10/23/56, Pikeville, KY

Style
Honky-tonk

Memorable songs
"Honky Tonk Man," "Streets of Bakersfield"

Awards
ACM—New Male Vocalist 1986; MCN—Vocal Collaboration 1989 (w/ Buck Owens)

If you were remaking the classic Howard Hawks Western *Red River,* you could cast Dwight Yoakam in both the Montgomery Clift and John Wayne parts. The guy's beautiful but he's tough, he has a cutting-edge contemporary bad attitude and a bone-deep respect for tradition. There's something extraordinarily theatrical about Yoakam, who came to country by way of the Los Angeles punk scene, and who came to LA from Pikeville, Kentucky, by way of Columbus, Ohio, where he spent most of his formative years, and where he's reported to have been part of a theater group. His first love and chosen profession, though, is country music, and he's given it the benefit of all his theatrical talents: bringing out the dramatic potential in a song; creating a vivid on- and offstage character; and playing out a fascinating drama of conflict and resolution in that area of a performer's life where the on- and off-stage merge.

That area, as it happens, is a particularly large and fertile field in the case of country music performers. Naomi and Wynonna Judd always brought their mother-daughter love and rivalry onstage with them and later added to it the poignancy of Naomi's illness. Johnny Cash brings his pill- and booze-tossed early life, and his religious conversion, Willie Nelson brings his weakness for women and the gypsy life, Merle Haggard his youthful prison days, Rosanne Cash the angst of her marriage and the pain and triumph of being a woman, Pam Tillis much the same except hers is the angst of being a daughter.

Dwight Yoakam, after an early and unsuccessful stab at Nashville, took his act out to the West Coast, where he worked as a trucker while playing local clubs and honky-tonks. He was surly, arrogant, and freewheeling, and at the same time uncompromising about his music; the combination played well in the punk clubs of LA. The same kids who followed groups like X and the Blasters found the same kind of hard-edged honesty in this honky-tonk cowboy.

That in itself wouldn't have been enough to recommend him to the powers that be in Nashville. Quite the reverse. But Yoakam and his producer/collaborator,

Pete Anderson, were making demo tracks that were too good not to pay attention to—especially since Randy Travis was starting to show that George Strait wasn't a fluke, and there was a real audience for this hard traditional stuff. Reprise, a division of Warner Brothers, was more West Coast than Nashville and liked Yoakam as their entry in the sweepstakes. He became one of the first of the post-Randy traditionalists. "Honky Tonk Man," originally a Johnny Horton hit, was Dwight's first Top Ten single, and the album it came from, *Guitars, Cadillacs, Etc.*, included such other country standards as "Ring of Fire" and "Heartaches by the Number." The title song of the album, with its celebration of "guitars, Cadillacs, and hillbilly music," was a masterful combination of tradition and cutting-edge attitude.

At the same time, Yoakam was developing an attitude as a nasty guy, a too-big-for-his-britches West Coast punk who said tactless and arrogant things, who needed to be taken down a couple of pegs.

And at the same time, Yoakum was about to launch a remarkable countermove on his reputation. Whether this was all worked out or whether Dwight was flying by the seat of his pants, or some combination of the two, is anybody's guess. Or maybe Shakespeare, a pretty fair lyric writer in his time, had a handle on the situation when he had Prince Hal, a punk prince if there ever was one, say, "I'll so offend to make offense a skill / Redeeming time when men least think I will."

While Yoakam was offending a lot of people in the country establishment—and while other Young Turks who were offending the establishment, such as k. d. lang and Steve Earle, were getting lopped off—Yoakam was dropping in at the Bakersfield office of Buck Owens and cajoling that legend into coming out of re-tirement.

In Shakespeare's story, Prince Hal comes out of the honky-tonks of East London to lead the English army to thrilling victory. In 1988, Dwight Yoakam appeared with Buck Owens at the CMA Awards show—as a last-minute substitute for Merle Haggard—and became the champion of real country music, the Bakersfield sound, the man who brought the man with the red, white, and blue guitar out of retirement.

Not bad, at all. As Gerry Wood put it in *Billboard,* "Dwight Yoakam and Buck Owens worked wonders on each other by combining talents and personalities. Owens got Yoakam to loosen up and have fun, Yoakam taught Owens how to have a ball onstage again."

Life on the edge, the classic rock image. Trial and redemption, the classic country image. Ladies and gentlemen, in living color and Sensurround, the Dwight Yoakam story.

Appendix

Jimmy Bowen

President, Liberty Records *(formerly Capitol)*

What's your job?

That's real simple. Taking care of music isn't hard—it's hard work. What's hard is finding music worth taking care of. That's my basic premise in putting a record company together. And it's my goal, in a very short period of time after taking over a label, to make sure that it's a solid organization, where you have promotion, marketing, administration, business affairs, finance—every leg of the table in place, knowing what they do and how they interact with each other. So that when you get lucky and get a piece of music that's worth taking care of, you max out that piece of music.

What did you start with when you came over to Capitol from Universal/MCA?

The first thing I had to do was to see if I had a franchise player on the roster. When I went to MCA, I had Reba McEntire and George Strait, and you go after them immediately, so you can turn the loser image into a winner image. When I got to Cap-

itol, I did the same thing. I went to see Garth Brooks work in front of the Statler Brothers. After fifteen minutes, I turned to my wife and said, "My God, this is the biggest ever." I came back the next day, called the department heads together, and said, "We have the franchise. Whatever you do, you do on this kid." I made every one of them see him within the next three weeks, so they'd see what I saw.

When you say everyone, you're talking about . . .

The VP of marketing sales, the VP of promotion, the VP of administration. Anybody who touches this music, who's part of this organization—you have to know that you've got your Joe Namath.

So that's what you do. You go and bang one home, so everybody takes you seriously, everybody realizes that you've got your shit together, and you're off and running. And that's what we did with Garth. You've got to get product out, and we set about doing that. And you've got to spend money to get product out, and we did that, and the product sold off, and we got more out, and it snowballed. You sit with the artist, and the artist's support

249

group, and you coordinate your people with their people, and you set out a plan, and you execute it.

What was the plan with Garth? You get him, you make sure everyone knows how important he is, and then . . . ?

The first thing we did was to decide when we'd have product from him, and when we'd release that product, so he'd know what his responsibility was. At that point, he was on his second single from the first album, so the plan was, we'd have two more singles. We decided that single three would be whatever it was, I think "Not Counting You," and single four would be "The Dance." That's the career record. He did a great video on it for us. That was all part of the plan. And we went out after this kid like he was the new Elvis. And that means we put money up to make sure his product was in retail locations, so when they saw him, they could go buy it. We went to radio and said we believe this is going to be the biggest act ever. Some in radio believed us immediately, some didn't believe until later. Now everyone believes.

We went after every major television show, and every minor television show. We got the easy ones; we didn't get the hard ones until after things started to explode. But the trick is going after all these things at the same time, so you hit it home quick, like they do it in pop music, not take forever like they used to do in country.

Explain the Garth Brooks phenomenon.

Well, I can't one hundred percent explain the Garth Brooks phenomenon. But first of all, you've got a twenty-eight-year-old with the mind of a fifty-year-old. He was a marketing major in college, and he understands how to market Garth Brooks. On the other hand, when he does his mu-

sic, no artist can be more sincere. I've never met an artist who has the song sense that he does. He's saying something to the baby boomers, the thirty-five to fifty-year-olds. They bought the lyric music of the seventies, and they're buying this kid's lyrics. He also reaches clear down into junior high with songs like "Friends in Low Places." And the last thing about Garth is that he's the most exciting in-person entertainer since Elvis.

Turning to your work as a producer. You're known as a coproducer, as a guy who lets his acts do what they want to do.

Well, yeah. I believe that the best way to produce is to help an artist do their music. The consumer doesn't give a damn who I am, they care about the artist. And if it's the artist's music, it's one of a kind. If it's my music, every artist who works for me sounds like me, and whatever I put around them. Afterwards, I can be an objective voice and fill in whatever gap is needed—but no more than that.

The artist you applied that to perhaps most strikingly is Reba, who found her own voice with you coproducing her.

Reba's a very intelligent woman, but she'd lived in a world where women didn't make decisions. When I met her, she didn't even have her own bank account. And I told her, "You can be a superstar. But you've got to know what a woman says to make other women want to go buy it. And that's something men are not good at. If you know that, I'll make sure you sound great, I'll help you choose what musicians to use, I'll be your objective voice. But it's got to work that way." The reason I coproduce is that I want them to take that responsibility. Then it doesn't get stale as quick, it doesn't get old as quick, because they're growing.

So Reba jumped in and did a great job. And the same thing worked with Hank Williams, Jr., and George Strait. And Allen Reynolds helps Garth Brooks do his music, he doesn't do it for him.

How did you get into the business end of music?

I started in 1956, in the Norman Petty studios in Clovis, New Mexico. Buddy Holly and the Crickets were there, and Buddy Knox and I had a band and put out some records. I had about an eight-month career, and then I started to notice there were more of us onstage than there were in the audience, and that's when I started to realize that wasn't my calling. I went back into radio for a year, and then in 1960 I went out to California. I got into publishing in Los Angeles, and then into record production—I'd decided that was what I wanted to do. I got lucky, and I got hired by Sinatra at Reprise Records, and after I'd been there for a while I got a chance to produce Dean Martin. I did a thing called "Everybody Loves Somebody Sometime" with Dean, and then I worked with Sinatra and Sammy Davis, Jr.—the Beatles were breaking, and I had all those old pop singers.

But you had some hits with them.

Oh, did I ever. And then when that era was over, I ran MGM Records in 1974–75, so with that, and my experience with Reprise, which was a young label when I started there, I knew something about putting labels together, and I was able to use that when I came here.

My son was born in 1974, and I went to the doctor's office, and he showed me an X ray on the wall of a three-year-old child who already had the lung damage equivalent to smoking three packs a day. So I said, this is it, I'm getting out of here. I moved to Arkansas for a year, before I

came to Nashville—back then they were nicer to you if you came in through the airport then if you actually moved here. I came here in October of '77, took over MCA in June of '78, worked there for four months, and then—

You slid past that. "Took over MCA" . . . that's a sort of major step. How'd it happen?

I've never been hired by anybody in Nashville. I grew up in an era where I knew all the label heads. We'd worked together, I'd produced records for them, we grew up together. When I came here, I was talking to Mike Maitland, whom I had worked for at Warner's, and I said, "Maitland, you've got to fix your label, it sucks." I got him some people, and then they decided not to do it, so Mike said, "Okay, why don't you do it?" And I said, "Oh, shit, this isn't what I came here to do. I wanted to come here to make music." But about that time, I was meeting with guys from the big labels, you know, RCA and CBS, and they were saying, "He won't produce for us, he spends too much money, and besides, we don't like the things he says." So I figured, hell, I'd better get my own label if I want to do any producing at all. So I took the job at MCA, and I worked there for four months, and then Mike came down with Alzheimer's, and they put another guy in who didn't know shit, and I quit. I can't stand to work for anyone who doesn't know anything about the record business.

Then two days later I took over Elektra for Joe Smith and ran that for four years. They had Eddie Rabbitt then, and I signed Hank Williams, Jr., and those two were our big sellers. Then they merged Elektra with Warner, and I figured if I'd wanted to be at Warner, I would have stayed there in '68, so I quit.

I didn't know where I was going, but

lo and behold, there's Irving Azoff at MCA, and he said, "Why don't you come over and fix our company?" So I moved over there in '84. I brought Tony Brown over from RCA the first year, and he became, I believe, the best producer in Nashville. Then they hired a guy there named Al Keller, who I didn't like—and as I said, if I don't like someone, I'm not going to work for him. So I set up my own company, Universal, as a joint venture with them. Then lo and behold, there's Joe Smith again at Capitol. And he had a shitty operation there, so I took my Universal artists, and we put them all together in a real big shitty operation . . . and then turned it into a major label.

So, is this something you think you'll do again? Do you like that challenge of going to a new place, like a Whitey Herzog or Bill Parcells, and building a winner?

Yeah, I could do it again. They tend to pay us more money to fix 'em than they do to run 'em. But I've always built a company that's good, even after I leave. Warner and MCA are fine record companies. They're solid. And I have to do it that way. If I'm in the studio, working on an album, I want to make damn sure I've got a solidly running company behind me.

You have a reputation for being a hard guy.

Oh, man, as far as being ruthless, I think I'm overrated. But part of that comes from the fact that if I walk into a record company and it's screwed up, I fix it. That means you have to get rid of a lot of people, that means you have to drop a lot of acts. You have to do a lot of things that, especially in a small town, will not make you friends. And after you've fixed four labels, you're going to have a lot of people who don't like you. I've fired some people two or three times.

Do you see country music as getting conservative in the nineties, dominated by the big four hat acts and shrinking radio playlists?

Well, just look at '91, and see how many acts had hits for the first time. I'll bet you'll find it's four times the number there were in '85. And radio . . . radio has never said we won't play great new acts, they've just said you have to give us the great new records, and then we'll play them. When I came here, country radio played oldies seventy to thirty over current records. Now it's fifty-fifty, and I believe soon it'll be seventy to thirty current over oldies. And it's because we have a lot of good producers in town, some good young acts, a lot of solid record companies, and we're giving radio decent music. They're not getting more conservative—hell, there are nineteen or twenty new acts this year—but they're playing hit records.

But aren't those new acts mostly like Joe Diffie, Alan Jackson . . . good-looking guys who wear cowboy hats and sing like George or Randy, whereas in '88 you had Lyle Lovett, you had Foster and Lloyd, you had a whole different range of acts?

But you have those today. Look at the new acts that have broken in 1991. Pirates of the Mississippi aren't a hat act, Billy Dean's not a hat act, the Headhunters aren't a hat act, Suzy Bogguss is a new Ronstadt. If you look around, there's more hair acts this year than hat acts. So the balance is always going to come.

What's the future?

Nashville will be the number one recording center in the nation by the year 2000, and you can mark that down and check it. Country music's going to continue to grow because we have better producers, better writers, better musicians— we're turning out better records to country radio, so they're going to stay strong. The record labels in Nashville are better structured than anywhere else in the world. They're bottom-line oriented, which is the way you stay in business.

Allen Butler

Promotion director, Arista Records

I don't strictly do promotion, in the sense that you may be used to—calling radio stations and asking them to play a record. Most promotion people in the business are handed the finished product and told, "Here, do something with this." Here at Arista, I'm involved much earlier on, from the time we sign the artist, through the process of looking for music, all through the process of recording, so I'm very familiar with the finished product by the time we get it. We have a very small roster at Arista because the way radio playlists are, you're only going to be able to break a limited number of songs at a given time. I work closely with Tim DuBois [Arista's president], and we try to identify what we feel will be the best songs for radio and the consumer at a given time.

While the act is in the studio, we're out talking to radio, and our basic pitch is that we've got a total commitment to making this act happen. It wasn't just some sort of internal politics, or somebody in house is gonna get thirty thou for producing them and that's all we care about. We're assuring the program directors that we've got a major marketing plan, we'll meet any demand for sales by making sure there is absolutely product in the marketplace. We'll create point-of-purchase display materials, such as posters and album-cover flats. We'll take the act out on a radio promotion tour, and in every market we'll have what

we call listening parties. We'll get a suite or a small banquet room in a hotel. We'll get a bunch of radio people in, we'll play the record for them, and if there's a video, we'll play that. We'll have the singer, or the band, there to schmooze with them. So everybody can see what it's all about and how much excitement there is for the project. This all starts about six weeks before the single comes out and goes right up to the time it comes out.

After that, the entire promotion department's function is to secure as much airplay, during the life of the record, as we possibly can. We have regional promotion people who cover about fifty to sixty radio stations each, and it's their responsibility to get a coordinated thing going across the country, so we see continued chart activity, which hopefully will result in sales.

That's what we do for every act. Alan Jackson was our biggest, and he was our first. But we do the same kind of promotion for everyone. Every act is unique—but we go on the premise that every act we sign has the promise of being an Alan Jackson.

What about, for example, a group that came to you with an established reputation, but they weren't selling records, and you had to build them back up: Asleep at the Wheel?

Okay. What you're dealing with in today's market is new-artist frenzy. Everyone wants the newest thing on the block. So a lot of artists that you'd consider standards, the cement of this format, are disappearing. They're not selling records, they can't get played on the radio. That was the situation with Asleep at the Wheel. Our idea was not to change them, or their creative integrity, because they do an unusual type of music, Texas swing, which nobody else does. You don't want to run off their core audience, which is pretty substantial, but you have to find music for them that radio perceives as music for the nineties. So it's a balancing act—a lot of gut instinct and guesswork.

And if it's a brand-new act that you've got to start from scratch?

We try to identify what market segment the act is going to appeal to. If it's, say, young females, then we would gear our promotional activities and press opportunities and all those things toward that demographic. We try to target our demographics and go after them.

How do you decide to let an artist go?

It's a business decision. If it costs a hundred thousand to record this act, and another hundred thousand in marketing and promotion, and you only sell fifty thousand units . . . it's a dollars and cents thing. You don't sell enough to recoup what it cost you to do business.

Does that mean you're only as good as your last record?

Not as far as we're concerned. If we go out and don't have the success we expected, then as soon as we realize that, we'll start asking questions. Do we need to change producers? Do we need to spend more money on marketing and less on promotion, do we need to spend more in promotion, do we need to do more videos? We'll reassess the entire situation from the ground up—including the possibility that there's just no more demand for the performer.

How is all this different from, say, a Waylon Jennings record in 1975?

Back then the business was artist driven; radio was artist driven. If a Waylon Jennings or Johnny Cash single came out,

they played it because it was Waylon Jennings or Johnny Cash. Today it's product driven: the quality of the record is what counts. The program director now—instead of just looking at a handful of records each week and saying here's a new Waylon, here's a new Willie, here's a new Kenny Rogers, now he's looking at fifty new guys.

Could there be another Loretta Lynn, driving from one radio station to another with a bunch of records in the back of her station wagon?

No; it's so controlled now they probably wouldn't let her into the station.

And if it were a legend trying to make a comeback—a Charley Pride, say?

They'd see him as a courtesy, because he's Charley Pride. But he still wouldn't get the airplay because they wouldn't feel the marketing and promotion clout behind him that they'd feel behind artists on major labels.

Tim DuBois is famous for the producer-created group. Is Arista looking to create another Restless Heart?

I'd say more accurately that we're looking for a niche that's not being filled. That's what we did with Brooks and Dunn. We saw all the duets in this format falling by the wayside. The Judds were breaking up, and some of the older duets were not seeing the status they had previously, so we saw a nice slot there. We took two guys who had come in looking for solo careers and put them together and said, "Why don't you two guys try to write together and see what happens." And it clicked. If it hadn't, we would have tried other combinations.

Marshall Chapman

Songwriter

I came to Nashville to go to Vanderbilt, but I really wanted to play music. I found myself playing places like the Steak and Ale, where they'd announce the tables through the same PA I was singing through—"Mr. Jones, your table for four is ready"—and I was out in the parking lot crying, and a friend told me, "Marshall, if you don't start writing your own songs, you'll be doing this for the rest of your life." Well, I was raised to be a Southern lady, so I guess I needed that permission. You mean it's okay? So I started writing songs. That was in 1974, I guess.

It seemed real easy at first. The first five songs I wrote were recorded in the order they were written. The first was called "A Woman's Heart's a Handy Place to Be." I'd moved out to California then, and I wrote this song on the beach, and I was so excited that I raced back to Nashville and went straight to Owen Bradley's office. I'd written a song, I was going to be rich. Somehow I got an appointment with Owen Bradley, and then I forgot it and stood him up. His secretary called me and said, "Let me tell you something—there are people who come to this town and try for years and *never* get a meeting with Owen Bradley. I can't believe you stood him up." So I said, "Oh, that's okay, I can come in this afternoon." I mean, I was such a little ass! Gidget goes to Nashville. So I came in, and I said, "Here's my song, and I want Loretta Lynn to cut it."

Well, you know, it doesn't work out that way, and I had to settle for some other singer. I was so depressed. Some girl I'd never heard of named Crystal Gayle.

Nashville was incredible back in those days. There was a real innocence. Waylon was innocent, Willie, everyone was innocent. There was a lot of drugs. Everybody stayed up all night for days. But the thing that made it so exciting was that the artists were getting control of their music. Nashville in the seventies was like the Paris in the twenties that Hemingway describes in *A Moveable Feast*. There was a place called the Ritz Cafe run by a woman named Mary Walton Caldwell, and she loved music people, and if you were a songwriter and broke, you could go in there and eat for free. So I'd go in, and Clive Davis and the governor are eating breakfast at the next table, and I'm there in my blue jeans and flip-flops and a T-shirt with no bra, and she's serving me scrambled eggs with béarnaise sauce. And at night I'm hanging out with Tompall and Waylon and those guys, and I'm just this crazy girl! I thought I'd died and gone to heaven.

I used to say I thought those were the greatest days, that I had more fun then; but I'm starting to have more fun now. It's a different kind of fun. I'm getting along. I get enough cuts to keep going, and I'm producing and marketing my own albums. It's a good time for songwriters. Singer/songwriters are getting a shot, you know, like Lyle Lovett and those people.

Garth Fundis

Producer

"My job is to help the artist live up to his/her potential or exceed that potential. That includes helping to choose material and acting as a liaison with the record company.

"I'm sort of a casting director for an

album, as though the album is a play, the artist is the star, and the songs are the supporting cast. An album is a piece of entertainment. It's got to have structure.

"That means a couple of things. One is that it's not enough for a song to be right for the singer; it also has to be right in the context of this album and this phase of the artist's career. When you're working with an artist like Don Williams, who's been doing this for a long time, a lot of the parameters have already been established in terms of musical styles and in terms of what the songs say. On the other hand, we deliberately kept Trisha Yearwood's first album simple. Trish has a lot more facets to her—she can really wail out on an R and B song—but we held some of that in reserve. There'll be more albums."

Garth Fundis is best known for producing Don Williams, Keith Whitley, and Trisha Yearwood. Other acts he's worked with include Steve Wariner, New Grass Revival, and Jamie O'Hara.

Fundis grew up as a rock and roller in a small town in Kansas in the sixties, and his first taste of country music came in 1969, when a band he had joined as lead singer and horn got a recording deal in Memphis, and he was brought down to add a couple of tracks. "That's where I met Allen Reynolds, Dickey Lee, and Knox Phillips, whose father was Sam Phillips of Sun Records. Allen Reynolds encouraged me to move to Nashville in 1971. I was still a singer then. I was also from the North, and the South in the early seventies was like a step back in time in relation to the social ideals I was used to. There'd been race riots in Nashville just five years earlier, in 1966. I wasn't totally comfortable there, but the music intrigued me, so I stayed."

He got a job with maverick producer Cowboy Jack Clement as a backup engineer—which meant in practice, in a studio like Clement's, doing a little bit of everything from gofer to engineer to arranger to backup singer, often on the same session—as was the case on Don Williams's "Amanda": "I wrote a high harmony line that Jack and Allen Reynolds thought would work, and they told me, 'Why don't you just go in there and do it?' So that's me on those harmonies.

"I learned a lot from Cowboy as a producer," Fundis recalls, "and the main thing was: don't miss the moment. Get everyone together, make them comfortable, and make sure the tapes are rolling. Always be prepared to capture the moment. But finally I left the studio—I got so I was starting to feel like a part of the furniture. I set up as independent engineer and engineered Don's records for several years. Eventually he asked me to be his coproducer, and the first sessions we did together included 'Tulsa Time' and 'Lay Down Beside Me.' "

How does a producer start working with an artist? In the case of Fundis and Williams, they started out their careers together. In the case of Fundis and Keith Whitley, Whitley needed a change. "Musically," Fundis says, "he hadn't found the right combination of songs and a personal style. He hadn't found the freedom to feel he was in a place to grow." Whitley had not found his commercial breakthrough yet, either. Like Vince Gill, he was one of those singers whom everyone admired, but who hadn't gotten that monster record yet: his biggest hit, "Miami My Amy," had peaked at number fourteen.

"Keith had finished a new album, but he didn't like it," recalls Fundis, "and he went in to Joe Galante of RCA and told him so. Fortunately, Galante backed him

—I mean, he could just as well have said, 'Christ, Keith, we've put a whole lot of money into this project, we've got a deadline to ship, we're going with this one.' "

In this situation, it was Galante who called Fundis and asked him to get together with Whitley and come up with a couple of songs that might work. Fundis brought "Don't Close Your Eyes."

"Keith was one of the easiest guys I ever worked with," Fundis says. "He knew exactly where he was at musically, and he loved country music. He was one of the strongest talents I ever saw, and he had a personal strength, too, but at the same time you always sensed a frailty. As I said, he *loved* country music, he loved being onstage, he even loved giving interviews, but for the rest of his life . . . he was a fish out of water. I can't tell you much about the problems he had in his life because I wasn't around for them. I never say him drinking—Keith wasn't a social drinker.

"We did that first album in two days, with Keith putting the vocals right in live."

The alternative to this approach is what's called "scratch vocals"—the singer sings a track that the musicians can use in doing their part of the recording, but it's not the vocal that will be used. That comes later, after all the musicians' work has been done.

"You can't demand spontaneity," Fundis says. "Different artists work in different ways, and you can't go in with preconceived demands. But I like to try to go for spontaneity. You have the musicians there, you have all the talent together, and you're never going to re-create that rapport again. Anyway, that approach certainly worked with Keith. When we played the tape back in the studio, I got goose bumps. There was no question but that we were going to use it."

With Trisha Yearwood, the artist/producer relationship had yet a different beginning. "A friend called and suggested I come down to a showcase at Douglas Corners, where Trish was singing backup for Pat Alger. Now, a show like that is going to be rehearsed for a couple of hours, if at all, so when I heard the inventive harmonies she was singing behind Pat, I was impressed. Then when he gave her a couple of solo numbers, she blew me away. I introduced myself after the show, and we talked.

"She was ambitious, gifted, and pleasant. People knew about her—she was talking to several labels, and several producers, and she wasn't about to jump into anything, but she was a big fan of Keith Whitley's, so we had that connection."

When Trisha and Garth decided to work together, again Garth's first move was to come up with a song. "I've got a file of demo tapes of good songs that have been pitched to me, and the first one I pulled and played for Trisha was 'She's in Love With the Boy.' She felt as strongly about it as I did, so we had a real base to start with.

"One good song gives you something to build on. Then, once you've found two or three songs that you both like, you can start to see a pattern. If an album is like a play, then that first group of songs is like the rough draft. After that, you start fleshing it out, you start finding characters that will work—and that can mean some good characters may end up on the cutting-room floor."

Fundis looks back over two decades as a producer in Nashville like this: "I've come around a lot on the question of art versus business. I believe you've got to indulge your own tastes, but at the same time you've got to pay attention to the boundaries of the music. The boundaries of country music are being pushed back all the time, and you can keep pushing at those boundaries, but you've also got to keep walking down the middle of the street. I used to think that if a song is good, that's enough; but you can't just think in terms of great songs—you've got to have radio songs. There are a lot of different people in the chain, and you have to depend on all of them being as excited as you."

Richie Albright

Producer, drummer

The new thing in Nashville—all these LA guys starting to come in—isn't all bad. It's done a lot of good in some ways. It's brought the budgets up to where you can cut some good quality records—$60,000 was plenty for an album as recently as the mid-eighties. Now it's $200,000.

But it was a lot different when I came to Nashville back in 1966. I came with Waylon—I'd joined his band out in Arizona—and I had long hair, which no one had in Nashville. That's really how the whole outlaw thing started, with the hair. When we first came to Nashville, I got a lot of "Baby what'cha doin' tonight?" That kind of thing. I got in lots of fights. But Waylon had no problem with it, he just said do your own thing.

Nashville may not have been the most progressive place in the world when I got here, but I wasn't disappointed with it, just because of the great music scene—the club scene, the jams.

We played all the time in those days.

When we came in off the road, I'd just back the trailer—a cut-down horse trailer—up to my apartment, and unload all the instruments, and set 'em up, and we just jammed the whole time I was here.

Kris Kristofferson used to come by. He was still a janitor then. He was a very bashful person, and I pitched a lot of his songs for him. I'd pitch 'em to Waylon, Waylon would like 'em, he'd take 'em to Chet Atkins and Chet would turn 'em down.

The music scene was really great. There was the Boar's Nest. There was this lady named Sue, who just gave her heart to country music, and her apartment was called the Boar's Nest, and that's where everybody congregated. Webb Pierce almost lived there, and George Jones . . . when the clubs closed at three o'clock, you'd go to Sue's house. She was just inducted into the Songwriters Hall of Fame. I lived in an apartment behind the Boar's Nest for about three years. Then Sue got sick, and the last two months she was alive Waylon and I put her up in a house I owned.

It's not the same today. Now it's guys who come into town with a marketing plan, and the smarts to pull the whole thing off, and they're doing it, and more power to 'em. But the old spirit's not gone. Willie Nelson's been having all those tax problems, but you're seeing a lot of his friends coming to the surface in his time of need. Most of them went to those tax auctions and bought the stuff he really wanted or needed, and have given it back to him.

Or take a young guy like David Lynn Jones—we've been working together lately, and he's never plugged into that New York manager and all that stuff, but his music says far more than anyone else is saying.

Richie Albright's list of the greatest songs of all time: "If You See Me Getting Smaller, I'm Leaving," by Jimmy Webb; "Honky Tonk Women"; Love of the Common People"; "Silver Wings."

Fred Koller

Songwriter

As a kid in Chicago, I started collecting records, and I started noticing that there were names in the fine print under the song title. I wasn't quite sure who they were, but I found out, and pretty soon I was buying records just because of who the writer was—I didn't even care who sang them.

I'd been playing guitar and writing songs in Chicago, and some local singers started asking if they could do some of my songs. So I hitchhiked down to Nashville. I was twenty-two, and I had a half a dozen songs, and I didn't have any idea of what modern country music was. I'd listened to Lefty Frizzell, the Sons of the Pioneers, Hank Williams, Sr. So most of the songs I was writing were pretty irrelevant to the current scene, and in fact the first few songs I had recorded were by acts like the Sons of the Pioneers, Tex Williams, Rosemary Clooney. It was pretty exciting, but you can't walk into a top producer's office and say, "Hey, I've got the new Rosemary Clooney cut," and be assured that they'll take you seriously.

What importance do you place on listening to what's on the charts and trying to write songs to fit in?

If your goals are to make some quick money, and you have your craft down, and you work at understanding the mar-

ket, you can do it. I know a lot of writers who have songs that were big hits two years ago, and a blinding array of ASCAP or BMI awards, and you sort of remember the titles, but you can't remember a thing about the songs. They're disposable songs. Of course you have to be aware of what's going on around you, but—well, my early experience was writing with guys like Shel Silverstein, who's more into the Ernest Tubb school of country narrative than he is into being trendy. I don't think he could write a song for, say, Diamond Rio. I mean, they might do one of his songs and have a hit, but I don't think he could sit down and tailor a song to them.

I've always tried to write songs—like "Jennifer Johnson and Me," which I wrote with Shel, or "Lone Star State of Mind" or "Angel Eyes"—that at least some people will still remember ten years from now.

To me, the audience for country music—the audience I write for—is an intelligent audience that wants an alternative to dumb rock and roll songs. I've always felt that country music doesn't have boundaries—not these days, anyway. James Taylor's lucky he's not starting his career today, because if he were, he'd be wearing a big hat.

Most pop music doesn't have as much furniture as country music. By furniture, I mean that in pop music, you tend to just get the who and the how, sometimes the why. In country, you also get the where.

A song like "She Came From Fort Worth," which I wrote with Pat Alger, is a piece of life that suggests a larger piece of life. She leaves her apron there for someone else to use. She knows she wasn't the first, and she's not going to be the last. All she wants to do is be out of Texas and be somewhere else. We chose Fort Worth for a reason. When I think of a fort, I think of an enclosure. If I said, 'She came from Teaneck, and Teaneck couldn't hold her,' it wouldn't have as much impact, although I'm sure there are just as many girls who blow off a gig in a diner in Teaneck.

You've written with everyone from Shel Silverstein to Sonny Throckmorton to John Hiatt to the late Keith Whitley. What are the advantages to cowriting?

It gives you a new kind of balance, a new person. For example, Lewis Anderson has written sweet songs like "Whatever Happened to Old Fashioned Love?" but when he and I got together, we came up with "Will It Be Love by Morning?" which has humor in it, but still keeps that pretty love thing, too.

What are the drawbacks to a songwriter of living in Nashville?

One problem is that you're trying to please someone besides the friends and neighbors, as we used to say—the real audience. If you're working for a publisher who's into pseudo-Eagles songs, and you want to keep that job, pretty soon you're writing for him instead of for the folks at Wal-Mart. And I've seen that happen over and over again: people coming into town with a fresh new way of looking at things, and then two years later, they've got a bunch of clever Nashville hooks. And you can understand why a guy wants to do that—he's got three kids and a wife, and he needs a hit. So you end up writing a song that's so dumb it needs a video to explain it. And it's a frustrating thing, because I love country music. I love hearing a Kathy Mattea or Bobby Bare or Lacy Dalton singing my songs, because I know they're going to do it with integrity.

But country music is going to last. There's always going to be a guy driving down the road in a pickup truck who doesn't want to hear a bunch of heavy metal guitars. There'll always be room for someone who sounds like Bobby Bare.

The 101 Album Country Library

We're not claiming that these are the 101 greatest country albums of all time. We'd simply put these forth as 101 albums that would be the solid cornerstone of any country collection. What we're saying about them is this: if we were over to your place for *cerveza* and *fajitas* or chicken fried steak and longnecks, and you put any one of these albums on, we would pause for a moment—even if we were talking about baseball—and say:

"Hey, yeah. Good choice."

1. John Anderson: *Greatest Hits* (Warner Bros.)
2. Asleep at the Wheel: *Greatest Hits Alive and Kickin'* (Arista)
3. Chet Atkins and Mark Knopfler: *Neck and Neck* (Columbia)
4. Bobby Bare: *Rosalie's Good Eats Cafe* (RCA)
5. Clint Black: *Killin' Time* (RCA)
6. Garth Brooks: *No Fences* (Capitol)
7. Mary-Chapin Carpenter: *Shooting Straight in the Dark* (Columbia)
8. Johnny Cash: *At Folsom Prison* (Columbia)
9. Ray Charles: *Modern Sounds in Country and Western Music* (Rhino)
10. Mark Chesnutt: *Too Cold at Home* (MCA)
11. Patsy Cline: *The Patsy Cline Collection* (MCA)
12. Mark Collie: *Hardin County Line* (MCA)
13. Rodney Crowell: *Diamonds and Dirt* (Columbia)
14. Lacy J. Dalton: *Hillbilly Girl with the Blues* (Columbia)
15. The Delmore Brothers and others: *Great Country Brother Acts of the Thirties* (RCA)
16. Iris DeMent: *Infamous Angel* (Rounder)
17. Steve Earle: *Guitar Town* (MCA)
18. Joe Ely: *Honky Tonk Masquerade* (MCA)
19. The Everly Brothers: *Cadence Classics* (Rhino)
20. Freddy Fender: *Before the Next Teardrop Falls* (MCA)
21. Flatt and Scruggs: *Folk Songs of Our Land* (Columbia)
22. Lefty Frizzell: *The Best of Lefty Frizell* (Rhino)
23. Vince Gill: *When I Call Your Name* (MCA)
24. Jimmie Dale Gilmore: *Fair and Square* (Hightone)

25. Vern Gosdin: *Chiseled in Stone* (Columbia)
26. Nanci Griffith: *Lone Star State of Mind* (MCA)
27. Merle Haggard: *Best of the Best of Merle Haggard* (Capitol)
28. Tom T. Hall: *The Year that Clayton Delaney Died* (Mercury)
29. Emmylou Harris: *Roses in the Snow* (Warner Bros.)
30. Emmylou Harris, Dolly Parton, Linda Ronstadt: *Trio* (Warner Bros.)
31. Highway 101: *Greatest Hits* (Warner Bros.)
32. Waylon Jennings: *Honky Tonk Heroes* (RCA)
33. Jim and Jesse: *We Like Trains* (Columbia)
34. David Lynn Jones: *Hard Times on Easy Street* (Mercury)
35. George Jones: *I Am What I Am* (Epic)
36. George Jones: *Very Special Guests* (Epic)
37. George Jones and Tammy Wynette: *Greatest Hits* (Epic)
38. The Judds: *The Judds Collection* (RCA)
39. Kentucky Headhunters: *Pickin' on Nashville* (Mercury)
40. Fred Koller: *Songs from the Night Before* (Alcazar)
41. Allison Kraus and Union Station: *I've Got that Old Feeling* (Rounder)
42. Kris Kristofferson: *Me and Bobby McGee* (Monument)
43. k. d. lang: *Shadowland* (Sire)
44. Jerry Lee Lewis: *Smash Hits* (Smash)
45. Lyle Lovett: *Lyle Lovett* (MCA)
46. The Louvin Brothers: *Tragic Songs of Life* (Rounder)
47. Loretta Lynn: *Greatest Hits* (MCA)
48. Kathy Mattea: *Untasted Honey* (Mercury)
49. Delbert McClinton: *The Best of Delbert McClinton* (Curb)
50. Reba McEntire: *For My Broken Heart* (MCA)
51. Roger Miller: *The Very Best of Roger Miller* (Heartland)
52. Bill Monroe: *The Columbia Historic Edition* (Columbia)
53. Michael Martin Murphey: *Cowboy Songs* (Warner Bros.)
54. Willie Nelson: *Red Headed Stranger* (Columbia)
55. New Grass Revival: *Friday Night in America* (Capitol)
56. Nitty Gritty Dirt Band: *Will the Circle Be Unbroken, Vol. 1* (United Artists)
57. Mark O'Connor: *The New Nashville Cats* (Warner Bros.)
58. The O'Kanes: *The O'Kanes* (Columbia)
59. K. T. Oslin: *This Woman* (RCA)
60. Buck Owens: *Live at Carnegie Hall* (Country Music Foundation)
61. Dolly Parton: *My Tennessee Mountain Home* (RCA)
62. Carl Perkins: *Original Sun Greatest Hits* (Rhino)
63. Webb Pierce: *The Wondering Boy* (Bear Family)
64. Elvis Presley: *The Sun Sessions* (RCA)
65. Elvis Presley: *How Great Thou Art* (RCA)
66. Charley Pride: *The Best of Charley Pride* (RCA)
67. John Prine: *Prime Prine* (Atlantic)
68. Jim Reeves: *Collector's Series* (RCA)
69. Riders in the Sky: *The Cowboy Way* (Columbia)
70. Marty Robbins: *Gunfighter Ballads and Trail Songs* (Columbia)

71. Jimmie Rodgers: *America's Blue Yodeler* (Rounder)
72. Ricky Skaggs: *Highways and Heartaches* (Epic)
73. Hank Snow: *I'm Movin' On* (RCA)
74. Jo-El Sonnier: *Come On Joe* (RCA)
75. Sons of the Pioneers: *Tumblin' Tumbleweeds* (RCA)
76. Red Sovine: *Giddyup Go* (Starday)
77. The Statler Brothers: *Best of the Statler Brothers* (Mercury)
78. Ricky Van Shelton: *Wild-Eyed Dream* (Columbia)
79. Gary Stewart: *Out of Hand* (Hightone)
80. George Strait: *Strait Country* (MCA)
81. Marty Stuart: *Tempted* (MCA)
82. The Texas Tornadoes: *The Texas Tornadoes* (Warner Bros.)
83. Merle Travis: *The Best of Merle Travis* (Rhino)
84. Randy Travis: *Storms of Life* (Warner Bros.)
85. Ernest Tubb: *Thirty Years of Hits* (MCA)
86. Tanya Tucker: *Delta Dawn* (Columbia)
87. Travis Tritt: *It's All About to Change* (Warner Bros.)
88. Conway Twitty: *Greatest Hits* (MCA)
89. Conway Twitty and Loretta Lynn: *Making Believe* (MCA)
90. Porter Wagoner: *The Cold Hard Facts of Life* (RCA)
91. Porter Wagoner and Dolly Parton: *The Best of Porter Wagoner and Dolly Parton* (RCA)
92. Hank Williams, Sr.: *Greatest Hits* (Polydor)
93. Hank Williams, Jr.: *Born to Boogie* (Warner Bros.)
94. Jason D. Williams: *Tore Up* (RCA)
95. Bob Wills and His Texas Playboys: *Anthology* (Rhino)
96. Gene Watson: *This Dream's On Me* (MCA)
97. Keith Whitley: *I Wonder Do You Think of Me* (RCA)
98. Tammy Wynette: *Greatest Hits* (Epic)
99. Wynonna: *Wynonna* (MCA)
100. Trisha Yearwood: *Hearts in Armor* (MCA)
101. Dwight Yoakam: *Just Lookin' for a Hit* (Reprise)

Index